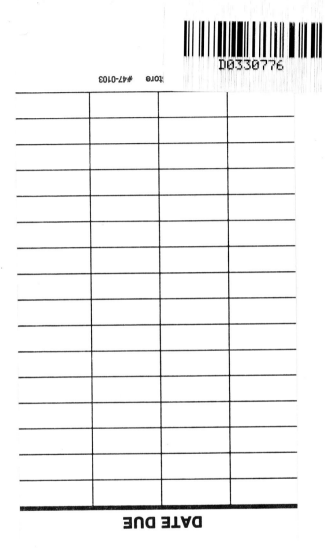

DATE DUE

GREAT CHAPTERS
OF THE BIBLE

Great Chapters of the Bible

G. Campbell Morgan

evangelical masterworks

FLEMING H. REVELL COMPANY
Old Tappan, New Jersey

ISBN 0-8007-1040-1

TO

EACH AND EVERY MEMBER OF

THE WESTMINSTER FRIDAY NIGHT BIBLE SCHOOL,

MY FRIENDS AND FELLOW STUDENTS OF THE WORD,

I DEDICATE THIS BOOK,

WITH GRATITUDE FOR THEIR PATIENCE AND CO-OPERATION

IN THE HOURS SPENT TOGETHER IN HAPPY FELLOWSHIP

CONTENTS

Foreword

THE Title of this volume may give pause. It may seem to suggest a comparison between the chapters dealt with and others in the Bible. No such comparison is intended. Every chapter, or section of the Sacred Writings, has its own greatness.

Nevertheless there are Chapters or Sections which stand out in the appeal they make to the human heart. The greatness of such passages is created by human necessity, rather than by their inherent quality. In that sense these are Great Chapters.

The selection of the first forty-five was not mine. It was made by the Westminster Friday Night Bible School. The last four were also among those selected in this way, but did not rank with the others as to votes cast for them. They were added to complete a Session of the School.

The selection was made by lists sent in of Twelve Great Chapters. Hundreds filled in these lists. These were then sorted, and the chapters receiving the highest number of votes were selected. In the selection the whole of the Literature was traversed, from the first chapter in the Bible to the last.

For me as Teacher the work has been a joy, and letters reaching me all the way through have proved that the studies have been helpful to many.

Necessarily the method has been that of Outline consideration, rather than detailed examination. This very fact may be helpful to further study of these Great Chapters, with their inexhaustible wealth.

G. CAMPBELL MORGAN.

GREAT CHAPTERS
OF THE BIBLE

GENESIS I—II, 3

WE are conscious that the first chapter of Genesis is a battle-ground. I am not approaching it in any controversial mood. We come to it as students, merely endeavouring to find out what it teaches. The line of supposed controversy around the chapter is that of conflict between its statements and science. I am not proposing to deal with that controversy in any way. There are two things, however, which I may say as revealing my own standpoint. I claim without argument at the moment, that there are absolutely no discrepancies between the Biblical statements and the ascertained facts of science. There may be many discrepancies between the hypotheses of scientists in their investigation of phenomena, and what the Bible says. It is equally true that there may be discrepancies between the ascertained facts of science, and what some people say the Bible teaches. Into these, I repeat, I am not going to enter.

It may be added by way of introduction, that it is impossible, of course, in one meditation to deal with this chapter completely. Adopting the figure of treating this chapter among others, as a mountain height of the Bible; it will be recognized that no mountain can be fully investigated in forty minutes. We may, however, see its contour in broad outline, and note its outstanding values.

Again, we are bound to recognize that this chapter is fundamental to the whole of the Biblical literature. As that. literature is read, whether it be history, prophecy, or poetry, no statement in this chapter is ever challenged, or called in question. Its statements are always assumed as accurate.

The chapter claims to be the solution of what some have described as " The riddle of the Universe." Taking it in its entirety, it introduces God, it explains the earth on which we live, and it interprets man. And that is all it does. It is of the utmost importance that we remember there is nothing final in this chapter on either of the subjects referred to.

There is nothing final about God. If we only had this chapter we should have a revelation of God, but not a full and complete one.

This chapter alone, does not attempt to give us all that there is to know about the earth.

And, certainly, the interpretation of man is neither full nor final. Everything is preliminary.

In considering the chapter we ought not to make excursions into later books, although under stress, we may find ourselves doing that at some points.

The chapter may be mechanically divided. It has three movements which may be expressed by the use of three words : Creation, Chaos, Cosmos. An account of the origin of the Universe; of a cataclysm overtaking the earth, and of the method by which the earth was restored from the chaos resulting from the cataclysm, into order.

The complete account of original creation is told in one verse, " In the beginning God created the heavens and the earth." That is a cosmic sentence, setting the whole universe within its sweep, and fastening attention upon what seems to be an apparently infinitesimal part of the universe, the earth. The second verse tells the story of the cataclysm,

" And the earth became waste and void; and darkness was upon the face of the deep; and the Spirit of God moved upon the face of the waters."

Then follows the account of the restoration of the order that had been involved in the cataclysm;

" God said, Let light be, and light became,"

and so on, down the poetic and remarkable story, which really ends at the third verse of the second chapter. That is why we include these three verses in the chapter. That is only to survey the story as a whole.

The fact that its cosmic sentence includes the universe, and names the earth, is a very arresting one. If we were reading this for the first time, we should almost inevitably be arrested by the fact that the writer, having written, " In the beginning God created the heavens," which evidently refers to the whole universe, and so includes the earth; then adds, " and the earth." Why name the earth? Evidently because the Literature which is to follow, deals specifically with the earth. To allow my imagination to have full play for a moment, I may say that I sometimes think when I have, to adopt a classical quotation, " shuffled off this mortal coil," and crossed the borderline, and entered into the life beyond, I shall have the universe before me, and the opportunity of investigating it all. Possibly I shall find that other worlds are inhabited by beings of whom we know nothing at present. Then my imagination carries me further, and I think it probable that all these worlds will have a Bible, or a revelation of God, which He has made to them. Other worlds, however, will not have our Bible, but I think every one of them will begin, " In the beginning God created the heavens," and then settle down to a reference to the particular world for which the revelation is made. To apply this flight of imagination to Mars, as we are sometimes talking of communicating with it, I think its Bible may begin, " In the beginning God created the heavens, and Mars." This is the Bible for the earth, and that is why it is immediately named. But the opening sentence puts the earth in relation with the universe as to its origin.

What then does this chapter say about God? The first revelation is found in the designation. I am not referring to our word, God. No philologist attempts to give us the ultimate meaning of that word. It is interesting to remember that in some form it is found in every branch of Teutonic language, and is always used with reference to a Supreme Being. It is further interesting to note that the word was originally used in the plural. It was when the Teutonic races came under the influence of Christianity that all branches took the singular number. We are concerned, however, with the word that Moses used, Elohim. In that word lies the first suggestion about God made in this chapter, and throughout the Biblical Literature. Elohim is a Hebrew plural. There are those who see in this the suggestion of the Trinity. Personally, I am never convinced that there is anything of value in that suggestion. The Hebrew language applies the plural in an intensive way when it is desired to signify that the thing referred to by the noun itself is superlative.

Of this word the singular is El, which simply means strength. We may employ the words might, power, force. The idea is the same. When that word is written in the plural form, it refers to absolute, unqualified, unlimited energy. That is how we are introduced to God. The statement is that in the beginning, that dateless date, which carries us behind all our guessing, even the guessing of the scientists which is colossal and amazing, accounting for everything, is Energy. That is the only designation of God employed in this chapter, occurring there no less than thirty-five times. Thus, as we read, we are conscious of the pulsations of infinite, unqualified, all-sufficient Energy; no weariness, no weakness, but power.

That, however, is not all that the chapter reveals of God. The designation is linked with a verb, " created." The Hebrew word here suggests causing to be. Now when it is said that Energy causes to be, Intelligence is postulated, and Volition also. Blind force does not create anything. Force, in order to create needs the direction of Intelligence, and the mastery of Volition. Thus the chapter declares that behind the universe and the earth there is absolute Energy, acting under the control of Intelligence and the direction of Volition. · We need not concern ourselves at this point about dates, or enter into discussion as to whether the days referred to were of twenty-four hours in length, or of longer periods. If we grant unlimited Energy, acting under complete Intelligence, and informed Volition, it is not difficult to believe that these were days of twenty-four hours; but it is equally possible to believe the days refer to longer periods. It is interesting that Moses in the great psalm which by general agreement was written by him, says,

" A thousand years in Thy sight
Are but as yesterday when it is past,
And as a watch in the night."

When we are endeavouring to think in the region of the Divine, it is well to cancel our almanacs. So far, then, the revelation of God in the chapter is that of a Being of unlimited Might, acting with Intelligence, guided by Volition, producing, creating, causing to be, originating.

From the chapter we learn something more than this. Might originating, postulates personality. It may be well to say here that finally we cannot comprehend the Personality of God by the study of our own. Personality in man is limited. In God it is infinite. Hebrew philosophy always recognizes that behind the concrete is the abstract. In other words, that thought precedes effects, and therefore postulates a Thinker. What then do we know about this Personality? So far as this chapter is concerned the answer is revealed in what His might, acting under the inspiration of His mind, and directed by His will, has created.

We turn, then, to contemplate the heavens, and once more to examine the earth in detail, watching the daisy growing, and the dewdrop sparkling. Such contemplation reveals clearly two things : order, and beauty. When we consider the heavens in all their far-flung splendour, and the earth in its minutiæ of perfection, we at least are driven to the conclusion that at the back of everything the Personality is a Mathematician and an Artist.

There seems to be another matter revealed, if only by suggestion. When we come to the description of the cataclysm, the declaration is made that the Spirit of God brooded upon the face of the abyss. That word is the word of Motherhood. The word, may we not say, of the out-spread wings of the hen that would gather her chickens beneath them. This may be but a hint, but in subsequent Biblical Literature it is verified. Thus the chapter reveals God as Might, directed by Intelligence, and acting in Sovereignty. That God is orderly, and full of beauty, and that God has the heart of Motherhood.

Then we turn to the earth. This is declared to have been set in relation with the cosmic order, a part of creation. It may be well here to pause for a moment or two with this Hebrew word *bara*, which does literally mean to originate, and in that sense to create. This word occurs in the chapter at three points. There is another word, *asah*, which does not mean to originate necessarily, but to form anew, or to give new forms to things already in existence. *Bara* never means that. It always means origination. This word is never used in Hebrew Literature of any other than God Himself. Man never creates; he makes; and therefore, the first declaration is that the earth is a distinct creation of God. We have no particulars within the time element. It is possible, and even probable that in the original creation the earth was the theatre of some special activity of God. As to what that was, we have no definite information. In a book published many years ago, called " Earth's earliest Ages," by George Pember, there was reverent speculation, almost amounting to certainty of interpretation.

Then we come to the second fact about the earth, namely, that it was overcome in some cataclysm. Our old version, " The earth was waste and void," is unfortunate. The verb rendered so is not part of the Hebrew verb " to be," but " to become." The old interpretation at this point was that the statement of the first verse is that God created the heavens and the earth, and that the statement of the second verse describes it as it was before He created it. One intelligent thought will show the absurdity of this idea, for it would suggest that the earth existed in chaotic form before it was created. That really denies the meaning of the word " created." To render it " The earth became waste and void," is to recognize that some cataclysm overtook it. I use the word cataclysm, because it literally means the overwhelming of waters. To glance on to the prophecy of Isaiah, we read,

"Thus saith Jehovah, that created the heavens, the God that formed the earth and made it, that established it, and created it not a waste." The words, "waste and void," do not describe the earth as God made it, but as it became through such a cataclysm. The description shows that after the cataclysm, that overwhelming of turbulent waters, the earth moved out of its true orbit in which it gained light in the heavens, and was wrapped in darkness, while the Spirit of God brooded over the face of the waters.

Finally, concerning the earth we have the story of restoration. "God said," nine times repeated, and after each saying, things happened. In glancing over this we find that the word already referred to, "created" does not occur beyond the original declaration for some time. The word *asah* is used, and is rendered "made." The light was not then created. The earth was brought back into right relationship with it. The firmament was not new. The separation of land and water was not the creation of land and water; and the coming of vegetation was not the beginning of vegetation. When we read of the sun and the moon, the statement is that God spoke, and the earth was swung back into its place in what we call the solar system. So with the light and the firmament, and the waters made to subside, and the dry land appearing, and vegetation manifesting itself again. This was all the work of restoration.

Then something happened. In the next stage the word is not *asah*, "made," but *bara*, "created." It is at the point where sentient life appears, fish, fowl, animals. This was a new creation. God is seen preparing the earth as a home for a new being, and so creating a new order of sentient life possible for this new being to live with and reign over.

This brings us to the last matter, that of the declaration of the chapter concerning man. Here the word "created" is once more employed. The declaration is that man was the result of special counsel within Deity, "Let Us make," the mystic plural. Further, the new being is to be "in the image and after the likeness" of God. Once more it is affirmed that the purpose of the being within the Divine economy is that of having dominion.

Thus to summarize. Man is a special creation of God, made in the image and likeness of God, and so offspring and kin of God.

The verses found at the beginning of the second chapter reveal God at rest. Of course this does not mean rest rendered necessary by weariness. It was the rest of a work done. The earth was restored. The new being was created, and placed in his new home.

In conclusion, we need again to remind ourselves that everything here is pristine, primitive, primeval. Every phase waits for further development and interpretation.

The chapter therefore is in some senses a cosmogony. If it be not accepted, then how are we to interpret the universe? Did someone suggest self-creation? The question arises, who or what was the self? That is an answer that cannot satisfy a rational being.

It is arresting that a phrase largely made use of forty years ago is hardly heard to-day. I refer to the phrase, " a fortuitous concurrence of atoms." We all understand that the word " fortuitous " simply means by chance, and not by design. Reason cannot accept that as a final interpretation of the universe.

Then, of course, there are those who say they do not know, and there is no knowing. Such describe themselves as agnostic. All we can say to that position is that real intellectuality cannot rest in ignorance. It must investigate.

To me, therefore, not because I am a Christian, but because I am a rational being, the solution of the riddle of the universe found in this chapter is acceptable as being simple, sublime, sufficient.

GENESIS III

THE third chapter of Genesis is one which all modern philosophy and modern fiction deny or ignore. We are also conscious in our approach to it, of questions that are being asked about it by devout persons, as to whether the story is literal, or allegorical. Let it at once be said, to treat it as wholly allegorical is to destroy the foundations of Bible history. The man cannot be treated as mythical without denying entirely the account of the race which follows throughout the Literature.

On the other hand, to make the chapter wholly literal is to deny its fullest value. For instance, if it be taken with strict literalness, then the promise made is literally the bruising of the heel of a man, while he is bruising the head of a snake. No one accepts that as the meaning of the statement.

The fact is that this is the story of actual events in physical life, of a spiritual nature. Spiritual evil is here represented as taking physical form to reach spiritual man through his physical being. We must therefore consider the physical facts, always observing the spiritual value.

Here in the Biblical Literature we meet sin for the first time, and we meet Satan for the first time. Evil had already been thrice recognized in the first two chapters. It is recognized in the second verse of chapter one, in the record of the cataclysm that overtook the earth. Again, it is recognized in the charge laid upon the man in chapter two, to dress the garden and to keep it, where the Hebrew word will be far more accurately rendered for the English readers, "to guard it." And again there is a recognition of evil in the limitation of liberty that was imposed upon man, of which limitation the tree in the midst of the garden was chosen as the symbol.

This chapter then is a microcosmic revelation of sin in human history as to its beginning. We have travelled far from these primitive simplicities, but we have not travelled any distance from their essential meanings. We live in the midst of life that is complex. Here all the complex is seen in its simplest form. In this chapter we have an account of the sources of the poison that has blasted human life, of its method, of its activity, and of its issue in human history.

In this record three personalities appear, Satan, Man and God. In the first chapter we saw two only : God and man. Here there appears another personality, and the three are seen in certain inter-relationships. In studying the chapter, then, there are three things for us to observe ; the Satanic method, the human experience, and the Divine action in consequence of human revolt.

In considering the Satanic method, necessarily we have first to observe the personality revealed. I do not propose to stay to argue as to the fact of such a personality. I may say in passing that to me it is always a curious fact that those who affirm the essential goodness of human nature, deny the existence of Satan. If we do not believe in the personality of the devil, then it is evident that everything dark, sinister, devilish, damnable, beastly in human life has come out of human nature. The Bible does not take that position. It affirms by this very chapter, and in all its subsequent teaching, that whatever it is that has blasted humanity, it did not originate in human life.

But to consider the personality as here presented. Our reading opens with the phrase, " Now the serpent." I cannot help saying that it seems to me that that is a somewhat unfortunate translation, because whenever we say serpent, we think of a snake, and that is not the essential meaning of the Hebrew word. It is quite true that the word is used for a snake, but it has another signification, and is used in other applications. The word *nawchash* literally means a shining one.

The personality that approached the mother of us all in the garden was not a snake, evidently inferior to herself, but a shining one, apparently superior. When Paul referred to the matter, he said among other things, " The serpent beguiled Eve," and later, in the same connection, he said, " Even Satan fashioneth himself into an angel of light." Personally I am convinced that it was in this guise he appeared to Eve.

Now observe his method. In doing so I will summarize, and then examine a little more carefully. In this connection let me parenthetically observe that I propose to waste no time apportioning blame as between the man and the woman. They were one. Later on in this book, in chapter five, it is said that God created man, " male and female created He them . . . and called their name Adam." Dan Crawford reading that once in a Northfield Conference stopped, and observed, " Please notice, not the Adamses." That was the genius of consecrated humour.

Man then was approached with a question, " Yea, hath God said, Ye shall not eat of any tree of the garden? " His second line of attack was a definite negation, " Ye shall not surely die." His last line of attack was an affirmation, " God doth know," that if you eat, you will be as gods.

The significance of the question was that in it a doubt was raised as to the goodness of God. While it was put in question form, it was not merely an enquiry. The enemy was not asking for information. The words were a satirical enquiry, having within them a suggestion. The suggestion was that God was unkind in withholding anything from them. To put the whole thing into a brief sentence, the first suggestion of evil made to man was that restriction is unkind.

We have exactly the same first suggestion of evil in the account of the temptation of our Lord, when the enemy said to Him, " If Thou be the Son of God," why be hungry? It was an attempt to cast a reflection upon the goodness of God.

Then the woman answered, and whereas it is but an impression it does suggest that the moment man begins to talk to the devil, he is likely to be outwitted. Said the woman, " Of the trees of the garden we may eat, but of the tree which is in the midst of the garden, God hath said, Ye shall not eat of it, neither shall ye touch it." This was not an absolutely correct statement. God had said, " Ye shall not eat " ; she superimposed upon the words of God the words, " neither shall ye touch it." It is ever so that when man is inclined to challenge restriction, he interprets restriction beyond that which is in the Divine Word.

The next line of attack was that of a direct denial of the Word of God : " Ye shall not surely die." If the first line suggested that restriction was unkind, the second affirmed that restriction was unreal. Evil is ever involved in a paradox of contradiction. First it says that restriction is unkind ; and then declares that there is no such restriction ; that God does not really mean what He says.

Once again we pass to the wilderness, and hear the voice of the enemy there saying to our Lord, " If Thou be the Son of God, cast Thyself down " ; angels will take care of You. In other words, trifle with the Divine arrangement and you won't die. Angels will guard You. Restriction is unreal.

Finally the affirmation of evil was, " God doth know that in the day ye eat thereof, ye shall be as God, knowing good and evil." Thus the declaration was blasphemy against God, as it suggested that restriction is unjust. Thus the enemy openly affirmed that the reason why God imposed restriction upon man was that He did not desire that he should be on an equality with Him. It is the suggestion of selfishness in the heart of God, that man is to be kept out of a kingdom which is his inherent right.

Again, we pass to the wilderness, and hear the final word of Satan to Jesus. If Thou wilt fall down and worship me, I will give Thee the kingdoms. This suggests that God was keeping Him out of His Kingdom, or compelling Him to enter it by ways involving suffering. Restriction is unkind.

This is not merely the Garden of Eden, it is London. It is not only the East End, it is the West End. It is not only the penitentiary, it is the university. These are ever the methods of Satan. He firsts suggests that restriction is unkind. That is the very spirit of the thinking of men to-day. They are advised to break through all bonds and bars and limitations, in the measure in which they are restricted. The second line is also very much in the ascendant to-day. It is affirmed that punishment is not a reality, that men do not really suffer through the breaking of law. Men are advised to get rid of their fear in the moral realm, and banish it, because there is no cause for fear. The ultimate blasphemy against God in Himself is still being proclaimed and acted upon. It is affirmed that the idea of God as moral Governor implicates His keeping of men out of that which they have a right to possess.

Here again in a serious connection, we quote Tennyson.

" A lie which is all a lie, may be met with, and fought with outright,
But a lie which is part a truth, is a harder matter to fight."

By which I mean that the terror of this story is that in every word of Satan there was an element of truth. God had said, " Ye shall not." The suggestion of the enemy was that this was unkind. Therein lay the danger. When the enemy said, " Ye shall not surely die," looking at human life on the level of the physical, it would appear to be true that they did not die physically in the day they ate. But they did die then. They died spiritually. The ultimate meaning of death is not the separation of spirit and body ; but the separation of the spirit from God. The word of the enemy then was a partial truth, that is, it was true in the realm of the dust, but it was untrue in the realm of Deity.

Finally the suggestion that God was keeping man out of some realm was correct patently, but the fact that God has one

passion, ultimately to lift man into the closest association with
Himself in all fullness of experience was ignored

Of all this we had a startling and terrible illustration in a
book written by Oscar Wilde, " De Profundis." Let me quote
some words from that which are the more terrible because, as events
proved, they were not sincere ; or if sincere, produced no effect
in the life of the writer :

> " I became the spendthrift of my own genius, and to
> waste an eternal youth gave me a curious joy. Tired of being
> on the heights, I deliberately went to the depths in the search
> for new sensations. Desire at the end was malady, or
> madness, or both."

There the whole thing is revealed. Restriction refused, in order
to experience, with the confessed result that the issue was " malady,
or madness, or both."

We then pass to the consideration of the human experience
revealed in the sense or consciousness of Eve ; and in the act
following thereupon, linked with the issue.

Her consciousness is clearly stated in the words that she
" Saw that the tree was good for food, pleasant to the eyes, and
able to make one wise." Perhaps the most illuminative
commentary on that statement is to be found in the writings of
John, when he refers to " the lust of the flesh, the lust of the eyes,
the vainglory of life." The word " vainglory " might have a more
literal rendering, which would reveal its meaning more accurately,
namely, braggadocia. Eve saw that the tree was " good for
food." That was the " lust of the flesh." She saw that " it was
pleasant to the eyes." That patently is " the lust of the eyes."
She saw it was desirable to make one wise. That is equally " the
vainglory, or braggadocia of life." Answering that consciousness,
she took of the fruit. That action was first of all volition upon the
basis of sight. She saw, and her will acted in accordance with
what she saw. That appears to be such a safe procedure, but it
is never so. It is merely a mathematical action of the mind ;
and however correct the findings may be, in the last analysis they
are never exact. I do not forget that mathematics is described
as the exact science. In my school days we learned geometry
by the method of Euclid, and in such study it was necessary to
begin with definitions. One of these earliest definitions was,
" A point is position, without magnitude." Face that, and it will
be seen to be absurd, impossible. Another was of the same
nature, " A line is length without breadth," which is equally

absurd. A yet simpler illustration of the inadequacy of mathematics is the statement that two and two make four. That is perfectly accurate ; but supposing in your outlook, some quantity is omitted from your calculation, then your mathematics will not only fail you, they may blast you. " She saw," and all she saw being put together, led her to a decision. For the moment, however, she was leaving out the supreme Quantity, which was God.

Therefore her taking was an act of rebellion, and consequently an act of suicide. There immediately resulted the sense of fear. That is the point at which fear enters the Biblical account of human history. Fear swept upon them, dejection overcame them ; and an overwhelming consciousness of the physical filled them with a sense of shame.

Then we come to the revelation of God in His action, after the rebellion of man. The Old Version and the English Revision say that He walked in the garden " in the cool of the day." The Hebrew word here is the word *ruach* ; and whereas that at times demands the rendering " wind," it is a word constantly used for spirit. Thus I would render it, " the spirit of the day."

In observing the Divine action, it is seen first how it vindicated that in God which the devil had challenged, namely, His goodness. Moreover it reaffirmed that which the devil had denied, the severity of God. And lastly it contradicted the blasphemy against God that He was unjust.

His goodness was vindicated in justice. It is a simple but sublime story of how God listened in each case to what had to be said, and accepting the statements, traced the actions back to origins. His first question, " Adam, where art thou? " was arresting. That was not the call of a policeman arresting the criminal. It was rather the wail of a father, who had lost his child. The answer of the man, that he was afraid because he was naked, and hid himself, is a very revealing one. He had become aware of the physical, when divorced from the spiritual. Therefore his shame.

Following that, the Divine investigation continued, " Who told thee that thou wast naked? Hast thou eaten of the tree? " The answer of the man was " The woman whom Thou gavest to be with me, she gave me of the tree." That was the answer of unutterable meanness, revealing the capacity of a man out of touch with God, for dastardly action towards a fellow being. Adam was the first cad, and there has been a long succession of them. But observe carefully that in the last analysis, the man was not blaming

the woman, but God. " The woman whom *Thou* gavest . . . me."
If the woman had been the occasion, according to this statement
God was responsible for putting her by man's side.

At once continuing the investigation, God turned to the
woman, and said, " What is this thou hast done? " Her answer
was again that of an attempt to place responsibility on another,
as she said, " The serpent beguiled me, and I did eat." God
did not argue with her. He did not rebuke her. He knew that
what she said was so, and what Adam said was true. Observe,
however, He asked no question of Satan, and conducted no
argument with him. Upon him He pronounced a sentence
in language of revealing symbolism. " Upon thy belly shalt
thou go, and dust shalt thou eat all the days of thy life."
Necessarily this was figurative language.

In all this the perfect justice of God is revealed. He heard
whatever had to be said. Thus goodness was vindicated in justice.
Moreover, severity was exercised in patience. On the serpent,
the curse ; on the man, the sentence tempered with mercy ;
and on the woman a sentence radiant with hope.

The sentence on the man was that the dignity of toil was to
remain, but was to be with the accompaniment of labour and sorrow,
which are beneficent in their intention and result. On the woman
the sentence was that out of the mystery of travail eventually there
should come the way of victory over the enemy ; and the
consequent delivery and restoration of man.

The final fact in the revelation is that of the Divine sovereignty,
and the underlying motive is that of grace.

This is the Bible account of sin and sorrow in its beginning in
human history.

GENESIS XXII, 1—19

IN our reading of this chapter we omit the last five verses (20-24) as they form an introduction to chapter twenty-three, rather than a constituent part of twenty-two.

While this chapter tells one great story, it is impossible to understand it, or to deal with it adequately, without recognition of previous facts in the history of Abraham. It is inseparably connected with the process. I think a great deal of confusion in the minds of many concerning the story here told, has been created by the fact that it has been considered as a lonely incident, rather than as a link in a chain.

There are seven occasions upon which we are told that Jehovah appeared to Abraham, or dealt with him in some way, in direct, personal, face-to-face communion. Of these, this is the seventh and final one. It is final in point of number, and certainly it is so in depth of value. In this experience Abraham was led into a new and more intimate fellowship with God than he had known before.

Let us rapidly review the previous appearances. Before doing so, we need to stay for a moment to consider the first purpose of God as revealed in the history of Abraham. He entered Canaan Anno Hominis 2083, that is in the year of man (and the calculation is based entirely upon the story from Adam and the Scriptural statements concerning ages). The purpose of Jehovah through him was that of the restoration of a lost order, and the establishment of the Kingdom of God as a revealing centre in the midst of human affairs. Abraham was not chosen in order that from his loins there might spring a people to be God's peculiar people, if by peculiar we mean a people to be the people of God, while the other peoples of the world were abandoned to darkness and to death. At the very beginning Jehovah said, " I will bless thee, and make thee a blessing." Thou shalt be a great nation, and " in thee all the nations shall be blessed." The whole human race was in the mind of God when Abraham was called. For the sake of humanity God needed an instrument, and the instrument must necessarily be of the human

race, in spite of all its failure. Ultimately that is the principle
lying at the back of the Incarnation. It would be of the uttermost
folly to say of God, that He could only do thus or so, that He was
compelled to adopt a certain method. We may, however, say
with confidence that this has always been God's method. He
reaches man through man.

It follows necessarily that if God needed a man, He must
find a man in sympathy with Himself. In the light of these facts
therefore we rapidly survey the seven occasions already referred
to, and notice what each appearance did for him.

The first Divine communication was made to Abraham with the
call to leave Ur of the Chaldees, and a little later to leave Haran.
When the call came to him to leave Ur he obeyed, but halted at
Haran until the death of his father, Terah. Then the call was
repeated, in obedience to which he went into Canaan.

Here then was a man who was brought into fellowship with
the discontent of God; discontent that is, with the order of life
that man had evolved for himself. This order had its manifestation
by this time in differing centres and schemes, the Chaldean being
one of such. The order was contrary to the Divine plan and
purpose for man. Abraham, in fellowship with God, shared the
Divine discontent, and was called to leave it.

The next appearing was the one in which God promised him
the land, where the Divine purposes were to be carried out. The
result of this appearance was the forward movement of Abraham,
as entering the land, he pitched a tent, and built an altar. Thus
he entered into fellowship with the method of God.

After some time had elapsed, God appeared to him again,
promising him a son and a seed. Thus Abraham was called into
fellowship with the patience of God.

Again after a time there came to him that night of strange
vision, a horror of a great darkness, the offering of sacrifice, and
the vision of a lamp moving between the pieces. Through this
God revealed to him the fact of the period of darkness that lay
ahead, and of the deliverance which would follow. Thus Abraham
was called into fellowship with the hope of God.

In the fifth appearance God made Himself known to Abraham
by the name El-Shaddai, the significance of which is not merely
God Almighty, as it is often said to be, but God, all-sufficient;

which includes not strength alone, but wisdom, and indeed, everything that is necessary for the accomplishment of the Divine purpose. By this appearance Abraham was brought into new consciousness of the all-sufficiency of God, for His own enterprises.

The sixth appearance was one in which Abraham challenged God, because it seemed to him that in an action contemplated, God was likely to break down in righteousness. " Shall not the Judge of all the earth do right? " To this God gave him complete answer in communion and in action; and so Abraham came into fellowship with the justice of God.

So we come to the story of this final appearance. It was a startling and remarkable call which now came to him. There was no word of promised blessing, no light of future victory shining through the darkness. Abraham had left Haran to find a land; he had given up kindred to become a nation; and now the call came to an action which seemed to make impossible the realisation of Divine purpose. No reassuring word was given to him of cheer and comfort, as on previous occasions. No vision was granted to him of emergence from the darkness of long affliction. There was no accompaying covenant to strengthen him for suffering and continuity of faith. There was no time of fellowship as under the oaks of Mamre. Rather there was a command, without reason given, without promise made, obedience to which threatened all the values of the past. " Take now thy son, thine only son, whom thou lovest . . . and offer him . . . for a burnt offering."

It is admittedly a strange story. Even Christian men have strenuously attempted to get rid of it. It has been suggested that no such command came to him from God, but that it was an expression of a devout thought of his own mind. That view simply contradicts the story, and cannot be entertained. On the other hand, multitudes of men and women have found unutterable comfort in this story. Our examination of it will follow two lines; first, the meaning of God; and secondly, the triumph of Abraham.

The meaning of God is not declared in the command which was given to Abraham. That will be found to be constantly true in the life of faith. There is always a meaning, but it is not revealed at the time when the command is issued. " The covenant is ordered in all things, and sure." Yesterday is linked with to-day. To-day has its explanation to-morrow. That surely is what Paul meant when he said, "To them that love God, all things work together for good."

Now let us at once daringly over-leap the centuries, linking the word of Jehovah to Abraham with a statement central to the New Testament. The word to Abraham was, "Take now thy son, thine only son, whom thou lovest . . . and offer him . . . for a burnt offering." The word of the New Testament is, "God so loved the world that He gave His only begotten Son." Thus while certainly Abraham could not comprehend the full meaning, God was calling him to fellowship with Himself in the only method by which it would be possible for the Divine purpose to find fulfilment.

The outstanding fact in the history of Abraham is that he obeyed. While Isaac was not slain, in the deep, essential spirit of Abraham, in his intention, volition, and surrender, the thing was actually done. In the previous hour of communion, Abraham had learned that the Judge of all the earth must do right; and therefore, without flinching, he went forward in obedience along a pathway, where there seemed to be no light, and which was one of personal, sacrificial suffering. Thus God was bringing him to the final stage of fellowship with Himself in His suffering.

Thus in effect, Jehovah was saying to His servant Abraham, that if there were to be full fellowship with Him, there must be fellowship in suffering. When He said to him, "Take . . . thy son, thine only son," He was calling him to do exactly what He Himself was doing, and in human history would subsequently do. Through such sacrificial suffering alone could the redemption and restoration of such a race be accomplished. Thus we see the God Who had led this man progressively along stages of understanding and fellowship, calling him into the ultimate fellowship of suffering.

And now to consider the obedience of Abraham, which in itself is one of the most wonderful stories of the Old Testament. Let us glance again for a moment carefully at verse three, and in doing so, watch the repetition of one little word, "and." "And Abraham rose early in the morning and saddled his ass, and took two of his young men with him, and Isaac his son; and he clave the wood for the burnt offering, and rose up, and went unto the place of which God had told him." That repetition of the word "and" reveals the adoption by the writer here of a Hebrew figure of speech which is called polysyndeton. Its intention is that of showing continuity and persistence. As reading this paragraph we watch Abraham, we see him desperately determined that nothing shall fail in his obedience. Every detail is attended to, as, in spite of all appearance, he follows the Divine pathway marked out for him, carrying out obediently, from the standpoint of what we have already described as volition, and surrender, the command of God.

Let us again observe the use of the same figure of speech as a method, in the statement, " *And* they came to the place which God had told him of; *and* Abraham built the altar there, *and* laid the wood in order, *and* bound Isaac his son, *and* laid him on the altar upon the wood. *And* Abraham stretched forth his hand, *and* took the knife to slay his son." All this emphasizes the same truth in that we see Abraham reaching the ultimate in obedience.

All this is so amazing from the standpoint of human understanding, that we are driven to enquire quite earnestly what was the secret of this determined obedience? The answer is found incidentally, and yet most explicitly, as we go back to certain words found in verse five. "*And* Abraham said unto his young men, Abide ye here with the ass, *and* I *and* the lad will go yonder *and* we will worship, *and* come again to you." In passing we may say that the same method of polysyndeton obtains here, the repetition of the " *and.*" That, however, which is full of significance is this, that he not merely said " we will worship," but " will come again to you." Carefully observe the plural " we " linked with two plural verbs, " will worship," and " will come again." Abraham was leaving behind the young men who had travelled with him. He was going away to build his altar, going away to lay the wood, going away to bind the boy, going away to slay him, going away to give up his only begotten son. He and Isaac were going away to worship. Yes, but he said, we " will come again."

Now there is nothing in the Old Testament which is a more remarkable revelation of the triumph of faith than that. In the eleventh chapter of the letter to the Hebrews, the writer refers to it, and he says that what Abraham did, he did, " accounting that God was able to raise him up, even from the dead." That statement flashes light back upon the story itself. Abraham was walking in obedience. To give up the son in whom all his hopes were centred, the son of his love, he was going through with it at all costs, but " accounting that God was able to raise him up, even from the dead." That word " accounting " is an arresting one in itself. It means he was arguing, arguing within himself, and on the basis of his argument, was coming to definite conclusion. Unquestionably his deductions were made as the result of the processes of the past. Abraham was saying within himself, I will obey at whatever cost. The one certain fact is that God cannot fail to fulfil His promises, and if I, in obedience slay my son, then God will raise him from the dead, rather than fail, either in His promises or His purposes.

Thus, as we have said, the accounting of Abraham was unquestionably based upon the knowledge he had gained of God by the previous revelations. All past experiences had prepared him for that line of argument which is the argument of faith. That is a revelation of the rationality of faith. The man who has no faith is breaking down rationally. Faith is for ever the action which results from reason, by the recognition of God.

It may be objected at this point that if this accounting amounted to conviction, then suffering was not involved. This, however, is not so. Faith never dulls feeling. Confidence never callouses the heart in the processes through which it is called to pass. Here again we may reverently quote from the Hebrew letter, when speaking of our Lord, it says, " Who for the joy that was set before Him, endured the Cross." The way to the joy was the way of the Cross; and the Cross was such that the only word that can describe it is the word " endured." Thus Abraham was being brought into fellowship with God, and that fellowship issued in triumph in his case, as he became the father of the chosen people, the ultimate flower and fruit of which people was the Son of God Himself.

The ultimate then in faith is that of such obedience to the call of God as brings the soul to the point of the giving up, not of something wrong, but of anything and everything, in order to the accomplishment of Divine purpose, though such giving up entails suffering, which is fellowship with the suffering of God, through which alone the redemption of man is possible. This is the ultimate in faith. Beyond this comes vindication by sight.

How often the human heart stops short in fellowship with God at that point. We see conditions as they are, and have fellowship with God in His discontent, and it may be, turn our back upon Ur. We agree with His method, because it is His method in our going out, even though we may not understand how the end is to be gained. We wait with patience, however long the darkness, believing the light will come. We rejoice in hope, because we believe in God. We commune with Him in prayer, honestly, and challenge Him at the point of our doubt, thus proving our intimacy with Him up to a certain limit. It is when we reach this point of sacrifice that we are in danger of halting; sacrifice of possessions, sacrifice of strength and virility, sacrifice of life itself.

When there fell from the lips of an apostle of Jesus the words, " Spare Thyself," the answer of Jesus was, " Get thee behind Me, Satan." The philosophy that expresses itself in the advice to " Spare Thyself," is the philosophy of hell. It is the philosophy which carries us all the way to the withholding of nothing which brings us into true fellowship with the God Who " spared not His own Son, but delivered Him up for us all," which is heaven's philosophy.

To dare to go forward at such a time as this is to see immediate results, and to come at last to complete realisation. Nevertheless let us ever be warned against daring, until God calls us to dare. When the sacrifice is necessary, He will give the command. That is the moment for daring. Until that moment comes, it is ours to go quietly forward with Him, and to wait patiently for Him.

EXODUS XII

THERE are senses in which this chapter may seem to lack the fascination and profundity of some others. As a matter of fact it is of fundamental importance, as all the history of the Hebrew people stands related to it. It gives us the account of the institution of the Passover, the annual religious rite which has ever been central to the life and history of the Hebrew people. It marks the occasion, describes the ritual, and declares the purpose of that Feast.

The year in which the feast was instituted was the year Anno Hominis 2513 (that is from the creation of man). This calculation is not based on Ussher's dates, although they were approximately correct. It rather accepts the chronology of the Bible from the standpoint of its own statements concerning the ages of men. That whole subject was exhaustively dealt with by Martin Anstey in his " Romance of Bible Chronology."

A brief glance back over the history is necessary to an understanding of this chapter. Abraham had entered the land four hundred and ninety years before the Exodus. It is good sometimes to remind ourselves of the apparent slowness in the Divine procedure, for we are often in danger of becoming impatient concerning the activities of God. By the measurement of our calendars they are admittedly apparently slow. It is well, though, at that point to remind ourselves quite seriously that the apparent slowness of God is always due to the actual slowness of man in his response to, and co-operation with, the Divine programme. An application of that may be made in passing, to the great fact of the Second Advent of our Lord. While many people are busily discussing the question of whether He is near, or far, it would be well to remember that there is good reason to believe that it might have already taken place if the Church of God had been true to her call and mission.

To return to the subject now being dealt with. Nearly five centuries before the Exodus, God's chosen man had been called, in order that through him a nation might be created for the blessing of all the nations. The long delay was due to the slowness of man. It is unnecessary to go into the details of that period.

All are familiar with them. Enough to remind ourselves that because of deflection from the pathway of faith, the people springing from the loins of Abraham had been down into Egypt, segregated in Goshen for at least two hundred and fifty years. Their presence there was due to failure, but in the Divine economy, was a method by which they were segregated from all possibility of contamination with surrounding nations. Thus through the strange fires of discipline they had been prepared for what was now to follow.

The time had now come when it was necessary for this people to be brought to a national constitution and consciousness. They had lived long in a slavery, which in process of time had become abject and cruel. By that baptism of long-continued suffering the fibre of the people had been stiffened; and even though they had lapsed into a condition of hopelessness, that very sense of their own insufficiency prepared the way for the action of God. God never comes a day too soon. He never comes a day too late. The interventions of God in human history always take place at the right hour ; whether they are brought about through souls loyal, or by others whom He girds, even though they have not known Him, as in the case of Cyrus.

The hour, then, had struck in the history of this people for a new and onward movement. Here then took place a supernatural intervention of God wherein and whereby the people who had been enthralled in bondage, were brought out into liberty. This chapter tells the story of the rite established in connection with this emancipation, which rite was to remain a memorial of that great event through all subsequent history.

It is impossible then to read a chapter like this in connection with the history preceding it, and with all subsequent history, without realizing of what supreme importance the things recorded therein must be.

The chapter opens with the words, "And Jehovah spake unto Moses and Aaron in the land of Egypt, saying." This shows that whatever follows is the record of the words of Divine authority. Jehovah now spoke to the people over whom He had watched through all the years, never deviating from His purpose, that purpose ever love-inspired, in spite of all their suffering. He spoke to them through a leader whom He had elected out of the midst of their bitter slavery. The whole story is full of fascinating beauty, and reveals how God works through simple methods which, at the moment, may seem to be entirely unimportant. A baby cried into the face of a woman, and as a result of that cry, was taken into the court of Pharaoh, and educated, so that a New Testament writer describes him as "learned with all the learning of the Egyptians." After forty years, he passed from the court to the splendid loneliness of the desert, and this through an act on his part which was characterized by zeal without knowledge. Here again God was seen over-ruling, and moving forward. After the second period of forty years in his life, his real work in the purpose of God commenced.

The first word of God to Moses in this connection constituted a command by which the calendar was changed. "This month shall be unto you the beginning of months; it shall be the first month of the year to you." The month in which the word was spoken was the month Abib, the month of spring. Before this, the year had begun in Tishri, the month of harvest. The cycle of the year henceforth for this people was to begin with the secret of their national life which they were now facing; and that secret was the action of God through which He delivered them from bondage, and took them to be a peculiar people unto Himself. As we have already said, they had been held by geographical and racial circumstances in separation from other nations. Now in a new way, they were to be themselves an actual nation, not like the other nations, but peculiar, as a nation having one King, Jehovah Himself; a Theocracy.

Here then we have the account of two inter-locking feasts. The first was the feast of Passover, and the second the feast of Unleavened Bread, which were always observed together. Passover became the great central religious feast of the year to the Hebrew people. There is a sense in which the Day of Atonement was a greater day, but from the standpoint of national existence Passover was the supreme feast. It is interesting to observe in passing that in the Bible we have ten recorded observances of the Passover.

Let us first consider this feast as to its simple ceremonial on the first occasion. The lamb selected must be a perfect one, without blemish. Such a lamb was to be slain; selected on the tenth day of the month, and slain on the fourteenth day. The blood of the lamb was to be sprinkled on the lintel, and on the side posts of the houses; never on the threshold. There was to be no trampling across that blood. The blood being thus sprinkled, the lamb was to constitute a meal, eaten within the house, with the doors closed. All this was certainly rightly intended to be symbolic. It is interesting to remember in passing, that this is the only religious feast of the Hebrew people observed in the night.

We may enquire now what it meant at the moment to these people. Jehovah's judgment was abroad in the land. After long patience with Pharaoh, whose heart God had rendered strong through the process; that is, had maintained him in strength of personality, enabling him to act for himself, during which process Pharaoh had calloused his own heart against the commands of God, Jehovah ratified his action, and hardened his heart. This is ever the method of God. He is patient, He waits, He pleads, He follows. But if man persists in hardening his own heart, there does come a moment when God ratifies that action. The final opportunity had been given to him; and now, because of his persistent rebellion, the judgments of God were abroad in the land. Inside the houses of the Hebrew people, with the blood sprinkled on the lintel and the side posts, families were eating the Passover feast in fellowship. Outside, the angel of death was smiting, but never entered a house on which the blood was sprinkled.

If we look at these groups gathered in the houses we see that they were all there in the attitude of pilgrims; their loins were girt; they stood with staff in hand, and sandals were on their feet. They were ready for the march. They ate the Passover feast in haste, while yet conscious of perfect security created for them by the fact that they had been obedient to the Divine command.

It is impossible to say how far they understood the ultimate significance of the thing taking place. In all probability they did not understand; but they acted in faith. We look back on the scene, and recognize how symbolic it was. The judgments of God were active, but safety was provided for men through sacrifice, according to Divine arrangement. We have no record of such a case as we may imagine ever happening; but for the sake of argument let us suppose that there had been one of the Hebrew people who said, This whole thing is without rationality. Nothing is going to happen. We need not obey this commandment. In such a case it is certain that the angel of death would have entered the house of a Hebrew as surely as he did the palace of Pharaoh. Such then was the spiritual value or significance of the rite. It spoke of shelter through sacrifice, and was a great foreshadowing, a shining out of principles through the simple observance of a ritual.

In close connection with this feast of Passover was the feast of Unleavened Bread. No leaven in any form was to be eaten at that feast. That is the first place in the Bible where there is any reference to leaven. The Hebrew word for leaven here means exactly what we mean when we speak of yeast. Yeast is the principle of fermentation; and fermentation has been defined, not by a theologian, but by a scientist, as chemical decomposition. Leaven is always an element of destruction.

In the New Testament it still has the same significance. The Greek word means exactly what the Hebrew word means, and refers to that which disintegrates, breaks up, and destroys.

If the symbolism of the lamb slain and the blood sprinkled spoke of safety through sacrifice when judgment was abroad; and the meal was to be partaken of by pilgrims ready for the march, ready for the next move under the shelter of that redeeming sacrifice; it was insisted upon that they ate no bread that was leavened, thus symbolizing the fact that nothing must be permitted which should disintegrate and break up the unity of the Divine purpose, either in individual life, or among the people who were now to be constituted a nation in the economy of God.

On that night then, " much to be remembered," that strange night, feasts were established, symbolic and suggestive to the nation which was about to emerge. The national life was based upon a Divine action, redeeming the people from slavery, bringing them under the authority of God, in a new and more intimate way; and reminding them that nothing was to be allowed to exist among them which should hinder the Divine purpose.

In the reading of the story it ever seems to me of the utmost importance that we should observe a matter which we may be in danger of over-looking. I refer to the declared statement as to the reason why these feasts were established. That reason is clearly declared in the words,

" And it shall come to pass when your children shall say unto you, What mean ye by this service? that ye shall say, It is the sacrifice of the Lord's Passover, Who passed over the houses of the children of Israel in Egypt, when He smote the Egyptians, and delivered our houses."

That is the statement to which I have referred as likely to be hurried over. The declaration is that when God established this ritual feast, He did so in the interests of the children. He was arranging for the generations that were to come. God's action was based upon the philosophy which we are so slow even yet to grasp, that the hope of the future is in the child; that if the child be rightly trained and informed, God's highway in human history is maintained.

Another illustration of it in the history of these people occurred later. When, after a period of sojourning in the wilderness they entered the land and crossed the Jordan, God commanded that the priests should take up out of the river-bed twelve stones, and build them as a memorial on the other side the river; and they were told that the purpose was that when the children should ask the meaning of the stones they should be told. God is constantly putting in front of the eyes of the children, things that make them ask questions; and there is no work more important that that of answering those questions, and so interpreting to the child the government and the method of God.

There follows the story of the Exodus itself, which is so familiar that we need not tarry with it at any length. Judgment fell upon Egypt, and then the strange remorseful appeal of Pharaoh was heard that the people should leave. So they passed out, and in that passing the national life began. They passed from slavery to freedom, from brutal oppression to life under beneficent authority, from degradation, which slavery always brings, to ennoblement, which life under true government ensures. Freedom does not mean license. It never means that every man is to go his own way. That is chaos, it is anarchy, it is hell. Freedom is life under law, which conditions it perfectly.

The chapter tells us that when they marched, there went with them a mixed multitude. There is always some weakness in the going of men, even in obedience to the command of God. These people were not of their flesh, not of their race. They were not the chosen of God. They caused trouble in coming days. We find that referred to in Numbers, the eleventh chapter and the fourth verse. The last reference to the mixed multitude is found so far on in their history as Nehemiah xiii. 3. The mixed multitude has always been a menace to the march of God and the people of God. It is so to-day. The organized Churches of to-day are crowded with a mixed multitude; and these for evermore hinder the progress of the people of God.

Thus we see the Exodus. Not yet have they received their constitution in detail. This will be given them from God through Moses. Here we see them on the march.

What an hour in human history that was all the following centuries prove. In connection with it this ritual of the Passover is described as an ordinance, a feast, a sacrifice. It is an ordinance, that is, an authoritative arrangement. It is a feast, that is, an occasion of rejoicing over deliverance. It is a sacrifice, that is, the recognition of the fact that their national life was due not to their own management, wit, wisdom, or cleverness, but to an act of God through which they were brought to Himself.

The New Testament refers to both these feasts as symbolic of the whole Christian economy. Paul said, in writing to the Corinthians.

" Purge out the old leaven, that ye may be a new lump, even as ye are unleavened. For our Passover also hath been sacrificed, even Christ."

Thus he refers to the feast of Unleavened Bread, and to the feast of Passover, showing how the Divine purposes symbolically suggested in these feasts to the Hebrew people, have been fulfilled, and are being carried forward through Christ and His Church.

EXODUS XX

THIS is pre-eminently the chapter of Law, containing the Ten Words which are basic to morality. This is universally admitted, even when the earlier commandments are either denied or ignored. The ten commandments fall into two distinct groups. The first group of four has to do with relationships between God and man. These to-day are very largely ignored. The second group of six has to do with relationships between man and man. These are accepted almost universally as basic.

It must at once be admitted that there are those to-day who minimize the value of some of the commands in this second group, but they are very generally accepted as of supreme importance.

While it is true that we have here the laws of the Hebrew people, it must not be forgotten that the very existence of this nation was, in the Divine economy, in the interest of all nations; and the laws, while given to the Hebrews, are wide as the race in their value and application.

In considering this chapter it is impossible to deal with the commandments in detail, although we shall pass them rapidly in review. Our purpose is rather that of seeing them in their setting, because for their interpretation the whole story is necessary. Let us then attempt to grasp the significance of this chapter in its revelation of law, proceeding from God, through His ancient people, for the government of human life. In doing so we have to remember that no such laws as these were necessary in Eden. They were rendered necessary by human failure. " The law came in beside," that is by the side of human sin, as Paul puts it. Thus it was given to man who had missed his way through loss of direct fellowship with God.

The chapter falls into four distinct parts, revealing :—

The source and origin of Law. Verses one and two.

The two-fold expression of Law. Verses three to seventeen.

The first effect of Law. Verses eighteen to twenty-one.

The way of the approach of the Law-giver. Verses twenty-two to twenty-six.

The first division is of supreme importance, for in these two verses we have a statement which conditions everything that follows. They reveal Moses as the scribe, recording the speech of God.

The source and origin of Law are revealed in the words, " I am Jehovah thy God." Whatever follows is thus introduced by a declaration concerning God Himself. He begins by using His name, adding to it a designation. The name Jehovah is here, as ever, full of significance, stressing not His sovereignty, not His might, but His attitude towards His people. The word *Yahweh*, being part of the verb to become, does not reveal essential Being, while it postulates it; but declares rather that this essential Being becomes whatever is needed to meet the requirements of those who are His. To use the thought and language of the New Testament, the name reveals Him as the God of grace.

Thus the first thought in this use of the Name, which must qualify all the laws, is that they proceed from this God of grace; but the designation added, " Thy God," interpreted by the first occurrence of that designation in Scripture (Genesis i. 1) speaks of His might and His wisdom. Thus, if there is a wooing winsomeness—and there certainly is—in the use of the Name, there is also the note of sovereignty and might in the Designation. If Jehovah stands for grace, God, used as it is here, stands for government.

Following this revelation of name and designation, an action is recorded, " Who brought thee out of the land of Egypt, out of the house of bondage." Thus, the basis of law in itself, is discovered in the name and designation; the basis of law in its application, is found in this description of those to whom it is sent. The laws are for those who are related to God on the basis of an action whereby He has brought them out of bondage to Himself.

This does not contradict that which has already been stated, namely, that the revelation of moral requirement is intended for all the nations. It does emphasize the fact that all the nations are to be reached through those who are thus redeemed. This is an abiding principle. The law of God demands first, subjection to God Himself. If we overleap intervening centuries, and stand in Palestine, in imagination, we find ourselves listening to Jesus. The day of Moses was passing. The new day was dawning. Our Lord was enunciating His ethic; and in doing so, putting it into comparison with this same law which came by Moses. My reference to the fact now is to note the same principle revealed in the words, " Seeing the multitudes, He went up into the mountain; and . . . His disciples came unto Him, and He opened His mouth and taught them." That is to say that all that followed of ethical enunciation, was given to those who were already submitted to Him as disciples.

The next section contains the Ten Words themselves with which, as has already been said, it is impossible to deal in detail, but we may summarize them.

The first four have to do with the relationship of these people, brought from bondage to God to be under His government, with Himself. In the first word, " Thou shalt have none other gods before Me," the word " before " does not mark precedence, as though it might be permissible to have some other god, if this God were given the primary place. It rather means in front of, or before the face of. Quite simply it is the law that claims that there must be no God other than " Jehovah-God." The first requirement of this Divine law is that man must sweep out anything and everything from the place where God alone should be. Thus every individual is brought into direct relationship with God. There is to be no interference between God and the human soul. It is a stern command, but beneficently so; for it is only in such direct relationship that man can ever find fullness of life.

The next command forbids the making of anything intended to represent God. It is a threefold requirement, " Thou shalt not make . . . nor worship . . . nor serve." In this there is the revelation of a sequence from which men cannot escape. Whatever be God to the human soul, the soul worships, and consequently, serves.

There is to be no attempt to represent God, because there can be no perfect representation of Him. That nearest to the likeness of God in creation is man himself. But man, having lost that image and likeness, there can be no representation which is accurate. Here inescapably, there breaks in upon the consciousness the value of the Incarnation. In Jesus, God's second Man, we have the perfect Image and Likeness of God, so that through Him we ultimately find and understand God. Jesus represented God on the earth level, being human; but from above the earth level, being Divine. Apart from Him, there can be no representation of God which will not mislead.

The third word commanded that there should be no profanation of the Name. This will at once be recognised as something of far profounder significance than the forbidding of what we commonly describe as profane swearing. The name of Jehovah God is profaned when it is used without the submission of life to all that it suggests and demands. To put this matter briefly. If in the sanctuary we say, " Our Father, Who art in the heavens, Thy name be hallowed, Thy will be done, Thy Kingdom come," and after the uttering of the words pass out into every-day life, without seeking that Kingdom, by doing that will, and by hallowing that Name, we are profaning the Name in itself. In the last analysis the blasphemy of the sanctuary is more dangerous than the blasphemy of the slum.

The final commandment on the first table is a double one. We often refer to it as the commandment to keep the Sabbath holy. That is not all the truth. The first part of the commandment is not that we should worship on the seventh day, but that we should work for six days. No one is really prepared for worship on the seventh day who has not worked on six days. It is equally true that no one can work in the full and glorious sense of the word who knows nothing of what it is to worship.

Thus the first four commandments condition relationship between God and man; and it is only as these are appreciated and obeyed, that those which follow can be appreciated and obeyed.

We turn then to the six commandments conditioning relationship between man and man. The first of these is, " Honour thy father and thy mother." This is a recognition of the fact that individual being is rooted in fatherhood and motherhood; and a requirement that this fact must never be lost sight of. Any human being who loses respect for father and mother is to be trusted by no other human being. Alas! that in many cases parenthood in itself is so utterly degenerate, that respect for it becomes well nigh, if not altogether, impossible. Nevertheless, even in such a case the Word does abide, and the very fact of relationship is one that must condition the attitude of children to parents. It is perfectly true that that does not tell all the story, but only that of human instrumentality, for every human life has direct personal relationship with God in the mystery of its being.

The next command forbids murder, and thus emphasises the sanctity of the individual, and its right to live. Every human being has such right, and therefore no other human being has any right to take the life of his fellow, until or unless he is under distinct Divine command, the instrument for carrying out the decree of

God. No man, on his own initiative, because of his desire for revenge or vengeance, has any right to rob another of life. I repeat, the command emphasizes the sanctity of individuality.

The next command, " Thou shalt not commit adultery," has a profound significance in its application to the family, as God's first circle of society. It is infinitely more than a law demanding personal chastity, being supremely one safeguarding the home. When we read of divorces, I wonder if we realize that the ultimate and most terrible side of the tragedy is the effect upon children. Whether the divorce is consummated here or there, for this reason or for that, those who are most likely to be permanently injured, and whose development along true lines is rendered difficult, if not impossible, are the children. In the economy of God, society is built on the purity and strength of the family. When that breaks down, the nation is blasted, and the race is damned.

In the command which forbids stealing, the rights of property are recognised and safeguarded. Perhaps no exposition of this is needed. It is clear-cut, definite, and final; that no man has the right to take for himself that which rightly belongs to his fellow man.

When we reach the next commandment forbidding false witness, we are moving out into the larger circle, including every form of social inter-relationship. No false witness means that in all our dealings with our fellow men, truth must be supreme. All our world troubles to-day, political and economic, result from a falling short in the recognition of the supreme importance of this commandment. The very term, " Secret diplomacy," may be a phrase to cover dishonesty in the supposed interests of prosperity. When the statesmen of the world gathered round the Green Table at Versailles, had there been no false witness, problems which are yet baffling us, would have found simple solution.

The last word, " Thou shalt not covet," is one of tremendous importance, as it deals with the inspirational centre of action, the realm of desire. Paul says that this was the command that convinced him that he was a sinner.

The philosophy of life revealed in this two-fold statement of law in the Ten Words is that when a man is right with God, he is right with his neighbour. That is what our Lord meant when He summarized the whole law in two commandments, " Thou shalt love the Lord thy God . . . and thy neighbour as thyself."

The next section in the chapter shows the first effect produced by this law upon these people. It was that of fear; and whereas all the surroundings of thunder and lightning, supernatural voices, and a mountain smoking were calculated to create fear, I believe the reason of that fear at its deepest was spiritual and moral. There was borne in upon them the consciousness of the holiness of God, and they were filled with appalling fear.

It was then that Moses said, Fear not, for God has come to make you fear. That is a fair summary of the thing actually said. In other words, the declaration was that God was creating fear in order to cast it out. The complete truth is revealed in that familiar couplet,

> " Fear Him, ye saints, and you will then,
> Have nothing else to fear."

The final paragraph gives the story of the erection of an altar. Moses addressing the people re-emphasized the first requirement of law, the necessity for loyalty to the one God. While no representation of God was to be made, an altar was to be erected; and the really arresting part of this story is the statement of the reason for the erection of the altar. It is found in these words,

> " In every place where I record My name, I will come unto thee, and I will bless thee."

Our general thought of the altar is that it is a way by which man may approach God. Now while there is an element of truth in that, the statement here is that it is the way by which God approaches man. While the altar is erected for burnt offerings of dedication, and peace offerings of communion; it symbolizes the way by which God may receive from man, and have communion with him.

The whole chapter is vibrant with thunder, and illumined with lightning, filled with voices and trumpets and terror, and a morality searching the soul, and filling it with fear; but in close connection God reveals the way by which He will approach man. It is the way of the altar.

It is interesting to consider the instructions concerning the altar. It must be of earth, that is, on the level of human experience; if of stone, no hewn wood is to be used, it is to have no graving upon it; nothing is to appear that marks an action of man, calculated to create pride in his heart. Still further, there are to be no steps by which man climbs to God. This means that He comes to our level, on to the earth. The principle of the Incarnation was shining through these instructions. The approach of God to man is always that of redeeming grace, in order to righteous government, and fulness of life.

" We have an altar," said the writer of the letter to the Hebrews, and linked the declaration with the name of Jesus, and His redeeming work. Through Him God approached man fully and finally, and that by the way of the Cross. Therefore through Him we have our access to God, and access to God ever means passing into the realm of love-inspired law, for the perfect conditioning of life.

Thus in Him there is fulfilment. We " are not come unto a mount that might be touched, and that burned with fire, and unto blackness, and darkness, and tempest, and the sound of a trumpet, and the voice of words; which voice they that heard intreated that no word more should be spoken unto them; for they could not endure that which was enjoined." We " are come . . . to Jesus the Mediator of a new covenant, and to the blood of sprinkling that speaketh better than that of Abel."

PSALM XXII

IN the Psalter, and perhaps in all literature, no single poem is to be found more poignant in expressing the experience of dereliction than is this psalm. The book of Job has dirges of dereliction, but it is certain that he never plumbed the depths of experience described by this singer. Nevertheless, the remarkable thing about this song of dereliction is that it merges into the note of jubilation. It is really the song of a sufferer who pours out his soul unto death. The moment of death is revealed in a broken verse, twenty-one, to which we shall come later on. Beyond that, the voice of the singer is heard again, no longer expressing dereliction, but in a pæan of victory.

The song is attributed to David. The only reason suggested against that view is that we have no circumstances recorded in the life of David which seem to explain such a song. There were hours of great suffering, but nothing that seems to fit such a song as this. Really, however, that objection has no value, because we are not supposed to have a full account of all his experiences. The song is also remarkable, in that it contains nothing in the nature of confession of sin. Sin is recognized, but not confessed as personal. Whoever the writer of the song may be, it came out of a double consciousness, that of God, and that of sorrow. It may be all unconsciously to the singer, the song was a great prophecy, finding its fulfilment in the climacteric sorrows of Messiah, and the ultimate result of them.

That our blessed Lord used the opening sentence of this Psalm on the Cross at once gives it a peculiar value, and suggests its Messianic character. In the hour of the uttermost in human dereliction, the opening sentence fell from His lips. Matthew records it, using the Hebrew form, " Eli, Eli, lama sabachthani?" Mark records it in its Aramaic form, " Eloi, Eloi, lama sabachthani?" I would at least suggest that when these words passed His lips, He was familiar with the whole psalm, and that in the cry we have a revelation of His own mind and thought at the time.

In the seventh and eighth verses of the psalm these words occur:—

" All they that see me laugh me to scorn;
They shoot out the lip, they shake the head, saying,
Commit thyself unto the Lord; let Him deliver him;
Let Him deliver him, seeing He delighteth in him."

Matthew, Mark, and Luke all tell of that ribald mockery; and Matthew employs these very words as the report of what men said around the Cross.

In verse eighteen, we read:—

> " They part my garments among them,
> And upon my vesture do they cast lots."

Luke records that as a fact in connection with the crucifixion; and John records it, and declares that the thing happened in fulfilment of these words.

In the twenty-first verse we find these words,

> " Save me from the lion's mouth;
> Yea, from the horns of the wild oxen Thou hast
> answered me."

Paul quoted these words as fulfilling his own experience when he found himself deserted, in fellowship with the sufferings of Christ.

In verse twenty-two the singer says:—

> " I will declare Thy name unto my brethren;
> In the midst of the congregation will I praise Thee."

The writer of the letter to the Hebrews quotes these words as being fulfilled in Christ.

Once more, in verse twenty-eight, is the statement:

> " For the Kingdom is Jehovah's."

John in apocalyptic vision saw that word fully accomplished through Christ.

This use of the psalm by New Testament writers shows that they recognized its Messianic value. Whereas it was almost certainly in its writing, the psalm of a lonely sufferer, whether that singer was conscious of it or no, the fact remains that only in Christ can we find One Whose experience perfectly fulfils that revealed in the song. Whatever may have been the experience of David, or some other writer, the suffering and the triumph described so transcends mere human suffering, and so ultimately sweeps in the whole world, that it is self-evident that in it there are meanings far beyond that of the experience of any merely human being.

The significance of the structure of this psalm is lost in our arrangement of it, and that in all our Versions. In the first movement of the psalm one voice is heard. In the second there are many voices. The first part is in the first twenty-five verses, and the second from verse twenty-six to the end. In our arrangement we find thirty-one verses. In the Hebrew psalm there are ten strophes; in the first part six, and in the second part four. Throughout the six the one voice is heard, the voice of one person. In the four strophes constituting the second part of the psalm, many voices are heard, first that of the singer in the beginning; and then other voices, until the ends of the earth are included.

The form of the verses are different. In the first six strophes we have five ten-line strophes (one to four, and six); while the fifth is broken in upon, and incomplete. That is the point where death comes, and leaves an unfinished strophe. In the sixth and final strophe the singer is heard beyond death. To indicate these strophe divisions by our verses; Strophe one is in verses one to five; Strophe 2, verses six to ten; Strophe three, verses eleven to fourteen; Strophe four, verses fifteen to eighteen; Strophe five, verses nineteen to twenty-one, and in that, in the Hebrew, there are only six lines. It is broken off like a broken column in a cemetery. Then the final Strophe is in verses twenty-two to twenty-five. Thus in the first movement the note of the psalm changes entirely, after the four strophes and the broken fifth; in the sixth and last, instead of travail there is triumph, instead of a dirge there is a pæan of praise.

In the second part we have four three-line strophes. The first is in verse twenty-six; the second in verses twenty-seven and twenty-eight; the third in verse twenty-nine, and the first sentence of verse thirty; and the fourth begins in the middle of the thirtieth verse and runs to the end.

The first part of the psalm, in which one voice is heard, falls into two parts, the first describing dereliction, verses one to twenty-one; and the second revealing jubilation, verses twenty-two to twenty-five.

In the section revealing dereliction, there are three movements, the first showing the singer in relation to God (1-6a); the second in relation to man (6b-18); the third an appeal to God (19-21).

The sense of dereliction with regard to God opens with the cry,

" My God, my God, why hast Thou forsaken me?"

The Hebrew word rendered " forsaken " literally means loosen, or relinquish, or let me go. The cry might be rendered,

" My God, my God, why hast Thou relinquished me?"

The Greek word employed in translating by the evangelists is one which literally means, " leave me behind." We might then render it,

" My God, my God, why hast Thou left me behind?"

The first impressive fact here is that the cry is not that of one who has never known God, but that of one who has known Him, has been travelling with Him, has been in fellowship with Him. The sense of the soul is that fellowship has been broken in upon. Observe still further that however much the sufferer for the moment, for some reason might be conscious of this break, his enquiry is neither rebellious nor complaining, and he still affirms relationship in the form of address, " My God, my God." Whenever we think of these words as passing the lips of our adorable Redeemer, these things should be borne in mind.

Now let us face a question which inevitably arises, and to which, let it at once be said, possibly there can be no final answer. The question is, Is there any reply to the " Why?" Personally I think there is, and that it is to be found in the context. After emphasizing the sense of loss, in pregnant sentences the affirmation is made, " But Thou art holy." That is the answer to the " Why." I submit that after those words there should be a full stop; the next sentence,

" O Thou that inhabitest the praises of Israel,"

being linked with what follows.

" Our fathers trusted in Thee;
They trusted, and Thou didst deliver them.
They cried unto Thee and were delivered,
They trusted in Thee, and were not ashamed.
But I am a worm, and no man."

The singer described himself in an appeal to God as " forsaken," and asks why. In what follows he looks back to what God has been to His people, and how He wrought deliverances for them. All this puts the singer into contrast with these things of past history and having asked " Why? " he has said that God is holy, while he is a worm, and no man.

There is an arresting significance in the use of the word " worm " at this point. The Hebrew word for " worm " is exactly the same as the word for " crimson." We read in Isaiah, " Though your sins . . . be red like crimson." Once more I reverently suggest that when our Lord employed the opening enquiry on His Cross, He did so with full knowledge of that which followed in the psalm; and the answer to the question is found in the affirmation of the holiness of God, towards One Who, at the moment, was crimson, the embodiment of sin, the incarnation of human failure.

The sense of dereliction with regard to man immediately follows as the singer described Himself as a reproach of men and despised of the people. From those opening verses right through verse eighteen He speaks of Himself as being the centre of ribald mockery, of cruel brutality, of appalling callousness. Men are seen waiting for His dying, nay, not even waiting for that dying, for they gambled for His garments ere He died. Thus humanity is seen around that Sufferer in all its ghastly failure, utterly blind to the real meaning of His suffering; mocking, brutal, callous.

Out of this double sense of dereliction came the great appeal beginning,

"But be Thou not far off, O Lord."

Thus, though in some senses forsaken, His consciousness was that of the distance of God. God had left Him behind, at a distance. He had relinquished Him, but He was there somewhere. This plaintive, pregnant passage runs on, until its last word, the end of the broken strophe,

"Save me from the lion's mouth;
Yea, from the horns of the wild oxen Thou hast
answered me."

That suggests a hiatus and an end, in which there merged the cry, and the declaration of assurance. It harmonizes completely with the historic account of how, at the very last on the Cross, the Redeemer said, "Father, into Thy hands I commend My Spirit."

Immediately there follows the arrestingly contrasting words,

"I will declare Thy name unto My brethren,"

and the note of jubilation is manifest. The result of the dereliction is the ability to make God known.

"I will declare Thy name unto My brethren;
In the midst of the congregation will I praise Thee."

Then the same voice makes its appeal to others. The language of the Sufferer beyond the suffering, beyond the dereliction is heard, declaring the result of it all; and now affirming that whereas He was forsaken of God, and despised of men, yet God had not abhorred the affliction of the afflicted, neither ultimately had He hid His face from Him. Rather, all the experiences were transmuted into the means by which there should be proclaimed to men a redeeming grace through which their right relationship with God might be established for ever.

In the second part of the psalm many voices are heard. The enlarging outlook is self-evident. First, there is a declaration of the result of the victory won to the individual. This is found in one verse, twenty-six. From that point to the end, the wider outlook is in view (27-31).

The individual application of the Messianic work, accomplished through suffering and leading to triumph, is revealed in the words,

> " The meek shall eat and be satisfied;
> They shall praise the Lord that seek after Him;
> Let your heart live for ever."

The juxtaposition of two words here is significant; the words " meek," and " seek." In the great Manifesto of Jesus we find the declaration, " Blessed are the meek," and also the command, " Seek first the Kingdom of God." These two words, indicate the people who are able to enter into possession of the values of the travail and triumph of the Redeemer. They are the " meek," who " seek." The meek are all such as have done with themselves and their pride, and who have denied self; while the seekers are those who do far more than indulge in speculations or admire ideals; those, in short, who treat the whole matter seriously, and with absolute devotion to the end.

Then the wider outlook.

> " All the ends of the earth shall remember and turn unto the Lord,
> And all the kindreds of the nations shall worship before Thee."

Three words will fix this upon the mind. The ends of the earth are to remember, to return, to revere.

The work of the Redeemer first recalls the people who have forgotten God to remembrance and recognition. Such remembrance will draw them back, and they will return to the Lord. Such remembrance and return will issue in reverence, which is worship in the full and perfect sense of the word.

Finally, everything is explained in the reaffirmation of the sovereignty of God,

"The Kingdom is Jehovah's;
And He is the Ruler over the nations."

The result of that recognition of sovereignty, as the result of the work of the Redeemer, is that "all the fat ones," that is, the vigorous ones, shall eat and worship; and those who lack vigour "all they that go down to the dust," who cannot keep their soul alive, "shall bow before Him."

Thus the whole earth, strong and weak, yielding to its sovereign Lord, through the redeeming work of the Messiah, is seen satisfied.

There is to be continuity too, for

"A seed shall serve Him;
It shall be told of the Lord unto the next generation.
They shall come and declare His righteousness
Unto a people that shall be born."

The ultimate phrase reflects the glory of God, "That He hath done it."

It is impossible to read this psalm, and believe that the singer understood all its meaning. It was a prophetic utterance. It was a case in which David, or some other poet, was caught up, borne along; and through personal suffering and deliverance from it through confidence in God, interpreted the ultimate, central, final sorrows of the Messiah; and how through them, and through them alone, deliverance should come to the meek, who seek; and the sovereignty of God, based upon His redeeming activity, should finally be universally established.

PSALM XXIII

THIS psalm has one theme. I think it may be expressed thus: the sufficiency of God for all human need. It is indeed an unruffled song of rest. All the circumstances of our pilgrimage, want and weariness, wanderings and perplexities, the shadowed mysteries of the valleys, and the thronging enemies, and the infinite Beyond, are recognised as we take our way through the song. They are only mentioned in order to negation. Want is cancelled, weariness finds a resting place in green pastures. Through perplexity there is guidance; and finally, the path runs on until it ends, not in a tangled wilderness, but in the King's palace.

The psalm is arresting because the note is strictly personal. There are great songs that are universal, in which we hear the cadences and the harmonies of massed humanity; but this is a solo. There are only two persons referred to in it from beginning to end; Jehovah and the singer. Once we see a group, or groups, somewhere in the neighbourhood, called " enemies," but they are at a safe distance because the singer is with Jehovah.

We have come to call it " The Shepherd Psalm," but let me at once say it is more than that. In our arrangement of it we have six verses. As a matter of fact there are actually three strophes. The first takes up verse one, and verse two, and the first part of verse three, ending with the words, " He restoreth my soul."

The second begins in verse three, and runs through verse four. The third occupies verses five and six.

Three strophes, and read thus, we see that they set forth three different lines of thought concerning God, under three distinct figures of speech. The first is the Shepherd; the second is the Guide; and the last is the Host. If we call it the Shepherd psalm, the Shepherd is also the Guide and Host. To limit the interpretation of this poetic gem to the activities of a shepherd is to put a strain on it that it was never intended to bear. Let us then follow its natural movement which presents Jehovah in three aspects, the Shepherd, the Guide, and the Host.

Whenever I read this psalm, I seem to hear two sayings of Jesus, and the first is this, " I am the Good Shepherd," and the second is this, " Fear not, little flock, for it is your Father's good pleasure to give you the Kingdom."

He said, " I am the Good Shepherd." Said the old Hebrew song, in those days long ago, " Jehovah is my Shepherd," and the decades had run on, and the centuries had run on, and there stood among the sons of men a Man of their own humanity, but infinitely more, and He said, " I am the Good Shepherd." John in the prologue to his Gospel, says that " The Son Who is in the bosom of the Father hath declared Him." Take the Greek word for that word " declared," and without translating, transliterate it, and it reads " He hath exegeted Him." Jesus is the Exegesis of God. " Jehovah is my Shepherd," " I am the Good Shepherd "; and if we want to understand all the fullness of that old Hebrew song, a fullness greater than the singer knew, we shall find it in Jesus.

And then in that second word of Jesus, the merging of metaphors exactly corresponds with the merging figures of this psalm. If a literary critic read that, he would probably be confused by it. I mean a merely literary critic, for such always breaks down, because life is more than language; and the great verities transcend the possibility of literature. The merely literary critic then, taking this saying of Jesus, " Fear not little flock, for it is your Father's good pleasure to give you the Kingdom," might be inclined to say that whoever wrote it, or uttered it, was getting his metaphors mixed. " Fear not little flock," and the figure is that of a Shepherd; " It is your Father's good pleasure," and suddenly the flock is forgotten, and the family is seen; " to give you the Kingdom," and we have still another figure of speech, no longer the flock, or the family, but a nation. But we recognise that though the metaphors merge, they do not mix; and in that great word of Jesus, He was revealing the threefold attitude of God towards His people. The figures exactly coincide with those of the psalm, when it is divided into its true Hebrew strophes, as I have been attempting to point out. " Jehovah is my Shepherd," " Fear not, little flock "; " He guideth me," " It is your Father's good pleasure." The Guide is the Father. Call to mind the word in Jeremiah, " My Father, Thou art the Guide of my youth." " Thou preparest a table before me . . . and I shall dwell in the house of Jehovah for ever." " To give you the Kingdom." Thus the figures of the psalm and the metaphors of the word of Jesus perfectly agree.

Now examine the movement. First of all the Shepherd is seen, caring for the flock. The Father is then seen, guiding on the pilgrimage. The King is finally seen, providing hospitality for to-day and all the coming ages. These are the great things revealed in the song.

The Shepherd is seen caring for the sheep of the flock.
" Jehovah is my Shepherd, I shall not want." That is the complete
affirmation, " I shall not want." Rotherham, perhaps taking a
little liberty with the tenses, yet reveals the essential value of
the statement as he renders it, " I have no want." It is not merely
an outlook on the future. It is the declaration of an abiding fact.
" I have no want," I have no lack. That is the meaning of the
word. " Jehovah is my Shepherd, I have no lack." Everything
is said there from the standpoint of the revelation of God under
the figure of the Shepherd.

Then follow the words:

> " He maketh me to lie down in green pastures;
> He leadeth me beside still waters.
> He restoreth my soul."

Here the thought is that of the Shepherd, choosing the
situations into which the sheep are brought. This is not a
pilgrimage, it is pasturage. The idea of a journey has not yet
emerged. The Eastern shepherd, when he leads his sheep from
place to place, is not taking them on a journey. The one purpose
of movement with the shepherd is the care of the shepherd for their
pasturage and rest. The purpose is the sustenance of life. The
Shepherd is never a guide in the sense to which we come in the
second strophe. Here God is revealed as choosing our situations, as
the shepherd always chooses situations in the interests of the
sheep. He takes the sheep where the pasturage is to be found, and
where the waters abound. So, " He leadeth me."

When we pass to the next strophe, beginning, " He guideth
me," the figure of speech has changed. That is why the revisers
have changed the word. The old version read, " He leadeth me,"
in both places. The revision has changed the word,

> " He guideth me in the paths of righteousness."

The thought embedded in the first word, " leadeth " is to
run as a river, as a stream. Of course it is a pictorial word. In
use it meant always to conduct in order to protect, and in order to
sustain. That is the first review of God, the Shepherd choosing
situations,

> " Jehovah is my Shepherd, I have no want;
> He maketh me to lie down . . .
> He leadeth me."

He creates or He chooses the situations, and then very
beautifully, the singer stresses the purpose of it all.

> " He maketh me to lie down in pastures of tender grass."

" Green pastures " is very beautiful but the Hebrew with a little more literalness, is, " in pastures of tender grass," just what the sheep need, " He maketh me to lie," rest, and sustenance.

" He leadeth me beside the waters of rest."

The idea of rest is found in both cases; the rest that comes from life sufficiently and perfectly sustained by the Shepherd. Travel back in imagination, in memory, some of you, to the Eastern land, and watch the shepherd with his flock, leading them here and there in order to reach the vegetation, the richest pastures, that their life may be sustained. That is the first picture of God, " Jehovah is my Shepherd." He chooses the situations into which I come, and He chooses them in order to the restfulness of my life, with the supply of the two things that are necessary for the sustenance of life in poise and rest and ease. That is the simple life, but it is the sublime life; it is the full life, it is the life of perfect rest.

And yet again. " He restoreth my soul." When we read that, we think of the sheep wandering. That is true, but there is far more than that in it. The word there rendered " restoreth " means He reneweth my soul, that is my personality. He reneweth continually. When there is weakness, He supplies vigour; when we wander, He recovers us. Any sheep in the flock, as the Shepherd watches, may sicken, and weaken, not having wandered at all. In that case He reneweth the life. Any sheep may break through a fence, and wander away where the thickets are. He goes after that sheep, and brings it back. He reneweth continually all the essential things of my personality.

Listen to Jesus. " Fear not, little flock." What was He saying to His disciples? Be not anxious, consider the birds, consider the lilies; your Father knoweth that you have need of food and drink and raiment. He knows. Then don't be anxious about them. Your Father knows that you have need. Seek His kingdom. " Fear not, little flock."

Now pass to the next. This strophe opens with the words, " He guideth me." To the Hebrew reader the word is arresting, and almost startling. Literally it reads,

" He driveth me in the paths of righteousness for His name's sake."

It is an interesting fact that the Hebrew word is also the word for a sigh. It came to be that because of the panting effect produced when driving has taken place. Does it seen as though all the gentleness of God was being denied? By no means. The gentleness is not forgotten, but the severity is recognised. Jehovah takes care of me personally. He is my Shepherd, making me to lie down in green pastures. My bread is given. My water is sure. But He driveth me. There is granite as well as grace in God. There is law as well as love; and there is law because there is love. He driveth me, where? "In the paths of righteousness." I cannot improve on that phrase, but I may make it a little blunter; "in right paths," and right paths are paths first of all, of purity and therefore of prosperity. The paths of righteousness are the paths that are right paths. That means they are pure and true. The element of holiness is there. Yes, but if they are right paths, they are paths of prosperity. Frances Ridley Havergal, in that little hymn,

"Light after darkness, gain after loss,"

and so forth, anticipating heaven's experience, says that when we reach the Land beyond, and review the pathway, we shall sing,

"Right was the pathway leading to this."

That is to say that the right path is the path of purity; but it is the path of prosperity. So He driveth me. We have left the figure of the Shepherd. In this country we talk about driving sheep, but this psalm was not written in this country, but in a land where shepherds never drive sheep, but lead them. They go before. This is not the shepherd, it is the guide; and as a father. It is a Father disciplining, love-impulsed; refusing to allow us to break from the right way.

"He driveth me in the paths of righteousness."

To travel in paths of righteousness is to confront difficulties, and so the psalmist goes on,

"Yea, though I walk through the valley of the shadow of death."

Quite rightly we think of death when we read that, but it is more than that. It is though I walk through gloomy ravines, though I walk amid the rocks where the shadows are so dense that I have lost any glimmer of light. There are experiences of life that are far more terrific than death can ever be. Some of you have passed through the gloomy ravines, through deep and dense darkness, the shadow of death. Yes, the valley of the shadow of death. If God drives me on right paths, there will assuredly be the valleys of deep darkness, and the possibility of prowling beasts hiding somewhere to come down upon me. What then?

"Yea, though I walk through the gloomy ravines of darkness,
I will fear no evil; for Thou art with me."

He drives me, but He travels with me.

And then this beautiful thing,

" Thy rod and Thy staff, they comfort me."

We nearly always interpret that as referring to the shepherd's crook. As a matter of fact these are not the instruments of the shepherd. The rod literally is the club; the staff is the staff of the pilgrim. The rod is for defence; the staff is for weakness and weariness. The pilgrim says, Yes, He is driving me, and here are the gloomy ravines, but I am not afraid; I will fear no evil. I would fear, I dare not go alone, but He is here; and I have seen in His hand the club that makes me secure against enemies; and I have seen the staff upon which I lean when I am tired.

" Thy club and Thy staff, they comfort me."

The comfort is the sense that the Divine Guide is the Companion on the pilgrimage; a complete Defence to me against all prowling enemies; and for evermore providing me with what I need when I am weary by the way.

Listen to Jesus. " It is your Father's good pleasure." If the Guide is driving, and if sometimes I have to say, the way is dark my Father, cloud upon cloud is gathering thickly o'er my head, and loud the thunders roar about me; I can always also say, Father take my hand, for He is ever there; not merely sustaining my life as a Shepherd, but guiding me on the pilgrimage, and guiding as a Father. He drives, and He accompanies, and defends, and strengthens me all the way.

And so we come to the last strophe.

Here we have the Host, and the Host is the King. He is seen providing hospitality. When? To-day. How long? For ever.

He provides hospitality on the pilgrimage.

" Thou preparest a table before me in the presence of mine enemies."

That is sustenance. He provides it.

" Thou hast anointed my head with oil."

That is gladness upon the pilgrimage. Thou hast anointed me with " the oil of gladness " above my fellows.

" My cup runneth over."

That is abundance, everything I need.

Then that beautiful touch,

" Surely goodness and loving kindness shall follow me."

Two qualities personified, as though they were attendants, waiting on me all the time; goodness in the widest sense; and mercy, or kindness.

The singer was conscious of the hospitality of God all the way. It is not merely the provision of all that which is necessary for life, that is the Shepherd. It is not merely the guidance that drives and accompanies; that is the Guide. It is hospitality all the way. That is the King.

And then at last, what? The end of the earthly pilgrimage is in the King's house, " in the house of Jehovah for ever."

Again, listen to Jesus. Just before He left the world, He said, " In My Father's house there are many abiding places," but I am going " to prepare the place for you." Again before He went He said, " I am with you all the days." Thus He brings us " to His banqueting house, and His banner over us is love."

We are not yet beyond the place where enemies are round about us. Then He spreads our table in the presence of our enemies. While we are still on this rough pilgrimage, or engaged in this severe warfare as the case may be, He does more than that. He anoints the head with oil. He gives songs in the night. He makes the darkest morning radiant with the rainbow. All the way, He is the Host; but the Host is the King, and the " cup runneth over." And all the way, two attendants are waiting on me, Goodness and Mercy.

Presently we shall go on, beyond the pastures of tender grass, and the still waters that have restored and have sustained us here; and presently we will be beyond the driving discipline that keeps our feet in the way, the paths of righteousness; and presently we will be beyond the place where the enemies are still lurking; but we shall never be away from the Shepherd, Father, King. We shall " dwell in the house of the Lord for ever."

" The Lord is my Shepherd, I shall not want."
The Lord is my Guide; I shall be rightly led.
The Lord is my King, I shall reach His palace by and by.

PSALM LI

THE Psalter contains seven psalms commonly and properly designated penitential. They are six, thirty-two, thirty-eight, fifty-one, one hundred and two, one hundred and thirty, and one hundred and forty-three. Five of these, the first four, and the last are attributed to David. Among these psalms the fifty-first is central and supreme as a psalm of penitence.

It is headed:

"For the Chief Musician. A Psalm of David; when Nathan the prophet came unto him, after he had gone in to Bath-sheba."

We may take it that such description correctly places the psalm in the life of David. Thus it was written in connection with what, judged by human standards, was the darkest blot on his escutcheon. When I say judged by human standards, I mean that some sins of the spirit are more terrible than those of the flesh, more damning to the soul of man. This, then is the song wrung out of the heart of David in connection with that dark hour. It is a remarkable revelation of the man.

The story is found in the second book of Samuel, in chapters eleven and twelve. From that story I want to select three sentences. Nathan was speaking to David and he said, "Thou art the man." David replied, "I have sinned against Jehovah." Nathan answered, "Jehovah also hath put away thy sin." When the prophet charged David definitely with the sin, he at once confessed; and upon the basis of that confession, the declaration was made with equal immediateness, "Jehovah also hath put away thy sin."

The grouping of these sentences reveals David, and shows him to have been "a man after God's own heart." Such a statement may for a moment somewhat startle. Let us, however, remember the facts and circumstances of life at the time. When we pass back into the period, and recall the relationship between kings and their subjects, we shall see what an amazing thing this was that David did; and indeed, we may come along down the line of human history, and test his action by that of other kings,

to have that amazement emphasized. Some years ago,
Dr. Margoliouth said of this action of David,

> "When has this been done—before or since? Mary,
> Queen of Scots would declare that she was above the Law;
> Charles I, would have thrown over Bath-sheba; James II
> would have hired witnesses to swear away her character;
> Mohammed would have produced a revelation authorising
> both crimes; Charles II would have publicly abrogated the
> seventh commandment; Queen Elizabeth would have sus-
> pended Nathan."

David confessed, "I have sinned," and added the arresting
words, "against Jehovah." That was the deepest note of this
psalm. The whole psalm constitutes an interpretation of the
spiritual consciousness which found expression in the words
spoken to Nathan.

In examining the psalm we first note its structure. As we
have it in our versions, it has nineteen verses. In the Hebrew
psalm there are four strophes, and four distinct movements. The
first strophe is contained in verses one to four; the second in verses
five to nine; the third in verses ten to fourteen; and the last in
verses fifteen to nineteen.

The first of these strophes deals with sin in relation to God.
The second deals with sin in relation to the sinner. The third
strophe is a great appeal. In the fourth we have a further appeal
in recognition of the wider application of sin, and of deliverance
from it, to others than the sinning one.

The whole psalm is in prayer form; prayer as confession
and appeal. We may notice, speaking generally, that David
does not promise God anything. He makes no promise of
amendment. He casts himself entirely upon the mercy of God.

> "Have mercy upon me, O God, according to Thy
> lovingkindness; according to the multitude of Thy tender
> mercies blot out my transgressions."

As we read these words we are reminded of the occurrence
of the giving of the Law as we have it in Exodus, and that it is
there recorded that Jehovah proclaimed His name, and declared
Himself to be, "A God full of compassion, and gracious, slow to
anger and plenteous in mercy and truth." These are the
conceptions of God to which David made his appeal.

This cry was wrung out of his soul as the result of his
consciousness of his sin in the presence of God. He uses three

expressions, " my transgressions," " mine iniquity," " my sin."
In doing so he was not repeating one thought thrice over. Each
word has a particular significance. " Transgression " refers to
definite rebellion and disobedience. That is the first thing in
his consciousness of sin, one therefore which includes guilt.
There may be sin which does not include the element of guilt.
When a man does something contrary to the will of God in
ignorance, there is no guilt, but it is still sin. David's first word
marks and confesses thàt his action was volitional disobedience,
and consequently he was guilty.

The word " iniquity " describes the result of the transgression
which is perversion, or distortion. The issue of his transgression,
he himself was perverted and polluted.

The final word " sin " includes all the fact. It expresses the
sense of failure and of ruin. David was thus facing the whole
thing in a three-fold way; saying, in effect, I wilfully disobeyed;
therefore I am perverted and polluted; and so to summarize,
I am a failure.

Now observe what he sought. As he used three words to
describe his consciousness of condition, he used three phrases
to express his consciousness of need, " Blot out my transgression,"
" wash me," " cleanse me."

The Hebrew word rendered "blot out" means simply to
rub out, to erase. In its figurative use it looks upon sin as a debt,
and as a debt inscribed upon some recording document. The
prayer is that such handwriting may be erased, blotted out in
that sense.

The literal meaning of the Hebrew word rendered " wash me "
is trample me. Behind that of course we recognise the Eastern
method of the washing of garments. The fabric was trampled
upon until the stains in it were trampled out. In that sense the
rendering "wash me" is perfectly correct, and cannot be
bettered in translation. If the first cry then was for erasure, as
the blotting out of debt, the second was for that washing which
removed defilement.

When we come to the word " cleanse me " we are in the
presence of something which is arresting. Edersheim said that it
is impossible to express with perfect accuracy in English, the
value of the Hebrew, because we have no word in the English
language that exactly fits it. Continuing, Edersheim says that the
only word that literally carries over the thought would be the
word " unsin." David, therefore, was seeking for a cleansing so

complete that the whole fact and issue of sin should be completely cancelled. Not only that the debt be erased, and the defilement trampled out, but the personality set absolutely free from the sin in every form.

We now turn to consider the ground upon which David made this appeal. The first word is the little word " For," which shows that he was proceeding from appeal to argument. So far he had appealed to the lovingkindness and the mercy of God to blot out his transgressions, to wash him throughly, to unsin him from his sin. He now stated the ground of his appeal;

" For I acknowledge my transgressions;
And my sin is ever before me."

Thus his appeal for Divine action was based upon the fact that he had confessed his own sin. The Hebrew word rendered " acknowledge " quite literally means I know it, I confess it, I make no attempt to hide it.

Another of the penitential psalms, thirty-two, also attributed to David, tells of his experience before he made his acknowledgment.

" When I kept silence, my bones waxed old
Through my roaring all the day long.
For day and night Thy hand was heavy upon me;
My moisture was changed as with the drought of summer."

Then he added,

" I acknowledged my sin unto Thee, and mine iniquity
have I not hid;
I said, I will confess my transgressions unto the Lord;
And Thou forgavest."

Thus it is evident that David was conscious that there could be no release, no cleansing until he himself confessed and acknowledged, without reservation, the fact of his sin.

That opens up a great subject, that of the confession of sin. When does confession of sin become of real value? It may be said, when it is confessed to a priest. That, however, I need not deal with here and now. Then it is said that confession becomes real when it is made to the man we have wronged. That may be a stern necessity, but that is not enough. Then when we confess the one to the other? This has no value at all, unless it is preceded by something deeper. Of course the apparently obvious answer is that confession becomes valuable when it is made to God; and that leads to the facing of the fact that confession to

God is only valuable after it has been made to oneself. David said, " My sin, is ever before me." The hour of moral cleansing and renovation comes when man, shutting all other out, says to himself, " I have sinned."

And yet, to look again carefully, we find that when David was thus confessing his sin to himself in the presence of God, he was doing it, recognizing that in the last analysis, the wrong he had done was wrong against God. It was here he said,

> " Against Thee, Thee only, have I sinned,
> And done that which is evil in Thy sight."

This conception is often challenged, and that quite naturally. It is said, Had not David sinned against Bath-sheba? There is a sense in which that may be admitted, but as a matter of fact, he had sinned with Bath-sheba. It is perfectly true that a man sins against a woman when he seduces her; but it is equally true that in the majority of cases they sin together. But had he not sinned against Uriah? Undoubtedly he had, but at least it should be remembered that his sin against Uriah was heroic and magnificent. As the result of his wrong-doing there were two ways open before Uriah. The one was that of his discovery of the sin, and the agony which it would cause him, and that of seeing Bath-sheba stoned to death. The other alternative was that he should die as a soldier on the high places of the field. David chose the latter for Uriah.

But now in the presence of God, David had come to the consciousness of the fact that the ultimate sin is against God; that when a man wrongs a woman, he hurts God; that when he wrongs a man the last agony is felt, not by the man he wrongs, but in the heart of God. This is the deepest sense of sin. It was this that made Paul describe himself as " the chief of sinners." It was this that gave such poignancy to the confessions of Augustine. David knew he had wronged Bath-sheba, and wronged Uriah; but realised in the last analysis he had wronged God. He ended this strophe by declaring that he made this confession that God might be declared as vindicated both in His punishment, and in His acts of mercy.

We pass to the second strophe, verses five to nine. Let us observe carefully how verse five begins and how verse six begins. Each opens with the word, " Behold," and in them two facts are declared:

> " Behold, I was shapen in iniquity;
> And in sin did my mother conceive me."

Here he was confessing the facts of his own being, that it was in essence, by inheritance, corrupt. The next statement, however, shows that in making this one, David was not finding an excuse for sin. We might think that this was so, if we stayed with that verse. But now listen to the next.

" Behold, Thou desirest truth in the inward parts;
And in the hidden part Thou shalt make me to know wisdom."

This is the other side of truth concerning personality. In the double statement two facts are faced. The first is that of the corrupt nature, but the second is that if shapen in iniquity, and conceived in sin, that is not all the truth. It is equally true that in personality there is an inner light, the demand for truth in the inward parts, the wisdom from God which is illuminative.

Looking thus at his own personality, he makes a new appeal for complete cleansing in the words,

" Purge me with hyssop, and I shall be clean;
Wash me, and I shall be whiter than snow.
Make me to hear joy and gladness;
That the bones which Thou hast broken may rejoice.
Hide Thy face from my sins,
And blot out all mine iniquities."

This was his cry for cleansing from inherited pollution, and for restoration to sensitiveness to the voice of wisdom, producing joy and gladness.

The third strophe is that of a great appeal, in which he seeks for " a clean heart," which is the embodiment in a phrase of all that he had already asked for; " a right spirit," which should be rendered " a stedfast spirit."

In the words, " Take not Thy holy Spirit from me," He asks for the maintenance of fellowship, and in close connection for the restoration of the joy which he had lost, finally seeking " a willing spirit," that is a spirit completely amenable to God. Every petition was that God would do for him what none else could do. All this was desired, in order that he might teach transgressors the ways of God, so that sinners should be converted to Him. In this way he saw that he would be free from blood-guiltiness; the reference being, not to the death of Uriah, but to harm rendered to others in any way.

The last strophe is characterised by selflessness:

" O Lord, open Thou my lips;
And my mouth shall show forth Thy praise."

He sought this action of God in order that he might be able to show forth the praise of God. He realised the condition upon which these blessings might be received, " a broken and contrite heart," that is, cancellation of the pride of personality, and complete submission to the will of God.

Finally, he saw the larger issue of all he was desiring for himself; the prosperity of Zion, and the building of the walls of Jerusalem.

The psalm in its entirety emphasizes certain great truths. The first is that sin in the last analysis, wrongs God. Moreover it destroys personality, and paralyses influence; and is utterly incurable by human action.

It reveals the abiding fact that God responds to confession and trust in His everlasting mercy. When a man says in complete sincerity, " I have sinned," the answer is ever the same, " Jehovah also hath put away thy sin."

Perhaps the central word of the psalm in some senses is,

" Create in me a clean heart, O God,
And renew a right spirit within me."

Kirkpatrick chronicles an arresting fact, that upon one occasion Voltaire sat down irreverently to parody this psalm; and that when he reached this petition, he was frightened, stopped his work, and destroyed his parchment. Whether the story is apocryphal or no, it remains true that to pray that prayer is a tremendous thing, and the whole psalm helps us to see what it really involves.

PSALM XCI

IN its recognition of human need, and its revelation of Divine resource, there is no greater statement than the opening verse of this psalm in all the inspired Literature. It is interesting to remark in passing, that all our great Versions have rendered it in exactly the same way, and these words do convey to us with unmistakeable accuracy, the thought of the singer himself. The statement places human life under final authority, "the Most High"; and within absolute power, "the Almighty."

This psalm has no inscription, either musical or interpretive in any way. It stands alone on the page. Its authorship is uncertain. The Talmud ascribes it, and psalm ninety, to Moses. There is general agreement among Christian exegetes and expositors that psalm ninety was written by Moses. There is not the same agreement about the ninety-first; but the authorship has no vital bearing upon its value. The one thing quite self-evident is that psalm ninety-one is related in thought to psalm ninety. If Moses wrote both of them we see at once the connection and sequence; or if not, if as some scholars think there are evidences that psalm ninety-one came from another pen, it is almost certain that the author was familiar with psalm ninety. The relationship between the two is indicated if we take the opening verse of psalm ninety, and that of psalm ninety-one, and read them together.

"Lord, Thou hast been our dwelling place
In all generations."
"He that dwelleth in the secret place of the Most High,
Shall abide under the shadow of the Almighty."

It is as though this singer, reading the psalm of the first, says; "Lord, Thou hast been our dwelling place in all generations." Is that *where* you live? Then this is *how* you live; "He that dwelleth in the secret place of the Most High shall abide under the shadow of the Almighty."

Yet there is a very striking contrast between these two psalms. In psalm ninety from beginning to end there is a minor note of sadness, and the sense of death. So patently is that so that it is a psalm constantly read in those sacred and solemn hours when we commit to the last resting-place the bodies or dust of our loved ones. "Thou turnest man to destruction," "We are

consumed in Thine anger," " We bring our years to an end as a
sigh," " The days of our years are threescore years and ten,"
" It is soon gone, and we fly away."

When we come to psalm ninety-one it is entirely different.
From beginning to end there is the major note of gladness, and
the sense of life, secure, victorious, in spite of all the prevailing
darkness. I should be inclined to say that if Moses wrote both
these psalms—and perchance he did—in the second he had
climbed to a higher plane of vision than he occupied in the first.
I am not suggesting that the first is not true, but it is possible to
have an outlook on life that is perfectly correct, and then to climb
a little higher, and gain a larger outlook; which does not contradict
the things you saw on the lower level, but sets them in different
relationships, so that the outlook is entirely different.

In this study I propose to look very briefly at the psalm as
a whole, watching its structure and movement, in order that we
may devote our attention to the opening verse in which all the
teaching is focussed. In the psalm as we have it, there are sixteen
verses. The song in Hebrew falls into four strophes.

The first strophe is in verse one. That is complete within
itself. Then there follow three strophes of interpretation. The
first strophe is one of inclusive affirmation,

> " He that dwelleth in the secret place of the Most High,
>   Shall abide under the shadow of the Almighty."

There is nothing else to say. All is said. Everything that
follows interprets what is so said. The first strophe of interpretation is found in verses two to eight. The next is in verses
nine to thirteen. The final one begins at verse fourteen and goes
to verse sixteen.

In the first of these strophes of interpretation the singer is
talking to Himself about Jehovah. It begins, " I will say of
Jehovah," and goes on, " He is my Refuge and my Fortress;
my God in Whom I trust." Then there is a sudden change in the
pronouns from the first person to the third. He suddenly speaks
to God.

> " For Thou, O Jehovah, art my Refuge."

Then he goes back, and again talks to himself.

> " Thou hast made the Most High thy habitation;
>   There shall no evil befall thee,
>   Neither shall any plague come nigh thy tent,"

and so on.

Thus he comes to the final strophe; and while he is still the singer, Jehovah is talking to him. The last strophe is the language of Jehovah; and the singer reports the answer God makes to what he has said.

" Because he hath set his love upon Me "—

" he," that is, the singer,

> " Because he hath set his love upon Me, therefore will I deliver him;
> I will set him on high, because he hath known My name."

The one theme of this song is that of protection in the secret place from all perils. This singer was not a man who had reached Elysian fields where asphodel was blooming, and there were no clouds. He was living in the midst of terror, of difficulty. Listen to the words which describe the perils of which he was conscious: " snares, pestilence, terror, arrow that flieth by day, destruction that wasteth at noonday, evil, plague, a stone, lion, an adder, a serpent, trouble."

Yes, but his song was not about the perils. It was concerned with protection from them. Glance down the psalm again, and note the words employed to describe that protection. " Refuge, fortress, pinions, wings, shield, buckler, angels, deliverance, honour, long life, satisfaction, salvation." Thus we find words that mark the perils, and words that tell of perfect protection from all those perils. That is the glory of psalm ninety-one.

Now let us consider the inclusive first strophe. The assurances of the song are all contingent upon the conditions which are revealed in this strophe. All the things which this man had to say to his own soul in the consciousness of peril, and of perfect protection from peril, were so for one reason. Who is the man who can read this psalm and claim it as his own? " He that dwelleth in the secret place of the Most High." That statement reveals a principle of perpetual application. The whole Biblical Literature, whether it be historic, didactic, or poetic, reveals the fact that the experience of privilege is contingent upon the fulfilment of conditions. Take the whole subject of prayer, so sacred a subject to all Christian men and women. Did not our Lord say, You shall ask whatever you will, and it shall be done for you? Can anything be more spacious? But we must not begin there. The conditions are, " If ye abide in Me, and My words abide in you."

So here, " He that dwelleth in the secret place of the Most High," is the man protected from peril. The assurances of the psalm are jubilant, vibrant, victorious, glorious; but they are the result of the fulfilment of the conditions, " He that dwelleth."

In this opening strophe two things are patent; first, the person of whom all these things are true, " He that dwelleth in the secret place of the Most High "; and secondly, the position described, " shall abide under the shadow of the Almighty."

" He that dwelleth in the secret place of the Most High."

We begin with the final words, " The Most High." The Hebrew word *Elyown* is the superlative of a word which means to ascend, *alah.* The Most High is the One in the ultimate height. Here let our imagination help us. When angels sang o'er Bethlehem's plains in celebration of the birth of Jesus, they sang, " Glory to God in the highest." That phrase, " in the highest " does not mark the degree of praise. It marks rather the place of God. Glory to God. What God? Who is He? He is in the highest, that is, He is the Most High. It is the idea of superlative height in authority. What are the things of authority to which we bow? The authority of our own desire, the authority of our own intelligence, the authority of our own will. Or to refer to external authority. Climb up and up, and higher yet; and presently we stand confronting the one Throne of the universe, the Throne of God. He is " The Most High." Thus relationship with the ultimate Authority is the secret of protection from all peril. Who is this man who sings this song? He is a man living in the secret place of the Most High, the man whose appeal is made to the Ultimate in authority, and who is submitted to that Authority.

A tremendous truth is here recognized, a truth about which our fathers talked far more than we do, that of the sovereignty of God. For the moment there is no suggestion made of wisdom, or power, although these are implicated. It is authority. Jeremiah broke out in a sentence than which there is none more sublime in the Divine Literature, " A Throne set on high from the beginning is the place of our sanctuary." The Ultimate in authority is the secret of protection, and of safety.

" In the secret place." There can be no better rendering I think than that; yet we pause to enquire what is the idea of the secret place? The Hebrew word rendered " secret place " means literally a hiding place. This word is variously rendered in the Psalter. In psalm eighteen I read, " He made darkness His hiding place." That is the same word, and so we may read, " He made darkness His secret place." In psalm twenty-seven, we read, " In the covert of His Tent He will hide me." The same word, " In the secret place of His tent." In psalm thirty-one, we read, " The covert of Thy presence," and again the same word, " The secret place of Thy presence." In psalm sixty-one, we read, " The covert of Thy wings," that is, " The secret place of Thy wings." In psalm eighty-one, " The secret place of thunder."

" He that dwelleth in the secret place." Where or what is that? Darkness is His secret place; or finally, thunder, the place of agitation, is His secret place. Those are the boundaries. Between them these; His Tent—figurative language, wherever He dwells; " The Presence," and from that we never escape; " Thy wings," the symbol of motherhood. The secret place, the place of darkness, the place of thunder, the place of the dwelling of God, the place of the presence of God, the place of the over-shadowing wings of God; he that dwelleth there is the person who sings the song. It is the man who is dwelling there, literally, who sits down there, that is, who remains there, is at home there— that is the man, the man related in his life to the ultimate authority is dwelling in the secret place.

Now what does the singer say about that man? " He shall abide under the shadow of the Almighty." Taking the same method, we begin with the description of God, " The Almighty." The designation implicates powerful impregnability, irresistible might, the ultimate in strength. The man who dwells in the secret place of the Highest Authority, is at the centre of all might and all strength. Do we wonder that Paul wrote, " If God is for us, who is against us? " Who can be superior to this environment of all Might which the soul finds in God, if he is dwelling in His secret place?

" He shall abide under the shadow." The idea of the word " shadow " is not that of a shade cast by a substance. Isaiah said of the Messiah, He shall be " as the shadow of a great rock in a weary and." The picture there is that of a great rock, casting its shadow, and in the shade of that rock the traveller may sit down and be protected from the heat of the day. That is not the idea here. The Hebrew word means to hover over. The figure of speech is pre-eminently that of motherhood. It emerges in Genesis when the Spirit of God brooded; and it comes out again and again in the course of the Hebrew poetic literature, the figure of spread wings. The singer sings about that, the outspread pinions; he abides under the shadow of the Almighty. " Almighty " fills me with the sense of fear, but this word " shadow " shows me Almightiness, acting with the tenderness of motherhood.

Finally, " He shall abide." The Hebrew word means quite simply, to stop, but we cannot always interpret by etymology. In Hebrew language the word was used as expressing the idea of passing the night.

> " He that dwelleth in the secret place of the Most High,
> Shall pass the night under the brooding wings of the Almighty."

That is the whole idea of the psalm.

As we said before, this psalm is not a psalm about still waters, but about storm and stress and strain. We know something about still waters. " He leadeth me beside still waters." But He does not always lead us there. Sometimes the waters are not still, they are storm-lashed. This psalm is the psalm of the storm; it is the psalm of the night. If we dwell in the secret place, we pass the night under the outspread pinions of God.

It is an arresting fact that when the devil attacked the spiritual centre of the personality of Jesus, this was the psalm he quoted. And in Jesus then, and always, victory came because He lived in the place here described. He dwelt in the secret place of the Most High. There was never a moment in the life of Jesus when His doing, His going, His coming, His speaking, His resting, His toiling, was not in keeping with that position. Everything was for ever related to the will of God. " I do always the things that please Him." He lived under the ultimate Authority; and so He abode under the shadow of the Almighty. But was that so in the moment when He said, " My God, My God, why hast Thou forsaken Me? " Assuredly. He spoke to God in the secret place of darkness and of thunder.

It is through Him that we enter that secret place. No one knoweth the Father save the Son, and he to whom the Son willeth to reveal Him, Come unto Me, He said in effect, and I will reveal Him to you; I will give you rest. No man cometh unto the Father but by Me. He that hath seen Me hath seen the Father. Through Him I have access to the secret place.

Access. That word arrests. We find it three times in Paul's writings. He says we have " access into grace." He says, we have " access to the Father." He says, we have access to the purposes of the ages.

They tell me that at the centre of the cyclone is a point of rest. That is the story of this psalm. Terrors, raging lions, snares and adders, pestilence, and things of dread and dire darkness. Surely, yes, but dwelling in the secret place of the Most

High, abiding under the outspread pinions of Almightiness, the soul is safe.

This is not the song of still waters. It is the song of the storm; and of the secret place; His Tent, His presence, His wings. The secret place is at the heart of the darkness, the place where the thunder is made.

Ellen Lakshmi Goreh interpreted the values of the psalm in Christian experience perfectly in her hymn:

" In the secret of His presence how my soul delights to hide!
Oh, how precious are the lessons which I learn at Jesus' side!
Earthly cares can never vex me, neither trials lay me low;
For when Satan comes to tempt me, to the secret place I go.

When my soul is faint and thirsty, 'neath the shadow of His wing
There is cool and pleasant shelter, and a fresh and crystal spring;
And my Saviour rests beside me, as we hold communion sweet;
If I tried, I could not utter what He says when thus we meet.

Only this, I know; I tell Him all my doubts, and griefs, and fears;
Oh, how patiently He listens, and my drooping soul He cheers.
Do you think He ne'er reproves me? What a false Friend He would be,
If He never, never told me of the sins which He must see.

Would you like to know the sweetness of the secret of the Lord?
Go and hide beneath His shadow—this shall then be your reward;
And whene'er you leave the silence of that happy meeting-place,
You will bear the shining image of the Master in your face."

PSALM CIII

THIS psalm is a pure song of worship. There is not a single petition in it from first to last. It is one of the psalms attributed to David, and in it he gave no expression of any desire; but from beginning to end, poured out his soul in praise and thanksgiving. Praise is the adoration of God for what He is in Himself. Thanksgiving is the adoration of God for what He has done for us. In such exercises the soul worships.

Worship, rightly understood in the simplest sense of the word, is a somewhat rare occupation. Of course there is a sense in which our services may be described in their entirety as Divine Worship. In them, however, we do, quite properly, more than worship. Nevertheless, the highest function of man's personality is not prayer, but praise. In another psalm (l. 23), we have a statement which is most arresting,

" Whoso offereth the sacrifice of thanksgiving glorifieth Me."

Reading it one wonders how it can be said that through any action of ours God can be glorified. Nevertheless the statement is made, and there can be no doubt that it is so. Perhaps the activity is rare because it is in some senses difficult. The difficulty may be illustrated by the fact of how few hymns we have in any of our hymn-books which are hymns of pure praise, that is hymns in which there are no petitions, but in the singing of which we are addressing God in terms of praise for Himself, and thanksgiving for His benefits. This is not at all to speak disparagingly of our hymn-books. The fact is equally true of the one hundred and fifty songs found in the Psalter. Every psalm and hymn addressed to God whether in prayer or praise, is of value. I am merely thinking of the exercise of praise in itself, as apart from prayer, which is of the nature of petition. This, I repeat, is a song of pure praise.

Every student of the Psalter must recognise that these songs were written principally for use in the Temple. There are certain musical notes which in themselves prove this; but apart from this, their very structure often is such as to lend itself to musical interpretation. This is remarkably so in this psalm. The chord

of the dominant is struck in the opening sentence, and repeated
in the closing sentence. It opens,

"Bless Jehovah, O my soul,"

and it closes,

"Bless Jehovah, O my soul."

Between this striking of the chord of the dominant at the
commencement, and its repetition at the close, all the movement
between is true to that declared intention.

An examination of the structure of the song will show two
distinct methods or movements. The first five verses constitute
a solo. No plural pronoun is found in them. From verses six
to eighteen the psalm becomes a chorus in which other voices
join, as the plural pronouns show. Then, from the nineteenth
verse to the end, we have again a great chorus, but the volume of
sound in the music is increased by angelic voices, reinforced by
the whole universe of God. Then suddenly, the plurality of human
voices, angelic voices and universal music, ceases, and the final
note is again sung as a solo,

"Bless Jehovah, O my soul."

The whole movement is one of praise uttered to Jehovah.
That is the only name of God employed in the song. It occurs
eleven times. God is never referred to by the words Elohim, or
Adonai. Once in the course of the psalm a similitude is employed
when it says, "Like as a Father pitieth his children." The praise
then is directed to God as revealed in the name which speaks for
evermore of His grace, as He becomes whatever His people need,
in order to the meeting of that need.

We are at once arrested by the background of this song
in so far as the conditions with which David was familiar are
revealed in it. Without dwelling upon this matter, we may group
certain words employed in reference to these conditions,
"iniquities, diseases, destruction, desire, the oppressed, our sins,
our iniquities, our transgressions, our frame" as "dust." These
are all things with which we are familiar, and express the consciousness of human frailty, human danger, human peril.
Nevertheless, the impression made upon us in the reading of the
psalm is not that of the fact of these things, but of the relation
of men to these experiences through the activity of Jehovah.
From beginning to end, triumph over these things is celebrated
through the grace of Jehovah.

In the first movement, as we have said, one man is singing.
In the course of it the name of Jehovah occurs twice, and linked

with it, a relative pronoun " Who " occurs five times. In the use of the name the Person addressed is referred to, and the repetition of the " Who " reveals the reasons for praise.

> " Bless Jehovah, O my soul;
> And all that is within me, bless His holy Name.
> Bless Jehovah, O my soul,
> And forget not all His benefits;
> Who forgiveth all thine iniquities;
> Who healeth all thy diseases;
> Who redeemeth thy life from destruction;
> Who crowneth thee with lovingkindness and tender
>   mercies
> Who satisfieth thy mouth with good things;
> So that thy youth is renewed like the eagle."

In all this it is interesting to note that the singer was talking to himself, and talking to himself about Jehovah. He was calling upon himself to praise and worship Jehovah, and he gave the reasons for so doing.

In considering the first call, " Bless Jehovah, O my soul," it is necessary to emphasize the meaning of that word " soul." The word so translated here is the Hebrew word *nephesh*. When to-day we speak of the soul we are really oftentimes referring to the spirit. This Hebrew word means far more than that. If we go back to its first occurrence in the second chapter of Genesis we have light upon its meaning. Man is there revealed as a merging of dust and Deity by the act of God; and it is said that when God breathed into his breathing-places the breath of lives, he became " a living soul," that is *nephesh*. Thus the word refers to complete personality. And so here the singer was calling upon himself in the sum totality of his being, to worship Jehovah. Then, recognising that within the unity of personality there are diversities, he added, " all that is within me, bless His holy name."

Thus a living being in this song was calling upon himself in the entirety of his personality, in the harmony of every distinctive element of that personality, to bless Jehovah. This, of course, is a perfect revelation of the true activity of worship. In such an act there is ever the symphony of the elements of personality occupied in adoration. Thus, in the opening call, unity of being addresses diversity of powers, and calls for perfect co-ordination, in order to worship.

The reasons for such worship are given, being introduced by the " Who," which relates the thought to the Person of Jehovah.

The first of these is,

" Who forgiveth all thine iniquities."

The first reason for adoration, always the first, is that of moral cleansing. That is where the activity of God on behalf of sinful man always begins. This fact is emphasized in many of the psalms; perhaps notably in psalm thirty-two, to which reference may be made.

The second reason is found in the words,
" Who healeth all thy diseases."

In reading this let us ever emphasise the word " all," including as it does diseases of the spirit, diseases of the mind, diseases of the body. Whatever there is in personality which is unhealthy, can only find healing by the activity of God. Sometimes it is good to remind ourselves that our words *holiness* and *health* derive from a common word in Anglo-Saxon, *halig*. We should be warranted in speaking of a man having a holy body, and a healthy spirit. The two words mean the same thing. Disease is failure, whether spiritual, mental, or physical. Here the singer declares that it is Jehovah Who healeth all disease. The simple meaning of this, therefore, is that whenever there is healing, it is Jehovah Who is the Healer. Here many will think merely in the realm of the physical, and therefore I pause at that point. If someone asks me if I believe in faith healing, I answer, Certainly not. There is no such thing as faith healing. If I am asked if I believe in Divine healing, my reply must be, I certainly do. There is no healing that is not Divine. I differ from some very excellent people who imagine however that God only heals in one way, and that His way excludes the use of all means. The name Jehovah is linked in the Old Testament once with a great word, Jehovah-Ropheka, which is rendered accurately, Jehovah that healeth. It is always, however, interesting to remember the place where it is used. It was when people were suffering from the result of poisoned water in a well; and Jehovah revealed to Moses the healing branch to be put into the well. He used means. One does not for a moment question the fact that there are times when God has, and does heal without the use of any means, but it is equally true that He heals through means. I owe my life on two occasions, first to the surgeon's skilful knife; secondly, to the physician and nurses' tender care. In each case God gave the healing, but He worked through means.

The next reason is revealed in the words,

" Who redeemeth thy life from destruction."

The word " redeemeth " here is one which means preserves.
It is not so much the idea of bringing life back from the realm
of destruction, but keeping it from that realm. The same idea
was found in psalm twenty-three, " He restoreth my soul,"
which we saw would have better interpretation by the rendering,
" He continually reneweth my personality." Thus the perpetual
sustaining and preserving of life through the action of Jehovah is
celebrated.

Again,

> " Who crowneth thee with lovingkindness and tender
> mercies."

This is a general statement, but of course great, as it shows
the life preserved from destruction, and crowned with all the
tenderness of the Divine lovingkindness.

At last we reach the words,

> " Who satisfieth thy mouth with good things."

Here we are halted by this word " mouth." The margin of
the Revised says, " Or thy years; or, thy prime," and then adds,
" Hebrew, thine ornament." Now, what is someone unacquainted
with Hebrew, to do with these suggestions? Well, let it at once
be said the word " mouth " is unsatisfactory. The word " years "
there has no warrant in the Hebrew. When we read " prime "
we have to ask exactly what we mean by that. It is perfectly
true that " ornament " is the literal translation of the Hebrew
word; but interpretation may go astray if it is governed merely
by etymology. The reference unquestionably is to the central
glory and force of personality. In that sense perhaps " mouth "
may be permissible, if it represents the clamour to be fed, that
which expresses desire. I believe in that word desire we have the
best interpretation of the Hebrew thought. It is ever the central
and greatest thing in personality. Not intellect, which is valuable
and necessary; not emotion, which is glorious and inevitable;
not volition, which is central and decisive; but that consciousness
which results from intellect, appealing to emotion, and leading to
volition; that which can only be expressed by the thought of
desire, or the consciousness of need, demanding supply. This,
says the song, Jehovah satisfies with good things.

To summarize therefore on this first movement; personality
is called upon to offer praise to Jehovah, because of moral cleansing,
the healing of disease, the preservation of life from destructive
forces, the coronation of life by love, and the satisfaction of life
in its deepest desire.

The second movement in the psalm is marked by general statements with plural pronouns, and constitutes, as we have said, a chorus. In it there are four movements, giving four reasons for united praise. These are indicated by the employment of the name Jehovah four times. The first reason offers praise for the government of Jehovah in verses six and seven. The reasons for praise for that government is found in the statement,

" He executeth righteous acts,"

which statement really emphasizes two facts; first, that His government is righteous, and secondly that it is actual. Jehovah does not merely make laws; He applies them. Moreover a special quality in the government of God is His care for the downtrodden and oppressed.

The next reason for praise is that of the patience of Jehovah; full of compassion, slow to anger, with mercy great as the heaven is high above the earth; He removes transgressions from us as far as the east is from the west.

The third reason for united praise is that of the pity of Jehovah, in verses thirteen to sixteen. Here it is that the similitude occurs in which God is referred to as a Father. Very beautiful is the declaration that

" He knoweth our frame;
He remembereth that we are dust."

How often in human judgment that fact of inherent frailty is forgotten. God never forgets it, and all His actions towards us are affected by that remembrance.

The final reason for the chorus of praise is that of the lovingkindness of Jehovah.

So we come to the last great movement. It begins with the declaration,

" Jehovah hath established His throne in the heavens;
And His Kingdom ruleth over all."

In these words the sovereignty of the God of grace is recognized. In view of it the singer calls upon the angels to join in the ascription of praise. And further, the ministers of God. That may, of course, still refer to the angels, but it may take in other beings than those of which we have knowledge. The appeal is intended to include all in the universe, who in any way fulfil the word, and do the pleasure of God, to join in the celebration of His grace and government.

Finally, feeling that there might yet be music not expressed by intelligent beings, the singer calls upon all Nature, inanimate as well as animate, to join the praise.

" Bless Jehovah, all ye His works,
    In all places of His dominion."

Suddenly, the chorus ceases, and the singer ends, standing in the midst of the resonant universe, with the personal,

" Bless Jehovah, O my soul."

This whole song expresses and emphasizes the truth that to know God is to be inevitably compelled to worship. If men do not worship, it is because they are ignorant of Him.

" Let those refuse to sing,
    Who never knew our God;
But children of the heavenly King
    Most speak their joys abroad."

The song teaches us, moreover, in its very method and movement that the worshipping individual is linked with the spheres, and is in tune with the Infinite. Wherever we truly worship God we are in harmony with the whole creation.

" The whole creation joins in one,
    To bless the sacred Name
Of Him Who sits upon the Throne."

We close our meditation by reminding ourselves of the opening call which teaches us that worship is not involuntary, is not automatic. It calls for preparation, and the co-ordination of all our powers. The sanctuary is never a lounge.

ECCLESIASTES XI, 9; XII

THE final division of the book of Ecclesiastes naturally begins with the ninth verse of chapter eleven. While the section in itself is brief in comparison with what has gone before, it contains the corrective to the false philosophy of life the results of which have been described in all the earlier movements of the writing. To understand it, therefore, it is necessary to briefly consider the book as a whole.

Its title, Ecclesiastes, was originally an attempt to translate into the Greek language the Hebrew title, and we owe it to the Septuagint Version. When Jerome translated from that version into the Vulgate, he retained the word, instead of translating into Latin.

The word itself simply means a member of the Ecclesia. The word Ecclesia was always used with reference to some select company. In the Greek cities the governing authority was called the Ecclesia. This, moreover, is the word employed for the Church in the New Testament. In general use it was applied not merely to governing bodies, but to any company devoted to some specific object. A member of such a body was an Ecclesiastes.

The title then suggests that this book was the work of a member of an assembly of thinking people, philosophers we may say, a company of those given to the discussion of wisdom. The Hebrew word, of which it is a translation is *Koheleth*, which really has the same significance. It is to Martin Luther that we owe the translation of the Hebrew *Koheleth* into our English "Preacher." This translation misses the real significance of the word. We come more nearly to the thought expressed by *Koheleth* if we render it "Debater." An Ecclesiastes was a member of an Ecclesia of thinkers who debated together, as they were engaged upon some quest. The word occurs nowhere else in the Old Testament. Whatever there is therefore in the book is the work of a Debater, one of an Ecclesia, one thinking about life, arguing about it, and expressing his opinion thereof.

We need not stay to discuss the question of authorship. That is referred to in the opening words, where the author is said to be "The son of David, the king in Jerusalem." The

word "king" there is in apposition to "son," not "David."
There can really be no question that the son referred to was
Solomon.

The whole movement of the book up to the point of the
section we are now considering, consists of a discussion of life
when it is lived wholly on the earth level. Throughout the book
one phrase recurs, "under the sun." As a matter of fact it is
found twenty-nine times, and twice we have a cognate phrase,
"under heaven." That is really the key to the interpretation of
all the earlier movements. They contain marvellous descriptions
of life, descriptions indeed which are quite up-to-date. They
harmonise perfectly with the pessimistic philosophy which
characterizes so much modern writing. The pessimism of this
writer, and of such modern writers, is entirely justifiable when life
is considered "under the sun," that is, on the earth level. The
Debater opens the discussion with the declaration of his final
finding concerning life on that level. "Vanity of vanities, saith
the Debater, Vanity of vanities, all is vanity."

It is well that we remember that this was the finding of a
most remarkable man. He was learned, he was thoughtful, he
was observant. He was a man who had entered into every possible
avenue of experience, "under the sun." The result is the
declaration that life is empty. There is nothing in it worth while.
The whole outlook is a merging of pessimism and fatalism at their
worst.

Someone may say that such a view seems to call in question
the inspiration of the writing. By no means. Here is a man
inspired to tell the whole truth about life when it is lived "under
the sun." That truth is that it is "vanity." The word occurs no
fewer than three and thirty times in the course of the writing.
It is a translation of the Hebrew word *Hebel*, that is Abel, the name
given to the second son of Adam, in the hour of a mother's
disillusionment. That then is the background leading to our
present section.

Turning from such description, the writer begins the final
movement with the arresting word "Rejoice." The key of this
section is found in the thirteenth verse of the twelfth chapter.
The Old Version rendered it, "Let us hear the conclusion of the
whole matter." The Revisers have translated, "This is the end
of the matter, all hath been heard." In either case the thought
is that now we may have a summary, the summing up of everything
concerning life.

That summing up is found in the words, " Fear God, and keep His commandments; for this is the whole of man." The word " duty " is not found in the Hebrew. To fear God, and keep His commandments constitutes the sphere, that is the whole. To live " under the sun " is to live in a hemisphere, and to do so is to find vanity. To fear God and keep His commandments is to recognize all that lies above the sun, and that in its bearing upon things " under the sun." So to live is to have the whole of life, and the finding of such life is never that it is vanity.

To examine the section carefully, let us notice its movement. It begins with general counsel to youth concerning life. The Debater having described his own experiences on the earth level, and declared that he had found all to be vanity, now addressed himself to youth, because youth is the time of vision, of choices which create direction for all the coming days. This appeal begins at the ninth verse of chapter eleven, and ends at the seventh verse of chapter twelve. As a matter or fact with that verse the book ends so far as the writer himself is concerned. Beginning at verse eight in chapter twelve we have an epilogue which almost undoubtedly was added by another pen. It is quite relevant, necessary, and important; and it continues to the end of the twelfth verse. In verses thirteen and fourteen everything is summarized, and in all likelihood, we have here once again the words of the Debater himself.

In the advice to youth there are two clearly defined movements. The first is found in verses nine and ten of chapter eleven; and the second in the first seven verses of chapter twelve. The first word of the first of these movements is the word " Rejoice," the first word of the second is the word " Remember." Thus when the philosopher turns to address himself to youth, he has two things to say, " Rejoice," " Remember."

With regard to the advice to youth to rejoice, it has been to me an arresting and a somewhat amazing thing how often expositors seem to have been befogged. In an old volume called " Darling's Encyclopædia of Sermonic Literature," it is interesting to see a list of the titles of sermons preached over a long period on this text. Here they are: " The judgments that attend sinners," " An exhortation to youth to prepare for judgment, a sermon occasioned by the late repentance and funeral of a young man "; " Consequences of early profligacy "; " The influence of conscience, and the credibility of a future state of retribution considered "; " Sinful indulgences in youth, with their fatal effects "; " The ironical permission "; " The vanity of childhood and youth, being some sermons with a catechism for youth."

The reading of those titles reveals an utterly false understanding of this whole passage. As a matter of fact there is nothing
in this advice which refers to evil in any form. Neither is there
any reference whatever to punishment. The word "judgment"
does not necessarily connote punishment. It is quite true that
punishment may be an activity of judgment, but not necessarily
so. There is no suggestion of a profligate life in anything said.
The advice is definite and positive. Let us listen to it.

The keynote is struck in the word "Rejoice." We may
render the Hebrew, not more satisfactorily, but with equal
accuracy, Be blithe, be gleesome, be merry. Quite literally the
Hebrew word means Brighten up. That advice someone suggested
that it was an ironical permission. As a matter of fact there is no
irony in it. Moreover the call is not merely to be blithe during
youth, but to rejoice in the fact of it. Youth is the time when
life is rising to the full, when dreams are being dreamed, or
visions are clearly seen; the time for building castles in the air,
which precedes the actual strain and stress of endeavour; the
time when holy, healthy, happy ambition is singing its song to
personality.

How this is to be done is then described. "Let thy heart
cheer thee in the days of thy youth; and walk in the ways of thine
heart, and in the sight of thine eyes." In other words, rejoice in
the fact of youth, and let all its forces and possibilities express
themselves to the uttermost.

Admittedly for the moment that sounds dangerous. It is not
so in the light of what follows. Therefore, stay for a moment and
face that. I am not among the number of those who ever speak
disrespectfully of the Victorian era. Nevertheless, I do realise that
there are multitudes of young people who were alienated from
religion because in the religious outlook of the times, that was
looked upon as dangerous advice, and youth was held within
restrictions unnatural to itself.

This advice is at once qualified by the words, "But know thou,
that for all these things God will bring thee into judgment." In
these words the principle is declared which will keep youth safe
while merry. In the midst of rejoicing, there must be remembrance of the fact of the Divine government. The Hebrew
word "judgment" is a word which connotes the making of law,
finding a verdict, pronouncing a sentence whether of commendation
or condemnation, and the executive action which accords with
these things. Therefore while life is to express itself in fullness,
it is to do so with a constant recognition of the authority and

executive action of the One from Whom all the forces of life have come. His government is in order that these forces may never be destructive, but constructive, and so co-operate in the realisation of life in all fullness.

Continuing, the writer says, " Therefore remove sorrow from thine heart, and put away evil from thy flesh, for youth and the prime of life are vanity." The word for " sorrow " there means vexation, or worry; and the reference to vanity is to the transitory nature of youth and the prime of life. All this may thus be summarized. Live fully; live richly; answer all the impulses of youth; but in all such things recognise the Divine government, and submit to its findings.

The second movement takes up and emphasizes what has thus been said. Youth and the prime of life are transient. It is important, therefore, that in them there shall be remembrance. " Remember now thy Creator in the days of thy youth." This designation of God is in itself arresting in its application, as it reminds us that all life's forces come from Him.

This advice to remember Him in all those quickly passing days is emphasized by a description, full of poetic beauty, of the days which are ever drawing nigh. This description of old age commences by looking at it under the figure of a storm. The darkening of the sun and the moon, and a prevalence of clouds and rain create conditions in the midst of which the zest of life has largely passed away. In that sense such days are evil days, in which a man will say, " I have no pleasure in them."

Turning from that more general description, the writer deals with it on the level of bodily experience. This passage, full of beauty, has been treated by some on an entirely anatomical basis. Others from beginning to end, allegorize. I think that its correct apprehension must have those two things in mind throughout.

The functions of bodily life are surely described, and whereas there may be differing interpretations, at least it may be suggested that " the keepers of the house shall tremble " refers to the days when arms are trembling, and losing their vigour; and " the strong men shall bow themselves," refers to the time when a man walks with bended knees; " the grinders cease, because they are few " refers to the failure of the possibility of the proper mastication of food; " those that look out of the windows be darkened," to the dimming of vision. The general sense of debility is then described in a statement that marks the fearfulness of age, the shutting of the doors in the street when the sound of the mills has ceased. Again old age rises at the voice of a bird, which indicates the light nature of its sleep. At this time also the daughters of music are brought low, which may either mean the loss of ability to sing, or of the power of hearing music. Another characteristic of old age is that of the fear of that which is high, and of terror of what may be in the way. The blossom of the almond tree may suggest the whitening hairs of age, or it may be the figure of sleeplessness, for the name of the almond tree is *sheked*, which means the tree of early waking. In this period the grasshopper shall be a burden, that is trifles shall create a sense of weariness; and finally desire fails, which is but another way of saying what has already been said, that the zest has gone out of life.

Here, however, all this failure of the physical is part of a movement towards the ultimate. In the words, " Man goeth to his long home," there is a flash of exquisite beauty. The journey through weakening powers is towards Home, and that, the Home that continues.

The description of death which follows is full of poetic beauty, and more especially so in the ultimate. " The dust shall return to the earth as it was, and the spirit return unto God Who gave it." That final outlook on dissolution can only be the outlook of one who in youth and prime, remembers God. If God be remembered in the days of vision and of strength; while the years of earthly decay are very real, and the consciousness very definite, these are but incidental, for all the feebleness is moving towards a dissolution when dust goes back to earth, but the spirit passes on to God.

In the epilogue the writer declares that the Debater was wise in that he did not finish with an earthly view. He still sought to find out acceptable words, and wrote them in the form of proverbs.

This brings us to the final finding, to which we referred at the commencement. The words " Fear God," mark a personal and essential relationship with Him; and the words, " keep His commandments " describe the consequence resulting from the maintenance of that relationship.

In the book of Proverbs much is said concerning the fear of God. In the seventh verse of the first chapter we read,

" The fear of the Lord is the chief thing in wisdom,"

that is to say, the chief element in a philosophy of life must be that of the fear of God. In chapter nine and verse ten we find,

" The fear of the Lord is the beginning of wisdom."

Whereas in our versions these two statements appear to be identical, they are not really so. The first speaks of the fear of God as the chief element; the second speaks of it as the starting point. Once more in the Proverbs we read,

> " The fear of the Lord is to hate evil " (viii. 13).

And yet again,

> " The fear of the Lord is a fountain of life " (xiv. 27).

All this helps us to understand the words, " Fear God."

Then " keep His commandments," that is, follow His guidance, walk in the way of His will. That is the whole of life.

Personality is in itself a mystery and a possibility. To discover its meaning by living on the level of the material alone is to be driven to the pessimistic conclusion that nothing is worth while, that all is vanity. To discover its meaning by allowing a complete expression of all its forces, always under the government and authority of God, is to find its interpretation in full-orbed realisation and beauty.

ISAIAH XXXV

IN the selection of great chapters by the Westminster Bible School four were chosen from the prophecy of Isaiah, namely, thirty-five, forty, fifty-three and fifty-five. This is an interesting selection, because it may be said that in these four chapters we have gathered the supreme values of this book of Isaiah. Chapter thirty-five leads straight to forty; while forty finds its ultimate in fifty-three, and fifty-three its result in fifty-five.

Chapter thirty-five is closely connected with thirty-four, and stands in startling contrast to it. Thirty-four portrays conditions of the utmost desolation. Thirty-five predicts the most glorious restoration.

We must, however, in order to anything like a right apprehension of the value of these four chapters, take a yet wider outlook. The book opens with the words,

> " The vision of Isaiah, the son of Amoz, which he saw concerning Judah and Jerusalem, in the days of Uzziah, Jotham, Ahaz, and Hezekiah, kings of Judah."

These four kings are named in their proper succession. In the reading of the book we find in chapter six a declaration of the death of Uzziah, and we may suppose that in the first five chapters we have the notes of Isaiah's ministry during the reign of Uzziah. In the book itself we have no note of any prophetic utterance during the sixteen years that Jotham occupied the throne. During the reign of Ahaz, whose death is recorded in chapter fourteen, verse twenty-eight, the prophet was commanded to cease his public work, when Ahaz refused to listen to the prophet's voice, or to accept the sign offered to him. It was an hour when the politicians were attempting to make the nation safe by entering into leagues with other nations. For doing this the prophet rebuked Ahaz, and offered the sign to show he had no need of such help. Upon his refusal to accept the sign, Isaiah was commanded to end his public ministry. From that point in the eighth chapter, up to and including the twenty-seventh chapter, we have the record of instruction given by the prophet to an inner circle of loyal souls. Then at chapter twenty-eight we find him breaking out again into public utterance in another hour of political peril; and from there, up to and including the thirty-fifth chapter, his ministry was again in public.

In that section, from chapter twenty-eight to thirty-five the messages were all, until we reach the thirty-fifth, messages of denunciation. They were concerned first in twenty-eight to thirty-two, with God's own people. Then followed a message in which Assyria, which had oppressed the people was denounced. In chapter thirty-four, the outlook is widened so as to include the world. It opens:

> "Come near, ye nations, to hear; and hearken, ye peoples; let the earth hear, and the fullness thereof; the world, and all things that come forth of it. For the Lord hath indignation against all the nations."

Thus the prophet's outlook was worldwide, and he saw judgment coming upon the whole earth because of its corruption and its sin. Having uttered this word of severest denunciation, he suddenly broke out into the message of chapter thirty-five.

Thus the outlook of chapters thirty-four and thirty-five is inclusive; and in these two chapters the great principles of the sovereignty of God in action are revealed. His judgments are unveiled.

Let it be borne in mind that when we speak of the judgments of God in that way, we must recognise that far more than punishment is included. Judgment may be, and under certain conditions must be, punitive. Judgment, however, in the full sense of the word, is government based upon righteousness, and expressing itself in justice. In that sense the judgments of God are revealed in these two chapters. We may summarise briefly by saying that in chapter thirty-four it is made clear that corruption, under the government of God, must issue in desolation; but because God is God, that is never the final word. That word is always the word of restoration.

To fix our attention then upon chapter thirty-five, we recognise the background of conditions which were present to the mind of the prophet when he uttered these words. That background is revealed in the phrase, " the wilderness and the solitary place." In that connection it should be remembered that the marginal reading, " the parched land" is certainly more accurate than " the solitary place." Immediately following, we have another word, " the desert." The things at which the prophet was looking were pictorially and symbolically described by these words " wilderness, parched land, desert."

If that is the background of the picture, in the foreground we have conditions revealed in the words, " gladness, rejoicing, blossoming, joy and singing, glory and excellency." These words are all found close to each other, and mark the startling contrast between the wilderness, the parched land, and the desert; and life which can only be described in these radiant words.

It is certainly an arresting fact, and cannot be over-emphasised in our study of the Divine Literature, that this is always the ultimate vision of the messengers of God to men. Such messengers never for a single moment condone sin, or call it by any other name than that which reveals it as disastrous failure and iniquity. But these messengers all and always see beyond the gloom to the glory, beyond the wilderness, the blossoming; and hear beyond the dirge of human agony, the song of restoration. This is true of the Hebrew prophets, rough, rugged, magnificent, daring oftentimes, in their invective against wrong. Everyone of them ended upon the note of restoration.

This is equally true in the writings of the New Testament. Paul, who ever looked with intrepid eyes into the appalling sin of the race, as witness his Roman letter, did nevertheless constantly rejoice in the hope of the glory of God. He saw that the groaning of creation moved through travail to emancipation and victory. The fact is equally patent in the teaching of our Lord Himself. He did not spare the word of denunciation, but said to the city that was central to the economy of God, " Your house is left unto you desolate "; but He also said, " Ye shall not see Me henceforth, till ye shall say, Blessed is He that cometh in the name of the Lord." Thus He looked through desolation to restoration. We may summarise everything by declaring that the Bible shows humanity marching through desolation, resulting from its rebellion against God; but the march ends in the garden city of God. All the beauty of the Apocalyptic vision is the culmination.

When we turn from these generalities about the chapter, and examine it, we find that it moves in such rhythmic splendour, and flashes with such suggestive beauty that very little in the nature of exposition is needed. However, let us break it up as to its movement. In the first two verses we have the affirmation of ultimate restoration. In verse three and the first part of verse four we hear the call to courage consequent upon the affirmation. In the brief word at the end of verse four, an inclusive declaration is made as to why we should have courage, and as to how the affirmed restoration will be brought about. Verses five to ten in poetic suggestiveness, describe the process.

In the opening affirmation of the first two verses the prophet illustrated the restoration in the realm of Nature. Whereas we are asked to look at the material earth, it is perfectly clear that the method was intended to illustrate moral and spiritual values. The word " wilderness " does not mean what it might seem to suggest. The Hebrew word so translated literally means pasture land. When we talk about wilderness we often think of a desert without vegetation. " The wilderness " is really the place of pasturage, but it is that place in a condition which can only be described as parched, that is, affording no pasturage.

The affirmation is that that parched pasture land " shall be glad." There is a sense in which it is impossible to improve upon that word " glad "; but for the sake of interpretation we may say that the Hebrew word means brilliant, or radiant. The pasture land, that is parched, and affording no pasture, is to become brilliant and radiant with beauty. It is not difficult to lift this material suggestion on to the highest level, and apply it to the spiritual and moral in life.

Again, the background is the desert, and the word indicates the same idea in another way; that is, it refers to a region of sterility; no life, no growth, no burgeoning or blossoming; death everywhere. That is to rejoice; and once again the Hebrew word is most suggestive. One almost hesitates to translate literally. If we do so, we should render it, The desert shall spin. The idea is that the desert will be seen rotating with life and motion. As a matter of fact that is more than poetry; it is science. Every movement of life is a spinning or whirling movement.

Then the result of that whirling of the life principle is that the desert breaks forth, it burgeons, it buds, it blossoms; and it does so abundantly, and with joy and singing. When we reach the fifty-fifth chapter we shall hear more of this singing of Nature, accompanied by the clapping hands of the trees.

But the prophet has more to say. " The glory of Lebanon shall be given unto it, the excellency of Carmel and Sharon." Once more we are arrested by these words. " Glory " literally means weight, the idea being that of copiousness or quantity.

In the picture we see life moving across the desert which had been sterile, and that in the copiousness of Lebanon. The other arresting word is the word " excellency," which perhaps cannot be improved upon; but I venture to change it to the word magnificence.

Then carefully mark the next declaration, " They shall see the glory "—which is the same word—" of Jehovah." That is the copiousness of Jehovah; and " the excellency "—or as we have suggested—" the magnificence of our God," that is, of Elohim.

The contrast between all this and the descriptions found in the previous chapter is marked. There, " the year of recompense " was portrayed, in which the streams were turned into pitch, and the dust to brimstone. Nothing could be more vivid as a description of uttermost desolation. Then we turn to chapter thirty-five, and see the pasture lands which had been sterile, radiant with beauty, as life moves throughout them. The desolation of death answers the movement of life, and all the glory and beauty is that of the copiousness of the life of God, and the magnificence is that of His excellency.

Thus the one outstanding truth is that the ultimate glory of restoration is that of the revelation of God in the fulfilment of His own purposes; " They shall see the glory of the Lord, the excellency of our God."

In view of that the prophet cried, " Strengthen ye the weak hands, and confirm the feeble knees. Say to them that are of a fearful heart, Be strong, fear not." That is the call to courage. The language is simple and yet graphic. The hands are weak; the knees are tottering; the heart is quite literally, liquid, that is, unstable. The conditions of fear are those of lack of virility. These words certainly describe the condition of many good people in the world to-day. We meet them everywhere. They cannot talk to us at any length without revealing their almost overwhelming sense of the appalling condition of things in the world to-day. I am not denying the fact of these conditions; but in view of this prophetic utterance, reinforced by the whole of the Biblical revelation, there should be no weak hands, or tottering knees, or unstable hearts.

It is perfectly true that as we look out over the world to-day we cannot but be conscious of the wilderness, the parched land, and the desert. It is for us, however, to listen to the affirmation of the prophetic word, that these conditions are transient; and though we may not understand the mystery, know that we are moving towards the realisation of the Divine purpose.

When we ask how is it possible to be free from dread, and even despair in the presence of conditions as we see them, the prophet immediately answers our enquiry. " Behold, your God will come with vengeance, with the recompense of God; He will come and save you." Who can make the desert blossom as the rose? Who can turn the parched wilderness into the place of springs of water? We cannot do it. But God can, and will. And He will do it along two lines of activity, first that of vengeance, which is punishment, and then that of recompense, which is reward. God, acting in judgment, will deal with sin for destruction, in order to the establishment of righteousness and beauty.

The prophet proceeded to describe the process. It is quite certain that the wilderness will never be made glad, and the desert blossom if affairs are left to human ingenuity and cleverness. It is only when God acts, that these things are brought about. The opening word of verse five " Then " links the declaration• of the Divine activity with the description of that which follows in the case of the people. " Then shall the eyes of the blind be opened, and the ears of the deaf shall be unstopped." In the activity of God, the first effect produced will be that men shall be brought to sensitiveness instead of dullness; eyes opened to see; ears unstopped to hear. " Then shall the lame man leap as an hart, and the tongue of the dumb shall sing "; that is humanity brought into the position of ability, instead of disability. When God comes with vengeance and with recompense, there follows a renewal of spiritual discernment; sensibility instead of dullness; and a renewal of power, ability instead of disability.

And still the prophetic word runs on. " And the glowing sand shall become a pool." The Hebrew word rendered " glowing sand " means quite literally the mirage. The mirage is something seen in the desert as one travels across it, an oasis with water and vegetation; but wholly deceitful, for when the point at which the mirage was seen, is reached, there is nothing still but desert." Thus the force of the figure is seen, " the mirage shall become a pool." Instead of the mockery of things which have no reality, there shall be the realisation of that for which men seek.

And yet once more, " In the habitation of jackals where they lay, shall be grass with reeds and rushes." And an highway shall be there, and a way, and it shall be called The way of holiness;

the unclean shall not pass over it; but it shall be for those, the wayfaring man, yea fools, shall not err therein. No lion shall be there, nor any ravenous beast go up thereon, they shall not be found there." Thus the protected highway for the pilgrim is seen; grass where there was desert, a place of springs of water where there was mirage; the character of that highway is that it is the way of holiness.

The whole message of this chapter considered against the background of the previous one is that the only hope of the world is found in the judgment of God, that is, in the government of God. Is is good, therefore, that we ever remind ourselves that that government has never ceased. God has not resigned. He has not vacated His throne. The force of evil has never been able to dismiss Him from the place of full and final authority. He is still reigning.

The process of His reign through human history is ever that of movement through desolation, which is the outcome of corruption towards restoration, resulting from holiness.

In this chapter we are told nothing of the method of God save this insistence upon the fact of His authority. We shall reach the story of how He will turn the wilderness into a place of gladness in subsequent chapters.

ISAIAH XL–XLI, 7

THE presentation of the Servant, Who is to be the Instrument of Jehovah through Whom the wilderness is to be transformed, begins at the eighth verse of chapter forty-one. There is the closest connection between chapters thirty-five and forty. The last words of thirty-five are :

" Everlasting joy shall be upon their heads; they shall obtain gladness and joy, and sorrow and sighing shall flee away."

The first words of forty are :—

" Comfort ye, comfort ye, My people, saith your God."

The central declaration of thirty-five is :

" Behold your God will come with vengeance, with the recompense of God; He will come and save you."

The central declaration of forty is :

" Behold, the sovereign Lord Jehovah will come."

Thus the chapters are linked together. Thirty-five sings of the fact that beyond the desolation there is to be restoration, that the wilderness and the solitary place are to be glad, and the desert is to blossom as the rose. Forty introduces the account of the method by which the wilderness and the solitary place will be made glad, and the desert will be made to blossom as the rose. The full story of that method begins in the eighth verse of that forty-first chapter, with the words : " But thou, Israel, My servant," and runs on to and through the fifty-third chapter, and chapter fifty-four, which begins, " Sing, O barren, thou that didst not bear."

If I may borrow a musical figure, I should describe the section we are now examining as the great introductory prologue to the oratorio of the Servant of the Lord. It has two movements. First, an announcement is made through voices. That occupies eleven verses. Then from the twelfth verse of forty, and running to the seventh verse in chapter forty-one, we have an argument through a questionary.

In the announcement through voices, we have six distinct movements. The first of these is contained in verses one and two. It is of the nature of a general statement, revealing the purpose of God concerning His people, and through His people concerning the whole wilderness. " Comfort ye, comfort ye My people, saith your God."

Comfort is the word revealing the purpose of God, but the comfort is based upon righteousness.

" Her warfare is accomplished . . . her iniquity is pardoned . . . she hath received of Jehovah's hand double for all her sins."

The final interpretation of that will be found in the fifty-third chapter, where we discover how the warfare is accomplished, and the iniquity can be pardoned, and the comfort come.

The second movement is contained in verses three to five. In it we hear the voice of the herald, " The voice of one that crieth." It is impossible to read these words without our minds leaping across the centuries to the story of Jesus, and the coming of John. The voice of the herald is a call to man to fulfil his responsibility in the presence of the Divine determination. The Divine determination is comfort. Because of that, man is called to prepare in the wilderness the way of Jehovah, to make straight in the desert a highway for God. We are again driven in thought to the New Testament. In the message of John the Baptist we find a full interpretation of how man is to prepare for the coming of God. God does not proceed to transform the wilderness into a garden save when man prepares a highway for Him.

The third movement is a brief one, occupying a part of verse six, " The voice of one saying, Cry." It is an authoritative command to make a proclamation, an announcement.

This is immediately followed by the fourth movement, in which the voice of the messenger is heard, in obedience to the voice of authority; enquiring, " What shall I cry? "

The fifth movement records the reply to that enquiry, and runs through to verse eight. It begins by facing the wilderness conditions and accounting for them :

" All flesh is grass, and all the goodliness thereof is as the flower of the field; the grass withereth, the flower fadeth."

That is the wilderness; withering grass, fading flower, the death of all life. These conditions are the result of the fact that " the breath of the Lord bloweth upon it." The breath of God blasts, and presently the breath of God causes the wilderness to blossom. It depends upon man's relation to the breath of God, whether he is blasted or blessed by it. The same principle is revealed in Malachi, where we are told that the sun-rising means healing for some, and blasting for others. The final note in the proclamation is that the word of God abideth for ever. Again the mind travels to the New Testament, to a letter in which Peter quoted this, " The word of our God shall stand for ever "; and added, " And this is the word of the Gospel which was preached unto you."

The sixth and last movement in the great announcement is found in verses eight to eleven. It records the fact and reason of the good tidings of the Gospel.

The fact to be announced is that of " good tidings."

" O thou that tellest good tidings to Zion, get thee up into the high mountain; O thou that tellest good tidings to Jerusalem, lift up thy voice."

Twice the phrase is repeated, " good tidings, good tidings." In the Greek version, the word used to translate the Hebrew word, is the word *euaggelion*, which is the word evangel, or Gospel, which is found in the New Testament. That is what Peter meant when he said, " This is the word of good tidings," the evangel, the Gospel, " which is preached unto you."

So far then the purpose is declared, that the wilderness is to blossom, that is, the message of comfort; the declaration is made that men must fling up the highway for God; and the determination of God is announced to carry out His plan as revealed, and to reveal His glory.

The reason for the good tidings is to be found in the fact that God is going to act. We are not told so far, how He will do so. Even though we cannot understand all the processes, the one thing that gives our hearts assurance is that it is God Who will act. In this passage declaring the fact, His three great titles are enumerated, or rather, His Name, and two titles : Elohim, the mighty One; Adonai, the sovereign Lord; these are the titles; Yahweh, the becoming God of grace, that is the Name. Thus might, and authority, and love are seen merging together, and the merging in action will make the desert blossom as the rose and the sterile pasture-land to be glad.

The second division in this section deals with the majesty of Jehovah, as revealing the reasons for perfect confidence, that in spite of all desolation there will be restoration.

The world outlook to-day is certainly not that of a garden blossoming with roses. It is rather that of a wilderness bristling with thorns. Who then is this Yahweh, Elohim, Adonai, Who claims that He will make the wilderness and the dry place glad, and the desert rejoice and blossom as the rose? This is the question which the movement now under consideration answers. I have described it as a questionary, and it will be noted that in the course of it fifteen questions are asked.

In the section we have four distinct movements, each one revealing God in a different way. In the first, verses twelve to seventeen, His splendid isolation as Creator is declared. In the second, verses eighteen to twenty-six, His transcendence of all similitude, that is, the impossibility of making anything that accurately represents Him. In the third, verses twenty-seven to forty-one, His immanence in strength is affirmed, and His nearness to all weakness, combined with His own freedom from weakness. In the last (xli 1-7), His action in government is illustrated.

Thus surveyed in its entirety, we have an announcement of comfort, a call to proclaim a Gospel, the central declaration of the action of God the Lord Jehovah; and a celebration of His majesty.

In the section dealing with the splendour of God as Creator, verses twelve to seventeen, we have three questions, every one of them compelling thought, " Who hath measured? " " Who hath directed the Spirit of Jehovah? " " With whom toòk He counsel? " More stately language in the setting forth of the majesty of God in creation, is impossible. It is this God Who in creation sought no counsel, asked no advice, because He needed none; Who lacked nothing in wisdom, and nothing in power. Who is the One to make glad the wilderness, and the desert to blossom. If we have that vision of God there can be no room for panic, however dark the outlook.

In the next movement, verses eighteen to twenty-six, we find no fewer than seven questions asked. The first two of them suggest the impossibility of representing God in any similitude. The last of them returns to the same implied conclusion. The four intervening are of the nature of appeal to the people addressed. Every question is one which actually involves its own answer; and the whole section is plainly intended to show the greatness of

God as being such, that there can be nothing comparable thereto; and consequently there can be no accurate likeness of Him.

In dealing with this the prophet indulges in satire, as he tells how men endeavour to represent God. The chief point in his description of such an effort is that men are anxious to make a God that they can keep by them, one that will not be moved or carried away. That idea is wrought out in fuller detail at a later point in the prophecy (chapter 46), where the prophet shows that if men make gods for themselves, when they make them they have to carry them; whereas the true God makes men, and carries the men He makes.

The prophet was addressing himself to God's people, hence the meaning of his questions, " Have *ye* not known? have *ye* not heard? hath it not been told *you* from the beginning? have *ye* not understood from the foundations of the earth? " He declares to them that God is the God " that sitteth upon the circle of the earth," that is that He is the circumferencing God. Moreover, He is governing among world affairs, for He " bringeth princes to nothing, He maketh the judges of the earth as vanity. Yea, they have not been planted; yea, they have not been sown; yea, their stock hath not taken root in the earth; moreover, He bloweth upon them, and they wither, and the whirlwind taketh them away as stubble." It is well for us to remember that this presentation of God is not out-of-date. It is all as true to-day as in the day when the prophet uttered the words.

Returning to the first question, " To whom then will ye liken Me, that I should be equal to him? saith the Holy One," the prophet re-emphasises the truth that the greatness and majesty of God are such that He cannot be represented accurately or adequately. So far we have been looking at the earth, and God sitting upon the circle thereof. We are now called upon to look beyond,

" Lift up your eyes on high, and see Who hath created these, that bringeth out their host by number; He calleth them all by name; by the greatness of His might, and for that He is strong in power, not one is lacking."

This is the God Who will make the wilderness blossom as the rose.

While it is true that man has never been able to create a likeness of God, God has given to man a Representation of Himself that is full and final. From the period of Isaiah's prophesying we overleap the intervening centuries, and find ourselves in an

upper room in the presence of a Man, radiant in the beauty of
His humanity, and yet with a light shining through His eyes
that never shone through human eyes before. Speaking to another
man, one Philip, He said, " He that hath seen Me, hath seen the
Father." In Him, then, there was given to men a similitude through
which God is perfectly known.

The next movement, verses twenty-seven to forty-one, was
again an appeal to the people of God,

> " Why sayest thou, O Jacob, and speakest, O Israel,
> My way is hid from the Lord, and my judgment is passed
> away from my God? "

It is at least arrestingly suggestive that the people are addressed
by the use of those two names, Jacob and Israel; a recognition
at once of frailty and of strength. These people are then reminded
of the abiding truth concerning God.

> " The everlasting God, Jehovah, the Creator of the ends
> of the earth fainteth not, neither is weary; there is no
> searching of His understanding."

Neither is that all the truth as it deals only with what He is
in Himself. Therefore it is further declared,

> " He giveth power to the faint; and to him that hath
> no might He increaseth strength."

This is illustrated superlatively in the statement,

> " Even the youths shall faint and be weary,"

that is, those who are supposed to be incapable of fainting or
weariness.

> " And the young men shall utterly fall,"

that is, those whose chief characteristic is virility. All strength
which is only human, breaks down.

> " But they that wait upon Jehovah shall renew their strength,"

that is, human life lived in fellowship with God is perpetually
reinforced. It is here that the wonderful paradox of processional
revelation is found.

> " They shall mount up with wings as eagles."

That, of course, is a perfectly natural and easy exercise if
we have wings.

> " They shall run and not be weary."

Running is always a more difficult thing than flying. Finally,

"They shall walk and not faint,"

It is the long persistent tramp which is the most difficult of all.

It is this God Who will make the wilderness glad, and the desert blossom as the rose. There is, therefore, no room for doubt or hesitation.

The final movement (xli. 1-7), consists of a great summons to silence, to strength, to approach, to speech, and to fellowship.

The whole of this appeal was illustrated by the then present situation. The prophet was speaking when everything looked hopeless. On the horizon was the enemy of the people, Cyrus, seeming to threaten their national existence. Of that outlook the prophet said,

"Who hath raised up one from the east, whom He calleth in righteousness to His foot? He giveth nations before him, and maketh him rule over kings; He giveth them as the dust to his sword, as the driven stubble to his bow. He pursueth them, and passeth on safely; even by a way that he had not gone with his feet."

Thus the majesty of God was revealed in a new way, in the fact that He was over-ruling all the forces surrounding His people, even though they appeared to be hostile to them.

So we ask once more, Who is equal to making the wilderness glad, and the desert blossom? The answer is found in this great argument by a questionary. He is the Creator, the Sustainer, the Unwearying, the Governing. Therefore, "Behold, your God," and beholding, know that the wilderness will yet be glad, and the desert blossom as the rose.

ISAIAH LII, 13–LIII

A CAREFUL reading of the prophecy of Isaiah shows that an examination of chapter fifty-three must begin at the thirteenth verse of chapter fifty-two, where the words, " Behold, My Servant," introduce the great unveiling which follows. Any approach to this section of Holy Scripture must be characterised by a reticence that amounts almost to reluctance. The reluctance is born of a sense of the almost overwhelming nature of what is found here. There is nothing, either in the Old or the New Testament more arresting than this portrayal of the Servant of the Lord, in which we are conscious of an appalling gloom, which nevertheless burns and shines with ineffable glory. Because the writing is here, reluctance must not prevent our examination, but such must be characterised by reverent reticence in a consciousness of the fact that we are dealing with matters too deep for final interpretation.

The opening words, " Behold, My Servant," reveal the nature of the vision, and demand attention. In the movement of the prophecy this passage is climacteric. This movement began in the fortieth chapter, the prologue to which is found in chapter thirty-five. There the prophet was lifted high above the gloom in the midst of which he lived, and saw a day of glorious restoration.

" The wilderness and the solitary place shall be glad, and the desert shall rejoice, and blossom as the rose."

Beginning at the fortieth chapter, the prophet proceeds to show how that day of restoration will come. A voice in the wilderness is heard calling upon men to prepare the way of Jehovah, for it is only through the action of God that the desolation can be transmuted into the glory of complete realisation. Following on he shows that this proclamation of an activity of Jehovah constitutes the Gospel of comfort, which is to be proclaimed; and in a stately passage shows the majesty of Jehovah as creating the ensuring certainty that these things will be so.

Thus to the prophet all the things in the midst of which he lived, of darkness and desolation, became radiant in the light of things, which, historically, were far away from him. As Peter has it, he " spake from God, being caught up and borne along by the Holy Spirit"; and saw the wilderness and the parched land made glad, and the desert rejoicing and blossoming with roses. He shows that Jehovah will move to the accomplishment of this great and glorious consummation through One described as "the Servant of Jehovah."

In the course of this whole section twice over the arresting words are found, "Behold, My Servant" (xlii. 1, lii. 13). As we follow through, we find that the title is applied to the nation, but also to a Personality arising in the life of the nation. The nation fails in the accomplishment of Divine purpose, but the Person carries out that purpose to complete realisation.

To glance at the two occurrences of the words, "Behold, My Servant," which in each case refer to the Person, we find that the first of these was quoted by our Lord in the synagogue in Nazareth, when He claimed their fulfilment in Himself, as He said, "This day hath this Scripture been fulfilled in your ears." The second introduces the section now under our consideration, which self-evidently has application to the travail and triumph through which the Servant of the Lord accomplishes the Divine purpose.

In order to an apprehension of the passage, we shall examine its natural divisions, which consist first of an inclusive exordium (lii. 13-15); secondly, of a section describing the travail of the Servant of the Lord (liii. 1-9); and finally of the section announcing His triumph (liii. 10-12).

The exordium is complete in itself. All that follows after, serves as interpretation of the declarations made therein. The first statement is "Behold, My Servant shall deal wisely," or as it reads in the King James' Version, "shall deal prudently." Both in that Version and in the Revision, an alternative rendering is found in the margin which makes the declaration, "Behold, My Servant shall prosper." Without any doubt that is the true meaning of the Hebrew word. Whereas it is so that at the base of the Hebrew word there is an idea of wisdom and prudence, the use of the word always was suggestive of success or prosperity, resulting from that wisdom or prudence.

The statement is immediately followed by the declaration, "He shall be exalted and lifted up, and shall be very high." To read that merely as a statement, would be to realise that it is a prediction of complete victory, and yet the introduction of the phrase "lifted up," is most arresting. In general terms, the whole declaration is that His prosperity will be gained by His exaltation, and that the exaltation will come by a lifting up; and that such exaltation by lifting up, will put Him into the place of full and final authority, that is, He will be " very high." When we follow on, we find a startling light upon the whole statement, in the words, " Like as many were astonied at Thee," which is immediately followed by a parenthetical statement, " His visage was so marred more than any man, and His form more than the sons of men." In these words there is a recognition of suffering, of sorrow, indeed, of agony. A visage marred, and a form marred, speak of the spoiling of personality.

The whole statement is mysterious, and we are driven to enquire what it is that the prophet means. Let us then bring together two statements thus, " Like as many were astonied at Thee . . so shall He sprinkle many nations; kings shall shut their mouths at Him; for that which had not been told them shall they see; and that which they had not heard shall they understand." Such marring of visage and form, creates astonishment; so, that is, that by that method, will the victory be attained.

We may say then that the lifting up referred to in the opening declaration is interpreted by these things that follow. The lifting up is the elevation of conspicuous sorrow, leading to the elevation of conspicuous sovereignty. The way to the sovereignty is the way of suffering.

From these great prophetic words, our minds travel on to some of the final hours in the life of our Lord, where we find this same double consciousness of sorrow and of sovereignty, and of sorrow leading to sovereignty finding expression in words which fell from His lips. Approaching the Cross He said, " Now is My soul troubled," and almost immediately afterwards, " Now is the judgment of this world; now shall the prince of this world be cast out. And I, if I be lifted up out of the earth, will draw all men unto Myself." Thus the historic utterances of Jesus harmonise perfectly with the prophetic foretelling; " He shall be exalted and lifted up, and shall be very high." Lifted up by conspicuous sorrows, but by them lifted into the place of conspicuous sovereignty, so that the kings of the earth shut their mouths because of Him. Thus, the exordium leads to the prophetic foretelling of the sorrows leading to the sovereignty; of the travail issuing in the triumph.

The account of the travail is one to be read with wondering awe, and most appropriately in solemn silence. Merely to aid in doing this, we venture reverently to break up the section into its three movements. We have presented to us first the rejected Person (verses one to three); then the vicarious Sufferer (verses four to six); finally, the atoning Lamb (verses seven to nine).

In presenting the rejected Person the prophet very clearly shows Him as seen by God, and then as seen by men. The Divine vision of the Servant of the Lord is contained in one simple and yet sublime declaration, " He grew up before Him as a tender plant." The poetic description refers to Him in all the beauty which is suggested by eternal youth. Thus God saw His Son. We remember how thrice during the period of earthly life the silence of eternity was broken by Divine attestations. In each case the attestation was that of the satisfaction of God in Him. The first was perfectly full and clear, " This is My beloved Son, in Whom I am well pleased." That was the Divine vision of the Servant of the Lord.

That, however, was not how men saw Him; and indeed, it is not how the world sees Him even yet.

In immediate and striking contrast to all that is suggested by the phrase " a tender plant," the words follow, " And as a root out of a dry ground; He hath no form nor comeliness; and when we see Him, there is no beauty that we should desire Him."

It will be seen that I have resolutely changed the punctuation of these sentences, in order to show the contrast of vision between the Divine and the human. This was the human view. No contrast can be more arresting then that between " a tender plant," and " a root out of a dry ground," a root lying on the pathway, not in the ground; something that men spurn, perhaps kick out of their way as they walk. In Him men saw neither form nor comeliness; and no beauty that made Him desirable.

The prophet certainly does not mean that the Servant of the Lord lacked either form or comeliness or beauty. What he did mean is that man was blind to His beauty. This was true, and remains true in the widest application. The ideals of beauty were false, and so they still are. To consult the world of art at the time when our Lord lived, is to discover the truth of this affirmation. It may truthfully be said that through His advent, art had its renaissance; but even yet much of its conception of beauty is entirely false. It was not, and it is not that there is no beauty in Jesus; but rather, that man is blind to beauty.

All concerning the Person is therefore finally summarised in the words, " He was despised and rejected of men; a Man of sorrows, and acquainted with grief." As a matter of fact His sorrows and His griefs made Him unacceptable to that world of art which refused to look upon anything which, in its estimation, was ugly or mutilated.

Having thus revealed the Servant of the Lord as personally rejected, the prophet proceeded to show that His Sorrows were vicarious. In the eyes of God, " A tender plant," in the eyes of men, " a root out of a dry ground " devoid of all beauty, " a Man of Sorrows, and acquainted with grief." What was He doing? The answer is found in the words, " Surely He hath borne our griefs, and carried our sorrows."

Here again men were blind to the facts, and the prophet says, " We did esteem Him stricken, smitten of God, and afflicted." More than forty years ago I sat in the City Temple, and heard these words read by Dr. Parker. He read the whole chapter without any note or comment, except that at this point he interjected three words. Let me repeat the sentences as they then fell from his lips. " We did esteem Him stricken, smitten of God, and afflicted "—' WE WERE WRONG '—" He was wounded for our transgressions, He was bruised for our iniquities; the chastisement of our peace was upon Him; and with His stripes we are healed." That was inspired exposition in the flash of a brief sentence. His griefs were not His own. His sorrows were not personal. They were all vicarious. Thus as art was at fault, and unable to detect His beauty, so theology and philosophy were at fault, unable to interpret His sorrows. The outlook of the thinkers upon His sorrows was that He was " smitten, stricken of God, and afflicted." It was the same philosophy which had mastered the thinking of the friends of Job. They gathered around him; they saw a man suffering; and they said, God is smiting him, because he is a sinner. That was the outlook of the thinkers, the philosophers and theologians in the presence of the suffering of Christ. Thus art was at fault in the consideration of His Person; and philosophy was at fault in the presence of His sorrows. Nevertheless, through Him art was reborn, and philosophy found the final interpretation of God.

And so we reach the final movement in the presentation of the travail of the Servant of the Lord.

" He was oppressed, yet He humbled Himself and opened not His mouth; as a lamb that is led to the slaughter, and as a sheep that before her shearers is dumb; yea, He opened not His mouth. By oppression and judgment He was taken away; and as for His generation, who among them considered that He was cut off out of the land of the living? for the transgression of My people was He stricken. And they made His grave with the wicked, and with the rich in His death; although He had done no violence, neither was any deceit in His mouth."

Thus, He is seen, silent in the presence of the wrong that was done to Him. It was the silence of One in perfect agreement with God, and with God's determination to make the wilderness glad. Surely this was,

" The silence of eternity,
Interpreted by love."

In this presentation the personal Sufferer, the vicarious Sufferer, the silent Sufferer, is revealed as an atoning Lamb ; for it was " for the transgression of My people was He stricken."

Then the note changes, and we reach the setting forth of the triumph of the Servant of the Lord. It begins with the statement " Yet it pleased the Lord to bruise Him." While it is true that the word " Yet " does not occur in the Hebrew, it is absolutely necessary in our language, in order to draw attention to the intended contrast. The declaration in itself lifts our contemplation to the level of the Divine. Whereas in the story of the travail we have seen the Servant of the Lord in the midst of the wrong done to Him by men, silently bearing the sins of those very men; we are now told that all of this was encompassed within the Divine will; " It pleased Jehovah to bruise Him; He hath put Him to grief." Thus the prophetic word harmonises with the apostolic word uttered on the day of Pentecost. The first reference to the Cross in the language of a man filled with the Holy Spirit, was made in these words, " Him, being delivered by the determinate counsel and fore-knowledge of God, ye by the hand of men without the law did crucify and slay." The prophet begins with the prediction of the wrong done by men, and ends with the affirmation of the Divine over-ruling. The apostle begins with the declaration of the Divine determination, and ends with the affirmation of the sin that caused the suffering of the Servant of the Lord.

It was in view of this consciousness of the relation of the sin of man, and the good pleasure of God, that the prophet broke out into the words which follow,

" When Thou shalt make His soul an offering for sin, He shall see His seed, He shall prolong His days, and the pleasure of the Lord shall prosper in His hands."

Thus the whole movement opened with the words, " Behold, My Servant shall prosper." This was then followed by the story of the travail and the prediction of the triumph. The whole of this is seen as being within the grasp of the Divine government, carrying out the Divine purpose. The result therefore is inevitable. When His soul, that is, His entire personality, was made an offering for sin, the purposes of God were assured of accomplishment. Through travail He came to triumph.

In that connection we read that great and glorious declaration, " He shall see of the travail of His soul, and shall be satisfied." Here we are in the presence of mysteries which cannot be finally explained, but which are radiant with the glory of eternal Grace. The satisfaction following the travail will be that of the right of the Servant of the Lord to justify many, as He has borne their iniquities.

It will be granted by all that in this section we reach the climax of Old Testament prophesying concerning the Messiah; and it may be well to remind ourselves of the marvel of it, that a foretelling so clear and definite, was given to the sons of men hundreds of years before its historic fulfilment. As Delitzsch says, " This whole passage looks as if it might have been written beneath the Cross on Golgotha."

In the light of that historic fulfilment of prophecy, of apostolic interpretation and all the witness of the centuries, we may gather up everything in the prophetic word, and express it in that wonderful sentence of Paul than which nothing could possibly be more complete or final, " God was in Christ, reconciling the world unto Himself."

Surely such a meditation appeals to us in the very words that Paul used in connection with that statement, " I beseech you, therefore, be ye reconciled to God."

ISAIAH LV

THIS chapter is complete in itself as a prophetic call and appeal. There is a sense in which it is by no means complete in itself. It demands all that has preceded it. It finds its reason in the fifty-third chapter. Let us make passing reference to the focal points of light preceding it which we have considered in this series. Chapter thirty-five confronted the desert, and foretold the garden. Chapter forty announced a Gospel consequent upon the activity of Jehovah. Chapter fifty-three unveiled the Servant of Jehovah passing through the wilderness of travail, and so preparing for the song of the garden. Chapter fifty-five is then the prophetic call, consequent upon all that has gone before.

This chapter opens in the wilderness where are thirsty, hungry, restless people. It closes in the garden where the hills are singing, and the trees of the field are clapping their hands. Throughout it employs figurative language to describe spiritual experiences. The prophetic word is addressed to the deepest spiritual necessities of human nature ; and calls men to those attitudes and activities wherein those necessities will be perfectly met and satisfied. That is to generalise on the chapter.

Its structure is that of first setting forth the conditions of the wilderness or the desert (verses 1, 2), finally describing conditions in the Garden of God (verses 10-13) ; while between these is found an argued appeal, setting forth the way out of the desert, and into the garden (verses 3-9). In that order let us consider the chapter.

The contrast between the conditions described at the beginning and those portrayed at the end is arresting and vivid. There is no straining after rhetorical effect, but the contrast is none the less patent and vivid.

In the first two verses let us take merely the phrases which describe the conditions. " Everyone that thirsteth," " Ye spend money for that which is not bread," " Your labour for that which satisfieth not." The conditions then are those of thirst, hunger, dis-appointment, which is restlessness. The prophetic word was addressed to human beings ; and at first calls them to the waters, though they had no money. It is self-evident that the prophet did not mean that these people were literally without money, because he immediately added, " Wherefore do ye spend money for that which is not bread." If, whether historically or prophetically the prophet was thinking of his own people in Babylon, as probably he was, they certainly had money. As a matter of fact, during that period of captivity, they were so materially successful in Babylon that in the case of multitudes of them they had no desire to return to Jerusalem ; and the records show that only a small minority did return. They had money, and were spending money, but they were still thirsty. They had no money that was current in the realm capable of providing the water that would quench the thirst of which they were conscious. The people were choked with the dust of material things, while yet conscious of a spiritual thirst for which they could find no water.

The prophet then changed the figure as he asked them why they spent money for that which is not bread. Materially there was fullness of bread. They were satiated with it; but there was no satisfying of that deeper hunger of the spirit.

And yet again, he recognised their energy, and their output of strength. They were labouring, but they were not satisfied. There was neither rest nor a sense of peace or poise, but rather that of feverishness.

That is a description of life without God ; thirsty, hungry, restless. Here men are living to-day, and perhaps those who are most conscious of these conditions are those who have repletion of material things.

Now turning to the conditions described at the end of the chapter, we find first a revelation of the secret of these conditions. The poetic illustration full of exquisite beauty is employed,

" For as the rain cometh down and the snow from heaven, and returneth not thither, but watereth the earth, and maketh it bring forth and bud, and giveth seed to the sower and bread to the eater."

Here the ministry of rain and of snow in co-operation with the forces of the earth are recognised, as bringing forth harvest.

The figure is then immediately applied :—

" So shall My word be that goeth forth out of My mouth ; it shall not return unto Me void, but it shall accomplish that which I please, and it shall prosper in the thing whereto I sent it."

Thus the fructifying power in human life is declared to be the Word of God. This, of course, has its application to the sacred Scriptures, but it means finally God's making known of Himself to the human soul. The co-operation between rain and snow and earth produces harvests ; and the co-operation between Divine revelation and human obedience brings forth all the things of fruitfulness in life. Thus the wilderness is made glad, and the desert blossoms as the rose. Thus the conception is that which Moses had uttered long before by Divine inspiration, and which Jesus repeated in an hour of fierce temptation, " Man shall not live by bread alone, but by every word that proceedeth out of the mouth of God." To live by bread alone is to live in the desert. To live by bread and the Word of God is to find life in all fullness and beauty.

This the prophet then sets forth once more with poetic beauty. He begins, " Ye shall go out with joy." The indefiniteness of that is in itself illuminating. " Ye shall go out," where? Anywhere, everywhere. The thought is that of progress and expansion, and this is to be for evermore with joy.

Again, " Ye shall be led forth," and the phrase itself suggests submission to guidance, and indicates progress ; and this is ever to be " with peace." In the going out there is joy ; upon the march there is peace. Men living in right relationship with God are evermore going out to something larger, something deeper, something grander, and therefore with joy ; while in the going they are conducted, led forth, and so with peace.

And still further, the prophet describes the experience of such people under such conditions,

" The mountains and the hills shall break forth before you into singing, and all the trees of the field shall clap their hands."

Moreover, on the way, life will be seen transmuted, and expressing itself at its highest ; no longer the thorn that curses, but the fir tree, full of life and beauty ; no longer the briar that hinders, but the myrtle tree full of exquisite loveliness. This is the glory of the garden of the Lord. The wilderness is glad. The desert blossoms as the rose. There is music everywhere.

Is someone inclined to say, All this is poetry? That is certainly true. Poetry is the interpretation of prose. The whole picture thus suggested is that of Godly life, life when fertilised by the Word of God, and lived in communion with Him.

There are multitudes of those who know nothing experi-mentally of this life. They would say, We never heard the mountains sing, or the trees clap hands. They are conscious of the mountains. They have seen them. They have even travelled through them ; but all the while were wondering perchance, if coal were there to mine, or copper to obtain. Mountains to them are mounds out of which they may gain something. They have not heard the mountains sing. The thought of the trees of the field clapping hands almost fills them with amusement. When the evening zephyr breaks across the trees, or the hurricane sweeps the forest, and all the little leaves are clapping their hands, they hear nothing. They see the trees, these people, but call them lumber in the States, and timber in the homeland. They have lost the capacity for the poetry of life, because they live immersed in things of the dust. Whatever theological objection may be raised to some of the suggestions he advanced, Wordsworth was right in the main when of childhood he said,

> " Trailing clouds of glory do we come
> From God, Who is our home."

There is at once pathos and tragedy in Tom Hood's familiar lines,

> " I remember, I remember,
>   The house where I was born,
> The little window where the sun
>   Came peeping in at morn ;
> He never came a wink too soon,
>   Nor brought too long a day.
> But now I often wish the night
>   Had borne my breath away.

> " I remember, I remember,
>   The fir trees dark and high ;
> I used to think their slender tops
>   Were close against the sky,
> It was a childish ignorance,
>   But now 'tis little joy
> To know I'm further off from heaven
>   Than when I was a boy."

There are people who hear all this music, and some of them may be living in the slums and tenement houses where there are no trees ; or, perchance in the more blighting and blasting sections where wealth abounds. Such people are in tune with Nature, because they are right with Nature's God.

We close with the central section in which the prophet shows the way from the desert into the garden. His first word is a call to attention, and that combined with a promise of life. With the listening soul God will make a covenant, which are the sure mercies of David. Then he refers to a Person, " I have given Him for a Witness to the peoples, a Leader and Commander to the peoples." Thus the call is a double one, first to listen, and then to look. The Person thus referred to is the Servant of the Lord Who through travail comes to triumph. But listening and looking must lead to endeavour. "Seek ye the Lord while He may be found, call ye upon Him while He is near."

Then in what is the seventh verse of the chapter, in clearest terms the way of seeking is revealed. " Let the wicked forsake his way, and the unrighteous man his thoughts ; and let him return unto the Lord, and He will have mercy upon him ; and to our God, for He will abundantly pardon." In these instructions we have first a declaration of human responsibility ; and secondly, a declaration of Divine activity. In other words, we are told what man must do, and what God covenants to do with man when he is obedient.

What, then, are the words revealing man's responsibility? " Let the wicked forsake his way, and the unrighteous man his thoughts ; and let him return unto the Lord." That is all man can do, but he must do that. The term " way " refers to the outward set of the life ; and the term " thought " to the weaving or plan which lies behind it. In these verses we have a psychological recognition of personality. The outward way is to be given up by the giving up of the inward thinking ; and in each case by a return to God.

It is conceivable that a man may say, Why should I give up my way and my thinking? Am I not capable of carving out my own destiny by doing my own thinking? The answer is No, a thousand times, No. That is the whole trouble with human life. That is where the Bible comes crashing across the pride of human life.

And still the question may be pressed, Why should men give up their own way, and their own thinking? The answer is found in the sentences immediately following, " For My thoughts are not your thoughts, neither are your ways My ways, saith the Lord."

Once again a question may arise, What is the difference between God's thoughts and man's thoughts, God's ways and man's ways? And once more the answer is found in the subsequent sentences,

" For as the heavens are higher than the earth, so are My ways higher than your ways, and My thoughts than your thoughts."

This is not a statement emphasising a distance between God and man, but showing a difference of conception and conduct.

Man's thoughts for himself are conditioned on the earth level, "What shall we eat? What shall we drink? Wherewithal shall we be clothed?" Or, in more vulgar parlance, "Let us eat and drink, for to-morrow we die"! That thinking is the thinking of the man with the muck-rake, with a gleam in his eye, proving his capacity for infinite things, and attempting to satisfy that, with the glitter of a straw among the muck. That is man's way for himself. God's thought for man is such as to give him the franchise of eternity, lift him to the infinity of the ages, call upon him to walk in fellowship with God.

When a man becomes conscious of the desert, and sees the glory of the garden, and desires to pass from one to the other, he may consent to give up his thoughts and his way, and returning to God, accept His thought and His way. The moment, however, that he does that he is conscious of sin. The very turning to God wakes within him a conviction as to the appalling failure of his life to that point. The question then arises, What shall he do with that failure? The answer is that he can do nothing. No soul can cleanse itself of sin, by telling someone else about it. What then shall he do? That is the point at which the Divine attitude and activity are revealed and declared. These are found in the words, " He will have mercy upon him . . He will abundantly pardon." Everything of redemption and renewal results from a Divine attitude and activity.

As we conclude our meditation upon this great chapter it is impossible not to make an application of it that is immediate and personal. It is conceivable that some entirely honest man will find a difficulty at this point ; the difficulty of being able to accept this declaration as to the attitude of God. At this point I do not propose argument, but rather illustration. I indulge in a reminiscence which carries me back to the year 1887. I was conducting Evangelistic Services in a little Chapel among the Yorkshire coalfields, employing the method of inviting men and women, anxious about spiritual things, to remain after the service and come into an enquiry room. On this occasion three days had passed, Sunday, Monday, Tuesday, and on the Wednesday evening one of the workers came and said to me, " I wish you would come into the vestry. There is a man there who came there on Sunday night, again on Monday, and yet again on Tuesday. He is there once more to-night, but he does not seem to be able to get through." I went into the vestry and found a fine, upstanding man of about forty years of age, a Yorkshire collier. I looked at him, and said, " My friend, what is the matter? " To which he bluntly replied, " I am in hell." I said to him, " Why don't you come out? " and he replied, " What is the way out? " I opened my Bible at this chapter in Isaiah, and pointed to the seventh verse and I asked him to read it. He did so, and then I said, " The first part of that verse tells you what you must do, and if you will do it, the second half tells you what God will do." He said, " Yes, I see that." I then asked him, " Are you prepared to do the first part? " He said, " Yes, I am." " Then," I said, " if you are, God will have mercy and He will abundantly pardon."

Then this man said a tremendous thing, one I have never forgotten, revealing the fact that he was not trifling, but thinking with undoubted seriousness. He bluntly said to me, " I don't believe it " ; and I asked him, " Why not? " He said, " Do you mean to tell me He will forgive me and pardon me and receive me now, after all the failure of life up to this point? " I replied, " He certainly will " : and then came this statement, " I don't believe it ; it is altogether too cheap."

I realised the greatness of this man's thinking, and that I was face to face with a soul conscious of need, and in agony. I shall always claim that I was very clearly directed by the Holy Spirit as to how to deal with him. I said, " Have you been to work to-day? " He said, " Yes, I have been down the pit." I said, " How far are you underground? " Said he, " About 800 yards." Then I asked him how he got home, and he told me he walked. I said, " How did you get on to the surface, in order to get home? " He said, " I came to the bottom of the shaft, entered the cage, and was pulled up." Said I, " How much did you pay to come up? " He replied, " Nothing," then staring at me, he abruptly said, " Oh, that won t do ; I didn't pay anything to come up, but it cost the Company . . . ! Oh, my God, is that it? You mean, it is cheap for me, but it was not cheap for God ! "

This man had seen to the heart of the Gospel. That is what I meant at the beginning when I said chapter fifty-five cannot be taken except as linked to chapter fifty-three, " He was wounded for our transgressions, He was bruised for our iniquities ; the chastisement of our peace was upon Him."

Verse seven may be described as the wicket gate through which men pass from the desert to the garden. It is so marvellously and simply hung that the weakest and most paralysed hand touching it, it swings toward the garden, but that wicket gate is hinged on Calvary's Cross.

MATTHEW V

WE recognise at once that this chapter is part of a larger whole, and cannot be considered alone. Fortunately, chapters six and seven are to follow in this series. The three chapters give us the great Manifesto of the Kingdom, as uttered by our Lord to His first disciples. It is necessary that we first, in the very briefest way, survey the whole Manifesto.

It begins with a Prologue (verses 1, 2) ; then follows the full Manifesto (v. 3—vii. 27); and it is completed by an Epilogue (vii. 28, 29).

The Manifesto in itself (v. 3—vii. 27), consists of a statement of foundation principles (verses 3-20); a complete Code of Laws (v. 21-vi); and final applications (vii. 1-27). In this chapter we have the Prologue (verses 1, 2), the section dealing with foundation principles (verses 3-20); and the first part of the Code of Laws (verses 21-48).

The Prologue is of supreme importance in order to an understanding of all that follows. It reveals the occasion upon which the Manifesto was uttered; the method which our Lord adopted; and so reveals the value of everything which follows.

As to the occasion. This is revealed in the phrase, " Seeing the multitudes," in order to understand which it is necessary to go back to the previous chapter and read the last three verses there.

" And Jesus went about in all Galilee, teaching in their synagogues, and preaching the Gospel of the Kingdom, and healing all manner of disease and all manner of sickness among the people. And the report of Him went forth into all Syria; and they brought unto Him all that were sick, holden with divers diseases and torments, possessed with demons, and epileptic, and palsied; and He healed them. And there followed Him great multitudes from Galilee and Decapolis and Jerusalem and Judæa and from beyond Jordan."

That passage reveals the fact of the crowds that were at this time following and pressing upon Him. They came from all the region round about. It was the vision of these multitudes which inspired our Lord's action at this time.

Then as to the method :

"He went up into the mountain; and when He had sat down, His disciples came unto Him; and He opened His mouth and taught *them.*"

The word "them" refers, not to the multitudes, but to the disciples. It is quite true that the multitudes gathered about and listened, as we discover when we reach the Epilogue, which among other things says :

"It came to pass, when Jesus had ended these words, the multitudes were astonished" (vii. 28).

Thus it is evident that they heard Him, but He was not addressing Himself to them, but rather to the disciples. Linking these two things together, however, His vision of the multitudes, and His action in addressing the disciples, we see that whatever He said to His disciples was said in the interest of the multitudes. They were in His heart.

Later on in the Gospel (ix. 36), we read that when He saw the multitudes He was moved with compassion for them. That was always true, and it was this very compassion which caused Him to call His disciples from the crowd, and speak to them.

These disciples were submitted to His Kingship, but so far He had not specifically given them the laws of His Kingdom. They did not know the demands His authority would make upon them. In this Manifesto then He revealed to them first the great principles underlying His work, and enunciated the applications of those principles in a Code of Laws. These principles and these laws are those which must govern human life in its entirety, if it is ever to solve its problems, and reach abiding peace and lasting beauty. The first necessity of obedience is submission to the King, and therefore to those so submitted He uttered His Manifesto.

So we come to the section revealing the foundation principles of the Kingdom (verses 3-20). To summarise : He first revealed the fact of the supremacy of character in His Kingdom in a series of Beatitudes (verses 3-12); He then revealed the intention of the character, that of influence (verses 13-16); and finally insisted upon the necessity for law (verses 17-20).

It is an arresting fact that when the King enunciated the principles and the laws of the Kingdom of God, He struck the keynote of the Divine thought and purpose in the very first word that fell from His lips, "Blessed." That is the purpose of God for humanity. One might, with perfect accuracy, render that word, "happy." As a matter of fact, taking the two words, "blessed" and "happy," as we use them to-day, both values are found in the word which our Lord employed. Blessedness to-day suggests a condition, while happiness describes a consciousness. I repeat then, that both ideas are in the word that our Lord used. Personally I always want to use yet another word, the word prosperous, for prosperity includes the condition of blessedness, and the consciousness of happiness. The nature of the blessedness or happiness, or prosperity, is revealed in the octave of Beatitudes.

An examination of these will show how entirely revolutionary in all the thinking of men, are their ideas of the secrets of prosperity. No blessedness is pronounced upon having anything. I have always been interested in looking at the Honours Lists in this country. In the days of my youth and young manhood an examination of them revealed the fact that they were conferred very largely upon those who had possessions of some sort. The coming of the War changed the character of these honours entirely, and they were conferred upon men who had rendered service, or had done something. This was a higher level. But in these Beatitudes we find no honour conferred upon any man for anything that he has done. The secrets, therefore, of prosperity, are not possession, or doing, but wholly those of character. This is fundamental in the Kingdom of God.

The next declaration revealed the fact that the character insisted upon has a definite intention, and that is the exertion of influence. The measure in which men and women approximate to the character revealed in the Beatitudes, is the measure in which they are exercising an influence in the world.

The nature of that influence was revealed in two figures of speech, those of salt and light. Salt is aseptic, that is it has a value, not for the cure of corruption, but for the prevention of its spread. That is the first effect of the influence exerted by those who are of the character described.

But the influence is also that of light, and our Lord used two illustrations to show the value of light; first, that of a city set on a hill, which means the illumination of vast expanses; and the second that of the lamp in the house, the illumination of the near and the immediate.

The last movement in the enunciation of principles was that of words insisting upon the necessity for law. He had not come, He said, to destroy the law or the prophets, but rather to fulfil. In this connection He uttered that arresting statement :

> "For I say unto you, that except your righteousness shall exceed the righteousness of the scribes and Pharisees, ye shall in no wise enter into the Kingdom of heaven."

Thus setting His seal upon the authority of the past, He declared that so far from abrogating any ethical requirement found therein, He was demanding a realisation in excess of anything provided therein. A much later illustration of the meaning of this is found in the writings of Paul, who, when looking back to the days when his life was conditioned wholly by the law and the prophets, declared that touching the righteousness which is in the law he was found blameless; and then added that he counted this to be loss, as of no value, now that he had come into relationship with Christ.

All this brings us to the definite enunciation of laws. In these we have an interpretation of the righteousness which exceeds. In what remains of this chapter we find the laws of earthly relationship, and in chapter six, the laws of heavenly relationship.

A very arresting fact faces us here. It is that of the comparative brevity of this Code. If we take this section in chapter five, and chapter six, we find there are only sixty-two verses. Nevertheless, there is no phase or condition of human life, individual, social, national, that is not conditioned within these enactments. The marvel of this fact is apprehended when we think for a passing moment of the laws found on the statute books of England. Yet they are all unnecessary if men would substitute for them these sixty-two verses of the New Testament. We remind ourselves once more that in these laws the authority of the Old is sealed, but they interpret and so enlarge it.

The first words are, " Ye have heard that it was said to them of old time." The Authorised Version rendered that statement, " It was said by them of old time." The change is really vital. The things referred to were not said by Moses, but to Moses. They were Divine in authority. Then the august majesty of the King is seen in that while recognising the Divinity of the authority of the law as given to Moses, He says, " But I say unto you." Moreover, nothing He said abrogates the past, but gives such an interpretation of the Divine intention that there can be no breaking of the ancient law, because the inspirational centres of life are now conditioned. These words of the King cannot be read with honesty without the heart becoming filled with fear and a sense of hopelessness.

Our examination of these laws of earthly relationship can only be that of a broad survey. It is very arresting to note that our Lord did not recite the ten commandments, but referred to two of them. To these He added two other words from the Mosaic economy, but not contained in the Decalogue. In the two commandments to which He referred, He revealed the foundations of human society, and in the two laws beyond the Decalogue, He recognised the pillars of human society; and then ended all by showing the ultimate secret of the true constitution of human society.

The two laws revealing the foundation facts of human society were given first by quotation.

" Ye have heard that it was said to them of old time, Thou shalt not kill."

" Ye have heard that it was said, Thou shalt not commit adultery."

If these laws are broken, society cannot be held together. If they are observed, then society can be built. The first of these is individual, and the second is social.

In the first forbidding murder, our Lord proceeded to interpretation. There must be no anger. " Every one who is angry with his brother." The Old Version read, " without a cause." These three words are now omitted, and upon scholarly authority. Some copyist had slipped them in, probably feeling that the thing was too difficult. We have another classic illustration of this kind of thing in Paul's first letter to the Corinthians, when he wrote, " Love is not provoked." The King James' translators tried to soften it by putting in the word " easily." The two ideas harmonise, Paul deriving from Jesus. The command is that there shall be no anger against a brother. There may be anger against sin, but not against the sinner, which is not a distinction without a difference. Where there is no anger, there will be no possibility of speaking disrespectfully, by calling a brother Raca, or of insulting him by calling him a fool. The ethic of Jesus demands therefore that the subjects of His Kingdom shall be such men and women that killing is impossible, because there is no anger, and no contempt, and no insult. Thus the law upon which He set His seal as a foundation law is one that recognises the sanctity of human personality, the right of every individual to live, free from molestation by another individual.

The next law enunciated was the Mosaic requirement, " Thou shalt not commit adultery." This law was not one providing for personal chastity merely. I am not suggesting that it has not that application; but the sin of adultery is never the sin of the individual alone. It is the sin that breaks up the family, which is God's first circle of society. Here the King's interpretation is one which makes the action impossible, as it declares that the secret of evil lies in the realm of desire; and where that is safe-guarded, there can be no overt act, reacting upon the sanctity of the family.

Thus the two laws quoted and interpreted, constitute the very foundations of human society, the first demanding the right of every individual to life, and life in its fullness; the second insisting upon the maintenance of the marriage relationship in purity, in the interest of the family. In this second application our Lord declared that mutilation is preferable to violation of the law.

If these be the foundations, there are two laws which con-stitute the pillars of society. The first of these our Lord enunciated by a quotation taken, not from the Decalogue, but from the wider Mosaic economy :

> "Again ye have heard that it was said to them of old, Thou shalt not forswear thyself, but shalt perform unto the Lord thine oaths."

This He emphasised by the command, "Swear not at all," declaring that heaven is God's throne, that the earth is His footstool. The first pillar of society then is truth in all simplicity, which needs no emphasis in the form of an oath. The con-sciousness of God, whether in the heaven or on earth, or in the matter of human personality, will produce truth within; and consequently speech characterised by simplicity of statement. We are all conscious of the value of simplicity in speech, even though we may not always practise it. When one says in order to produce conviction in another, "I will take my oath that it is so," doubt is immediately created in the mind of the one to whom the thing is said. The taking of an oath always postulates the possibility of deceit.

Once again we have a quotation from the wider law :

> "Ye have heard that it was said, An eye for an eye, and a tooth for a tooth."

That is a law demanding strict justice, which is the second pillar for the building of society. This is most remarkably inter-preted by the King as He declares that in order to an ultimate strictness in justice there is to be personal non-resistance. Of this He gives illustrations full of poetry, but remarkably practical. If a man takes my coat, I am to let him have my cloke also. If a man compels me to go a mile, I am to go two. At first one wonders if these things do stand for strict justice. Let them be considered. If justice demands the coat, the demand is certainly met if the cloke be given also. If justice demands that I go a mile, I certainly have fulfilled its demands if I go two. In every case an over-plusage upon strict justice ensures a fulfilment about which there can be no question.

It is necessary in this connection to remind ourselves once again that these laws are the laws of the Kingdom; that is to say, they are applicable within the realm of those who are submitted to the Kingship of Christ. To apply them promiscuously to the rebellious may be to encourage that which is not true, and to violate justice.

The final movement here reveals the great secret of that which holds society, thus founded, and thus being built, in security.

Here, once more, the quotation was from the wider Mosaic requirements :

"Ye have heard that it was said, Thou shalt love thy neighbour, and hate thine enemy."

In the Kingdom where righteousness exceeds, hatred is forbidden, and love becomes supreme. Love is to be manifested towards enemies; prayer is to be offered for those who persecute; and salutations are to be given, irrespective of worth; and all this, because the subjects of the Kingdom are to manifest the character and conduct of God Who "maketh His sun to rise on the evil and the good, and sendeth rain on the just and the unjust." Love is never governed by calculating caution. When society is completely mastered by love, all its problems will be solved.

A consideration of these laws of earthly relationship, if we are perfectly honest, can only produce one effect, and that is the consciousness of our helplessness. If this is all the King has to say to me, I admit the perfection of the ideal, but find it condemning me for my failure. Has He more to say? He has. We find it in the sections which follow.

MATTHEW VI

IN this chapter we find the final things in the " Laws " of the Kingdom. In the previous chapter we found the laws concerning earthly relationships. Here we have the laws showing heavenly relationships. We ended our previous study by saying that the laws of earthly relationship reveal our helplessness, and the consequent necessity of something more. That something more is now revealed. If we have none other than the revelation of heaven's ideal for earthly conduct we are hopeless, not because we fail to recognise the glory and beauty of the ideal, but because we are conscious of inability to realise it.

The chapter falls into three sections : the first being a declaration of an abiding principle (verse one), which flashes its light back on all that has already been said, and forward on all that is now to be said. Then follow the laws concerning spiritual activities (verses two to eighteen). Finally, we have the laws revealing the true attitude towards material things as the result of obedience to those concerning the spiritual activities (verses nineteen to thirty-four).

The general principle is expressed in the words,

" Take heed that ye do not your righteousness before men, to be seen of them ; else ye have no reward with your Father which is in heaven."

The King James Version reads : " Take heed that ye do not your alms before men." The Greek MSS. upon which we place dependence in translation, read, " righteousness," instead of " alms," and it is generally agreed that there is no doubt that this is what our Lord actually said. We come to the subject of alms later, but it is only one aspect of righteousness.

Already the declaration had been made that the righteousness of this new Kingdom must exceed that of the scribes and Pharisees. We now reach the section in which that earlier declaration is interpreted, as it shows how, or in what way righteousness will exceed.

Therefore our Lord commenced with this declaration of principle, that righteousness must have a true motive. This He revealed by warning His subjects against a false motive; and incidentally revealing the true motive. The false motive is revealed in the words, " before men, to be seen of them." A form of righteousness which results from this inspiration, Christ dismisses as being entirely worthless. We are all familiar with the old saying, " Honesty is the best policy." I remember long years ago that that was the heading on one page of a book which we used to call a copybook. I wrote it over and over again, and then showed the page to my headmaster. I have never forgotten what he said to me. Pointing at the statement, he said, " You see what that says, Honesty is the best policy? " I replied, " Yes, Sir," to which he in turn replied, " Well, don't forget that the man who is only honest because it is good policy, may be the biggest rogue in the world." He was quite right. So here, if men are doing right to gain the good opinion of other men, if these other men are not watching, the right doing may cease. This is proven in many simple ways. One has known of people who in their homes in the country will not do certain things which they seem quite ready to do when they are visiting London; and there are people who will not do things in London, which they seem free to do when off on holiday. The motive is wrong if it be that of desiring the good opinion of men.

There is only one motive which produces true rightness of action, and that is a recognition of the Divine authority, and a desire to be well-pleasing to the Father. This is the great principle laid down.

In the application of this principle three subjects are dealt with; alms in verses two to four; prayer in verses five to fifteen; and fasting, in verses sixteen to eighteen.

We are arrested here by the fact that these are not subjects usually dealt with in a study of ethics. This in itself gives pause, as it suggests a recognition of spiritual values as being of supreme importance in matters of moral moment.

The word " alms " refers to an activity which is distinctly outward, but which ever springs from an inward impulse. Prayer is distinctively a spiritual thing, an activity dependent upon a recognition of the Godward aspect of life. Fasting, according to this teaching, is pre-eminently something which is inward and secret, being a condition for prayer, and issuing in the giving of alms. To summarise : alms is an outward action; prayer is a heavenly activity; fasting is an inward attitude. We shall find as we examine, the close relationship of the three.

Our Lord described the popular method of alms-giving, and poured upon it a withering sarcasm. Referring to the method of those whom He styled hypocrites, He declared that the reason of their giving was "that they may have glory of men." This He immediately followed by the sentence, "Verily I say unto you, They have received their reward." That is to say they get what they want. They seek glory from men, and receive it, and that is the end of the whole business. The true alms-giving is that which is done secretly so far as men are concerned, but with the consciousness of co-operation with the Father. Thus in dealing with righteousness our Lord commenced with alms, because that is the outward expression of life within His Kingdom.

Having thus dealt with the outward expression of righteousness our Lord proceeded immediately to the subject of prayer. In this the same principle is applied. Once more He referred to a prevailing method at the time, that of such as stood to pray in the synagogues, and at the corners of the streets. It is well that we remind ourselves that there is nothing inherently wrong in praying either in the synagogue or at the corner of the street. What was wrong was that these men were doing it "that they may be seen of men." Here once more we have the note of sarcasm, "Verily I say unto you, They have received their reward." If men are praying with the thought in their heart that others are watching them, and they are doing it in order that they may be approved of the watchers, again they obtain what they are seeking. They are seen of men, and that is the end of the business. A story comes back to one of a happening some years ago in the city of Boston, when at a public function, an eminent clergyman was asked to pray, and he did so. The diction was wonderful, the language unimpeachable, the periods rhetorically excellent. Next morning one of the great Boston papers referred to this by saying, "At this point the Rev. Dr. —— made the most beautiful prayer that was ever offered to a Boston audience." Exactly! "Verily, they have received their reward."

Over against this false motive and method in prayer our Lord then gave the true method. .We may summarise His teaching first by saying that He insisted upon privacy, directness and simplicity; and then gave a perfect pattern.

Privacy is at once suggested as necessary in the words, "Enter into thine inner chamber and . . . shut thy door." It is when this is done that prayer becomes vital. In this privacy prayer becomes direct, that is, without vain repetitions, and so is characterised by the uttermost simplicity.

This command does not forbid united prayer, but it does help us to recognise that even in united prayer there is a sense in which our soul must realise the presence of God alone, and deal with Him directly. Fellowship in prayer becomes valuable in the proportion in which each one in a meeting for prayer, is enabled to forget every other, and deal with God. The fellowship is created in the spiritual realm by the harmonising of the praying of the units into the unity of intercession. In our meetings for prayer we are always more or less in danger of wondering what someone else may be thinking about the prayer we utter. Such consciousness of others has two apparently contradictory results, each of which is destructive of the power of prayer. One may be a desire to impress the listeners with the prayer we offer. The other is that for fear of those who are listening, we do not pray at all. The first are those who are proud of their praying. The others are too proud to break down in prayer.

Thus whether for the fellowship meeting or in loneliness, the final secret of prayer is that of the consciousness of God, and of direct dealing with Him. Where there is such consciousness, there is no necessity for vain repetitions. The things the soul has to say to God can and will be said with the uttermost simplicity. We are never heard for our much speaking, but for honesty, and simplicity of statement.

It was here and now that our Lord gave to the subjects of His Kingdom this pattern prayer. An examination of it in detail of course is impossible. Our familiarity with it, however, with constant repetition, will enable us to speak of it generally, and thus endeavour to understand something of its greatness.

The opening of the prayer by implication is a theology or revelation of truth about God. He is " Our Father Who is in the heavens." For the moment I resolutely translate literally, using the plural as it is in the Greek New Testament, " heavens." Therein is a doctrine, therein is the recognition of the omnipresence of God. He is in the heavens; all heavens. To adopt the Hebrew view of the heavens; this refers first to the heaven of the atmosphere; secondly to the heaven of the stellar spaces; and finally to the heaven which is the place of the supreme manifestation of God, and the dwelling place of the blessed.

Then of course the designation " Our Father " is at once a revelation of character, and a recognition of His nearness. To apply this implicated truth to the matter of prayer is in itself a revelation full of meaning. The boy or the girl of your love may be on the other side of the world. It is a long way as earthly matters go. But God is there as well as here; and when we cannot touch our absent ones with the hand that would touch them so tenderly, we can move the " Hand that holds the world," to bring the help they need. Thus prayer is addressed to a Father Who is transcendent, and yet for ever immanent.

Another matter of supreme importance is the recognition of the fact that in this pattern prayer there are two realms of desire, and the order of petitions is arresting. The first part of the prayer moves in the realm of desire, not for anything to meet our personal need, but for the accomplishment of the purposes of God in the world. The case may be bluntly stated thus. In the earliest petitions we are not asking God to give us anything, but we are praying to God on behalf of God. This manner of praying is the outcome of the supreme passion of the subjects of the Kingdom, that God may regain His lost world. To pray this prayer always leads to service on the earthly level in order to the accomplishment of the desires expressed.

Then the prayer turns to the necessities of our human life; sustenance, and restoration, and discipline. The bread that is necessary for daily life, which includes material and spiritual things; forgiveness of our debts, always contingent upon our having the forgiving spirit; and a recognition of the necessity for discipline, with the holy fear which shrinks from the testing, and yet has, as its supreme passion, deliverance from evil.

In looking at the prayer as a whole we must ever remember that which has so constantly been pointed out, that it is entirely a social prayer. It is true, as has been said, that one of the first necessities for prayer is the inner chamber and the shut door. It is true that when we arrive there, and have shut the door, we take in with us, in sympathy and desire, all others. There is no pronoun in the prayer in the singular number referring to us. They are all plural.

In this connection it is at least interesting to observe that only one of these pronouns is in the nominative case, that is, there is only one of them in which those who pray are the subjects of the sentence. All others are possessive or objective, and principally objective. We look with interest to see the point at which in prayer we may refer to ourselves as active. It is found in the words, " Forgive us our debts, as we also have forgiven our debtors." The only right we have to speak of our action in the presence of God is when we tell Him that we are forgiving others. That petition is really a very searching one. We say, " Forgive us our debts, as we also have forgiven our debtors." Do we really mean that when we say it? How do we forgive the man who has wronged us? Sometimes we say, " We will forgive, but we can never forget." Is that how we desire God to forgive us? It is not to be forgotten that this was the one petition in the prayer, upon which our Lord made comment after He had given the pattern. " For if ye forgive men their trespasses, your heavenly Father will also forgive you."

Turning to the subject of fasting, the method of the Lord was the same in that He described the prevalent custom, that of the sad countenance, the disfigured face, in order that those who fasted might be seen of men. Again we have His note of sarcasm, " They have received their reward." The man fasts and looks sad in order to impress other men he is fasting. Again Jesus says he gets what he is seeking. Men do see him. He is noticed, and that ends the business.

The true method of fasting is then revealed.

" Thou, when thou fasteth, anoint thy head, and wash thy face."

To do this is to hide the fact of fasting from our fellow-men. Fasting is the practice of self-denial to the point of sacrifice. This is the deepest thing in the cultivation of the spiritual life. It must be, however, a matter between the soul and God. Then there is true value in it.

These three subjects have to do with the relationship of man to God. Alms in the true sense are always a direct outcome of life lived in right relationship with God. Necessarily this is so in the matter of prayer. And according to this teaching of Jesus, fasting must be so also.

In experience we discover that if God is put out of count, these things will fail in inverted order. That is to say, the first failure will be in the realm of fasting, the culture of the inward life of sacrifice and self-denial. When that fails, prayer weakens, and ultimately ceases. When these things of fellowship with God cease, alms will also cease.

Then we come to the laws defining attitudes towards material things, growing out of the experience of these spiritual exercises.

We are still living in a world where material things are necessary. We are still in contact with the earth. What then is to be the attitude of the subjects of the Kingdom to these material things? The answer is found in this section, and falls into two parts; the attitudes of the subjects of the Kingdom first towards wealth (19–24); and secondly, towards necessities (25–34).

The attitude towards wealth is to be that of freedom from covetousness. This is revealed first in a negative command :

" Lay not up for yourselves treasures upon the earth,"

Immediately followed by a positive command :

" Lay up for yourselves treasures in heaven."

Here again the gentle yet searching sarcasm of Jesus is revealed in His description of what happens to treasures which are wholly upon the earth. The moth can destroy all purple and fine twined linen; rust, the slowly burning fire of Nature, can destroy all piled up metal; and thieves can break through and steal whatever is hoarded. Treasure piled up on the earth level is a subject to the ravages of moth, rust, thieves.

Treasure laid up in heaven is beyond the reach of moths, or rust, or thieves. On another occasion our Lord said,

" I say unto you, ... make to yourselves friends by means of the mammon of unrighteousness."

That is the right use of wealth. Continuing, He revealed the issue.

" When it (that is the mammon) fails, they (the friends made by its use) shall receive you into the eternal habitations."

Thus He revealed the right attitude towards wealth, ending with the statement, " Where thy treasure is, there will thy heart be also "; and illustrating the whole business by the figure of the single eye, that is, the eye free from astigmatism. All this ended with the superlative declaration, " No man can serve two masters."

Finally, He laid down the laws which condition our attitudes towards things absolutely necessary. That attitude is revealed in the thrice repeated injunction, " Be not anxious." Our attitude, then, towards necessities is to be that of being without care.

This He illustrated as He argued that anxiety is unnecessary in the case of the children of such a Father. Look, said He in effect, at the flowers, and look at the birds; and mark how they are clothed and cared for by your Father.

Therefore anxiety is unworthy in the subjects of such a King, and within the borders of such a Kingdom.

Moreover, and finally, anxiety is unfruitful. It never realises anything in the realm of our need. We cannot add a cubit to our stature by being anxious. Thus we detect here again a tender and beautiful satire of all carking care, which so often blights our lives. We hear His voice in this great ethical Manifesto, saying about these things, " Be not anxious." " Your Father knoweth."

Nevertheless in this connection He revealed the necessity for a true anxiety, as He said, " Seek ye first His Kingdom, and His righteousness." Whereas I have used the word anxiety, even that does not mean restless care, but rather ceaseless effort.

In this consideration of the super-earthly relationships, we are brought face to face with the fact that when we are careless of human opinion, but for ever careful as to the thought and purpose of our Father, we have found the secrets of obedience to the ethical demands of our Lord.

MATTHEW VII

IN this chapter we have the last movement in the Manifesto
of the King, with an epilogue, declaring the result produced
upon the multitude who had listened as He thus taught His
disciples. In this movement we have certain final applications
of the things already said. These applications move in two realms;
first revealing the true attitude of the subjects of the Kingdom to
others, that is, to outsiders (verses 1–12); and secondly, the
relation of the subjects of the Kingdom to eternal things.

In dealing with the subject of the attitude of the subjects
of the Kingdom to those outside, He uttered words which at
first blush seem to constitute a contradiction. Of course there is
no contradiction, but the appearance is found in the fact that our
Lord said first, " Judge not, that ye be not judged," and then later,
" Give not that which is holy unto the dogs, neither cast your
pearls before swine." The first is a command not to judge, and
the second is a command which necessitates in some form, an
activity of judgment. The two things are really complementary,
and should be carefully considered.

First, then, judgment is forbidden, and secondly, discrimination is enjoined. In order to an understanding of this it is
necessary that we are careful in our interpretation of the meaning
of judgment. The word rendered " judgment " here is one that
is capable of many varied applications, but always has the same
central value. The Greek word means quite simply, to distinguish,
or to decide, but has varied shades of value in its use. While
somewhat mechanical, it may be suggestively helpful to indicate
the varied words by which this verb is translated : avenge,
conclude, condemn, decree, determine, esteem, judge, go to law,
sue at the law, ordain, call in question, sentence to, think. It
is self-evident that while all these words have a common, underlying conception, in order to understanding of the meaning of
the word at any point, we must study the context.

What then is the peculiar value of the word here? The
later command which makes an action of discrimination and
distinction necessary, shows that when our Lord says, " Judge
not " He certainly does not mean that we are not to use our reason,
and come to decisions as the result thereof. There is no doubt

therefore that the word is employed here in the sense of a censorious criticism which condemns. We might appropriately
interpret the command by reading it, " Condemn not, that ye be
not condemned."

In uttering this command, our Lord gave two reasons against
such censoriousness as finds verdicts and passes sentences upon
our fellow-beings. One is that if I apply my judgment to my
fellow man, my fellow man will apply his judgment to me. Let it
at once be said that there is no action against which any individual
has a right to protest more earnestly than that of being judged
by another individual, who cannot, by any means, know all the
truth about the one he is judging. Therefore, because we are
inherently limited in our knowledge of our fellow-beings, we must
never judge them with a judgment which is condemnatory.

A further reason why we should not judge is our inability
to form a correct judgment, not only because of our limited
knowledge, but because of what our Lord here refers to as a beam
in the eye. Two words arrest us here, " beam " and " mote,"
being the only place in the New Testament where they occur.
The word " beam " quite literally means a trunk of a tree, or a
vast piece of timber. " Mote " means more than a particle of
dust; it signifies a chip, a small piece of timber. The illustration,
of course, is perfect, as it represents a defect of great magnitude
in ourselves, which prevents our being able to deal with a defect
of lesser magnitude in others.

The beam is really the spirit of censoriousness that watches
for something evil in another, to fasten upon, and condemn.
That very spirit distorts our vision, and makes impossible any
correct dealing with something wrong in our brother. The
implication of all this is that the only thing we ought to want to
do is to remove the mote in our brother's eye, and that it is
impossible so to do if we approach him in a spirit of censoriousness,
already condemning what we behold.

Too often this has been taken to mean that if a man is
committing some vulgar form of sin, he cannot correct a man who
is committing what is considered to be a less calamitous sin. It
may at once be said that no man living in vulgar sin ever attempts
to correct his brother. The meaning, as we have said, is far more
searching than that. The beam is ever that of the attitude which
beholds the mote, and assumes the right to condemn.

In the last analysis then, by these words our Lord dismisses
every man as inadequate to form a correct opinion about his
brother which involves condemnation. We are not to usurp the

throne of God, Who alone judges righteous judgments. No man is able to do anything to remove a mote from the eye of his brother, save as he is free from all desire to condemn him.

This leads us to the command, " Give not that which is holy unto the dogs, neither cast your pearls before the swine." We are at once arrested by the amazing nature of these words from the lips of our Lord. I refer to the words, " dogs," " swine." There is no doubt that Peter heard Him use these words that day, and we find an echo of them in his second letter, in chapter two, and verse twenty-two; " The dog turning to his own vomit again, and the sow that had washed to wallowing in the mire."

The vivid description refers to people who are so definitely and positively hostile to God, as to have no sense of the value of holy things, or the beauty of pearls. In the presence of this fact there must be on the part of the subjects of the Kingdom an attitude and activity of discrimination. We are the custodians of holy things, and pearls of great price. We are not to give these holy things to dogs, or cast these pearls before swine.

The question arises as to whether the subjects of the Kingdom have ever been guilty of doing these things. I fear it must be admitted that they have often failed at this point. We are giving holy things to dogs, and casting pearls before swine when we admit those who are openly hostile to Christ, to service for Christ. I cannot agree with any who say that if they put a man to work for Christ, they will gain him to the side of Christ. We have no right to put any to work for the King, until such an one is definitely committed to the King by submission. All detailed applications may be seen in the light of a very outstanding general one. It has sometimes been affirmed that it was a great move forward for the Christian emprise when the Roman emperor, Constantine, espoused the cause of Christianity. As a matter of fact that was one of the darkest hours that ever came to the Church. The action of Constantine was based entirely upon political expedience, and dragged the whole Church into an atmosphere of paganism. In that hour the Church consented to give that which is holy to the dogs, and cast her pearls before swine. Whenever the spiritual powers of the Church are yielded to the mastery of the forces of the world in any way, the result is that these forces turn again, and rend the Church. It was a recognition of these things that created the attitude of the Covenanters in Scotland, and those who stood for the principle of the spiritual authority of the Church in this country in 1662. In all this is revealed the necessity for discrimination in our attitude to those who are outside the Kingdom.

The distinction between censoriousness and discrimination is so fine as to create a difficulty, which may well fill us with fear. Let me state that in another way. How are we to live in a world like this, observing these two principles which are apparently contradictory, but are really complementary? How are we to act in obedience to the first word, that we are not to pass final judgments of condemnation upon other men; and at the same time, to discriminate so carefully as ever to guard holy things from dogs, and pearls from swine? These questions are necessary and vital.

The answer is found in the words of our Lord which immediately follow. "Ask, and it shall be given you; seek, and ye shall find; knock, and it shall be opened unto you."

We enquire again, Who is sufficient for the life free from censoriousness, and at the same time equal to discrimination? The answer is found in these words, which admit us at once to the place of relationship with spiritual forces.

These words of Jesus constitute at once the great charter of prayer, and the charter of scientific investigation. To take the latter first. Science as we know it to-day, is the activity which is for ever asking, seeking, knocking. These activities all recognise some spiritual realm which can only be reached through them, but which being reached, enables us to discriminate; and at the same time delivers us from any final attitude of censorious condemnation.

In the three words, "Ask," "seek," "knock," we find a gradation of thought. The Greek word here rendered "ask" is one which recognises the dependence of the soul. "Seek" suggests effort. The combination of the two shows us that in prayer and in investigation there must ever be this merging of dependence and of effort. The final word "knock" is the mingling of these two things.

Whatever wider application we may properly make of these words of our Lord, their first application is to this very business of living in such relationship with those outside the Kingdom that we are neither censorious, nor lacking in the true principle of discrimination.

In response to this recognition and use of the spiritual world in dealing with God, He revealed the attitude of God. If we ask, He is willing to bestow. If we seek, it is He Who provides the answer to the quest. If we knock, it is He Who opens the door. Continuing, the very character of God is revealed by our

Lord's use of the word Father. The Father is One Who knows how to give good gifts to His children.

To summarise on this, when we ask, how can we live as commanded in a world like this? The answer is, " Ask," " Seek," " Knock." Your Father is there, and all wisdom and power necessary for life are at your disposal. When we ask, when we seek, when we knock, we are putting ourselves in contact with final Wisdom and ultimate Power. At the centre of this Wisdom, for ever inspiring it, and to this Power for ever directing it, is found the heart of God. Thus it is revealed that if we are going to live as we should in a world, and amid people largely hostile to the Kingship of God, we must ourselves keep in touch with the loving heart of God, Who is always ready to give what we ask, to reward our quest with conquest, and to open the door when we knock.

This in itself makes this ethical code of our Lord different from any other that has ever been offered to the world. Nowhere else can we find prayer introduced as the secret of behaviour. This is the ultimate ethic, the ethic of the King, and the ethic of the final Kingdom.

At this point we reach what we have come to describe as the Golden Rule. Let us carefully observe that in our Lord's uttering of it, He began with the word " Therefore," and thus connects the demand it makes with what had immediately been said concerning the method of life resulting from asking, seeking, knocking. Whatever there may be of responsibility revealed in the Golden Rule, the resources at our disposal for obedience have already been discovered in these words concerning the possibility of relationship with God through prayer.

It is a very arresting fact how wide an appeal the idea of the Golden Rule has made to humanity. In this connection it has been said that the ideal is not peculiar to the teaching of Jesus, but that it has found expression in other teachers. Let us glance at some of these.

Hillel, the founder of the Pharisaic School of theology, said, " Do not do to thy neighbour what is hateful to thyself."

Socrates said, "What stirs your anger when done to you by others, that do not to others."

Aristotle said, " We should bear ourselves towards others as we would desire they should bear themselves towards us."

Confucius said, " What you do not want done to yourself do not do to others."

Now admittedly all these sound like the Golden Rule, but when we come to consider them carefully, we find a profound

difference. Each one of these is negative or passive. Christ's
command is positive and active. The motive in Hillel's command
was that of protecting self from what is hateful. That is equally
true of Socrates' injunction, of Aristotle's advice, and Confucius'
instruction. Thus there is a sense in which all these words are
self-centred and self-seeking. In the word of Christ we are
commanded to go and do to others as we would desire they should
do to us, were we in similar conditions. It is a command gathering
up all the notes of the love-mastered life, and condensing them
into a word.

Thus we have surveyed in broad outline His teaching with
regard to the relation of the subjects of His Kingdom to those
outside.

Let us now rapidly survey the final section dealing with the
relation of the subjects of the Kingdom to eternal things. There
are three indicating sentences, " Enter ye in " (verse 13); " Beware
of false prophets " (verse 15); " Not every one that saith unto
Me, Lord, Lord " (verse 21). These words constitute a threefold
charge, and introduce the teaching which shows the relation of
those within the Kingdom to eternal and abiding things.

In the first of them our Lord goes back to the very beginning,
the way into the Kingdom, the entry by the strait gate. In this
connection He reveals two ways of life, the broad and the narrow;
but carefully observe what He says in each case. It is not enough
to read them, and to think of the way of rebellion as a wide gate
and a broad way; neither is it enough to think of the way of
submission as a narrow gate and straitened way. These things
are true, but they are not all the truth. Of the way of rebellion
He said, " Wide is the gate and broad is the way, *that leadeth to
destruction.*" Of the way of submission He said, " Narrow is
the gate, and straitened the way, *that leadeth unto life.*" The
issue constitutes the final test of value. There is the wide gate
and the broad highway of life apparently unyielded to any restriction
but watch it; and all the time it is narrowing, until the ultimate is
destruction. The King's highway is entered through a narrow
gate, and is straitened, but watch it, all the way it broadens
until at last it comes to life in all its fullness. Thus finally our
Lord takes His subjects back to the starting point, and so suggests
that if the start be what it ought to be, the programme and the
progress will be according to Divine purposes.

Then when the feet are on the straitened way, and moving on
into the fullness of life, instruction and guidance are necessary.
It is said in apostolic days the early disciples continued stedfastly

in the apostles' doctrine. Hence the necessity for being careful in the matter of those to whom we go for teaching.

Furthermore, His words were full of solemn significance as He warned His subjects against the valuelessness of all profession which was not reinforced by action. He spoke of a day when there would be those who would address Him as Lord, and declare the things they had done. As a matter of fact it would be found these people had done everything except the will of God; and to such He will have to say, " I never knew you."

All this teaching He ended in words of august majesty. Referring to what He had said in the phrase, " These sayings of Mine," He declared the value of such sayings, under the figure of building. Our Lord here recognised that every man is building, and insisted upon the supreme importance of the foundation upon which the building rests. He claimed that the day of testing of the building is not that of sunshine, but that of tempest and of storm; and affirmed that those who built upon His sayings will find what they build stands unmoved, while those who build on any other foundation will find their building swept away. Men and women who build on His sayings, build for the eternities, and no storms can destroy what they build.

In the final words (verses 28-29), Matthew records two things, first the effect produced upon the multitudes who had listened : and secondly, the reason for the effect. The effect produced was that of astonishment, or amazement; and the reason was that " He taught them as One having authority, and not as their scribes."

The arresting thing in this statement of authority is the comparison suggested in the words, " not as their scribes." The scribes were the authoritative teachers. His authority was not that of any official position. It was the authority of the inherent unanswerable truth of everything He said.

That authority abides. It may be possible to declare that the idealism is such that is unattainable. Indeed it is so, until some change takes place in man. It is not possible, however, to question the perfection of the idealism.

We close this survey of the Manifesto by reminding ourselves that He Who uttered it, did finally provide all that was necessary for yielding obedience to its demands.

MATTHEW XXVII

IN dealing with this chapter it is necessary first to recognise once more that it is part of a larger whole. The final section in the Gospel according to Matthew occupies the last three chapters, twenty-six, twenty-seven, and twenty-eight. It will be conceded that there can be no intelligent reading of either chapter without at least a consciousness of what is found in the others. In this complete section the theme is that of the travail and the triumph of the King, Matthew's Gospel being pre-eminently the presentation of our Lord in His Kingship. The account of the travail is found in chapters twenty-six and twenty-seven. Chapter twenty-eight is the record of His triumph.

In order, then, to a consideration of chapter twenty-seven I propose first to summarise what is found in chapter twenty-six. It opens with a remarkable statement showing that our Lord fixed the hour for the Cross, as against the decision of the rulers. To His disciples He said,

> " Ye know that after two days the Passover cometh, and the Son of man is delivered up to be crucified."

This statement simply meant that they knew that the Passover would be observed in two days, and He told them that it was then that He would be delivered up to be crucified. At that very time the rulers were deciding that He must be put to death; but also declared that it must not be at Passover, " lest a tumult arise among the people." The Kingly majesty of that paragraph must not be lost sight of.

At that point in his narrative Matthew inserted the account of the supper at Bethany, which had taken place four days earlier.

He next recorded the account of the Passover itself, the observance of the old feast, and its passing; and the institution of the new feast ; and declared that the whole observance ended with the singing of a hymn, which undoubtedly was the whole or some parts of the Great Hallel, which consisted of psalms one hundred and thirteen to one hundred and eighteen. A study of these psalms, remembering that our Lord, in all probability, joined in singing them, is very suggestive. Among other words found in them, are these :

> " Bind the sacrifice with cords, even unto the horns of the altar."

Then followed the experience of Gethsemane, and the arrest of our Lord.

The account of the trial before the priests is then given, and the story of the denial by Peter.

This brings us to our chapter where the story runs on, first with the account of the doom of Judas, and then that of the trial before Pilate.

The actual story of the crucifixion begins at the twenty-seventh verse ; and in its entirety, runs to the end of the chapter.

The trial before the priests was absolutely illegal from the standpoint of Jewish law; and that before Pilate was the most terrible travesty of justice in all the history of humanity.

In our present meditation, then, we confine ourselves largely to an examination of this last section. In doing so there are three movements; the first dealing with the crucifixion, that is, the human side (verses 27-44); the second revealing the Cross, that is, on the Divine side (verses 45-56); and the last dealing with the burial of our Lord (verses 57-66).

Considering first, then, the crucifixion, or viewing the Cross on the human side, we have an appalling revelation of human sin and failure. When on the day of Pentecost Peter became the first interpreter of the great events in the life and death and resurrection of our Lord, he referred to the Cross in arresting and remarkable language. He was then speaking to people who had been present, and were familiar with the facts to which he referred. He referred to the Cross in these words :

" Jesus of Nazareth, a Man approved of God unto you by powers and wonders and signs, which God did by Him in the midst of you, even as ye yourselves know; Him, being delivered up by the determinate counsel and foreknowledge of God, ye by the hand of men without the law did crucify and slay."

Thus the man who, at Cæsarea Philippi had vehemently protested against the idea of his Lord's going to the Cross, the man who in the last hours with profane lips had denied his Lord, this man had now seen the Cross in right relationship. In referring to it he did not begin on the level of the human, which is sin; but on the level of the Divine, which is grace. " Him, being delivered by the determinate counsel, and foreknowledge of God," was the Divine side of the Cross. " Ye by the hands of men without the law did crucify and slay," was the human side.

In the light of that Pentecostal interpretation we come back to our chapter, and begin where Peter ended. That human side is revealed in verses 27 to 44. The appalling action of men began with the mockery of Jesus. Those ribald soldiers, who in all probability knew little of the facts of the case, perhaps only that they had a prisoner charged with sedition, who had claimed to be king, and had failed; indulged in brutal mockery as they placed upon Him a robe of scorn, crowned Him with thorns, and put a reed in His hands as a sceptre. All that took place in that inner court of the Prætorium, who shall describe !

Then, as they bore Him away to the place of crucifixion, they, perhaps out of some pity, impressed one Simon, to carry His Cross.

Arrived at Golgotha, they crucified Him. Matthew, however, does not even state the fact in that form. He refers to the crucifying as something accomplished. This reverent reticence with regard to the physical Cross is found in each of the Gospel narratives, and supremely so in this account by Matthew. Whereas it may be a purely imaginative thing to say, it ever seems to me as though Matthew said in effect, ' No, I cannot describe it. They did it.' It would have been a great advantage if that reticence had been observed down all the running centuries. No painting of the crucifixion, and no verbal description of it has been, in the deepest sense, really helpful in understanding the Cross. Not that the physical was anything less than appalling, but that it is possible to be so occupied with it as to lose the sense of that which is infinitely more terrible, the spiritual side of it.

As we look at Him, the One Whom they had crucified, we see others sharing the same experiences. Nay, would it not be a more accurate statement to say we see Him sharing in their experiences. " He was numbered with transgressors."

And yet on this human side, the most devilish part of the story is that of the raillery heaped upon Him as He hung there in the midst of the thieves. It began with the mob passing by, wagging their heads at Him. They had evidently understood the claim to Kingship which He had made, even though they might not ever have agreed with the claim. The thing He had said in the earliest year of His ministry had quite evidently become widely known. It had been specifically repeated against Him at His trial; and they now flung it at Him :

" Thou that destroyest the temple, and buildest it in three days, save Thyself . . . . If Thou art the Son of God, come down from the Cross."

That was the raillery of a mob, ignorant, swept by passion, as the result of the rule under which they were living, which was false and degraded. That is the supreme instance in all history of the fact that the voice of the people is not necessarily the voice of God. God pity the man, whether he be king, or president, or prophet, who depends upon the voice of the crowd.

The raillery, however, was not confined to the populace. The chief priests, with the scribes and elders, joined therein. It is very arresting at this point to remember that when our Lord began to show His disciples of all He must pass through, He carefully indicated the nature of the hostility massed against Him, when He said, that He must " suffer many things of the elders and chief priests and scribes." In these words He included the threefold authority exercised by the Sanhedrim. The elders were the civil rulers. The chief priests were the religious rulers. The scribes were the moral rulers. Now in recording the fact of the Cross, Matthew names these as joining in the mockery of the Crucified.

The first thing they said was, " He saved others; Himself He cannot save." Nineteen hundred years have run their course, and with the light of them shining upon this record we realise how the thing said in mockery has been revealed as the deepest revelation of truth concerning Him. He could not save Himself, because He would save others. They were mocking, but the centuries have changed the mockery into the essence of the Gospel.

The next recorded word of mockery is :

" He is the King of Israel; let Him now come down from the Cross and we will believe on Him."

In that they lied. Our Lord had once said in the course of a parable :

" Neither will they be persuaded if one rose from the dead."

He did not come down from His Cross; but He did rise from the dead, and still they did not believe.

The cruelest taunt of all was found in the words :

" He trusteth on God; let Him deliver Him now, if He desireth Him; for He said, I am the Son of God."

Thus we see the " Intelligentsia " around the Cross, and many of them are still there, and saying the same things.

Finally, Matthew says :

" The robbers also that were crucified with Him, cast upon Him the same reproach."

This, then, is the crucifixion, viewed from the human side. It is that of man's rejection of light and love and life; an account of the darkest hour in all human history, and the severest condemnation of fallen human nature.

Turning from this we face the Cross from the Divine standpoint. As we do so the first thing that impresses the truly devout and waiting soul is that of the apparent non-interference of God. There the perpetual problem of suffering is focussed. Considering the things we have seen from the human standpoint, it would seem as though God must rend the heavens and come down, and blast those who were guilty of this iniquity. Yet we remember again the words of Peter, " Delivered by the determinate counsel and knowledge of God "; and we discover that so far from it being correct to speak of the non-interference of God, the deeper truth is that there God was Himself in Christ, suffering with human sin. Even in the tragic cry, that ever haunts the soul with mystery :

" My God, My God, why hast Thou forsaken Me? "
impossible of final explanation as it may be, it remains true that God in Christ, was acting in order to human redemption.

As to the facts recorded, the first was that of the darkness. To this Watts referred in those well-known lines :

" Well might the sun in darkness hide,
And shut his glories in;
When Christ, the mighty Maker died
For man, the creature's sin."

That deep darkness that fell upon the Cross, and continued for three hours, indicated first, perchance, the Divine anger with sin; but also something of the Divine tenderness towards the Sufferer in the darkness.

Then the cry to which we have already referred is full of light, even though it be a mysterious utterance. There upon the Cross our Lord quoted the first lines of a song that in all probability He had often heard chanted in the synagogue and temple worship, a song wrung out of the soul of a sufferer long before. It was the cry of a soul that had lost God, and become aware of the loss; and that is hell. Another psalm may tell the story of that cry :

" The pains of hell gat hold upon me."

Yet once more we must never forget the word already quoted more than once. " God was in Christ." If that cry was the cry of supreme human dereliction, it was the cry of God, as He entered into that experience of dereliction.

Then Matthew records the fact that He cried with a loud voice. He does not tell us what He said, but we learn from John's account that the words He uttered were, " It is finished," words revealing a sense of complete accomplishment and victory. Matthew points out that the cry was uttered with strength. It was not the cry of defeat, but of conquest.

Finally, Matthew records the fact that He " yielded up His Spirit," or quite literally, He dismissed His Spirit. Here again, as no evangelist described the crucifying, no evangelist refers to the passing of His Spirit as dying; but always in terms that suggest volitional and conquering activity.

In connection with this story of the Cross Matthew records certain supernatural signs. The first was that of the rending of the veil of the Temple. One often is inclined to wonder what effect that really had upon the authorities. For what long years that veil had hung between the Holy Place and the Holy of Holies, excluding man from access to the immediate presence of God. Now, suddenly, not by human hand, but by supernatural action, that veil was rent in twain, from the top to the bottom. At the same time Nature was convulsed. " The earth did quake, and the rocks were rent." In that convulsion " tombs were opened." In this connection Matthew is careful to point out that no bodies emerged from those tombs until after Jesus had risen. All these supernatural signs were demonstrations of the fact that God was abroad, and acting.

In the presence of these wonders, the watching centurion was so impressed that he cried, " Truly this was the Son of God."

The last tender touch in the narrative tells of the watching women.

The final paragraph in the chapter is full of beauty. It has to do with the dead body of Jesus. I refer to it in that way, because that is what Joseph asked Pilate to grant him, and what Pilate gave him.

Mark Anthony said of Cæsar :

" Now lies he there,
And none so poor as do him reverence."

Whatever ignominy and shame may have been the portion of our Lord in the Cross, that line could not have been written of Him, for He still held the place of love in the hearts of many.

As we contemplate for a moment the dead body of Jesus, we go back in memory into the stories of His public ministry, and to things He said in the presence of dead bodies. When He came into the chamber where the child of Jairus lay dead, He said, " She is not dead, but sleepeth." Later on in His ministry we hear Him refer to the death of His friend, Lazarus, and saying, " Our friend Lazarus is fallen asleep." In the first case men laughed Him to scorn. In the second His disciples utterly failed to understand His meaning; and He had to adopt their language, and say plainly, " Lazarus is dead." With these things in memory, we look at the dead body and say, He is not dead. He is asleep.

The story of the dead body of Jesus falls into two parts; the first records the ministry of love (verses 57-61); and the second, the activity of hate (verses 62-66).

The ministry of love is seen in the action of Joseph of Arimathæa, providing for Him the rock-hewn tomb, and wrapping the body with care, and the touch of infinite love. It is always to be remembered that after the spear had pierced His side, no hands touched Him other than those inspired by love. Disciples took Him from the Cross, prepared Him for His burying, provided the burying-place, and laid Him there, and left Him. Thus love had its radiant manifestation.

Then the strange manifestation of the ultimate in hatred. On the next morning the chief priests and Pharisees, haunted by some fear, went to Pilate. To him they said :

" That Deceiver said, while He was yet alive, After three days I rise again."

This always seems to me a remarkable thing. His enemies remembered what He had said, even when His disciples for some reason, seem to have forgotten it. It is impossible to listen to the words of Pilate when he granted their request for a guard, without finding in it a touch of scorn for them. Said he :

" Ye have a guard, go your way, make it as sure as ye can."

Thus we have attempted to survey this marvellous chapter. We do not forget as we close, that the story is not ended here. Here we leave the dead body of the Lord, saying, The King is dead. When chapter twenty-eight is read, we shall have to say, The King is alive for evermore.

In the presence of this chapter in its entirety, we exclaim :

" O love of God, O sin of man,
In this dread act your strength is tried;
And victory remains with Love,
When He, our Lord, was crucified."

If that verse sets forth the truth as a general statement, I cannot refrain from ending on a more personal word. To do that I borrow from old John Newton, and what he sang I make the language of my own experience.

" In evil long I took delight,
Unawed by shame and fear,
Till a new object met my sight,
And stopped my wild career.

" I saw One hanging on a tree
In agonies and blood,
Who fixed his languid eyes on me,
As near His cross I stood.

Sure never till my latest breath,
Can I forget that look;
It seem'd to charge me with His death,
Though not a word He spoke.
    *   *   *
A second look He gave, which said,
' I freely all forgive;
This blood is for thy ransom paid;
I die that thou may'st live.'

Thus while His death my sin displays
In all its blackest hue;
(Such is the mystery of grace),
It seals my pardon, too."

LUKE II

THE greatness of this chapter consists in the fact that it contains the record of the first thirty years in the life of our Lord; and it is the only record we have of those years. The chapter is great also because of its method. If we treat it as literature merely, it is almost unique for its beauty. The method of the writer is at once scientific and artistic. Luke was himself a scientist in his age, and an artist; and both these gifts of his personality were consecrated to the sacred work of delineating the personality of Jesus.

The scientific method is observed in the way in which he deals with his subject. He first chronicles the birth of the Person. This, in all its details, occupies the first thirty-nine verses. Then in brief sentences he tells the story of the growth of the Baby for the first twelve years (verse 40). He then pauses at the next point of importance in the development of personality, which in our modern terminology we should speak of as adolescence, the Boy being twelve years of age; and he gives a portrait of Him then, full of revealing beauty (verses 41-51). Finally, in another equally brief statement of simple and sublime sentences, he tells the story of the development of personality, from adolescence to manhood (verse 52).

In this survey of the chapter we shall not attempt anything like detailed examination, but rather endeavour to gain a consciousness of its revelation in broad outline. In doing so we shall see, as I have already intimated, science and art consecrated to this presentation of the first thirty years in the life of our Lord.

We may pause here to say that the central value of this chapter is focused in one verse :

" For there is born to you this day in the city of David a Saviour, which is Christ the Lord."

In these words we have the sum total of truth concerning the fact of the birth; and in remembrance of it we come to understand most clearly the story of the growth and development of the Person. From the standpoint of the economy of God— by that I mean the government of God in the world and in human affairs—that is the central declaration.

Before proceeding to examine the chapter, it is necessary that we remind ourselves that it tells us nothing concerning the Baby, except that He was born. There can be no proper understanding of the things recorded in this chapter save upon the basis of a recognition of the pre-natal facts recorded in the previous chapter.

When Luke approached the study of the Person of Jesus in order to write the record of it, he began where all true writers of biography begin, enquiring concerning these pre-natal facts. In the previous chapter then we are told that the Baby was the Child of a Virgin, and that His conception was by the act of the Holy Spirit, and the overshadowing of the Most High. Thus we are considering the story of a Person entering into human nature, and human history by the act of God which, using the word in our ordinary sense, can only be described as supernatural.

We take our survey of the chapter in two movements, the first having to do with the birth, and the second with the development.

In the consideration of the birth, at the risk of repetition, it is of supreme importance that we remember the declaration already referred to. "Unto you is born a Saviour." The declaration is not that a teacher was born, nor an example was born; though of course these things are supremely true. The One upon Whom we are called to look in these thirty years is One designated by heaven as "a Saviour."

As we survey the whole, we discover that there are three view-points from which the great fact is considered. They are those of Rome, of Heaven, and of Jerusalem.

Everything is set in relation to Rome in the opening sentences.

"It came to pass in those days, there went out a decree from Cæsar Augustus."

The approach from that standpoint occupies the first seven verses.

Verse eight opens :

"There were shepherds in the same country, abiding in the field . . . and an angel of the Lord stood by them."

That is the second point of approach, containing Heaven's interpretation; and that occupies verses eight to fourteen.

From verse fifteen, the point of approach is Jerusalem and the Temple. That runs on through the thirty-ninth verse.

First, then, the facts as related to Rome. Cæsar Augustus had issued a decree that all the economy, that is, all the Roman Empire was to be enrolled. Luke is careful to give us the exact date of that enrolment. It may be said in passing that there was dispute for long years concerning Luke's date; but the most recent scholarship has declared his absolute accuracy in this regard.

As we read, we see two people starting on a journey in obedience to the fiat of Augustus, and their journey led them to Bethlehem. These were the days when the doors of the temple of Janus had been closed for ten years, and they remained closed for between twenty and thirty years after that. That fact means that it was a period in which there was no war in the Roman world. The known world was completely subjugated to Roman rule. The absence of war was the result of human inertia, by reason of the fact that humanity had been subdued to one central authority. The Cæsar named was the first Roman imperator. He had become the most successful among the imperators or generals, and had gained the mastery of the world. In obedience to a decree issued by this man, we see a man and a woman travelling along the road that led from Nazareth to Bethlehem. If we could listen across the centuries we should hear the tramp of millions of feet, all going to certain centres, in obedience to this command. Among the rest, then, these two were travelling, going to Bethlehem, by the edict of Cæsar.

As we look again at the two in the light of facts recorded in the previous chapter, and employing the delicate and beautiful language of Luke, we see that the woman was " great with child," and know that the time was at hand " that she should be delivered." Rome was unconscious of those two, and cared nothing about them, except that they were in bondage to its decree. And yet, as we look, we see that the woman walking on that road, was the temple of the Son of God, as she bore the body necessary for the carrying out of His mission, and contributed to its forming and fashioning. The Judæan hills were unconscious of it, and Rome had no suspicion of it. The ultimate Autocrat was thus being borne along Roman roads.

Upon their arrival in Bethlehem we are told that there was no room for them in the kataluma. I have adopted the Greek word in order to point out that it does not represent an inn in the sense of a caravanserai. The kataluma was an enclosure of walls, into which cattle were driven for the night. There was always water there, but no food, and no host. That Bethlehem kataluma offered no hospitality to this woman. She found her refuge then in some outhouse of a dwelling where there was a manger.

The Son of God is thus seen, coming into human history in human form. In doing so He passed the city of Cæsar, and the palace of Herod, the dwelling places of the rich, and the hovels of the poor; and entered upon His human life, finding only a Mother and a manger.

That is the story of the birth from the standpoint of Rome's authority. It was by the edict of Cæsar that she was compelled to take that journey at that time; and in the hour of all hours that should be the most sacred, she was alone. There was no physician there, and no woman near to help. Luke, with artistic delicacy tells the story :

"She brought forth her Firstborn Son, and she wrapped Him in swaddling clothes, and laid Him in a manger."

With holy reverence I declare that we need not be sorry for that Baby. He found as He entered upon life on the earthly level, all that any boy needs, a Mother and a manger. The dignity of the entry is manifest. He passed all human positions of elevation, and entered human life on a level so low that no other baby ever came into the world on a lower one.

Then continuing, Luke shows what Heaven's attitude was towards that birth. Its messenger, "an angel of the Lord," accompanied by a multitude of the heavenly host, announced the real meaning of the thing that had happened. The angel sang the solo :

"Unto you is born this day in the city of David a Saviour, which is Christ the Lord."

Then suddenly the heavenly host celebrated the significance of the fact. The first note in their song ascribed glory to God,

"Glory to God in the highest."

That was the ascription of praise to the One Who occupied the highest position of authority, far above the throne of the Cæsars.

Then the song celebrated the meaning of the birth, so far as earth was concerned.

"And on earth peace among men, in whom He is well pleased."

Thus the angels were not only celebrating the birth of the Baby but greeting the new race that would result from the coming into human history of that Child. They understood that the ultimate issue of that birth would be the re-birth of men who would fulfil the Divine purpose, and be men well-pleasing to God; and their song declared that in this race there would be the realisation of peace.

All the world to-day is talking about peace, and it may surely desire peace; while all the time the world is everywhere preparing for war. It is good in this connection that we remember this announcement of the angels, and understand that the world will never find peace save as the result of its occupation by a race pleasing to God, after the pattern of the Man of His right hand. Thus the song of the angels spanned all the centuries from the birth of the Baby to the consummation.

Finally, Luke gives the fact of the birth from the standpoint of Jerusalem. This story begins with the account of the shepherds who were almost without doubt Temple shepherds, watching over flocks destined to sacrifice.

After the lapse of eight days the Baby born was circumcised, and received His name, in accord with Jewish law. It must never be lost sight of that it was by the rite of circumcision that every Hebrew boy entered the stream of national life; and it was at that point his name was given to him.

Then when the Child was forty days old, He was taken to Jerusalem and presented in the Temple. We pause here to notice carefully how Luke states that fact.

" When the days of their purification according to the law of Moses were fulfilled, they brought Him up to Jerusalem, to present Him to the Lord (as it is written in the law of the Lord, Every male that openeth the womb shall be called holy to the Lord)."

The words in brackets are full of significance. If we turn to the Hebrew Scriptures in the book of Exodus and in Numbers, we find that according to the first Divine intention, the firstborn in every family was to be set apart to the service of Jehovah. That was the service of the priesthood. Later, by Divine arrangement, the tribe of Levi was appointed to that office, and one Levite represented one firstborn. When this requirement was carried out, it was found that there were not enough Levites to meet the requirements, and so other arrangements were made. With that historic reference in mind, we see Jesus presented in harmony with the first Divine intention. He was not a Priest after the order of Aaron. He did not belong to the tribe of Levi; but He was the Firstborn. Thus we see Him from the standpoint of Jerusalem and the Temple, received into the national life by circumcision, named by a name chosen by heaven to represent His function as Saviour, and presented to God as the Firstborn.

Then Luke tells the stories of Simeon and Anna; Simeon singing his Nunc Dimittis; and Anna, worshipping and testifying. These two certainly represented an elect remnant in Jerusalem, who amid all the chaos of the times, were waiting for the consolation of Israel, the coming of the Messiah.

The next movement in the portrayal is that of the account of twelve years. He says, " The Child grew." Growth is ever the outcome of life, and is effortless. By that I mean it is unconscious of any volitional impulse. During the period of growth there is no responsibility. Luke carefully, however, analyses the growth, referring first to the physical in the words, " waxed strong "; secondly, to the mental in the words, " Becoming filled with wisdom " ; and finally, to the spiritual in the words, " The grace of God was upon Him." Thus He is presented to us for those first twelve years of natural development by growth.

At about twelve years of age the Jewish boy still comes to his barmitzvah, that is, to the hour when he becomes a son of the law. There can be, however, little question that Jesus had had His barmitzvah in the synagogue at Nazareth, and so by that Divine arrangement had become a Son of the Law. This meant He was no longer responsible to others in matters of religion. Luke gives us a picture of Him at that point. His tarrying in Jerusalem was voluntary. We see Him in the Temple in the presence of the doctors, or better, teachers, doing what, as a Son of the Law He had a perfect right to do. It is more than probable that He was One among a group of boys who were there on that occasion. Such boys asked the doctors questions, and replied to questions the doctors might put to them. We have no account of any question which these doctors asked Jesus, nor of any questions He put to them. Luke tells us that they were amazed at Him, that these reverent and scholarly teachers of the law were astonished at His understanding and His answers.

Mary and Joseph are introduced here in a very interesting way. They had started home without Him. I can never read this without feeling that that fact was a testimony to their confidence in Him. When, however, they discovered He was not with them on the homeward journey, they turned back with some perturbation. When He was found, Mary addressed Him by a word of tenderness, which I ever feel would find its best translation by the use of the Scotch word bairn, which really means one I have borne. The Greek word employed by Mary was an equivalent of that.

Then came the first recorded words of Jesus :

" Wist ye not that I must be in the things of My Father? "

In these words we find a consciousness of relationship, " My Father " ; and a recognition of the responsibility of relationship, " I must be in the things of My Father." These first uttered words constitute a keynote to everything that followed in the life and ministry of Jesus.

This brings us to the final movement, again characterised by remarkable brevity and equally remarkable revelation.

" And Jesus advanced in wisdom and stature, and in favour with God and men."

A change will be noticed here in the Revised Version from the reading of the King James' Version. There the statement was that He " increased," and that misses a suggestion of the utmost importance. Increase may refer to growth merely, or to some enlargement by accretion. The Greek word employed by Luke indicates a volitional attitude and activity, to which we get much nearer in the Revisers' " advanced." When we speak of advancement we do not refer to a matter of growth merely by the propulsion of life, but to progress, which is at the centre volitional. The Greek word is *prokopto*, and if we take that word to pieces it means quite literally to hew the way on, to hack forward, to drive ahead.

For twelve years Jesus had grown without volitional responsibility. From this point, as a Son of the law, He had to act alone, and fight His own way through. This applied to the whole of His personality; and here again the scientific method of Luke is manifest.

" He advanced in wisdom," that is a reference to the mental, and means that He had to face problems, to seek for knowledge, and to think His way through.

" He advanced . . . in stature," which is a reference to the physical. It was necessary for Him to observe the laws of health, and He did so. He had to seek for culture through the practice of restraint and He did so.

Finally, " He advanced . . . in grace with God and men." The Old rendering " in favour with God and men," is, I think, a most unhappy translation. By that I mean in reading it we might quite naturally think that it means that that advancement meant God and men grew—shall I venture to say—more fond of Him. That is by no means the meaning of the statement. The same word " grace " is employed as was used by Luke in declaring that in the early years the grace of God was upon Him. The Greek preposition here for " with " is *para*, which means by the side of. The statement then is that He advanced in grace by the side of God and men. He maintained His fellowship with God, and He maintained His fellowship with men; and the fellowship was characterised by grace.

This record of the thirty years by Luke as to its essential revelation, is condensed in the words of Luke's friend and teacher, Paul, when in simple and sublime sentences he wrote,

" When the fulness of the time came, God sent forth His Son, born of a woman, born under the law."

To this Paul immediately adds those revealing words, declaring that the purpose of this birth and life was:

" That He might redeem them that were under the law, that we might receive the adoption of sons. And because we are sons, God sent forth the Spirit of His Son into our hearts, crying, Abba Father."

From this statement of Paul take two sentences; the first of which covers all the ground of Luke's narrative, " God sent forth His Son "; and the second of which shows the result of that sending forth, " God sent forth the Spirit of His Son into our hearts."

LUKE XV

EXCEPT for the first three verses, which contain Luke's introduction, and one connecting sentence at the beginning of verse eleven, this chapter is the record of words actually spoken by our Lord, and for all they are intended to teach, they are supreme and superlative. The chapter stands out among the mountain-peaks of the Biblical literature, first on account of its matchless pictorial beauty, but ultimately and principally because it brings to focus truths concerning God and man which are fundamental on these matters.

Whereas the key to interpretation is found hanging at the portal, there is a sense in which much more is needed in order to complete understanding. To gain this, it would be good to read chapters fourteen, fifteen, sixteen, and seventeen so far as verse ten. That section constitutes one continuous story. It is the account of the last Sabbath in the life of Jesus, of which we have any record, prior to the one which opened Holy Week, and led to the Cross. Necessarily it is not possible now to cover the whole of the ground; but it is important to notice that chapter fourteen ends with the paragraph giving the account of our Lord's enunciation of the terms of discipleship, in language perhaps more severe than He had ever employed; although we must remember that He never suggested to men that following Him was an easy thing.

In this paragraph three times over we hear His voice saying, " He cannot be My disciple "; and if we set that statement in relation to what He had been saying, we shall see how severe these terms are. The last words recorded as falling from His lips were,

" He that hath ears to hear, let him hear."
There chapter fifteen begins, and really runs on in close connection with the words :

" Now all the publicans and sinners were drawing near unto Him for to hear Him."

He had uttered the terms of discipleship, as we have said, in language revealing the severe nature thereof; and it is arresting to observe that the people who most needed Him, were the people most eager to hear Him.

We have no detailed description by Luke of how He received these people, as they pressed upon Him, but the story he tells us becomes a revelation of it. Standing by, and watching all, the Pharisees and scribes said :

" This Man receiveth sinners, and eateth with them."

There is no doubt that that is what they saw Him doing at the time. These men, righteous in their own estimation, and needing no repentance therefore; held that unwashed multitude, ceremonially unwashed, and perhaps many of them literally unwashed, in supreme contempt. They massed them all in that one word, " sinners."

They saw Jesus receiving them, that is, taking them to Himself, as though He were their Friend, and they were His friends. He was not standing aloof from them in any way; nay, He was positively eating with them. Their statement with regard to Him was one of profound disapprobation.

These then were the circumstances which called forth these remarkable words of our Lord. Luke says, " He spake unto *them* this parable," and the pronoun " them " refers principally to that company of critical Pharisees and scribes. Of course He spoke in the hearing of these people thus designated, " sinners," and for their sakes also; but He certainly had in view the self-righteous, who held sinning men in utter contempt. They were men who lacked compassion, because they knew nothing of the heart of God.

The teaching then was intended to give these scribes and Pharisees the reason for His attitude towards sinning men. In effect our Lord said to them, You are watching something that you do not understand; and He proceeded to interpret what they were seeing. There is no doubt these watchers, if they were concerned about Jesus at all, imagined that His attitude towards these sinning people was one which would result in His own pollution; and the whole movement and force of His teaching was to show that so far from that being the case, the result would rather be the restoration of the lost.

In examining the teaching then, the first thing to be noted, is that we have here not three parables, but one. Luke distinctly says:

" He spake unto them this parable,"

and all that followed in His teaching to the end, constituted a parable. It may be perfectly proper to speak of three parables if we remember that in the last analysis the three constitute a triptych. There can be no true interpretation of the teaching which neglects any one of them. The three are needed for the revelation of the thought of the Lord.

Summarising ahead, we may say that the one theme of the parable is that of the grace of God. If it shall be objected that the word grace is not found in the discourse, the reply is that if the word be absent, the fact of grace is there from beginning to end. Thus the parable was intended to teach these rulers something of the deepest truth concerning God. They knew His justice, they knew His righteousness, they knew His holiness; they did not know His grace. This He was unveiling to them; and at the same time, if they had but eyes to see, He was revealing to them the truth about the people that they held in contempt. He was showing them that if these people had no place in their heart, they had in the heart of God.

The parable then has a threefold movement, showing first a shepherd suffering in his quest for a lost sheep; then a woman seeking for a lost coin until she find it; and finally a father singing with joy when his boy returns to him. The parable is unified in the fact that it deals with lost things, a lost sheep, a lost coin, a lost son.

The teaching also shows the value of the individual as distinguished from the mass. Whereas it is perfectly true and must be ever remembered, that He loved humanity in the mass, in this story the individual is in mind. A man had lost one sheep. A woman had lost one drachma. A father had lost one boy. Thus emphasis is put upon the value of the individual, and by so much as that is recognised, the value of the multitude is realised.

Again, the parable is not merely about lost things, but about lost things sought, lost things found, lost things restored. The shepherd seeks the sheep. The woman seeks the silver. Then let us pause carefully. The father is not revealed as seeking the son, but as receiving him when he, the son, seeks the father.

The Christian Church has been divided for centuries between two schools of theology, which we describe as Calvinist and Arminian. In the days of my youth there was real bitterness between these. Thank God it has largely passed away to-day, as men are recognising that there are truths that cannot be finally interpreted, and which while seeming to be contradictory, are nevertheless complementary. The Calvinist insists upon it that there can be no hope save as God seeks the lost. He is perfectly right in his contention. The Arminian, recognising the fact that the first approach is that of God to man, insists upon it that there is no hope for the man until he returns, seeking God. He also is perfectly correct. The Calvinist will find his place in this story as he contemplates the first two phases of it. The Arminian will find his place in it, as he dwells upon the last phase. It is a great thing to recognise that both conceptions find their place in this one parable.

It is self-evident that in a broad outlook such as we are now able to take, we can only see the parable in outline. In doing this we glance first at the picture of the Shepherd. All readers of the story recognise at once that this is a picture of the Son of God Himself. He had used the figure of speech before this. When after the confession at Cæsarea Philippi He was instructing His disciples, He definitely employed it (Matthew xviii). Yet again, when in the midst of controversy with the rulers concerning what He did for the man born blind, He spoke of Himself as " the good Shepherd," declaring what that meant as to His mission. In this parable, in general terms, He employs the same figure of speech. The method was characterised by simplicity, and yet in the light of all the facts, and in the interpretation already referred to, found in John x, we know something of what that shepherding meant. I said, we know something of it; whereas it is true that,

> " But none of the ransomed ever knew
> How deep were the waters crossed;
> Nor how dark was the night that the Lord passed through
> Ere He found His sheep that was lost."

Thus, then, in the first movement of the parable He was interpreting His own mission. It was that of seeking the lost sheep.

The second phase is the picture of a woman seeking a coin. We are at once arrested by this change from the picture of a shepherd to that of a woman. To this seeking woman, the piece of silver was still of value, but it was lost; it was no longer current coin. Let it be remembered that from the first page of the Bible God is revealed in the fact and mystery of Motherhood. This is clearly suggested in the first chapter of Genesis, when referring to the Holy Spirit it is said, " The Spirit of God brooded over the face of the abyss." The word " brooded " there refers to the outspread wings of motherhood. Whereas the fact of the Father-hood in God is found enshrined in the Old Testament literature, in the words:

> " Like as a father pitieth his children,
> So Jehovah pitieth them that fear Him ";

so also is His Motherhood in the equally arresting words:

> " As one whom his mother comforteth, so will I comfort you."

When we pass beyond this parable into the realm of the apostolic interpretations of Christ and His work, we find the whole Church is spoken of as the Bride; and in that suggestion is revealed the fact that the Church is the instrument of the brooding Spirit of God. Here, then, is a picture of the Spirit of God acting through the Church, seeking for the coin that has lost its value. Thus, if the first phase of the parable unveils the Son as the Shepherd, the second unveils the Spirit acting through the Church.

When we come to the final phase we find ourselves once more in universal agreement as to its intention. It is that of the revelation of God as the Father.

The first movement here is that of a revelation of the father supplying the son with substance. All that the son wastes in a far country in riotous living is substance which his father has bestowed upon him.

Then we come to the moment when that substance has been wasted, and we read:

" When he had spent all, there arose a mighty famine in that country."

That is not the declaration of a mere coincidence, but the announcement of a persistent fact. Men may be in the midst of plenty, but if they have spent all, they might as well be in the desert. The fact is illustrated persistently and perpetually. It applies to our condition in England to-day. The nation is not without resources equal to the banishing of all hunger, but men, women and children to-day are hungry, because they have no resources enabling them to provide what is necessary. I am not discussing our economics. I do not understand them. I do know, however, there is something radically wrong. When we hear of bank reserves it may be that we are referring to facts which are unavoidable; but, if so, they are unavoidable because of some failure somewhere. When we lift this fact on to the spiritual level it is even more self-evident. When men have wasted the substance with which God endows them, there is famine everywhere.

Now taking the story as our Lord certainly intended us to take it, on the natural level in order to the interpretation of the spiritual, we must never forget that while the son was away from the father's house, the father was suffering. The son suffers, but his suffering is never so great as that of the father and the mother, who are left to mourn his absence and his loss. There is something terrible in the word lost, specially when we speak of a lost son; but it is good sometimes to ask ourselves when we are conscious of sorrow in the presence of the fact, who are we sorry for? It is perfectly right that we should have sorrow for the son; but our deeper sorrow should be for the father who has lost his son. This deduction from the story is not only a fair one, but is inescapable.

Then the moment comes when the boy, reduced to the nakedness of his own personality, remembers and returns; and here we are face to face with a picture of amazing beauty. As we watch, the first thing we see is an old man running. We are inclined to say that there could be nothing more characterised by the lack of dignity. The reference to the father begins by the declaration that he saw him while he was yet afar off. That to me does not merely mean that he saw him on the way home when he was yet at a distance. I think it means that he had seen him all the time he was in the far country. It is certainly true that lost men and women are never lost sight of by God.

Then did we suggest that the picture of this father running was undignified? We recall the suggestion. A human father is never more characterised by true dignity than when his heart speeds his feet to welcome back his sinning boy.

Meeting him, he flung his arms around him, and as the Greek says, " kissed him much," or as we might say, smothered him with kisses.

Here again we might be inclined to say that the father was acting lovingly but not wisely. The boy was unkempt, all the marks of his dissipation still upon him. Would it not be wiser to put him on probation before embracing him? At least would it not be better to wait for his acknowledgment of guilt before putting the arms around him? The answer of the Father to such wisdom in effect is this, My son will confess most easily and fully when his head is pillowed on My heart, and when My kisses are rained upon him. That is the picture of God.

Lifting our eyes from the pictures presented, we look again at the company of self-satisfied men who had been watching and now were listening; and we look again at our Lord as He was seen by these men, receiving that polluted crowd of men, and sitting down and eating with them. In the story we have His interpretation of what He did. His attitude and activity were those of God. The Son, seeking as a Shepherd; the Spirit seeking as a mother; the Father suffering while the boy is away; and singing when he comes home.

Finally, our Lord talked to those men about an elder son, and what He had to say concerning him was an intended contrast between the self-righteous who lacked compassion, whether Jew or Gentile, and sinning men and women.

This son was devoted to his father's law, but was out of sympathy with his father's heart; and therefore was utterly unable rightly to value his brother. If we see men through God's eyes, we never could hold them in contempt, however low they may have sunk, however corrupt they may have become. It ever seems to me that in this final movement in the words of our Lord in which He gave utterance to no angry word for the failing son, but only revealed the foolishness of his attitude, He was making an appeal to these watching scribes and Pharisees to come into sympathy with Him in His mission, by understanding the heart of God.

I am constrained to conclude this broad survey of this wonderful chapter by reference to something which I heard Samuel Chadwick say many years ago, at the Northfield Conference. He read the story of the prodigal son, and having completed the reading he said, " I propose to preach to you this morning about the third Son in this story." Then he went on to say that we have two sons, one who by disobedience broke his father's heart; and one who, while keeping his father's law, had no sympathy with his father's heart. Then there is a third Son, and He the One Who uttered the story. He was the Son of the Father, Who both kept the Father's law, and understood His Father's heart; and so was able to reveal the whole truth concerning God in the presence of derelict humanity, and to make possible the restoration of the lost.

It is good to close such a meditation with enquiries addressed to ourselves. How far are we in fellowship with God as revealed in this story? Are we able to suffer with the Son as He takes the journey to find and restore? Are we diligently searching with the woman, until lost things are found? And, finally, are we able to rejoice with the Father when men and women, however low they may have sunk, are brought back again to the Father's home and the Father's heart? The answers to these questions will reveal the truth about our relationship to Christ.

LUKE XXIV

THE chapter opens with a " But," which at once suggests relationship with what has gone before, and yet that what is to follow is to be of a different nature. At the end of the previous chapter we leave the body of Jesus lying in the tomb of Joseph of Arimathæa. That is not the end of the story, and Luke leads to the end by the use of this word, " But," and proceeds to the presentation of the living Lord.

In doing so he gives the account of incidents on the first day of resurrection, and then, omitting all references to the next forty days, records the ascension. In common with the other evangelists, he does not record the fact of the rising, but refers to the resurrection of the Lord, thus necessarily implicating the fact. In this narrative the incidents of the first day occupy the first forty-nine verses; and the declaration of the ascension, verses fifty to fifty-three.

The account of the ascension is brief, and this at least suggests that when writing this first treatise, he was already intending to write another; for in the Acts we have a more detailed account of this ascension. Here, then, we have Luke's presentation of the last facts on the earth level, about Jesus.

When we examine this story of the first day, we find the record of things happening in the early morning, one story concerning the afternoon, and finally the account of what happened in the evening. We may thus divide the section into three parts; the early morning, verses one to twelve; the afternoon, verses thirteen to thirty-two; the evening, verses thirty-three to forty-nine.

As to the morning. We first see the women and the angels, verses one to seven; then the women and the disciples, verses eight to eleven; and finally, Peter alone, verse twelve.

The picture of the women finding their way to the sepulchre is full of beauty. Their quest was the quest of love. They were intending to find the dead body, and honour it. This becomes the more radiantly beautiful when we remember what inevitably must have been their state of mind at the time. It was not only that in the death of Jesus they had lost their dearest Friend. It was that in His death their highest hopes were extinguished. It may be admitted that they were mistaken, and that they ought not to have been. Indeed, presently the angels and the Lord Himself told them so. There is no doubt, however, that this was the fact concerning them. They still believed in Him personally, and loved Him with a great love; and in the inspiration of that belief and love they were on their way to do the last honours to His dead body.

When they arrived at the place of the tomb, they found the stone rolled away from the entrance, and two men standing there in dazzling apparel. In passing, it is interesting to remember that Luke records in his second treatise that after the ascension two men appeared to the disciples. A good deal has been said as to whether these were angels or men. Certainly other of the evangelists refers to those seen as angels. The matter is of no vital moment. That which is important is that they were heavenly visitors; and that the message they delivered to the women was of the nature of a tender rebuke.

" Why seek ye the living among the dead? "

or as the marginal rendering has it, which I prefer,

" Why seek ye Him that liveth among the dead? "

That was heaven's word about Jesus. He was living, and those women were reminded of what He had said to them before His death. Another incidental matter suggests itself; it is interesting to note that these heavenly visitors knew what Jesus had been teaching His disciples for at least the past six months before His crucifixion.

Then follows the simple statement, " they remembered." Evidently they had forgotten in the midst of their sorrow that He had distinctly foretold them that beyond the suffering and the death, He would be raised again. Perchance they had never caught the significance of His statement, notwithstanding the fact that if we study the records we shall find that He never referred to His death, without declaring the fact of His resurrection. Their failure to understand was thus tenderly rebuked by the heavenly visitors. It is as though they had said to them, If you, on the earth level have not listened, or have failed to understand; we in the heavenly places, have listened and have understood. The resurrection gave cause for no surprise among the inhabitants of heaven. May we not daringly affirm that heaven would have been surprised if there had been no resurrection.

Immediately following the meeting with the heavenly visitors, we see the women hurrying away to tell the disciples what had happened. The statement that these disciples " disbelieved them " is perhaps not to be wondered at, because they, in common with the women, had failed to apprehend His teaching on the subject.

The last reference to the morning has to do with Peter. Luke does not give us a full account of what happened. To find that, we must refer to John. He does tell us, however, the bare fact of Peter's hastening to the tomb, and seeing the grave-clothes lying, in such form as to create in his heart wonder at what had happened. Notice that it does not say he was wondering *what* had come to pass, but wondering *at* what had come to pass. The form of statement suggests that what he had seen was proof of the resurrection; and it was that fact that filled him with wonder. The word Luke uses to describe this wonder does not suggest perplexity, but rather admiration, and in that sense marvel, or wonder. Having seen that which produced the wonder, Luke says he departed to his home. It may be that Peter had a house in Jerusalem, but it is hardly probable. John had, and I understand this to mean he went to John's home, the place where he had found refuge, when, in the dark and terrible night, amid the storm, he had denied his Lord, he went out and wept bitterly. These were the events of the early morning as reported by Luke.

Then follows Luke's account of something which took place in the afternoon.

" Two of them were going that very day to a village named Emmaus, which was threescore furlongs from Jerusalem."

We should remember that this was not the Sabbath Day, but the first day of the week; and the journey these two were taking was a journey of sixty furlongs—in our measurements, about six miles and a half. As they walked along the road, they were communing, talking together of all the things which had happened in Jerusalem. How natural the story is. At the moment there was nothing to talk about other than these things; and as they went, what was there to say about it? The one grim and ghastly certainty was that Jesus had been killed. There were certain reports already circulating that He was alive, but no evidence that these reports were true. One can imagine these two saying to each other, Let us get away from the city. Let us escape somehow, or in some measure, from the scenes which have been so terrible.

As they proceeded on their way, a Stranger joined them, and to me personally there is no story more full of beauty than this of the way in which He dealt with these men. As He joined them He did so in such form that they did not recognise Him. One of the outstanding mysteries of these post-resurrection stories is that He was able thus to come near without being recognised, and yet presently to demonstrate the identity of His personality. In the early morning Mary had supposed Him to be the gardener. So these two did not recognize Him. He first asked them what they had been talking about. Quite evidently the nature of their conversation was revealed in the sadness of their faces. When He asked His question, they stood still in amazement that anyone should be in ignorance of the great events of the past days. They expressed their amazement in their question, which we may render simply thus, 'Art Thou the only one in Jerusalem Who does not know the things that have been happening there?' Then we are at once arrested by His question in reply, "What things?" He Who had been at the centre of everything, and around Whom all conversation gathered, asked these men, "What things?" It is quite evident that He intended to compel them to express in their own language, not for His information, but for their sakes, their conception of what had taken place.

Cleopas, one of the two, replied. The reply immediately revealed how that their love for Him, and their faith in Him personally were unchanged. Cleopas spoke of Him as "Jesus of Nazareth, a Prophet mighty in deed and word." The language was the expression of the utmost confidence in Him as to His message and intention. Then the next words revealed the point of their disappointment and despair,

"We hoped that it was He Which should redeem Israel."

That past tense in the use of the verb to hope, revealed the fact that hope had perished; and the light of hope which had shined upon them as they had listened to Him in the days of His earthly ministry, was blotted out, and they were filled with despair. They had lost their Lord through death, but it was not merely the loss of Jesus personally, terrible as that was to them from the standpoint of personal attachment; but it was that when they saw Him put to death, they felt that all expectation that it was He Who should redeem Israel, perished.

Continuing, they admitted that they had heard some rumour that He was alive. This is revealed in the clear statement,

> " Certain women of our company amazed us, having been early at the tomb; and when they found not His body, they came saying, that they had also seen a vision of angels, which said that He was alive."

This evidently had not carried conviction. The report of the women had, however, been ratified by certain who had been to the tomb, and found it even so; but the end of it all as they stated it was this, " Him they saw not."

The picture of these men is very natural and very wonderful. Their hearts were loyal and filled with love, and they still believed in Him, but they had been driven to the conclusion that He had failed, and consequently their hope could not be realised. The lights that had been shining upon the dark sky for them had been put out in murky blackness.

Then the Stranger began to talk to them, and as the angels had done with the women, so this Stranger began with words of tender but definite rebuke:

> " O foolish men, and slow of heart to believe."

He did not, however, refer to His own teaching, but to all that the prophets had spoken. He charged these men with failing to believe their own sacred writings. In those writings they might have found the declaration that the Messiah must suffer, and through suffering come into His glory. They who had accepted Him as Messiah, and had seen His sufferings, yet were unable to believe in His glory.

Then,

> " Beginning from Moses and from all the prophets, He interpreted to them in all the Scriptures the things concerning Himself."

One seldom reads this without having the feeling that it must have been great to hear Him do that. And yet, let us not forget that before He left them, He had told His disciples that the Spirit should come and guide them into the truth. And so it happened, and in the apostolic writings of Peter, and of John, of Paul, and of James, we certainly can find the essentials of what He taught these two on the way to Emmaus; how that in Him all that Moses and the prophets had foretold, had come to fulfilment.

When they arrived at Emmaus, the shadows were beginning to fall, and as Luke has it:

" He made as though He would go further."
It was then that they said to Him:

" Abide with us; for it is toward evening."

Let us bear in mind at this point, that they did not know Who He was. They had listened to the marvellous things He had been saying to them about the Messiah, but they did not recognise Him. Their appeal to Him was born out of their respect for this Stranger, and their desire to offer Him hospitality. The road beyond Emmaus was a dangerous one, infested by robbers. It was not safe for a man to travel alone that road in the night. Therefore they besought Him to go in and stay with them. We all love, and must for ever love Lyte's great hymn, " Abide with me." Everything in it is true, but it is well that we should remember that when we sing that hymn, inevitably we are thinking of the gain to ourselves of having Him as Guest. These men were not doing so. They were thinking rather of His safety.

And so the three of them entered the house, and we see them acting as hosts, while He was Guest. Until suddenly He became the Host, and they the guests. The revelation of Him came as He took in His hand a loaf and broke it. With their illumination He vanished. In that moment of realisation, all that He had been saying to them on the highway became filled with new meaning, even though as He had spoken, He had produced within them a strange moving of heart, to which they referred in the words:

" Was not our heart burning within us, while He spake to us in the way, while He opened to us the Scriptures? "

It is evident that they hastened back over the six and a half miles, and Luke gives the dramatic and beautiful story of their arrival. When they entered where the other disciples were gathered, before they could tell the story that was filling them with wonder, they heard the news declared thus:

" The Lord is risen indeed, and hath appeared to Simon."

It is interesting here to observe the proof of the resurrection stated by this company. " He hath appeared to Simon." There is a beautiful reticence about that statement. It is impossible to escape from wonder as to where He appeared to him, but we are not told. The certain fact is that somewhere He had seen him; and the implicate is that He had seen him alone. When Paul massed the evidences of the resurrection in his Corinthian letter, he named the fact, " He appeared to Cephas." There can be no doubt that in that private interview, everything was settled that had come between Peter and his Lord. It may be permissible reverently to speculate on the subject of that solitary interview. I can almost imagine our Lord saying to him, " Simon, six months ago I told you all that would happen, but you rebelled against what I said to you. You even rebuked Me for declaring the Cross to be necessary. I then rebuked you, Simon, for minding the things of men, rather than the things of God. Simon, I have been to the Cross; I am alive again, and because I have been to the Cross, and am alive, I am able to speak to your troubled heart the word of pardon and of peace.' These sentences are speculative, and may be forgotten; and yet I think in essence they are true.

So we come to the evening of that first day. Suddenly, as they were talking of these wonderful matters, in the language of Luke:

" As they spake these things, He Himself stood in the midst of them."

He came with the old, commonplace greeting of the city street, of the market place, and the country-side, " Peace unto you." Yet, by reason of the marvel of His coming, the ordinary became extraordinary. They had never heard that greeting in that way before. The fact of His standing amongst them, when the doors were closed, and had not been opened to admit Him, filled them with terror. Then, in order to demonstrate the actuality of corporeal resurrection, He showed them His hands and His feet. Even then, some of them doubted for very joy. Therefore He took another method; and asking for something to eat, He sat down in their presence and partook of it. Thus He proved to them that He was no phantom, no phantasy, but actually the same Jesus Whom they had come to know so well and intimately in the days before His Cross.

Then, with these men gathered around Him, He gave them light on their own Scriptures. In doing so He referred to all those Scriptures when He used the terms, " The law . . the prophets . . . the psalms." These constitute the divisions of those Scriptures. The law was the Torah, the first five books; the prophets, or Nebiim, covering part of the historic books, and all that were commonly called prophets; while the Psalms referred to the Kethubim, or writings, which division was often designated the Psalms, because in it they took the first place. Thus, we repeat that He referred to the whole of their Scriptures, and declared that He Himself was the Subject of them, and that in Him fulfilment was found of all their teaching.

Then He opened their minds that they might understand the Scriptures. On the way to Emmaus He had opened the Scriptures to two. Now He opened the minds of all. The word in each case is the same, and means to disentangle, and bring into true and right relationship.

The last movement in the chapter records the ascension. He is seen leading His disciples out from Jerusalem as far as Bethany. There was far more, however, in that action than that of geographical movement. He led them out from everything in city and Temple that was effete, and gathered them about Himself. The last vision they had of Him was that of lifting His hands in Priestly attitude of blessing upon them. So they saw Him finally borne from earth away until their earthly eyes could see Him no longer. What they did was the natural and inevitable outcome of what they had heard and seen. They worshipped Him, and returned.

JOHN I

THE sublimity of this chapter must be recognised by any thoughtful person who has once read it. Its profound significance will grow the more often it is read and pondered.

It falls into three parts. In the first eighteen verses we have what we have now come to speak of as the prologue. It is unquestionably the exordium, which at once introduces everything that is to follow, and summarises the results of all subsequently recorded. From the nineteenth verse to the thirty-fourth, we have the writer's statement concerning the introductory ministry of John the Baptist, the herald of the Word. From the thirty-fifth verse to the end of the chapter, we have the record of incidents in the first three days of the earthly ministry of the Lord.

In order to an approximately correct apprehension of the value of the prologue, it is necessary that we submit it to a careful analysis as to its structure, distinguishing between its principal statements, and those which are secondary or subordinate.

When this is done, we find that if we link together, verses one, fourteen, and eighteen, we have a statement complete in itself, which really introduces us to the study of the book, as it summarises, or perhaps we should say reveals, the secret of everything that follows.

Glancing for a moment at verse fourteen we find certain words are printed in brackets. This is so in all the great Versions; and unquestionably they ought to be so placed, constituting as they do, an ejaculatory parenthesis to the main statement. Verses two to thirteen contain what is, from the standpoint of the main statements, another parenthesis; and we have still another in the portion contained in verses fifteen to seventeen. Thus, in the eighteen verses, we may say at once that we have three parentheses. It is important that we should recognise that the parentheses are rightly placed, and full of significance; but do, nevertheless, constitute a turning aside from the main line of statement.

We are proceeding upon the assumption, without argument, that this book was written by John the disciple and apostle of our Lord. In the days of my youth it was very confidently affirmed that it could not have been written by John, and that it was written at least two hundred years after the events. It is interesting to remember that the most recent findings of competent critics put it back to a much earlier date. Burney considers it was written no later than 75 A.D., and Torrey in his most recent book, places it at an earlier period than that. The one thing, however, about which there is general agreement is that it was the last written of the four Gospel narratives. We may, therefore, assume that John had read the writing of his fellow-apostle, Matthew, and those of Mark and Luke. Here, however, shall we say, thirty or forty years after the crucifixion, John, looking back to those days which he remembered so well, selected from them certain outstanding facts in the life and ministry of our Lord, and his treatise opens with that which is, so far as he was concerned, the summing-up of the whole of the facts concerning Jesus. It is possible that this prologue was the last thing he wrote, that having completed his scheme, he ended by this statement of final findings concerning the Person of our Lord. That is by no means certain, and is only stated by way of suggestion.

In the story as written by Matthew we see Jesus as King. In that from the pen of Mark we see Him as the Servant of the Lord. In the writing of Luke He is revealed as God's archetypal Man in all the perfection of His Personality. When we come to the Gospel of John it is as though he says to us in effect, Let us see Who this King really is, Who this Servant of the Lord is, Who this Man manifest in earthly glory really is. The answer to such an enquiry is found in the principal statement of the prologue, which it may be well to set out, omitting the parentheses referred to.

> " In the beginning was the Word, and the Word was with God, and the Word was God . . . And the Word became flesh, and tabernacled among us . . . full of grace and truth . . . No man hath seen God at any time; the only begotten Son, Which is in the bosom of the Father, He hath declared Him."

Let us examine this a little more in detail. In the first verse there are three clear statements.

> " In the beginning was the Word."
> " The Word was with God."
> " The Word was God."

This threefold statement might have been written by someone who had never seen or heard of Jesus. There are those who claim that the statements are the result of the influence upon John of Greek philosophy. Personally I do not accept that view for a moment. They certainly are statements in complete harmony with Hebrew philosophy. I admit that a Greek philosopher may have written such sentences, but submit that they exactly accord with the view of Hebrew philosophy. Hebrew philosophy did not begin by asking a question, but by making an affirmation. It assumed the fact that God is. Yet the assumption was the result of a process of thought, and the thought of the philosopher moved along these lines. Every phenomenon is the outcome of thought. Thought postulates a Thinker. That Thinker is named God.

That philosophy lies at the back of these opening sentences. " In the beginning was the Word," that is, the Word as wisdom, thought, conception. " And the Word was with God," that is, the conception demands One Who conceives, and such an One is named God. " And the Word was God," that is, the thought and the Thinker are necessarily one in essence.

Passing to verse fourteen, we read first, " The Word became flesh." No Greek philosopher ever imagined such a thing. No Hebrew philosopher, merely upon the ground of his philosophic thinking ever did, or could have, come to such a conclusion by deduction. This is the record of an event, something which took place, some breaking in upon human life and human history of a new fact.

There are really three statements in this verse, though not so clearly and sharply defined as those in the first verse. If we supply the subject in the last two of them, and the subject and predicate in the third, we may set them out thus,

> " The Word became flesh."
>
> The Word " pitched His tent among us."
>
> The Word was " full of grace and truth."

Here then we have a summary of the central mystery and manifestation of the Christian religion.

Passing to verse eighteen we read,

> " No man hath seen God at any time."

Both Hebrew and Greek philosophy would be in perfect agreement as to the accuracy of that declaration. Then follows the statement,

> " The only begotten Son, Which is in the bosom of the Father, He hath declared Him."

Again, that is a summary of the result of the fact declared, that the Word became flesh.

The correlation of all these statements is very arresting. Taking those of verses one and fourteen, let us set them out as the three of verse fourteen answer the three of verse one.

" In the beginning was the Word,"
" And the Word became flesh."
" And the Word was with God,"
" And the Word . . . pitched His tent among us."
" And the Word was God,
" And the Word . . . was full of grace and truth."

Again, let us observe the relation between the first half of verse eighteen and verse one, and the second half of verse eighteen and verse fourteen.

" In the beginning was the Word, and the Word was with God and the Word was God."
" No man hath seen God at any time."
" The Word became flesh, and pitched His tent among us . . . full of grace and truth."
" The only begotten Son, Which is in the bosom of the Father, He hath declared Him."

If we examine the parentheses, we shall see their relation to the main statements. After the philosophic declaration of verse one, the writer turns aside to show the relation of the Word to two creations. As to the original creation he says, " The same was in the beginning with God," and declares that by Him all things were made, and without Him nothing has been made that has been made. The idea is that original creation and progressive creation have all been under the control of the Word. Further, he says that in Him was life, that is all life; but that the distinguishing element of life in man was light. Such is a very incomplete summary of the declarations concerning the relation of the Word to the first creation.

Then follows a statement which brings us face to face with a new creation. The Word is declared to have been in His own world, but that His world did not know Him. The ministry of John the Baptist is referred to as that of one bearing witness to the Light which lighteth every man. The reference is found in the words, " There was the true Light . . coming into the world." In other words, the Light which had not been apprehended or extinguished, was seen coming into visibility. Even then, coming into His own world, His own people failed to receive Him. Nevertheless His coming was victorious, in that those who did receive Him, by believing on His name, were born into a new life. Thus the parenthesis refers to the Word in relation to the first creation, and in relation to a new creation.

The brief parenthesis in the midst of verse fourteen was evidently an exclamation on the part of the writer as to what was seen. The vision was that of glory, glory of the very essence of the Father, and it is described in the one pregnant and complete phrase, " full of grace and truth."

In the final parenthesis we find the meeting and merging of two witnesses. The first is John the herald; the second is John the evangelist. In their testimony they are united. The herald completing the witness of the past economy; the apostle uttering the witness of the new.

To summarize. In verse one, eternal facts are declared. In verse fourteen, a temporal manifestation of the eternal facts is recorded. In verse eighteen, the value of that temporal manifestation of the eternal facts is declared.

The writer then gave a condensed record of the ministry of the herald, its principal value being in what that herald had to say concerning himself in answer to enquiries instituted by those in official positions. He first affirmed " I am not the Christ." In answer to their consequent enquiry, " Art thou Elijah? " he replied, " I am not." When they further asked him, " Art thou the prophet? " he answered " No." This naturally led to the enquiry, " Who art thou? . . . what sayest thou of thyself? " In reply he quoted to those doctors of the law who would be familiar with their own sacred Scriptures, the words :

" I am the voice of one crying in the wilderness, Make straight the way of the Lord, as said Isaiah the prophet."

By this quotation he distinctly announced the fulfilment of the prophecy of Isaiah concerning the Messiah, as he claimed to be the Voice, announcing the coming of the Word.

On the day after his answers to this deputation, he formally identified Jesus as the Messiah, in the words,

" Behold, the Lamb of God, Which taketh away the sin of the world."

The relation of this to the prophecy of Isaiah is very significant. If these men had turned to that prophecy they would have discovered that the Voice announced the advent of the Servant of the Lord, and that the portraiture of that Servant of the Lord found its ultimate in the fifty-third chapter. Thus the herald has declared that the One described in the prologue as " The Word made flesh," is " The Lamb of God, Which taketh away the sin of the world."

The rest of the chapter is occupied with incidents occurring in three successive days, clearly marked by the writer.

" On the morrow," that is, on the day after the herald had publicly identified Jesus as the Messiah, he is seen in conversation with two of his own disciples, when Jesus passed along the way, and John indicated Him again, as he said, " Behold the Lamb of God ! " Immediately these two left John, and went after Jesus.

In the rest of the narrative we see five men, Andrew and John, Simon, Philip and Nathanael. These were the first followers of the Messiah. It is not within the purpose of a survey of the chapter to deal with this wonderful story in detail. Glancing rapidly over it, we see the differences between these men. Andrew, a strong soul, determined to investigate, and presently showing his concern about his brother. John the poet, the dreamer, the writer of this narrative. Simon an elemental human, with all the essential things of human nature within his personality, but lacking the principle which would weld the elements into strength. Philip, the quiet, unobtrusive man, as subsequent events show, capable of thinking big things, but not finding it easy to express them. Nathanael, a man perfectly characterised by Jesus as guileless.

Thus the story of the chapter proceeds upon its way with sublime simplicity. " The Word made flesh " and tabernacling in human form, is seen proceeding along the pathway of earthly service, without fanfare of trumpets, taking things as they came, coming into contact with human nature, and beginning the mighty work of so dealing with it as to produce a new creation.

If we follow Him on these three days we listen to Him, and to the actual words that are recorded as having fallen from His lips. " What seek ye? " " Come, and ye shall see." " Thou art Simon the son of John; thou shalt be called Cephas." " Follow Me." " Behold, an Israelite indeed, in whom is no guile." " Before Philip called thee, when thou wast under the fig tree, I saw thee." " Because I said unto thee, I saw thee under the fig tree, believest thou? thou shalt see greater things than these. . . Verily, verily I say unto you, Ye shall see the heaven opened, and the angels of God ascending and descending upon the Son of Man." Seven recorded sayings, spoken to Andrew and John, to Simon, to Philip, to Nathanael. Let them be carefully pondered, the first words recorded, as having fallen from the lips of the Word made flesh in public ministry.

In our survey of the chapter it is self-evident that we have been able to do no more than breathe its atmosphere, and get some impression of its glory. To return in conclusion, to the central statement of the prologue:

" The Word was made flesh, and dwelt among us . . full of grace and truth."

In those words we have in some senses a complete statement concerning the Christian religion. The teaching of Jesus was of course of supreme importance. The deeds of Jesus were also full of significance. The Cross of Jesus, combined with the resurrection, is central and ultimate to the Christian religion. Nevertheless the matter of ultimate importance is to know Who is this One Who taught and wrought and died and rose? Who was it that uttered the teaching? Who was it that wrought the wonders? Who was it that went to Calvary? It is only when we recognise that He was " the Word made flesh," that we feel the full weight of His teaching, or gain the sense of the value of His deeds, or are able to interpret His Cross and His resurrection. This One was indeed:

> " God manifestly seen and heard,
> And heaven's Beloved One."

That is the deepest fact of the Christian religion.

When men begin to try to account for Christianity in the realm of scientific examination and philosophic speculation, they must utterly break down. It cannot be that the Infinite can be apprehended by finite thinking. Sometimes the poets do better than the philosophers, even though we may charge them with being imaginative. It is with this in mind that I dare to end by quoting from George Herbert, lines of dreaming beauty, but to me full of illuminative suggestiveness.

> " Hast thou not heard that my Lord Jesus died?
>   Then let me tell thee a strange story;
> The God of Power, as He did ride
>   In His majestic robes of glory,
> Resolved to 'light, and so one day
> He did descend, undressing all the way.
>
> The stars His tire of light and rings obtained,
> The cloud His bow, the fire His spear,
> The sky His azure mantle gained;
> And when they asked what He would wear,
> He smiled, and said as He did go,
> He had new clothes a-making here below."

" The Word became flesh."

JOHN III

THE third chapter in the Gospel according to John is one of the most familiar in the New Testament as to its first part. A great many people if asked what the chapter is about would reply, Nicodemus, and they would be perfectly correct. There is more, however, in the chapter than the story of Nicodemus, although all that remains grows out of that story. By way of introduction, let us point out the movement of the chapter.

In the first twenty-one verses we have the account of the conversation of Jesus with Nicodemus in the night, on the occasion of the first Messianic visit of our Lord to Jerusalem. The story of that visit begins in the previous chapter. We are there told how He came and cleansed the Temple; and, moreover, that He wrought signs, but we are not told what signs they were. Evidently they made a great impression upon many, according to the concluding statements of the second chapter.

In verses twenty-two to thirty we have the fact recorded that after the visit to Jerusalem our Lord tarried, possibly for a considerable period, in Judæa; and in that connection we have the account of the great recessional words of the herald.

The rest of the chapter, verses thirty-one to thirty-six, consists of some reflections of John the writer, on the ministry of Jesus.

In the chapter taken in its entirety we discover a remarkable unity as it discloses the central verities of Christianity. These verities are found in certain outstanding declarations around which all the rest of the chapter gathers. These statements are three in number. Two of them fell from the lips of our Lord Himself. The third is found in the final paragraph in which the writer is referring to the ministry of our Lord. Let us first read these sayings.

The first of them is found in the third verse:

" Except one be born from above, he cannot see the Kingdom of God."

The second is found in verses fourteen to seventeen:

" And as Moses lifted up the serpent in the wilderness, even so must the Son of Man be lifted up; that whosoever believeth may in Him have eternal life.

" For God so loved the world, that He gave His only begotten Son, that whosoever believeth on Him should not perish, but have eternal life.

" For God sent not the Son into the world to judge the world; but that the world should be saved through Him."

The third is found in verses thirty-five and thirty-six:

" The Father loveth the Son, and hath given all things into His hand. He that believeth on the Son hath eternal life; but he that obeyeth not the Son shall not see life, but the wrath of God abideth on him."

These are the great sayings of the chapter, and I repeat what I have already said, that if they be carefully pondered, we find in them declarations of the essential things of the Christian faith.

In the first of these sayings we have a statement of Christ made to Nicodemus. This man had come to Him in the quiet and silence of the night, undoubtedly with a sincere motive, and an honest enquiry. He had been impressed by the signs which Jesus had wrought in the city, and had made a true deduction from them, namely that He was sent from God. Himself a teacher, or as our Lord described him, " the teacher of Israel," desired to know what this Messenger from God had to say. The words we are considering constituted the first answer of Jesus to him; and indeed, it was an answer that was complete in itself. Other things were said to Nicodemus after, in response to his further enquiries, but all the ensuing conversation was in interpretation of this one saying.

This first word of Jesus then to this man was His first and fundamental word to humanity as a whole. We have printed it in a very literal translation which is found to deviate slightly from the Versions. The word " man " does not occur in the Greek text and the Greek word *anothen* does not mean *again*, not even *anew*, but " from above." It may have the sense *from the beginning*, but here, as in other places in the New Testament, certainly it means " from above." The omission of the word " man " in the rendering shows the statement to be what it really was, a generalisation. " Except one," that is, any individual, " be born from above." That is Christianity as to human necessity. In the second statement to which we come presently,

"As Moses lifted up the serpent in the wilderness," and so on, we have an interpretation of Christianity from the standpoint of heaven's activity.

As to the fact of human necessity, the first word of Christ spoken to Nicodemus was one that brought him, and indeed, must bring us, face to face with what can only be described as a revolutionary suggestion, involving a conception of the Kingdom of God itself, which must have been, at any rate to Nicodemus, entirely new. He had come honestly, an observing man. John intentionally put him into contrast with others as is seen if we read the final statements of chapter two, in close connection with the beginning of chapter three. There were certain who, in a certain way, believed in Christ, to whom Christ could not commit Himself. To this man, however, He did commit Himself, answering his implied request for help when he said, "We know that Thou art a Teacher come from God." This first word of the Lord to him then was one that told him that he could not understand, could not apprehend the Kingdom of God in itself. The implicate was, as we have seen, that the thinking of Nicodemus, in common with the men of his time concerning the Kingdom of God, was entirely false. We know that their thinking was material, that they were looking for the establishment of an earth order, while they were unmindful of the spiritual necessities of life. As a matter of fact, it was this false conception on the side of those in authority which issued in the crucifixion of our Lord. Therefore it was that when an honest enquirer sought for teaching, the first necessity was declared to him as being that of capacity for understanding the true nature of that Kingdom. This necessity was that of a new life altogether, issuing in a new vision.

Edersheim interprets this word of Jesus by saying that our Lord declared that men need to be, in order to become. All human thinking had proceeded upon the idea that if men by their own efforts could bring about a certain order, then they would be what they desired to be. This fundamental word of Christianity reveals the fact that the first necessity is that of the being what we should be in order that circumstances may become what we desire they should become.

All this may be made clearer by a consideration of the time in which these words were uttered. If we glance at the world background as it then existed, we see men attempting, in many ways, to realise life at its highest, and everywhere failing. The three great forces operating in that period, and so far as the localized ministry of our Lord was concerned, centralised in Judæa, were the Roman, the Greek, and the Hebrew.

As to the Roman world, it sought to bring in conditions which should be of the best, by the arrangement of human life under a strong and stern government. We cannot study the history of the Roman people and empire without being conscious that up to a certain point, they had been marvellously successful in that effort. The idea was that men could enter into life fully, under the government of authority and force.

On the other hand, the Greek outlook which was concerned with culture, attempted a realisation of life along those lines. Again we recognise how marvellously they wrought. The evidences are still available in the realm of art. Moreover, Greek philosophy seeking the perfection of personality, taught that the highest possible thing for man was self-expression in fullness of experience.

The Hebrew ideal was that of religion, expressing itself in ritual, rules, and regulations, conditioning human conduct in order to the well-being of humanity as a whole.

Now for a moment look at the actual condition of the world at the time. Neither Roman government, nor Greek art, nor Hebrew ritual, was helping men to rise into anything like the full beauty and glory of life. Everywhere men were debased, spiritual conceptions were almost dead, and the very ideal of morality was degraded. Those familiar with the times, whether under Roman rule, or in the midst of Greek artistry, or at the heart of the Hebrew religion, will at once recognise the accuracy of these statements.

Into the midst of this world came Jesus, and speaking on this occasion to one enquiring soul, He declared that the fundamental necessity in order to the realisation of life individually, and therefore socially and racially, was that of a re-birth, the impartation of new life, enabling men first to see clearly the ideal.

" Except one be born from above, he cannot see the Kingdom of God."

It is well that we carefully observe that Nicodemus did not challenge the statement. What he did do was to question the possibility of the thing referred to taking place. He asked:

" How can a man be born when he is old? "

and he illustrated the difficulty as he saw it, in the realm of the physical.

" Can he enter a second time into his mother's womb, and be born? "

These questions meant, How can it ever be possible that a man can begin his life over again?

This question was, when rightly apprehended, an honest and indeed a profound question. It involves the fact of personality as the result not only of the beginning in birth, but development through all the passing years. How can it be possible to deal with personality so that there shall be that which is equivalent to a new beginning, a new birth? The physical illustration which Nicodemus used might be stated thus, Can a developed and full-grown man be pressed back into embryonic conditions in his mother's womb? If that cannot be done with the physical, how can it be done with the side of personality which is more difficult to deal with, namely the mental and the spiritual?

Turning back from this statement of difficulty by Nicodemus, we face the facts of life as they are patent to-day. What is the matter with the world? and for the moment I am using that phrase, the world, in its narrowest sense, as applied to peoples who are supposed to be civilised. What is wrong with us, causing all our long continued struggle for better conditions, and our absolute inability to produce them? The supreme difficulty is that men do not see the Kingdom of God. The ideal after which they are striving is incorrect and incomplete. It does not include the whole fact of human life. In order to clear vision, a miracle of regeneration is necessary.

That is what Christianity is saying to the world in the name of her Lord and Master. It declares that it is useless offering the world the ethic of Jesus, because it is unable to understand it. It is useless attempting to interpret the beauty and glory of the Kingdom of God, because men are incapable of appreciating such beauty. When the ancient prophet speaking of the coming Servant of the Lord declared that there was no beauty that men should desire Him, he was not declaring that there would be no beauty in Him, but that men would be blind thereto. That is an essential element of the great fact declared by Jesus to Nicodemus in the words:

" Except one be born from above, he cannot see the Kingdom of God."

It is not our purpose now to follow the conversation with any detail. Suffice it to say that our Lord continuing, first affirmed the necessity for a new birth of water and the Spirit, in order to enter into the Kingdom of God. He then admitted the impossibility of the new birth physically, but implicated its possibility spiritually as He said:

" That which is born of the flesh is flesh; and that which is born of the Spirit is spirit," the patent meaning and value of which is that whereas no man could enter into his mother's womb and be born a second time physically, there remained a possibility of his being born again spiritually.

Continuing, He illustrated by the figure of the blowing of the wind. The consideration of this figure will show that it teaches that as in the blowing of the wind, so in this work of the Spirit there are things we may know, but there are things that are beyond the possibility of our apprehension, or interpretation; thus calling upon Nicodemus and all men, to obey the law of that which is known, and thus bring themselves into relationship with the operation of the Power that is beyond the possibility of their understanding.

Then Nicodemus asked his second question, "How can these things be?" This question must not be confused with the first questions Nicodemus asked. They had to do with the apparent impossibility as to the fact. This practically admitted the tremendous nature of the suggestion, but raised the question of the difficulty of process.

Our Lord's answer to this question brings us to the second of the great sayings of Jesus to which we have referred. He commenced His reply to Nicodemus with a touch of gentle and yet definite irony, as He said:

"Art thou the teacher of Israel, and understandest not these things?"

Continuing, He asked him if He had told him earthly things, and he could not believe, how would he believe if He told him heavenly things. The earthly things were the things on the earth level of experience. The heavenly things were the things of the Divine activity already referred to as fact, under the illustration of the blowing of the wind. Having asked him the question our Lord did proceed to tell him the heavenly things, which make possible the new birth, which He had declared to be a supreme necessity.

Employing the story of the Old Testament for the sake of illustration, He declared that the way by which men could find this new life, the life of the ages, eternal life, would be by the lifting up of the Son of Man. It would be very questionable whether Nicodemus at the moment understood exactly what our Lord meant by that phrase concerning the lifting up of the Son of man. There came a day towards the end of our Lord's life and ministry when He said:

"I, if I be lifted up from the earth, will draw all men unto Myself."

One wonders whether Nicodemus was there, and heard that great utterance. Even if he were, it is doubtful whether he grasped its significance, although he might recall the words spoken to him in Jerusalem long before. Still glancing on, we see this very man Nicodemus, with tender hands, helping Joseph of Arimathæa to wrap the dead body of Jesus in the cerements of the tomb. He certainly then did not understand. But when presently the One Who was dead was found risen from the dead, there would inevitably come to him an understanding of how through the laying down of His life, and His taking of it again, it was possible for man in his spirit life to be born from above. Thus in the illustration used, the great provision was revealed.

But the statement was not yet finished. The words immediately following are, " For God so loved the world." It is important that we should not omit that little introductory word, " For," which links the great declaration to be made with that already made. Thus:

" As Moses lifted up the serpent in the wilderness, even so must the Son of Man be lifted up; . . . For God so loved the world."

Exposition of that would be almost an impertinence. The matter is so clear and self-evident that the lifting up of the Son of man was caused by the fact of God's love for the world. The lifting up of the Son of man was the great provision made for human life. " God so loved the world," was the reason why that provision was made.

And once again in words commencing with the little word " For," and so linking what is said to what had been said, our Lord continued:

" For God sent not the Son into the world to judge the world; but that the world should be saved through Him."

This completed the revelation of heavenly things as it revealed the intention of the love of God in the lifting up of the Son of man.

Thus to summarise, in these sayings of Jesus we see Christianity facing the supreme necessity of human life:

" Except one be born from above, he cannot see the Kingdom of God ";

Christianity revealing the heavenly activities that meet the human need, the Son of man lifted up, because God loved the world, and His intention was that of saving the world.

So we come to the last of the three sayings referred to, the expository word of John concerning the work of our Lord; and from that saying we take merely its first declaration.

" The Father loveth the Son, and hath given all things into His hand."

Concerning this statement, " The Father loveth the Son," we call to mind that which is recorded later on in the Gospel, that Jesus Himself said:

" Therefore doth the Father love Me, because I lay down My life, that I may take it again."

That interprets the word of John:

" The Father loveth the Son, and hath given all things into His hand."

It is unnecessary to dwell upon that. The statement is final and supreme, and is thus interpreted by the words of our Lord.

Thus, once more to summarise in conclusion. The verities of our faith, of our mission, and of our message are all here declared. We first affirm the necessity for a new birth. Nothing else will meet the deepest need of human nature. No strenuous effort after good government, no attempt to ennoble by the subtleties of art, no attempt to realise life by the practices of ritualistic religion, are of any value. That is the message with which Christianity confronts the world.

When the necessity is realised, and the human mind enquires How can this be? the answer is to be found in the declaration that God so loved the world that He gave His Son to be lifted up, in order to the accomplishment of this impartation of life.

Thus Christianity is seen, cleansing the nature by a new birth, changing the person by the operation of a new life, and conditioning the whole by the mastery of the redeeming Lord.

JOHN XIV

IN dealing with this chapter and the following one, difficulties are created by the fact that neither is complete in itself. Chapter fourteen needs thirteen to a correct apprehension of its value; and fifteen demands sixteen in the same way.

At the thirty-sixth verse of chapter thirteen there begins a continuous account of the teaching of Christ, called forth by questions asked, or things said to Him by His disciples. Beginning there, we may set out the sequence thus; the question of Simon Peter (xiii. 36–xiv. 4); the protest of Thomas (xiv. 5-7); the appeal of Philip (xiv. 8-21); the enquiry of Jude (xiv. 22-31).

While this whole section is required, there is a sense in which chapter fourteen is complete in itself. The final words of chapter thirteen record things said to Peter personally. The pronouns are in the singular number. The opening words of chapter fourteen were words addressed to the whole of the disciples, this being revealed by the use of plural pronouns. This change from the singular to the plural does not mean, of course, that Peter was excluded from what our Lord was saying, but that all the others were included. So far as Peter is concerned, the connection is vital, and full of revealing beauty. Having told him personally that before the light of morning broke he would have denied his Master thrice, including him with all of them, He charged them not to let their hearts be troubled. So far as Peter was concerned, it is as though He said to him, I know the worst that is in you and how you will break down; but if you will trust in Me, I will realise all the highest and the best.

As we shall consider this chapter around these questions and words of the disciples, it may be well first to set them out in order, without note or comment.

SIMON PETER: " Lord, whither goest Thou? "

THOMAS: " Lord, we know not whither Thou goest; how know we the way? "

PHILIP: " Lord, show us the Father, and it sufficeth us."

JUDE: " Lord, what is come to pass that Thou wilt manifest Thyself unto us, and not unto the world? "

As we thus group them, a simple matter, and yet an important one, arrests our attention. Every one of these men addressed Him as Lord. Simon Peter called Him " Lord." Thomas called him " Lord." Philip called Him " Lord." Jude called Him " Lord."

The earlier part of chapter thirteen tells how when He had washed their feet, He had said unto them:

" Ye call Me Master and Lord; and ye say well; for so I am."

When they came to ask Him their questions, each one of them addressed Him in that way. Of course they had constantly called Him " Lord "; but the very circumstances make this an arresting fact. To them the hour must have been in many ways a strange one. The Passover Feast had been observed, and the New Feast instituted. Judas had been excluded. There must have rested upon them all a sense of solemn awe, and of much bewilderment. They were conscious of ignorance and perplexity; and in these four sayings they expressed the same; and at least in the case of one of them, in tones of protest. Nevertheless, each addressed Him as Lord, thus revealing their sense of relationship to Him. This very fact brings into prominence another fact, that, namely, of their freedom of utterance in His presence. They evidently spoke, without restraint, the things that were in their hearts. Peter's question would seem at first to have been a very simple one. As a matter of fact it was a very profound one. Thomas practically introduced his question by a protest against something his Master had said, declaring that they did not know where their Lord was going; and consequently could not know the way. Philip's word was the revelation of his sense that there was indefiniteness in what his Lord was saying. What Jude said revealed the fact of the perplexity of his mind in the presence of the Lord's new attitude towards the world.

These two things are certainly impressive, first their reverence for His authority; and secondly, the freedom with which they were able to speak to Him of the things that were troubling them.

And yet another matter of a general nature arrests us as we read this story. All the things they said to Him reveal the fact that in the presence of His imminent death, their minds were occupied not with matters upon the earthly level. Every utterance was born of the sense of infinite things, the things beyond, the mysteries that lay out of sight. It is quite evident that these men knew that what He had been telling them for six months was coming to pass. On the human level they saw Him surrounded by His enemies, and hemmed in on every side; and knew that the issue must be His death. Whenever men and women stand in the presence of death, this sense of that which lies beyond death in some way takes possession of the mind. So it was with these men. We hear the questioning of troubled hearts, peering out into the mystery of the life beyond, and speaking to Him as the result of that attitude of mind.

When Simon Peter said, " Lord, whither goest Thou? " he was not asking a geographical question. He knew full well that Jesus when He left that upper room, would inevitably be arrested, arraigned; and as He had been telling them from Cæsarea Philippi, would pass to suffering and to death. It was this consciousness which caused him to ask, " Whither goest Thou? " It is the very question that men and women are constantly asking, as they watch their own loved ones passing away from them. Whither away? What lies beyond?

The first movement in our Lord's answer was a very personal one as we have already said. He said, " Whither I go, thou canst not follow Me now; but thou shalt follow afterwards." To that Simon Peter replied, evidently realising that our Lord was still referring to His death:

" Lord, why cannot I follow Thee even now? I will lay down my life for Thee."

It was a great word, which taken in conjunction with the question he had asked, practically meant, Even though I am in ignorance of whither Thou art going, I am prepared to go with Thee. It was a perfectly sincere word, but one that proved his ignorance of himself? Our Lord's answer to him reveals this as He said:

" Wilt thou lay down thy life for Me? "

Is that your intention? Is that your understanding of yourself? I know you better than you know yourself. Before the light of morning breaks you will have denied Me thrice. Then continuing, and gathering all the disciples into His speech, He said:

" Let not your heart be troubled, ye believe God, believe Me."

Let it be carefully observed that so far He has not answered Peter's question, " Whither goest Thou? " Now He proceeded to do so.

" In My Father's house are many mansions; if it were not so, I would have told you; for I go to prepare a place for you."

That was the first line of His answer. " Whither goest Thou? " " I go to prepare a place for you." In saying this He still did not refer to any particular locality; He included all the universe; for that is the meaning of the phrase, " My Father's house." In the Father's house are " many abiding places." The earth itself is one of these; and He told them that if the earth were all, He would have said so. He was leaving it to enter another abiding place, and in doing so to prepare for their coming. Thus, in language characterised by the uttermost simplicity, He had revealed the sublime conception of the whole universe, as constituting the house of His Father, and had declared that in that house there are many abiding places. He was leaving these men to pass on to some other abiding place, to which they were presently to come. He did not attempt to tell them where that would be, for that was a secondary and unimportant matter. It was enough for them that He would be there, and that when they came, He would receive them. We may say in passing that He has fulfilled that in the case of every soul who, trusting in Him, has crossed the border line, and left behind this abiding place. Every one of His own that has come to the margin and crossed over, He has received on the other side. Ultimately that word of Jesus will apply to the final gathering of the elect at the Second Advent; but it has been true in the case of every individual who has, in His faith, come to the end of the pilgrimage. All such are absent from the body, and present with the Lord.

His final word in this connection was:

" Whither I go, ye know the way."

He did not say that they knew the place. Peter had wanted some definition of place, and in effect the Lord's reply to him was this, Do not let your heart be troubled about that kind of thing. My Father's house has many places for abiding. You know I am going to die, and are wondering where I shall be beyond death. The one thing of which you are to be sure is this, that if I am not in sight, I am still in the Father's house.

To that place, wherever it may be, He passed, as He said, to prepare a place for them. This of course did not mean in our earthly and material sense that He was going to prepare in the sense of equipping or furnishing a new region. Rather He meant that when the hour for their passing came, they would come to a place prepared for them by the fact of His presence there. He was going before, in order that when they arrived, even though all the surroundings might be unfamiliar, they would indeed feel at home because with Him.

That final word in answer to Simon Peter, "Whither I go, ye know the way," occasioned the protest of Thomas:

"Lord, we know not whither Thou goest; how know we the way?"

In these words Thomas revealed the same idea which had inspired the question of Peter, his ignorance of locality, and he argued that if the locality were not known, it was impossible to know the way by which men should travel to reach that destination. Thomas knew, as Peter did, that Jesus was about to die, and like Peter, was attempting to know what lay beyond death. He was asking for a statement of locality, and declaring that lacking that, there could be no understanding of the way.

To that word of Thomas came the answer:

"I am the way, and the truth, and the life; no one cometh unto the Father, but by Me."

By implication our Lord revealed the fact that in some new sense He was going to the Father. In such an answer any particular locality is excluded, but all the universe is included. In the light of this the stupendous nature of His claim is revealed. He was the Way to the Father, and He explicitly said, " no one cometh unto the Father, but by Me." Moreover, He said, " I am .. the Truth," that is, the Truth concerning the Father, and consequently the Truth concerning the whole universe. And yet again, "I am ... the Life," that is the very Life of the Father in which all the universe is sustained. If we would have a further interpretation of the tremendous nature of this word of Christ, it will be well to turn to Paul's letter to the Colossians, and its teaching concerning the relation of Christ to creation, and to all things.

It was at this point that Philip uttered the words:

"Show us the Father, and it sufficeth us."

There are senses in which this out-cry can only be apprehended as we remember the man who uttered it. Suffice it now to say of him that the cases where he appears in the writings of John reveal him as a quiet, silent sort of man, it may be slow in the up-take, and certainly not able to express himself with facility. As is so often the case, this kind of man, who cannot talk glibly, is thinking profoundly. In that hour of stress and strain, Peter having asked his question and been answered; Thomas having made his protest, and received reply; suddenly Philip said in effect, Yes, Lord, Thou speakest about going to the Father, but that is the ultimate problem. The very method of Philip's outburst seems to show that he felt that however great the problems of where our Lord was going, and of how to reach that place, they were only secondary to another. The supreme matter is that of being sure of God. "Show us the Father." In that word of Philip one hears the great, oft-times ignorant, but none the less definite cry of humanity.

Thus to understand the greatness of Philip's cry enables us to grasp the tremendous significance of the two-fold answer of Jesus thereto. He first of all declared that those who had seen Him had seen the Father; and then further, promised that He would send the Paraclete to interpret Him to them. He thus claimed that through His coming, ignorance of God would cease as a necessity of human experience. He would reveal the Father, and the Spirit would interpret the revelation to men.

Humanity is still asking for God. To that quest Jesus is the full and final answer. If man's vision of Him is not clear, the work of the Holy Spirit is that of making that vision clear. This is a matter of profound and abiding importance. All human interpretations of Jesus ultimately fail, and failing, so fail to see God. It is only through the Spirit's interpretation of the Christ, man comes to the revelation of the Father.

It was in this connection that He said that amazing thing to them that they should do greater works than He, seeing that He was going to the Father. His reference to His works was unquestionably to the things they had seen Him do on the earth-level; the things which perhaps we may refer to as miracles, operations in the realm of the supernatural. It is always a greater work to lead a soul into right relationship with God than to raise the dead physically. These greater works His followers have been doing through all the centuries, since He returned to the Father, and poured upon them the Holy Spirit.

Finally, Jude uttered his question, being evidently impressed by something which seemed strange to him. He had apprehended through the period of his association with his Lord, the fact of His great love for the world. It seemed to him that now, by these very hours in which he had left the world and devoted Himself to His disciples, He was abandoning the world. Why was He doing so?

Our Lord's answer to him was in some senses an involved one, implicating great truths. He declared:

"If a man love Me, he will keep My word; and My Father will love him, and We will come unto him, and make Our abode with him."

The emphasis throughout is that upon the fact of a new and intimate fellowship to be established between His Father, Himself, and His disciples. They were to remain in the world, and through them the truth concerning Himself and His Father would be manifested to the world. As He went on, He showed that so far from abandoning the world, the ultimate meaning of everything was that the world may believe, and that the world may know.

It was as though He said to Jude, I am not abandoning the world. The world is to have a new, a fuller revelation through those who love Me, and are working with Me in the fellowship of the Holy Spirit.

Then there fell upon their listening ears the great final word of peace.

" Peace I leave with you; My peace I give unto you; not as the world giveth, give I unto you. Let not your heart be troubled, neither let it be fearful."

His final word was a revelation of His sense of power over the forces that were against Him. Said He:

" The prince of the world cometh, and He hath nothing in Me."

This was followed by His declaration of ultimate purpose, " That the world may know," and of immediate procedure, " even so I do." That " even so I do " referred to all to which He was now passing, the Cross, which should be the place of His victory over the forces of evil that had blasted the world, and so the way to the Father, and all that His going to the Father meant for the disciples and the world.

It is interesting to notice how this chapter opens, and how it closes. The first words spoken to troubled hearts were:

" Let not your heart be troubled."

The last words spoken to those same men were words disturbing them, and calling them forth to new experiences:

" Arise, let us go hence."

We conclude our survey of the chapter by noticing something which is certainly interesting. In the fourth verse it is recorded that our Lord said to these men, " Ye know the way." In the seventh verse He said, Ye know the Father. In the seventeenth verse He declared that they knew the Holy Spirit. Now as a matter of fact these were the very things they did not seem to know.

Yet He declared that they did know them. In other words, it is true that these men knew more than they knew they knew. They thought they did not know the way, but they did, because they knew Him. They thought they did not know the Father, but they did, because they knew Him. They thought they did not know the Spirit, but they did, because they knew Him. What they needed was to explore the things they really knew, in order to discover how wonderful they were.

It is impossible to read this chapter without feeling its challenge, and being conscious of its encouragement. The men we have seen are remarkably representative men. As we have observed them gathered around the Lord, we have discovered their sense of His authority, in spite of the perplexities that were confronting them. We have listened to them talking to Him with a great freedom. All of which calls us to the same attitude of submission to His authority, and remission of all our perplexities to Him. We seem to hear Him saying to us also, " Ye believe in God, believe also in Me." It is in such fellowship that we learn the secret of the untroubled heart.

JOHN XV—XVI, 16

CHAPTER fourteen ended with the words of our Lord, "Arise, let us go hence," and undoubtedly at that point He and the disciples left the upper room. Where they went is open to question. There are those who believe that He led the disciples to the Temple, whose outer courts at that time of the year, as Passover approached, were left open during the night. There are others, who are inclined to the opinion, which I share, that they left the city, and that somewhere on the slopes of the hill, leading down to the brook Kidron, He uttered this great and final discourse.

In considering chapter fourteen we saw that the questions asked by His disciples were concerned with super-earthly matters, in view of the approaching death of their Lord. The fact which now arrests us is that in this discourse, having answered their questions, the Lord sharply brought them back again to the earth level, and their responsibilities in the world. There is a sense in which it may be at least suggested, that in doing so, He was giving a yet fuller reply to the suggestion of Jude that He was withdrawing from interest in the world. The whole burden of this discourse is that of a revelation of their coming relationship with Him in service. In the course of it He distinctly told them that He had chosen them that they should bear fruit. It is as though He was saying to them that while they had been looking on to that which lay beyond this life, and that quite properly, it was important that they should come back to the level of their present position, and coming responsibilities. In thus calling them to that level of consideration, He employed a great figure of speech, that of the vine; and then in prolonged discourse, interpreted that figure of speech.

First of all, the figure was given in all simplicity, and yet in all suggestiveness and sublimity. It is, therefore, of the utmost importance that we tarry with the figure in itself. In doing so, we must remind ourselves that it was no new figure of speech of which our Lord made use. We may listen to the declaration, "I am the Vine," accepting it as figurative, and attempt to interpret by what we know of the vine in itself. To do that, however, would be to miss one of the most important elements in our consideration.

Unquestionably the figure is first one from Nature, but it had already passed into use in a certain way, which must affect our consideration of it, as the Lord used it. In the Sacred Literature of the Hebrew people the figure is definitely found, and that in interesting relationships. At the time of our Lord's ministry, on the gates of the Temple there might be seen a golden vine; and its presence there was a revealing one. The vine had become, very definitely, the symbol of the national life. As to when it was so definitely adopted it is impossible to make a statement. If, however, we glance back to the Literature, we find the idea first suggested by Asaph in psalm eighty. A reading of that psalm will show that in some hour of national calamity, the singer spoke of the nation under the figure of a vine, which God had brought out of Egypt, and planted in the land. Certainly it is at that point that the figure of the vine emerges in Biblical Literature, and possibly as the direct result of that song, in time it became accepted as symbolic of the nation.

Quite evidently the prophets were familiar with the fact, and employed it. If we glance at them so far as is possible in a chronological sequence, we find both Hosea and Isaiah who were contemporary, employing it in that application. Hosea declared that Israel had become a luxuriant vine, bringing forth wrong fruit. Isaiah, in his song, beginning:

" Let me sing for my well-beloved a song of my beloved concerning his vineyard,"

quite definitely, and in interpretation, makes the vine the symbol of the national life. Jeremiah employed the same figure in one terrific statement, in which he declared that the nation had become " a degenerate vine." Ezekiel made use of it three times in the course of his prophesying, first in evident satire, when speaking to the people who were glorying in the fact that the vine represented the nation, asked them what was the good of the wood of the vine, declaring that its only value was that of fruit. It will be found that he, on two subsequent occasions, employed the same figure. The one certain thing is that in the time of our Lord the vine stood for the symbol of the national life.

Let this, then, be remembered as we listen to Him saying:

" I am the Vine, the true," and "I am the Vine, ye are the branches."

Moreover, our Lord Himself had already made use of the figure only a few days before that, when dealing with the rulers in the Temple He had uttered the parable of the vineyard, and of those husbandmen who had failed in the cultivation of the

vine. In connection with that parable it was that He uttered the
solemn words which excommunicated the Hebrew nation from
the office to which they had been called, and in which they had
failed; that namely of the representation of the Kingdom of God
to the world at large. It is well to remind ourselves in passing that,
that excommunication was final, and that because all in which the
nation had failed was now to be realised and fulfilled in Christ
Himself, and those associated with Him. In the words of excommunication He declared that the office should be now given to
" a nation bringing forth the fruits thereof." To this fact Peter
referred, when in his letter to members of the Church of God
he wrote:

> " Ye are an elect race, a royal priesthood, a holy nation,
> a people for God's own possession."

Having thus used the figure on this public occasion in the
Temple, He now, with His disciples gathered around Him, uttered
these words, " I am the Vine, the true." In our Versions we
translate His words, " I am the true Vine." While I do not
suggest that that is inaccurate, in the interest of adopting and
using an English idiom; I cannot help feeling in this case something
is lost by changing the form in which the words were actually
uttered by the Lord. " I am the Vine, the true." In that form
there is a suggestion of contrast, which is in danger of being
missed in the more general form. That suggestion of contrast
pointed at once to a recognition of failure, and a claim of fulfilment.
The nation whose symbol was the vine, had failed to fulfil its true
function; but now He, the Son of God and the true Messiah
claimed that in Him there would be fulfilment.

If we pause to glance again at the Old Testament literature
and the references already given, the fact of the failure of the
Hebrew nation is revealed. The passage in Isaiah v. is really the
central and classic one on the subject of the vine in the Old
Testament. In that passage, referring to the nation, especially
Judah, because he was a prophet to Judah, he declared that in
planting it as a vine, the act of God had been in order that it
should bring forth grapes, but it had brought forth wild grapes.
The vine planted to bear fruit, failed to bear the fruit it was
intended to bear.

After thus employing the figure, the prophet interpreted it
as he declared what the fruit was that God intended the nation
to bear. " He looked for judgment," " He looked . . . for
righteousness." Instead of " judgment " He found " oppression,"
and instead of " righteousness " He heard " a cry " of the
oppressed.

Two words in this interpretation reveal the Divine purpose and ideal. They are the words righteousness and judgment. The Hebrew nation was created in order that all the nations might be given righteousness and judgment. In other words, the Divine intention was that through that nation the principle of life which is righteousness, and the consequent practice of judgment should be revealed to humanity as a whole. In its history the nation had entirely broken down in this matter. Within its own borders, instead of righteousness, oppression existed, and for lack of judgment or equity, the cry of the oppressed was heard. Therefore the nations of the world were not being supplied with the things essential to their being, and their well-being. Because of this failure the nation was rejected as the vine of God.

Thus again we listen to the words of Jesus, " I am the Vine, the true," thus claiming to be the One through Whom the Divine purpose would be fulfilled, and righteousness and judgment placed at the disposal of the world. When we pass on into the completion of the discourse contained in the sixteenth chapter, when speaking of the world our Lord said that when the Spirit of truth was come, He would convict the world in respect of sin, of righteousness, of judgment. The conviction concerning sin is conviction of failure and breakdown. The conviction concerning righteousness and judgment is conviction concerning the two great matters essential to human well-being, for which the world was, and is, supremely waiting. His claim then was that through Him these matters of righteousness and judgment should be realised, manifested, and placed at the disposal of the world. Interpreting His statement concerning the work of the Spirit in the world, He had declared that the revelation of righteousness should come through His going to the Father; and of judgment as possible, because of His victory over the prince of the world, through whom all the misgovernment and misery of human life had occurred.

Thus He stood in the midst of human history and declared that God's purpose was not failing, that His intention would be carried out, that He was the Vine through Whom these things would come to complete fulfilment. The majesty of the claim is self-evident; and the high privileges and responsibilities of His own are revealed in the fact that He incorporated that group of men with Himself as the instrument of Divine realisation as He said, " I am the Vine, ye are the branches."

In the uttering of those words our Lord revealed in the most remarkable and complete manner, the unity which would exist between Himself and His own. Other New Testament figures of speech set forth the same truth, but none more succinctly or perfectly than this.

For a brief moment let us listen to Him without prejudice, and attempt to understand in the simplest way, what He said. First, take the sentence, " I am the Vine," and in connection with it another " I am the Vine, ye are the branches." Now how do we mentally interpret that? If we were attempting to interpret it to children, we might draw a picture of a vine. Having drawn it, how should we explain its suggestiveness? I think we should be at least in danger of failing. We might point first to the main stem of the vine, and then to all the branches, and we might say that that main stem of the vine represents Christ, through Whom all the life forces pulse; and then we might naturally enough say that the branches represent His people. Now, whereas there are elements of truth in such an explanation, it fails to grasp the full significance of the first declaration. Our Lord did not say, I am the main stem of the vine, but " I am the Vine." What, then, is the vine? Everything: root, stem, branches, tendrils, leaves, fruit. Thus in the first declaration our Lord claimed that through Him there would be the carrying out of the Divine purpose. The nation had failed, but He, after the flesh the Child of the nation, the Seed of David, would not fail.

That being borne in mind, we may properly consider the second declaration, " I am the Vine, ye are the branches." Now it is impossible to find any figure of speech at once more suggestive, more complete than that. If He be the Vine in its entirety, every branch becomes part of Himself. To that first group of men He declared that they were so bound up in His life as to be one with Him, and one with Him in order to the fulfilment of the Divine purpose.

This being recognised, we at once look at the branches, and discover that they are the instruments for the bringing forth of fruit. The fruit is the outcome of the whole life of the vine. The branch is the instrument for the providing of fruit. The world is waiting for righteousness, and judgment as the practice of it, through Christ, as He is in Himself, and as He is fulfilled in purpose through those who are united to Him, as branches in the vine.

Thus there emerges our Lord's conception of the function of His Church in the world. In that connection His words are full of arresting solemnity:

" Apart from Me, ye can do nothing."

The Church cannot bear the fruit the world is waiting for if severed from Christ.

In this connection let me say with reverent reticence that the implicate of all this is a very arresting one. It is that while He declared " Severed from Me, ye can do nothing," it is equally true that apart from His Church, He cannot accomplish His purposes. As branches in living union with the vine are for the bearing of fruit, the vine must have branches for the growing of fruit. If our Lord has been and still is being limited in any measure it is because the branches are failing. To change the figure, and maintain the teaching. The Church is the body of Christ. It is only through her eyes that He can look upon men; only through her hands He can touch them; only by her feet that He can run on His errands in the world to-day.

We pass now to a very rapid survey of the interpretation found in what remains of our Lord's teaching. To begin with, He declared that of this vine His Father is the Husbandman. It is at least an arresting fact the only place where this word " husbandman " occurs is in the parable in Matthew, in which, while dealing with the wicked husbandmen, who had failed to produce fruit, He compelled them to the finding of a verdict, and the passing of a sentence upon themselves. These having now failed, He now says, " My Father is the Husbandman." It is as though He had declared that in the new economy, all intermediation ended, Himself and His own are to have direct dealings with God. In those dealings there will be the operation of pruning and cleansing, in order to the bearing of fruit.

The responsibility devolving upon us is that of abiding. Concerning that I want to say two of the simplest things. The first is that abiding does not mean making an effort, but ceasing to make an effort. Effort is necessary to come into any place or relationship. Effort may be necessary to leave that place, or to sever that relationship. The second thing is that abiding does not necessarily mean consciousness of the fact, in what I may speak of as the upper reaches of consciousness. Nevertheless it is always there, and in any crisis that underlying consciousness manifests itself.

When we abide, the first result is that we may demand what we will, and it will be done. This means that to abide in Him is to desire only the things which are in harmony with His will and purpose. Under the mastery of that inspiration, prayer becomes such definite co-operation with God, as to bear fruit.

It was in connection with this teaching that He declared to these men that henceforth He would call them no longer slaves, but friends. In the realisation and maintenance of that relationship of intelligent co-operation lies the secret of prevailing prayer, and of fruit-bearing.

Such a relationship maintained must mean to the disciples suffering in a world wrongly constituted. This must be inevitable, because the world loves its own; and those living in fellowship with Christ and God do not belong to the world. Their outlook is not the worldly outlook. Their inspiration is not the worldly inspiration. The world is living wholly in the realm of the material. Christ and His own, touch the world familiarly, but always from the standpoint of relationship to the spiritual and the heavenly. He reminded them that all this had been demonstrated in the fact that He had been persecuted by the world, and that therefore they could not hope to escape the same experience.

It was in this connection that He declared to them that it was better for them that He should go away. The world is revealed in its darkness and hostility. They are to bear fruit for the world. They could only do so in the fellowship of the Holy Spirit; and His going away was the means by which that Spirit would be granted to them in fullness. The result of the coming of the Spirit for the world would be through them in co-operation with the Spirit, the truth concerning sin, righteousness and judgment would be made known to the world. This is what Peter meant when subsequently he said:

" We are witnesses of these things, and so is the Holy Spirit."

Finally, He revealed the relationship they would bear to the Paraclete, and the Paraclete to them. This He began by saying to them:

" I have yet many things to say unto you, but ye cannot bear them now."

That however was not the final word, but rather this:

" Howbeit, when He, the Spirit of truth is come, He shall guide you into all the truth."

This great word found its fulfilment on the day of Pentecost, and processionally through all the following period. The work of the Spirit is ever that of guiding the Church of God into the truth, revealing to them the way, interpreting to them the Christ Himself. His final words were:

" A little while, and ye behold Me no more,"

a reference to the fact that by the way of the Cross He was passing out of the vision which they had had of Him in the days of His flesh. And then:

"And again a little while, and ye shall see Me,"

a reference to this very clear and final interpretation of Him which they would receive by the coming of the Holy Spirit. So ended the great discourse.

Necessarily the rest of this chapter sixteen must be read. We find the disciples arrested by His term " a little while." He interpreted His meaning to them, and then uttered that stupendous word that covers all the facts of His mission.

"I came out from the Father, and am come into the world; again I leave the world, and go unto the Father."

"I came out from the Father," that is the story of the nativity; "I am come into the world," that includes all the fact of His ministry; "I leave the world," that refers to the fact of His Passion consummated in resurrection; "I go unto the Father," that is the declaration of His coming ascension, as the result of which the Spirit was to be given, and that little group of men, representing the sacramental host through the coming age, are made one with Him.

JOHN XVII

TO approach this chapter without a sense of awe, would demonstrate ignorance of its setting, or unfitness for its consideration.

Our Lord's public ministry was completed. He had no more to say to the world. That is what He meant when, in the course of this communion with His Father He said that He had accomplished the work the Father had given Him to do *on the earth*. He had not then accomplished the full work which He came to do. That accomplishment could only come as He was lifted up out of the earth. On the earth level His work was over. He had wrought His last wonder. He had uttered His last word to the listening multitudes. Furthermore, He had no more to say to His disciples. His final word to them was full of significance,

" Be of good cheer; I have overcome the world."

Nothing remained now but the lifting up out of the earth by the way of the Cross and the Resurrection. To that His face was set. Clouds were gathering around Him. He knew the force of the storm that was about to break upon Him; and it was with that knowledge, and in that connection He entered into communion with His Father.

The record of this communion falls naturally into three parts. In the first movement (verses 1–5) it was communion concerning Himself. In the second movement (verses 6–19), His communion was concerned with the group that were round about Him at the time, the men, as He said, whom the Father had given Him " out of the world." The third movement (verses 20–26) records communion concerning all who were to believe on Him through the apostolic word, that is the whole Christian Church.

For the purpose of our present meditation, I do not propose to attempt any examination of the details of this threefold movement. It is my intention rather to consider the chapter in the light of its revelation of our Lord's desire for, and interpretation of, the unity of His Church.

In some senses this is indeed the master thought of this chapter. It is self-evident that as He was going away to complete His mission on the Cross, and beyond that, to carry on His work through the coming age, this was the desire of His heart concerning that Church. The fact of that unity had already been revealed in the great allegory of the Vine. In this hour of His communion with His Father there is granted to us an unveiling of His thinking concerning it.

Three matters therefore demand our attention; first, that of the nature of the unity of the Church; secondly, that of the method of that unity; and thirdly, that of the purpose thereof. Our method will be that of taking out certain sentences which bear on these aspects of the unity from the words of our Lord.

As to the nature of the unity, we glance on to verse 21:

" That they may all be one; even as Thou, Father, art in Me, and I in Thee, that they also may be in Us."

The unity of the Church, therefore, which He desired, was a unity on the pattern of the unity in Deity; that is, the unity existing between Himself and His Father. That unity being a unity in essence, was a unity of thought. Let it at once be said that a statement like this reveals a fact that transcends the possibility of our complete apprehension. Here a higher type and method of life is revealed than anything we can find in what we commonly speak of as the realm of Nature. There is nothing whatever in Nature comparable to this kind of unity. Necessarily although the statement of our Lord here, referred only to His Father and Himself, we find ourselves in the realm of the mystery of the Trinity. Of that mystery we have no perfect analogy in Nature. The unity between the Father and the Son is that of two personalities, having identity of consciousness. We may pause here to remark that our use of the word personality may limit our thinking, because we interpret by what we know of personality in human life. Here we have two consciousnesses that for ever merge in perfect harmony, so that the thinking of the Father is ever the thinking of the Son, and the thinking of the Son is ever the thinking of the Father. The great fact is disclosed by suggestion, even though we may not be able fully to apprehend it. His desire therefore for His Church was that it might consist of men and women of whom this is true, multitudes of individuals, yet sharing a common life, creating a common consciousness.

If we glance further down to verse 23, we read:

" I in them, and Thou in Me, that they may be perfected into one."

Here the thought is that of unity of essence, which we have already referred to, and taken for granted. This is the secret of the unity of consciousness, both in Deity, and in the Church.

In the apostolic writings, perhaps especially in those of Paul, we are constantly finding remarkable interpretations of things said by our Lord. A careful study of the first and second chapters of the Colossian letter will show how, in the course of his argument, Paul used the word " mystery " three times. If the process of thought by this repetition is followed, it will be found that he first uses the word in connection with the Church, " the mystery," which is the Church. Then he uses the word in connection with the individual Christian experience, " The mystery . . . Christ in you, the hope of glory." Until a little later he speaks of " the mystery of God, even Christ." In this line of argument we have the apostolic interpretation of this conception of unity, as revealed in the words of our Lord. If we take that statement of Paul, beginning at the point where he ended, we have first the fact that Christ is the Mystery of God; secondly, that Christ formed in the believer constitutes the mystery of individual experience; and finally, that the whole body of those in whom Christ is thus formed, constitutes the mystery of the Church. Thus the unity of the Church is of the essence of the unity in the Godhead.

In this thought of our Lord we have revealed then the deepest truth concerning the unity of the Church; and when once we grasp the fact of that unity, we shall cease to be very much concerned about matters of uniformity, or unanimity. Uniformity is after all a matter of ecclesiastical arrangement, and there may be room for infinite variety there. Unanimity is a matter of mental apprehension, and because of the finiteness of human thinking, may be unattainable at present. Unity, however, is a matter of the essential spirit life as revealed in the unity between the Father and the Son.

Such consideration is in itself full of significance, as it gives an interpretation of individual Christian experience, showing that no human being can be a member of the Church who is not born from above. Nothing less than that new birth can bring men and women into living union with Him and the Father, or with each other. It is only by the communication of this new Divine life that there can be any entry upon, or realisation of unity.

And once more on this subject of the nature of the unity, we shall discover in the words of our Lord a threefold progressive unity. Glancing back to verse eleven, where He was praying for the first group, everything He asked for them has equal application to every subsequent group of believers. He said:

" And I am no more in the world, and these are in the world, and I come to Thee. Holy Father, keep them in Thy name which Thou hast given Me, that they may be one, even as We are."

Here the reference to the unity between the Father and the Son was not so much to the vital and essential things with which we have already been dealing, as to the level of experience and manifestation. The Father and the Son were one in thought; They were one in purpose; They were one in will; They were one in ministry and service. The Father and the Son never acted in separation from each other. The thinking of each was ever the thinking of the other. The purpose of the Father and the purpose of His Son were identical. The will of the Father and the will of the Son had no rupture. The work of the Father and the work of the Son were the same. " My Father worketh even until now, and I work," He said to His critics at the beginning, and the statement clearly indicated identity of action.

His prayer then for that first group of men was that they might be one in that way, one in thought, one in purpose, one in will, one in service. All those born again from above are become united with the thought of God and His Son, the purpose of God and His Son, the will of God and His Son, and the service of God and His Son. In the Church, the realm of human experience is to be lifted into fellowship with the Divine, and must react on the matter of inter-relationship within the Church. We are one with each other, because we are one with the Father and the Son; and the unity existing between us is that of the unity existing between Them.

This whole conception and fact gives weight to the apostolic injunction with which we are familiar:

> " Be ye stedfast, unmoveable, always abounding in the work of the Lord."

Let it be emphasised, " in the work of the Lord," which is far more than attempting to do something for the Lord. This petition used in reference to the first group has persistent application to every subsequent group, that is to say, to any and every local church.

When later He prayed, thinking of the whole Church, He said:

> " That they may all be one; even as Thou, Father, art in Me, and I in Thee, that they also may be in Us."

It is quite evident that His thought then was sweeping across the whole age. We realise that.

> " Part of the host have crossed the flood,
>   And part are crossing now,"

while many of us are still in the midst of life and service. He prayed for a unity running through the decades and the centuries, until the hour of His Advent, a unity binding all believers together, however separated by time, or by space. The emphasis of thought here is upon the continuity of the union of all believers with Him and with the Father, this of course creating and conditioning the unity existing between all Christians from then until now, and to the consummation.

The last phase in the revelation of progressive unity is found in verses 22 and 23:

" And the glory which Thou hast given Me I have given unto them; that they may be one, even as we are one; I in them, and Thou in Me, that they may be perfected into one."

In these words our Lord was not referring to an immediate realisation of the perfection of unity, but to a process which should lead to the ultimate realisation. His eyes were looking on towards the consummation, towards an hour in which that which is now perfect in certain senses, having been processionally maintained in perfection, in other senses, shall come at last to a final realisation and manifestation of perfection in unity.

We may take this threefold revelation of progressive unity, and express it thus. Jesus prayed first for the local Church, then for the catholic Church, and then for the perfected and glorified Church; and in every aspect the thought is that of a unity, the nature of which is discovered in the unity between Himself and His Father.

The method of the unity is full of arresting significance. There are times when surveying the history of the Church, or looking round about upon present conditions, we might be tempted to wonder whether the desires of our Lord, as revealed, are possible of realisation. Therefore it is well to note carefully what He says on this matter. In verse 20 we read:

" Neither for these only do I pray, but for them also that believe on Me through their word."

We have already more than once quoted these words. We quote them again to emphasise the fact of His intercession. If we had no other warrant than this for being sure of the possibility of realisation in itself, it would be enough. His intercession was based upon His accomplishment of the Father's purpose in and through Him. In the process of this prayer He referred to His work. It was that of giving eternal life (verses 2–4); it was that of manifesting the name of God (verse 6); it was that of giving men the words of God (verse 8).   On the basis of His accomplishment of all these things, He prayed this prayer.

Moreover, the method of the unity is not only that of the intercession of our Lord, but that of the gift which He bestows upon men (verses 22–23).   The gift He bestowed was that of the perfect vision of the Father which transfigures all life by a revelation of the unity of all being.

Finally, therefore, the method of the unity is the declaration of the name of the Father through the Son.   This He refers to as accomplished, " I have made it known "; as progressive, " I will make it known "; and as to its result, " that the love wherewith Thou lovedst Me may be in them."

Finally, we discover the purpose of the unity.   This is to be found revealed in verses 21 and 23:

" That the world may believe,"
" That the world may know."

The first is progressive, and the second is final.   " That the world may believe."   The demonstration of the Divinity of the mission of Christ is to be found in the vital unity of the Church. The process of the world's believing depends upon the manifestation of the unity of the Church with God and with His Son; and consequently, the manifestation of the unity within its own borders.

Then when looking on to the consummation of unity in the perfected Church, made up of perfected individuals, perfectly realising communion with each other, perfectly co-ordinating; then will come the demonstration that is beyond question, " that the world may know."

We have not yet reached that consummation.   Nevertheless the measure in which the world believes is the measure in which it has the demonstration of the nature and power of the Father and the Son through the Church.

When Tennyson wrote:

" We have but faith, we cannot know,"

I am ever inclined to feel that the statement is inadequate.   At any rate it may certainly be declared that because we have faith, we know; and it is certain that the world will come to know in proportion as it believes; and it will come to believe, and so to knowledge, in the measure in which the unity of the Church becomes a revelation of God.

It is impossible to follow the revealing thought of this chapter without some sense of humiliation taking possession of the soul. We cannot be surprised if sometimes the world says to us, When you have settled your differences within the Church we may consider your message.

Nevertheless, I am not inclined to leave the matter on a note that sounds like one of despair. The unity of the Church is a fact, and a fact which has affected, and still is affecting the world. Realising in many senses the failure of the Church to manifest this fact of unity, it is well to remember that the fact is still in existence.

More than half a century ago I was standing with my father, as he was talking to one of the world's great saints, Robert Chapman. My father was speaking in tones of sadness concerning the breakup of the Church into its various and ever-varying sections, when Robert Chapman said this to him,

"Yes, that is true, but it is good for us to remember that God holds in His own hand the golden bowl of the Church's unity unbroken. The earthly replica committed to us we have smashed to atoms."

The Lord's prayer that the Church might be one was certainly answered in its deepest meaning. The Church is one. Deeper down than all our differences is this unity, and it is the power that is bringing men into the realm of belief, and the power, therefore, which is moving towards the world's certainty about Jesus.

Perhaps the final note in our meditation should be concerned with the matter of individual responsibility. The question each should ask is, How far am I, as a living member of the Church of God, helping to the realisation of the ideal, and its manifestation to the world? Perhaps the whole matter may be expressed in simplest fashion by the citation of a couplet which, though lacking in poetical accuracy, does give expression to a matter of supreme importance:

"What sort of a Church would my Church be,
If every member were just like me?"

JOHN XIX

THIS chapter is one of the great chapters concerning the mystery of the Cross. In our series of studies we have already considered Matthew xxvii, which was concerned with the same subject. In this chapter, then, we have John's account of the Crucifixion and burial of the One Whom he described at the beginning of his treatise as "the Word made flesh." As in the case of the Matthew chapter, consideration of this one, demands a recognition of more than itself, in order to a complete understanding of what it records. The full account of the death of our Lord requires chapters eighteen and nineteen. Very briefly, then, let us first summarize the content of chapter eighteen, and the first part of nineteen, as introducing the actual story of the Cross.

In chapter eighteen we have the story of the Garden, of the betrayal by Judas, of the coming of the cohort to arrest our Lord, and of Peter's sincere but mistaken impulse when he drew a sword, and smote the servant of the high priest. These matters occupy the first eleven verses. From verse twelve to the sixteenth verse of chapter nineteen, we have John's account of the trials of our Lord, first before the priests, in the course of which the voice of Peter is heard thrice denying his Lord, and then before Pilate. The supreme matter of this chapter then begins with the declaration that after the trials, Pilate delivered Jesus to those who were clamouring for His blood, to be crucified.

Whereas there are very clearly marked differences between Matthew's story and this of John, the similarity between them is equally evident. In essence they both present the Cross in the same way. John, as I think we shall see as we proceed, admits us to the inner mystery more definitely than does either Matthew, or Mark, or Luke. Nevertheless the general outlook of John is identical with that of Matthew. As in Matthew's account, so here, the two sides of the event are clearly marked, the human and the Divine. Therefore we may make our division of the story, and our method of consideration the same as those employed when considering Matthew's story.

We have first of all the Crucifixion in verses 16 to 27, that is, the human side; then in a brief paragraph of only three verses, 28–30, we have the Cross, that is, the Divine side. The final section in the chapter, verses 31-42 are concerned with the dead body of Jesus, and what men did with it.

In this meditation I do not propose to consider the story in detail, but rather to contemplate its presentation of the Cross, reverently and quietly both on the human and Divine sides. The human revelation deals with the Cross from the standpoint of earthly history and earthly attitudes, a; an earthly activity. The Divine unveiling is granted to us, and in it we are able to rise above the earth level, and see it from the heavenly standpoint.

The first matter in the record in verses 16 to 18 is that of the deed in itself, and the first statement in connection with that immediately arrests our attention.

" Then, therefore, he delivered Him unto them to be crucified," (16a).

Carefully considered, this is followed by a most suggestive, and indeed an arresting declaration. " They took Jesus therefore." The idea of the Greek verb there is that they received Him. Pilate delivered Him up, and on the basis of that, they took Him. The statement means that Pilate handed Jesus over into the hands of those who, through hatred and clamour and madness, had cried out for His death. " They received Him," and from their standpoint they did so, intending to do with Him as they willed. In a sense, moreover, that is what they did. It is well here however to pause and remember that even then, so far as human compulsion was concerned, He need not have gone to the Cross. Only a little while before as Matthew records (Matthew xxvii. 53) in the garden, in rebuke of Peter, He had said:

" Thinkest thou that I cannot beseech My Father, and He shall even now send Me more than twelve legions of angels? "

In this statement He revealed His consciousness that He was not caught in a trap laid by men. This gives the full interpretation of the statement, that when they received Jesus, " He went out, bearing the Cross for Himself, unto the place called The place of a skull, which is called in Hebrew, Golgotha." " He went out for Himself." Our thinking is always at fault if at this point we conceive of our Lord as a Victim. He is rather seen as a Victor, proceeding on His own triumphant way. It is quite true that on what we may speak of as the human level, judged by the statements possible to the mere historian, who can only see the things on the earthly level, they took Him to the place of crucifixion. Once more, we seriously remind ourselves that so far as their action was concerned, He need not have gone. As in the course of His ministry more than once, when they would have used violence to Him, He passed through the midst of them, and they could lay no hands upon Him, so it might have happened now. Whatever follows, therefore, is to be viewed in the light of this declaration that He, Whom John ever saw as " the Word made flesh," went forth bearing His own Cross.

Once again we are impressed here, as indeed in the story of each evangelist, with the solemn reticence of the method employed to describe the fact of the crucifying. John merely writes, " They crucified Him." " *He* went out "; " *they* crucified Him." He moved towards the ultimate in His work, of His own volition, fulfilling by that action what He had said to them on an earlier occasion, " No one taketh My life from Me . . I lay it down of Myself." If it may seem as though this were an over-emphasis, let it be at once declared that it is of supreme importance that we for ever get away from the idea of the Cross that speaks of it, or approaches it, in any sense as an hour of defeat in the work of our Lord. He is seen moving along a fore-ordained path in fellowship with the eternal counsel and purpose of God. " He went out, bearing the Cross for Himself "; " They crucified Him."

When referring to the action of men, John says:

" They crucified Him, and with Him two others, on either side one, and Jesus in the midst."

Thus He is seen in the midst of two others. From the other evangelists we learn that these were malefactors, robbers, violent characters, who according to the testimony of one of them in his dying hour were receiving the just rewards of their deeds. When they crucified Jesus they put Him in the midst; and on the earthly level there is significance in that fact. In Roman executions, the chief criminal was always placed in the centre. Thus they gave Him the place, when they crucified Him, of the One supreme in guilt. This was an unjustifiable action from the human standpoint. Witness the trials before the priests and Pilate, that no one had been able to suggest that He had ever used violence to His fellow men, or wronged them in any way. Yet they gave Him the place of the supreme malefactor.

Here, almost with bated breath, I would say from the standpoint of His intention of bearing sin, that was His right place. " Behold, the Lamb of God, Which taketh away the sin of the world." He was the incarnate Representative then and there of all human sin, and thus what was an insult from the standpoint of the human, was the recognition of an appalling and supreme fact in the Divine procedure.

Continuing to look at the deed on the human level, we are arrested by the story of John concerning the superscription they had placed over His head. It is well to notice that John tells us that Pilate wrote that himself. Whereas that may mean that he ordered it to be written, John's method of statement inclines me to the conviction that he took the stylus in his own hand and wrote the superscription himself. One cannot read it without wondering what really was in the mind of Pilate. It is perfectly evident that he wrote it out of supreme contempt for the Jewish people, and hatred of their priests. Nevertheless when the priests protested, he said, " What I have written I have written." One is inclined to speak to Pilate imaginatively across the centuries and say, ' Yes, Pilate, what you have written you have written; but when you wrote there was a Power behind you higher in authority than you or your Imperator, and you wrote better than you knew.' The ultimate value of the superscription is its revelation that Jesus was a Fulfilment of the purpose of God in the Hebrew nation from the very beginning. That nation had failed, had rejected Him and cast Him out; and yet out of all the failure, Behold, the King of the Jews, and therefore the One Who in fulfilment of Divine intention was the desire of all nations.

Still looking on the human side, we turn our eyes to the watchers. John refers only to soldiers and friends. The soldiers were dividing the spoils. Four men had evidently been employed in the act of crucifixion, and these took His garments and divided them into four parts, until their eyes fell upon that wondrous robe woven from the top to the bottom. As their eyes rested upon it they said:

" Let us not rend it, but cast lots for it, whose it shall be."

John who watched all, evidently saw the fulfilment of great words of the Old Testament Scriptures, with which he was familiar, to three of which he referred:

" They parted my garments among them,
     And upon my vesture did they cast lots " (Psalm
         xxii. 18);
" A bone of him shall not be broken " (Exodus xii. 46);
and
" They shall look on him whom they pierced " (Zechariah
         xii. 10).

The friends of Jesus consisted of four women named, His Mother, her sister, the wife of Clopas, and Mary Magdalene. John, of course, was there also. Although we have no means of definitely knowing, it is almost certain that other disciples at a distance were also watching. The stories of Matthew and Mark are certainly those of eye-witnesses. Thus while soldiers gambled, lovers watched.

Now we pass to the second movement in the story, which while very brief as to its wording, is of supreme importance.

It opens with the words:

" After this, Jesus knowing that all things are now finished, that the Scripture might be accomplished, saith, I thirst."

The words " After this " refer of course to the crucifixion, and to what John tells us of our Lord's committal of His Mother to the care of John. Between that and this statement in all probability very nearly three hours had passed, the whole period of the darkness. We think of those passing hours with profound reverence. Moreover our thinking of them is quite hopeless in one sense. We cannot fathom that darkness. Let it be remembered that John has not recorded the cry that escaped His lips at the close of the three hours, that haunting cry:

" My God, My God, why hast Thou forsaken Me? "

into which there was gathered up and expressed, so far as it ever can be expressed, all that those three hours had meant. John takes up his story at the close of that period, and it is of the utmost importance that we notice the way in which he records the cry of human suffering, " I thirst." He is careful to point out that He did not say this until " knowing that all things are now finished." He knew that for which He went to the Cross, whatever it was, was completed, before He said, " I thirst." Thus, in a very remarkable way, we are admitted to the mind, or perhaps we should say, the consciousness of Jesus at the end of those three hours. This consciousness was not in any sense that of defeat, but rather that of complete victory in accomplishment. The word " finished " in the statement, " Knowing that all things are now finished," is the same verb employed when presently He said, " It is finished." The point of emphasis at the moment is this, that He knew all things were finished before He said, " I thirst."

At this point, quite properly, the objection may be made, that when He said this He was not dead; and the question asked as to whether it is not true that we are saved by His death. The very pertinence of the question leads to the discovery of the fact that when we speak of being saved through the death of our Lord, we must remember that the reference is not primarily to His physical death, but to something far more profound, some mystery of death in the darkness, which was already accomplished.

My mind goes back to an occasion some years ago, when John Henry Jowett preached from the text, "It is Christ that died." No one who heard that sermon I think will ever forget the power of the message in which he showed that in the profoundest sense of the word, that death was lonely and unique; something infinitely beyond the merely physical.

I, at least, am entirely incompetent to attempt anything like a philosophic interpretation of the fact, but the fact is that whatever the transaction of the Cross was in the economy of God, it was accomplished before the hour of physical dying. The word accomplished means not merely over, but completed, rounded out to perfect realisation. It was when our Lord knew that this was so that He said, "I thirst."

After receiving the vinegar, He said, "It is finished." He knew it was finished before He said, "I thirst." He declared it to be so after that cry of human agony had escaped His lips.

Here, I repeat, we are in the realm of infinite mystery because:

"The light . . . is too bright,
For the feebleness of a sinner's sight."

If here we are conscious of blindness, it is caused not by darkness, but by the excess of light. Out there, somewhere in the loneliness of complete isolation, God in Christ wrought and completed that which He came to do, when He was born of a Virgin into human history, when He was "made flesh." The Infinite is seen in perfect co-operation with the finite, and revealing the infinite things through the finite. The Divine touched, dwelt, and acted within the human. There came the moment when the Flesh, the human, said, "I thirst"; and the Word, the Divine, said, "It is finished."

Then came the last act. He yielded up His spirit. No man took His life away. His dying on the human level became the sacramental symbol of the death in the realm of the Divine. This being accomplished, He "gave up His spirit." When He had completed that for which He had passed to the Cross, He yielded up His spirit. In passing it may once more be observed that neither Matthew nor Mark nor Luke nor John speak of what we describe as dying, as dying. They all speak rather of the action in which He yielded up His spirit. Moreover, another of the evangelists tells us that He did so with a word of perfect fellowship with God of assumed and eternal relationship with Him, as He said:

"Father, into Thy hands I commend My spirit."

In conclusion, we glance at the last section of the chapter, which has to do with the dead body of Jesus. As we look at this we see that which was an offence to the Jews, His enemies, precious to His lovers.

His enemies linked Him with the malefactors, and observing punctiliously the ceremonies and ritual of a decadent religion, sought burial, " that the bodies should not remain upon the cross on the Sabbath." They went to Pilate, in order that these bodies might be put out of sight. To them the dead body of Jesus was an offence.

On the other hand we see the lovers of the Lord, Joseph or Arimathæa, a disciple in secret " for fear of the Jews." He was evidently a wealthy man, who had prepared for himself a tomb in a garden. Into that garden, and into that tomb they took the dead body of the Lord. There ever seems to be a poetic significance in the declaration of John:

" In the place where He was crucified there was a garden."

At least we may observe that wherever the Crucified has come, gardens have sprung into beauty. In this act of burial Joseph was joined by Nicodemus, another disciple in some senses in secret, at least he is never seen with the company of the disciples until now.

Gathered around that dead body, His enemies thought everything was over, and they were glad. His lovers thought that everything was over, and were sad. But love performed the last sweet rites for that dead body. It is worthy of observation that after His enemies had nailed Him to His Cross, no hand other than the hand of a lover touched the body of Jesus. Loving hands took Him from the Cross, carried Him to the garden, wound Him round as the manner of the Jews is to bury, and laid Him in the tomb.

There this chapter ends, with a dead body in a rock-hewn tomb, in a garden. If that were all, the flowers in the garden must perish, and the rock crumble away, and the sacred dust be lost. If that is the end, then we are of all men most pitiable. But thank God, the story is not over. Chapter twenty completes it.

JOHN XX

WE ended our study of chapter nineteen in the Gospel of John, standing by a new tomb in a garden, around the dead body of Jesus. In ending that study we said that if that were the end, we were of all men most pitiable; but the story was not over. Chapter twenty completes it. We now come to that chapter. It gives John's account of the central fact in the history and ministry of our Lord.

In the Revised Version the chapter begins with the word, " Now." As a matter of fact there is no such word in the Greek New Testament, but it certainly is rightly introduced, being at once adversative and connective; that is to say, indicating the fact of continuity, and yet of something entirely fresh. John's writing is certainly continuous, and may thus be rendered as to the close of the one chapter and the beginning of the other.

" There, then, because of the Jews' Preparation (for the tomb was nigh at hand) they laid Jesus. On day one of the week came Mary Magdalene early."

The break between is so evident that the introduction of the word " Now " or " But " is of value. The whole character of the chapter is thus suggested as being one of continuity and yet change. The necessary and inevitable issue of the Cross was the resurrection. That is continuity. The fact of the resurrection, however, stands in striking contrast to that of the Cross. The writer now calls us from the gloom of the tomb to the glory of the resurrection.

With this chapter the systematic work of John's writing comes to conclusion. There is another chapter of the nature of a postcript, which we shall have under consideration later. The last two verses of the chapter constitute the writer's interpretation of his work. The ultimate climax is reached in the confession of Thomas and the answer of Jesus (verses 28–29).

The Gospel opened with the impressive and inclusive declaration:

" In the beginning was the Word, and the Word was with God, and the Word was God . . . And the Word became flesh, and dwelt among us, and we beheld His glory (glory as of the Only Begotten from the Father) full of grace and truth . . . No man hath seen God at any time; the only begotten Son, Which is in the bosom of the Father He hath declared Him."

Beyond that opening statement, John's writing proceeded in a selection of signs by way of interpretation and demonstration. The account of the final sign occupies these two chapters nineteen and twenty. We refer to it in this way because in the earliest Messianic visit of Jesus to Jerusalem, when He had cleansed the Temple, and was challenged as to His authority, His answer was,

" Destroy this Temple, and in three days I will raise it again."

In these words He declared that the ultimate sign of His authority would be that of His death and resurrection. The former part of His prediction concerning this sign had been fulfilled in His death. The latter part was fulfilled in His resurrection. That, of course, is to generalise on the chapter, in order to see its relation to the whole purpose and movement of the Gospel.

When we were dealing with the fact of the resurrection as recorded by Luke, we saw that he gave us incidents of the first day, some in the morning, some in the afternoon, some in the evening, made no reference to intervening days, but briefly referred to the fact of the ascension.

Now when we turn to John we find he has an octave of days, referring first to the first " first day," and then to the second " first day," and giving us one incident occurring in the interval. With regard to the " first day," he gives us incidents of the morning and the evening. We may then set out the movement of the chapter thus: Incidents of the " first day " (verses 1–23); Thomas in the interval (verses 24–25); Incidents on the eight day (verses 26–29).

Referring to the " First day," John says that Mary Magdalen came to the tomb " while it was yet dark." We must remember that the Jewish Sabbath ended at sunset, so that from the stand-point of religious observance, the statement, " While it was yet dark " would suggest that the approach of Mary took place in the night period. Matthew refers to her coming:

" As it began to dawn towards the first day of the week." Mark says:

" When the Sabbath was passed."

and then records the coming not of Mary alone, but of a group, " when the sun was risen." Luke says, also referring to a group of them, that they came " at early dawn." Careful consideration of these statements will show that there is no contradiction between them. The one certain thing is that the coming of Mary Magdalene

took place in the earliest period of that day, " while it was yet dark."
The record of that first day has a threefold movement. In the
first we see the empty tomb (verses 1–10); in the second the living
Lord (verses 11–18); and in the third the living Lord and the
company of His disciples (verses 19–23).

As we gather to the empty tomb, while it is yet dark, we
see one woman there. She is Mary of Magdala. She was a woman
who had been delivered from a sevenfold demon-possession by
our Lord. When she arrived she found the stone—that had been
so carefully rolled into position at the opening of the rock-hewn
tomb, and sealed with the seal of Pilate, to break which was death—
rolled away. Evidently she did not then stop to see anything more,
but ran to find Peter and John. This in itself is an interesting
fact. We have no reason to suppose that Peter had a house in
Jerusalem, but we know that John had. Quite evidently then
John had found Peter after the denial, and had taken him to his
own home. Evidently Mary knew that Peter was there, and to
find them she hurried away. Arriving, she told them the
astounding news:

" They have taken away the Lord out of the tomb, and
we know not where they have laid Him."

It is to be observed that the idea of resurrection does not
seem to have entered into her mind. She was conscious of the
fact of the loss of the dead body of the One Whom she still described as " the Lord." This is another evidence of the fact that
when the disciples had seen Jesus put upon His Cross, they had
lost all hope, that is, hope of His being able to do what they thought
He would do. He was dead, and that seemed to end everything.
Nevertheless to Mary He was still " the Lord." The statement,
" While it was yet dark," while having reference to the time,
in the case of Mary, and indeed, of all the rest, had a deeper significance. Everything was dark to them, as they had lost Him in
death. And now she had lost even the sacred body.

Directly they received the news, Peter and John started for
the sepulchre. Very natural and very beautiful is the story of
how John outran Peter. The characteristics of the two men,
moreover, are clearly seen. When John came, evidently looking
into the tomb, he saw " the linen cloths lying." It is clear that
he recognised that the body of Jesus was gone, but the wrappings
which had been around the body were still there. The Greek
word rendered " lying " is a very suggestive one, describing them
as undisturbed. The word used there for seeing is the same as
the one used in the case of Mary, but John saw more than Mary
did. She saw the stone gone. John saw " the cloths lying."

Then Peter arrived, and he is the same impulsive man as we have been made familiar with in the story of the years of his discipleship. When he came, he did not stand outside, but went into the tomb; and we are told what he saw, but the word used for his seeing is not the same. The verb used of the seeing of Mary and of John describes the ordinary casual observation of that which is apparent. The word used concerning Peter's looking, however, is one that means to observe closely, to inspect. Mary had seen the stone rolled away, a perfectly patent sight. John had also seen linen cloths lying, a self-evident thing. Peter went in and stared at those linen cloths, and as he looked, observed what John is particular to tell us that the napkin which had been about His head was lying in a place by itself. Again we have a very significant declaration here. In the burying of a dead body, according to the custom of the Jews, a separate wrapping was always provided for the head, and was folded around the head. What Peter saw was that that napkin was still there, folded as it had been around the head of Jesus. Thus Peter, carefully examining, saw the undisturbed grave cloths.

Following on, the narrative tells us that John now went in; and again we are told of something that he saw, but the word used is still a different one. No longer is it the word that marks casual seeing, nor is it the word employed of Peter's careful inspection. It is rather a word that suggests apprehension, and John links it at once with another, as he says, " he saw, and believed. What then did he believe? The only thing which was possible, in view of the evidences, namely that the body of our Lord had not been taken away, but that He had risen. Looking at those undisturbed grave cloths he apprehended their significance, and believed. It is most significant that John, the writer of this story adds at this point that very interesting declaration that " they knew not the Scripture that He must rise again from the dead."

Thus we realise that no human eye saw Jesus rise, but what they saw brought conviction that He was risen. From the evidences before them they knew that it was impossible that foes had stolen the body, for they could not have done so and left the grave cloths undisturbed as they were.

The next incident recorded is that of the actual appearance of the Lord Himself to Mary. Peter and John had left, but Mary had tarried. She, too, had had the evidences which they had had; but evidently they had not brought for her full understanding of their significance. Therefore, she tarried by the side of the empty tomb in profound loyalty and love. When they had left her, she did that which was natural, and to be expected:

" She stooped, and looked into the tomb."

When she did so, she saw angels, one sitting at the head and one at the feet, where the body of Jesus had lain. She does not seem to have been surprised at the vision of angels, nor embarrassed by their question:

"Woman, why weepest thou?"

Out of the fullness of her heart, she told them that which was her supreme consciousness at the moment.

"They have taken away my Lord, and I know not where they have laid Him."

Thus evidently she still had no apprehension of the fact of resurrection; and therefore told heaven's messengers that earth had desecrated the tomb by stealing the body of her Lord.

Then lifting herself up from the stooping position she had occupied in gazing into the tomb, and turning back toward the garden, she saw Someone standing there, Who asked her the self-same question which the angels had asked:

"Woman, why weepest thou?"

In all the full flood of her sorrow and perplexity, and not seeing clearly:

"Supposing Him to be the gardener," she said:

"Sir, if Thou hast borne Him hence, tell me where Thou hast laid Him, and I will take Him away."

What a natural and beautiful story this is. She was not calculating on her physical strength. She felt equal to anything if she could get into contact with that dead body. He was still to her, her Lord, even though dead, as she thought. Mary of Magdala is here seen, not only true till death, but beyond death.

What follows defies interpretation in certain ways. The simple record says that Jesus uttered the one word, "Mary." How often He had called her by that name in the days that were past. How familiar it must have been to her ears. Now He used it once more unquestionably in the old familiar tone. No one could say "Mary" to that woman as Jesus said it; and so in a moment she knew Him. Dropping into the Aramaic of her mother speech she said, "Rabonni," which was more than Rabbi, which might have meant Master, or Teacher. It was the form that introduced the personal note, "My Master."

When she had thus recognised Him, He said, "Touch Me not." As a matter of fact the words would be far more accurately rendered, Do not take hold of Me. I do not believe that the reference was to physical contact, but rather that He intended to say to her in effect, Do not try to hold Me in the way in which you have held and known Me in the past. Mary had lost Him in the way in which she had been accustomed to have Him; but presently she would gain Him in an intimacy far nearer and tenderer than had existed in the past. The commencement of that new relationship, however, could not be until after His ascension, and His sending forth of the promised Comforter. The message that she bore to the disciples after the interview was not that He was risen. That they knew already. It was rather that of His coming ascension.

The day wore on, and at its close the disciples were gathered together, "assembled, for fear of the Jews." Suddenly Jesus stood in the midst of them, and said, "Peace unto you." It was the ordinary salutation with which they had long been accustomed to greet each other; but now it came to them thus in a new way. They were afraid, and He said "Peace."

Presently He repeated the same words, but with a fresh significance. In connection with its first utterance He had showed them His hands and His side. Now again uttering the words, He said, "As the Father hath sent Me, even so send I you." The sequence of these two things is arresting. First the greetings of peace, because He was there, Master of the grave, superior to all opposing forces; but bearing in His hands and side the marks that told of His Cross. Then again, "Peace unto you," coupled with the words, "As the Father hath sent Me, even so send I you." They were to have peace because He was risen; but they were to go by the way He had gone, of which going the wound-prints constituted the sign.

Having uttered these words,

"He breathed on them, and saith unto them, Receive ye the Holy Ghost."

The breathing was symbolical, suggestive, prophetic. They did not then receive the Holy Spirit. He had commanded them to tarry until they had received Him. The action, therefore, was prophetic of that which was to be fulfilled later, and all that which would be for them, their moral and spiritual equipment for their service in the world. As the result of the reception of the Spirit it would be true that, whosesoever sins they forgave should be forgiven; and whosesoever sins they retained should be retained.

In these words and this action there was recognised the fact of the message that they were to deliver to men, and the conditions they were to lay down, upon which the remission of sins might be obtained; and failing to fall in with which, sins must be retained. We may summarise by saying that the conditions were those of repentance towards God, and faith in the Lord Jesus Christ. As they went forth, bearing that witness, and men repented and believed, they had the right to declare the sins of such to be remitted; and they had equally the right to declare that in the case of men who refused to repent, and did not believe, sins would be retained.

The incident of the interval between the two days is that of Thomas. We are told that on the first occasion Thomas was absent. The question naturally arises as to why he was not there. I can only reply to it from the standpoint of personal conviction. Thomas was the man who but a little while ago, when Lazarus lay sick, and Jesus insisted upon going to him, had said:

"Let us also go, that we may die with Him."

He had been perfectly sincere in the saying of it, but he had failed. He had run away with all the rest. I cannot escape the conviction that in that interval Thomas was filled with despair in the presence of his own failure.

Nevertheless he could not wholly break with the past, and presently we see him on the next " first day " gathered with them.

Into that gathering the Lord came once more, with the same salutation, but without any question He came specifically for Thomas, for immediately singling him out, He offered him the evidences he had demanded. In reply Thomas it was who uttered the full confession concerning Christ:

"My Lord, and my God."

The whole story ends with the last beatitude of Jesus:

" Blessed are they that have not seen, and yet have believed."

These words were not words applying to the rest of the disciples then gathered about Him, because they had seen. No, He was looking through and on the the whole company of those who, not having seen, yet resting upon the record, have believed, and so have entered into fellowship with the risen Christ.

ACTS II

PERHAPS there is no chapter in the New Testament which has been read more often than this. Moreover, I think it is impossible to read it without being conscious of its mystery and its majesty.

There is a sense in which it is complete in itself, although it leads on to everything that follows in this remarkable book; and as has so often been pointed out, the book itself, while complete in its value, is unfinished. This could not be otherwise, seeing that it contains a record of the commencement of those things which are still going forward. For nineteen hundred years things have been happening in the world as the result of the coming into human history of the Son of God; and in this book we have the account of the beginning of these things. Our chapter then deals with the beginning of these beginnings, and, moreover, reveals the secrets of all that has followed.

We are at once arrested by the opening sentence of the chapter, which reads in the Revised Version:

" And when the day of Pentecost was now come."

A reference to the margin is here of great importance. There the fact is indicated that the literal translation of the Greek would read:

" When the day of Pentecost was being fulfilled."

That really is the key to the chapter and to everything that follows in the book.

The words, " the day of Pentecost " referred to an established Jewish feast, and the statement is really a declaration that that which took place in Jerusalem was the fulfilment of everything that had been suggested by that feast.

It is not necessary to strain interpretation to recognise that all the Jewish feasts were in a certain sense predictive. All of them pointed on to some fulfilment in the future. The whole Jewish year was marked by religious observance. The new year opened with Passover and the Feast of Unleavened Bread. These feasts reminded the people that their life was rooted in their deliverance by God from slavery; and that it was to be characterized by complete separation from evil. All the ritual of these feasts looked on to something waiting for fulfilment. Paul makes use of both in the course of his writings; to Passover, when he said:

" For our Passover also hath been sacrificed, even Christ";

and to that of Unleavened Bread in close connection, when he said:

" Wherefore let us keep the feast . . . with the unleavened bread of sincerity and truth."

Fifty days after this feast of Passover came Pentecost. It was the feast that marked the gathering of the harvest. Passover symbolized the beginning of all things, rooted in redemption. Pentecost spoke of finality and realisation.

Thus this full significance of the opening sentence must be realised if we are to understand the story. " The day of Pentecost was being fulfilled." The colours of the old economy, radiantly beautiful, full of suggestiveness, were fading away, eclipsed in the glory of the new, the dawning of the day in all its fullness. The prophetic value of the ancient symbolism was now being merged into the historic realisation of everything which that symbolism had suggested and foretold. On that day there was given to the world a phenomenon, an outshining, a manifestation; something entirely new and mysterious from the standpoint of human thinking. No more remarkable day had ever come in the history of the world, with perhaps one exception, but the two should ever be linked together. The other day was that on which a Baby was born into human history, Who was God incarnate. On this day the outcome of that Birth and of that ministry, and of the Cross which followed, culminating in resurrection and ascension, came Pentecost.

In order to our consideration we may describe the movement of the chapter as four-fold; the phenomenon in history, in itself (verses 1–4); the phenomenon in its first effect upon the world (verses 5–13); the interpretation of the phenomenon under the guidance of the Spirit (verses 14–36); and the immediate issue, the beginning of the things which have continued until this time, (verses 37–47). Or to put that more briefly; the phenomenon in history (verses 1–4); in its first effect (verses 5–13); in its interpretation (verses 14–36); and in its issue (verses 37–47).

As to the first movement. The disciples of Jesus were gathered together in Temple courts. In passing I may say that there may be some difference of opinion on that point. It has constantly been said that they were gathered in the upper room. A most careful examination of the whole story, however, will reveal the fact that the upper room was merely a place of tarrying for some of the fellowship; but their meeting-place day by day was in the Temple. Luke tells us in his Gospel (xxiv. 52):

> " They worshipped Him, and returned to Jerusalem with great joy and were continually in the Temple, blessing God."

In the first chapter of the Acts at the fourteenth verse, speaking of that company, he says:

> " These all with one accord continued stedfastly in prayer, with the women, and Mary the Mother of Jesus, and with His brethren."

That describes the composition of the company. In our chapter we are told that:

> " They were all together in one place."

The place is not named, and it has been generally referred to as the upper room. A glance on to the forty-sixth verse, however, will reveal another statement of Luke:

> " And day by day, continuing stedfastly with one accord in the Temple."

Moreover, a consideration of the facts themselves will surely lead to the conviction that the place of convocation was not in any upper room. There were at least one hundred and twenty of them together; and moreover, presently more than three thousand people were gathered about them. This certainly could not have been in the upper room. All this is technical, but interesting, and, I think, important. Taking the wider outlook of the whole economy of God, what more fitting than that the fulfilment of Pentecost should take place in the Temple.

The record declares that while these were thus assembled, there came:

> " A sound as of the rushing of a mighty wind."

This was an appeal to the senses in sound, for Luke does not say that there was a mighty rushing wind, but a sound like one. Co-incident with that sound there was an appearance of fire which, disparting, sat in the form of tongues upon each one of the waiting disciples. It was one fire; Luke refers to it by the singular pronoun " it "; but disparting, became many " tongues." This was an appeal to the senses through sight. Neither the sound of the mighty rushing wind, nor the appearance of tongues was intended to be permanent. That which was symbolized by these things was permanent, and that permanent fact is declared in the statement:

> " They were all filled with the Holy Spirit."

The Spirit could not be seen or heard with the seeing and the hearing which in themselves are of the material world. Therefore in connection with His coming, two signs were given, which did appeal to these senses; the one, the sound attracting the crowds to the place where it had its centre; the other, possibly unseen by the crowds, but certainly seen by the disciples, the disparting fire. It is of importance to realise that which we have already stated, that the signs were transient. The fact which they symbolized is permanent.

And yet another sign was granted to the crowds. When attracted by the sound of the mighty rushing wind, they gathered about this group of men and women, they found them all using their voices. Luke is careful to show in what way they were thus using their voices, as he says that men in the crowd declared that these people were " speaking in our tongues the mighty works of God." The words they were uttering, then, referred to " the mighty works of God." That phrase is a very arresting one; and indeed, is found in only one other place in the New Testament, and that is in the Magnificat of Mary, as given to us in the Gospel of Luke. That is how she in her singing described the activities of God. This then is what these disciples were doing. They were not preaching the Gospel in our sense of that great phrase. They were not attempting to interpret the mystery in the midst of which they were living; but in the full consciousness created by the fullness of the Spirit, with eyes open to see as they had never seen, and ears attuned to hear as they had never heard, with all their being stirred to its depths by the inrush of this life of God through Christ, they were uttering words of ecstatic joy as they celebrated the mighty works of God. Such was the phenomenon in itself. The crowd heard these men and women giving vocal evidence of the presence of the unseen One as it was symbolized by the sound of the wind, and the appearance of fire.

The marvel of it all to the crowd was that as they listened, they heard:

" Every man . . . in his own language wherein he was born."

The effect produced is very carefully declared by Luke. Indeed, his words are characterized by scientific accuracy and artistic beauty, and he traces all the effects produced upon the crowds in the use of three statements. First, he declares that they were " confounded." Presently he states that they were " amazed "; and finally, he says that " they marvelled." These words describe a mental process. First, they were confounded. That means mental arrest. Secondly, they were amazed. That means mental defeat. Finally, they marvelled. That indicates mental awe. They were confounded, that is they were arrested and perplexed. They were amazed, that is, they could not understand or explain the things in the midst of which they found themselves. They marvelled, that is, for the moment, at least, they stood in awe in the presence of the strange phenomenon; and some of them, perhaps most of them, enquired as to its meaning.

We next find an attempt made by some of them to explain the thing they saw. This they did as they said:

" They are filled with new wine."

In other words the only attempted explanation of Pentecost by the outside world was that this group of people were drunk. There was something about them that commanded attention, arrested a city, and which was of such a nature that the people were unable to interpret; and when they tried to do so, the only solution which occurred to them was that the manifestation was that of drunkenness. It was, of course, merely a suggestion, and yet there are senses in which it was nearer the truth than some people may imagine. Let me hasten to say at once, however, that the suggestion was as far from the truth as is hell from heaven. This apparent contradiction needs explanation. That is found when we remember that when people take stimulants to produce intoxication, what they are seeking for is exhilaration, the lifting of themselves out of experiences of dullness. We know perfectly well that the result at the moment is such a sense of exhilaration; but that it ever reacts in a yet more appalling sense of dejection. The filling of the Spirit lifts out of all dejection, and maintains the life on the level of victory. We are at once reminded of Paul's words to the Ephesians:

" Be not drunken with wine, wherein is riot; but be filled with the Spirit."

When Peter rose to speak, he did so in answer to the question raised by the crowd, " What meaneth this? " This leads us to the section giving an interpretation of the phenomenon, through the illumination of the Spirit. This section then must for ever remain full of vital importance. It is the record of the first Christian message in all its fullness; and in all essential particulars, is a revelation of what Christian preaching ought constantly to be. The boundaries of preaching are indicated; the passion of preaching is revealed; the purpose of preaching is found; and the issue of preaching is seen. Peter began with a fine courtesy, which is ever an element in true preaching. He answered the question asked by the crowd, beginning with a reference to the suggestion made by some that the people were drunk, dismissing it with tender irony, pointing out that the hour of the day was too early for that to be so.   In the positive interpretation there are two movements, the first showing the relationship of what they saw to the prediction of the ancient Scriptures; and the second declaring how that prediction had been fulfilled through Jesus of Nazareth.

As to the first, he took them back to Joel, quoting words with which those who listened were probably quite familiar, linking what they saw with the prediction by the pregnant phrase, " This is that."   In effect he was saying to these people that they ought not to be surprised at what they saw, if they had really believed in the prophetic word of their own Scripture.   He commenced this part of his message by addressing them as:

" Ye men of Judæa, and all ye that dwell at Jerusalem." Then in the second movement, he spoke to them as " Ye men of Israel," and in briefest and yet plainest way told them the story of the ministry and work of our Lord.

In doing this he was careful to begin at the point with which they were all familiar.

" Jesus of Nazareth, a Man approved of God unto you by powers and wonders and signs which God did by Him in the midst of you, even as ye yourselves know."

He thus fastened attention upon the Person, naming Him as He had been so constantly named during the period of His public teaching.   By doing this he reminded them that they were familiar with this Person, that they had watched Him, and listened to Him, that they had seen works done by Him, which could only have been done because God was with Him.   This it will be remembered is what Nicodemus had discovered in the early days of that teaching ministry:

" We know that Thou art a Teacher come from God; for no man can do these signs that Thou doest, except God be with Him."

Peter claimed that they were familiar with One Who thus had been demonstrated by God to them, as he said that all the powers and the wonders and the signs had been wrought by God through Him in their midst.

Next, still holding attention to the Person, he said:

" Him, being delivered up by the determinate counsel and foreknowledge of God, ye by the hand of men without the law did crucify and slay."

In that statement there was no wavering. Peter had now passed far beyond his questionings and his vacillations concerning the Christ. In these words he took them back to the thing that perchance hundreds and thousands of them had witnessed at Golgotha. In referring to these things, however, he did not begin by referring to their failure. He began by the remarkable declaration that what they had seen was something which could only be described in the words:

> "Him, being delivered up by the determinate counsel and foreknowledge of God."

Then he referred to their own wrong-doing in the matter, as he said:

> "Ye by the hand of men without the law did crucify and slay."

Thus the fact of the Cross was declared from the Divine side:

> "Delivered up by the determinate counsel and fore-knowledge of God";

and from the human side, crucified and slain by the men of Israel through the hand of the Gentiles.

The Cross having thus been referred to, Peter, still keeping attention fixed upon the Person, said:

> "Whom God raised up, having loosed the pangs of death,"

and with an aside of majestic satire for all the forces of evil, and a fine contempt for death, he said:

> "For it was not possible that He should be holden of it."

In connection with that reference to the resurrection he went back again to their own Scriptures, and made remarkable quotations therefrom.

Continuing his main argument at the point of the resurrection, he said:

> "This Jesus did God raise up, whereof we all are witnesses. Being therefore by the right hand of God exalted, and having received of the Father the promise of the Holy Spirit, He hath poured forth this."

In these words he declared that the issue of the resurrection was the exaltation of our Lord, and the fulfilment of the prophetic word of long ago.

It is good to summarize on this whole movement. Said the crowd, "What meaneth this?" Said Peter, "This is that" foretold in prophecy; and He, the Man crucified, raised and exalted, "hath shed forth this."

The rest of the chapter is occupied with an account of the immediate issues of the Pentecostal effusion and the Pentecostal interpretation. The first effect declared is that of conviction. Using the figurative language of Luke, " they were pricked in their heart." They found they were face to face with an activity of God which fulfilled their ancient prophecies, in spite of, and even through their own sinful action. Thus convinced, they enquired, " What shall we do? "

The answer given to that enquiry was immediate and definite.

" Repent ye, and be baptised every one of you in the name of Jesus Christ for the remission of your sins, and ye shall receive the gift of the Holy Spirit."

That is to say, they might share in all they had seen, as they fulfilled the conditions thus stated. There was immediate obedience on the part of three thousand of that multitude, and the new life began for them also.

As we ponder this chapter, inevitably the question arises as to how it impresses us. What are we inclined to say as we read it? The first answer to that will be that we feel its wonder and its glory. That being so, is it possible to ponder the chapter without finding that it produces within us a sense of loss somewhere? And further, out of that sense of loss, does there not arise within us a desire for something approximating to that which is here revealed?

What is lacking? We hear no sound of a mighty, rushing wind. We do not need to. We have seen no fire parting asunder, and tongues sitting upon the Christian assemblies. It is quite unnecessary that we should. These things were transient.

That which is permanent is the fullness of the Holy Spirit, placed at the disposal of the children of God. If there be any lack, it is found in us, in some reserve which we practise, some holding back from complete surrender. At that point our general meditation must cease, and its application be made in the Secret Place, and in the conscious presence of God.

ROMANS V

THE letter to the Romans is pre-eminently the document of Salvation. There is no writing in the New Testament which, from the standpoint of interpretation, deals as fully with the subject. It is, in common with all the New Testament epistles, a document for the Church, rather than for the outside world. By that I mean that if someone should ask me, What shall I do to be saved? I should not reply, Read the Roman letter and find an answer. I should rather say, The way of salvation is that of repentance toward God, and faith in our Lord Jesus Christ; but if you would understand what salvation really is, then read this letter.

Paul was a Jew by race, a Greek by all the early influences that had been brought to bear upon his opening years in Tarsus, a Roman by citizenship; but he was supremely Christ's man, and all the things referred to were qualified by that final fact. It was from the standpoint of his Jewish training that he looked out upon the world, viewing the Gentile world of which he was a citizen, and the Jewish world of which he was by race a member. His outlook convinced him of the overwhelming disaster of sin, but he wrote as one who knew the superabounding remedy of grace. He did not minimize sin, as the earlier part of his letter makes perfectly clear. He looked with intrepid eyes into the darkness of the world; but he looked upon it with eyes lit with hope, because he knew that God's remedy for sin was full, and met all the need.

As he looked at the Gentile world, he summarized everything as he said that they had been disobedient to the light, holding down the truth in unrighteousness. He looked upon the Jewish world and found it equally involved, and perhaps more guilty because of the greater light it had received. Finally, he summarized as he declared that the whole world was guilty before God.

All this being so, the purpose of this letter was that of interpreting the provision made for the world, in its dire necessity. That whole provision was found in Christ, and Paul wrote from the standpoint of conviction that the only solution of human problems must come through Him, that there could be no staunching of humanity's wounds save in the blood that He shed, that there could be no hope for newness of life and the realization of ideals but in living relationship with Him.

Roughly gathering up the teaching of the letter we may say that it shows that the provision of grace is revealed in a threefold movement, which may be expressed by the use of three words: justification, sanctification, glorification.

The chapter now under consideration completes the section in which Paul was dealing with justification. The great question was as to how it could be possible for God to be just, and yet justify the guilty. From the standpoint of human wisdom that is an insuperable problem. It is utterly impossible for any earthly judge or jury to justify the guilty, without violating justice. Yet that is what the Gospel proclaimed God as doing, and the way of His action is revealed in one phrase:

" Through the redemption that is in Christ Jesus."

A further question is raised as to how man may appropriate the provision thus made. The answer is contained in the simple phrase " by faith." These things having been dealt with, in chapter five we have a revelation of the privileges and responsibilities of those appropriating the provision.

The chapter falls naturally into two parts. The first eleven verses give us the privileges and responsibilities from the personal standpoint; and the rest of the chapter, from verse twelve to twenty-one, deals with the racial application. In saying that I am not suggesting for a moment that there are no personal applications of the second part; but it is important that we realise that in that part the apostle was looking over the whole of human history and human affairs, and seeing the working of the Divine grace therein.

In considering the first movement there is a technical matter which should be examined, though in the last analysis perhaps it is not of any vital importance. I refer to the difference between the King James' and Revised Versions. The King James' Version throughout translates the passage as though the apostle were dealing with the great privileges that have come to us through justification;

" Therefore being justified by faith, we have peace with God, through our Lord Jesus Christ; By Whom also we have access by faith into this grace wherein we stand, and rejoice in hope of the glory of God."

The Revisers' rendering of the passage is such as to emphasize the responsibility resulting from the privileges;

> " Being therefore justified by faith, let us have peace with God, through our Lord Jesus Christ; through Whom also we have had our access by faith into this grace wherein we stand, and let us rejoice in hope of the glory of God."

The difference is unquestionably due to the MSS. The reading which finds translation in the Revised Version is found in all existing Greek MSS. earlier than the ninth century. The earliest trace of the reading, " we have peace " is found in the Sinai MS., and an examination of this shows that it appeared in the form, " Let us have peace . . . let us rejoice," but that this at some time was amended. As we have already said, the real value is not seriously interfered with, because if we accept, as I personally think we are bound to do, the Revised rendering, it implicates the blessings received through our access into grace, and simply urges a fulfilment of the responsibilities created thereby.

I proceed therefore upon the assumption of the accuracy of the Revised rendering. That being so, Paul was doing here what he did on other occasions, in other applications, urging the necessity for appropriating and acting upon the blessings received. He did that when he wrote, You have put off the old man; put off the old man. The thing is done; now act accordingly. Exactly the same thought is here. Being justified, we have peace. Therefore let us have peace; that is, let us appropriate the thing that is ours. Let us live according to the privilege created for us.

Everything therefore begins with the fact stated, " being therefore justified by faith." The context explains that, as it shows how God can be just and justify; and man can appropriate the provision by faith. Having then passed into this experience of justification through the act of faith in the redemption that is in Christ Jesus, there are two privileges implicated, and two corresponding responsibilities declared. The first privilege is that of access into grace, and the second that of the hope of glory. The responsibility consequent upon them are that we have peace with God, and that we rejoice in hope. Having access into grace we find everything suffused with the radiant light of glory. That is what salvation really means. Access into grace always means passing into the light of glory.

The word grace here is used, with all its fullness in the background, but in one particular sense, that of favour. Through the redemption that is in Christ Jesus, and by faith, we have access into the realm of the Divine favour. We stand no longer as suppliants outside, but are admitted into the closest and most intimate relationship with God. That being recognized, all the other values of the word grace may be considered. To stand in the Divine favour is to live in the realm of all perfection and beauty; to share the Divine passion to communicate such values to others; and finally to have fellowship with the Divine activity, by which the desire is fulfilled, that namely of the Cross.

Thus it follows inevitably that we are brought into the realm of the hope of glory. It is of supreme importance that we carefully note what the apostle says at this point. It is that we " rejoice in hope of the glory of God," which means far more than that we rejoice in hope of our own personal glorification. That, too, is included, but the essence of the hope is that God will ultimately be completely glorified. The hope of glory following upon access into grace knows nothing of selfishness. Grace, which in some senses is the fire of the Divine purifying making beautiful all that it touches, also burns up the dross, the things that are out of harmony with the Divine nature. Having access into that grace, we rejoice in the assurance of the ultimate victory of God. When it is written concerning our Lord:

" Who for the joy that was set before Him, endured the Cross,"

His joy was that of the certainty that through the Cross endured, at last the prayer He taught His disciples would be answered; the name of God would be hallowed, the Kingdom of God would come, the will of God would be done on earth as in heaven. The privileges then are thus summarized. Having access into grace, the glory of God becomes the one hope of life.

In view of these privileges, the responsibilities are stated and are self-evident. The first is expressed in the words:

" Let us have peace with God."

We are brought into the place of reconciliation by grace. Let us live accordingly. This means that we are to see to it that nothing is permitted to interfere between us and God, which breaks in upon peace, which creates any measure of conflict as between us. It is not enough to talk about peace with God, and to treat it as a great benefit conferred. From the Divine standpoint the fact has been made possible, in that God has swept away every reason for conflict. We are ever in danger of allowing something to intervene which creates distance, and even conflict between us and Him. How often God has to say, as He did to His people of old:

"The Lord hath a controversy with His people."

It is this possibility that gives urgency to the injunction:

"Let us have peace with God."

The second responsibility is revealed in the words:

"Let us rejoice."

Whereas rejoicing in the possession of such privileges would seem to be inevitable, we are reminded by the apostle that rejoicing is not merely a privilege, it is a duty. It is perfectly true that to feign rejoicing is futile and reprehensible. We have no right to pretend to joy if we lack it. The smile that is forced is always in itself a lie, and consequently has no value. The point of responsibility, of course, is that we see to it that the condition is maintained, which makes the rejoicing inevitable. That condition is the one already dealt with; peace with God. If that peace be maintained, so that nothing is permitted to break in which creates conflict, we shall still have sorrow, but in spite of the sorrow, the joy will remain. Paul and Silas in Philippi's prison, knew sorrow. There was nothing in their circumstances such as to make for joy; and yet they were filled with joy. Even then they were rejoicing in hope of the glory of God, though their backs were bleeding from the lictors' rods, and their feet were fast in the stocks, and there was no light in the dungeon. Being at peace with God, they sang in the night. Thus in those first two verses of the chapter essential and eternal matters are dealt with.

In the next section the apostle passes to temporal conditions and experiences. He begins with the arresting phrase, "And not only so." That is to say that the responsibilities of standing in grace which are those of maintaining peace with God, and rejoicing in hope, lead to a further responsibility, and this Paul expresses in the arresting words:

"Let us also rejoice in our tribulations."

In that word we have in a very remarkable way, a revelation of the distinctive Christian note. We can find nothing approaching it in any other realm of human thinking, however high, however noble. It ever seems to me in the original Stoic philosophy men reached the highest outlook on life possible to the activity of the human mind, unilluminated by Divine revelation. In a rough and ready manner we may say that that Stoic philosophy is expressed oftentimes to-day in a familiar saying, " What can't be cured must be endured." That is exactly what these men said. But those who have access into grace say something far more arresting than that, which we may express also in simple fashion. We rejoice in what has to be endured, because in it we have discovered the process that cures.

This is what Paul then explains, as continuing, he says:—

" Knowing that tribulation worketh patience; and patience, probation, and probation, hope; and hope putteth not to shame."

Thus he comes back to hope, showing that the ultimate hope is the result of tribulation. When he says that " patience " worketh " probation," it is important that we understand the meaning of probation in this connection. It has the sense of proof, and I think would have been far more helpfully rendered by the use of that word. Observe the movement then. " Tribulation worketh patience." We may at once say tribulation never works patience unless we are at peace with God, and then it does; and the patience resulting in the experience of tribulation, in fellowship with God, becomes the demonstration of things, the proof. Out of that proof or certainty, hope ever springs.

And still continuing, the apostle shows the secret of all that experience as he says that these things are so:

" Because the love of God hath been shed abroad in our hearts through the Holy Spirit which was given unto us."

And still continuing, he declares that the supreme proof of that love is that:

" While we were yet weak, in due season Christ died for the ungodly."

That is the supreme proof of love.

Finally, the apostle takes the wider racial outlook, the two forces of sin and grace still being in view. In doing this he has two pivotal view points, the beginning of history in the first man, Adam; and its new beginning with the second Man, Jesus. Surveying the whole period, and indeed looking prophetically to the consummation of all things, he employed a threefold contrast, first between the trespass that issued in sin, and the free gift which is to correct the result of that trespass; secondly, between the condemnation resulting from the trespass, and the justification resulting from the free gift; and finally between the reign of death, and the reign of life. There is a threefold movement on the one side, " trespass," " condemnation," " death." There is a threefold movement on the other side, " the free gift," " justification," " life."

With regard to the trespass and the free gift, the comparison is made in verses twelve to fourteen. Sin entered by one man. The free gift of God comes through one Man. The whole teaching is that however terrible the result of sin, the provision of grace is more than enough to meet it, correct it, and remove it.

The comparison between condemnation and justification is equally clear and forcible. Through the condemnation of one, condemnation fell upon all related to him. Through the work of One Who in Himself needed no justification, justification is placed at the disposal of all those under condemnation, who become related to Him by faith.

The final comparison is between the reign of death and the reign of life through the operation of grace. As sin reigned through all human history, so grace also reigned; and now in Christ Jesus comes to all the fullness of its power.

It is interesting to carefully mark that in each one of these comparisons, the apostle emphasizes the fact that the power and activity of grace is mightier and more than that of sin. Notice the words:

" For if, by the trespass of the one the many died, MUCH MORE did the grace of God, and the gift by the grace of the one Man, Jesus Christ, abound unto the many."

Or again:

" For if, by the trespass of the one, death reigned through the one; MUCH MORE shall they that receive the abundance of grace and of the gift of righteousness reign in life through the One, even Jesus Christ."

And even once more:

" Where sin abounded, grace did abound MORE EXCEEDINGLY."

In this historic and racial outlook the supreme declaration is that which we have just quoted:

" Where sin abounded, grace did abound more exceedingly."

Here, whereas in our translations the verbs employed are the same, they are not the same. When speaking of sin, the Greek word suggests not merely abundance, but growth and fecundity. When referring to grace he used a verb which would ever seem to be one coined to meet a need. The revisers have employed four English words to express it, " did abound more exceedingly." To take the Greek verb to pieces, we find it composed of a word meaning superabundance, prefaced by a prefix meaning more. Thus we may say that the word means to more than superabound. To abound means plentifulness. Superabundance means more than plentifulness. More than superabundance introduces the conception of such superlative provision that there can be no measurement of it.

Thus surveying history, the apostle saw the working of sin in all its terrible force and fruitfulness; but he also saw that throughout the whole of it, grace had been more and mightier than it; and wherever sin manifested itself, it was still held within the controlling power of grace in the ultimate government of God. Necessarily the supreme, not illustration only, but activity, is seen in the Cross, where sin came to its direst expression and apparent victory; but where grace over-ruling, became triumphant in the provision of redemption.

ROMANS VIII

IT is almost a commonplace of exposition to say that the eighth chapter of Romans has clearly defined boundaries, which may be expressed thus, No condemnation; no separation. It opens with a declaration that there is no condemnation, and closes with the affirmation that there can be no separation. To speak of this as a commonplace of exposition does not suggest for a moment that it is either false, or lacking in value.

A consideration of the chapter demands that it be set in relation to the whole letter. It constitutes the climax to the constructive arguments of the writer. Through the remaining chapters he is making applications.

The chapter in our Version opens:

" There is therefore now no condemnation."

In the Greek the first word is " Therefore ";

" Therefore there is now no condemnation."

The " therefore " necessarily links the chapter with all that has preceded it. We remind ourselves once more, as we did in considering chapter five, that the letter is pre-eminently the document of salvation. In it we have an exposition of the Gospel, which is the Good News concerning the way of human salvation. The very word salvation suggests danger, but declares a way of deliverance; postulates failure, but promises realisation. At the very forefront of the letter Paul described the Gospel as

" The power of God unto salvation,"

declaring that he was debtor to the Gentile world, literate and illiterate; that he was ready to proclaim the Gospel, and that he was not ashamed of it. Proceeding to show the need for salvation, he did so as he declared the moral failure and dereliction of humanity through unrighteousness; the implicate of the argument being that righteousness is the supreme thing for humanity, individually, socially, nationally, internationally. Peace is the result of righteousness; and as Isaiah had declared long before:

" There is no peace, saith my God, to the wicked."

Surveying the condition of the Gentile and Jewish worlds, he declared that all the world was guilty before God. In this declaration he wrote as one recognising God as the ultimate Authority.

The way of salvation was then shown to be that of faith in a Divine provision of grace, that provision being interpreted as an action wherein and whereby God has placed righteousness at the disposal of man, and that He has done this in such a way that He can be at once just, and the Justifier of the guilty who believe. God violates no principle of moral law, and does no violence to His own essential, eternal character of holiness when He extends pardon and peace to sinning men.

The salvation thus provided for man first deals with his past as justification, then with his present processionally as sanctification, and finally with his future in glorification.

This chapter then falls quite naturally into three parts. In the first seventeen verses the experience of sanctification is described. In verses eighteen to thirty the process resulting from sanctification, and leading towards glorification, is dealt with. And finally, in verses thirty-one to thirty-nine we have the outlook of the believing soul upon life.

Concerning the experience of salvation everything is contained in the first great utterance.

" There is therefore now no condemnation to them that are in Christ Jesus."

In the King James' Version this statement is followed by the words:

" Who walk not after the flesh, but after the Spirit."

These words have been rightly omitted by the Revisers, seeing that they are evidently an interpolation upon the text. The fact they declare, however, is stated quite clearly in the fourth verse:

" That the ordinance of the law might be fulfilled in us, who walk not after the flesh, but after the spirit."

In the first inclusive statement then no condition whatever is referred to. It has to do with the Divine provision in itself. And yet there is a condition clearly revealed in the statement, and it is found in the words, " to them that are in Christ Jesus." The only place in which the sinner can find himself set free from condemnation is " in Christ Jesus." The experience is described in the phrase, " No condemnation," and the sphere in which that experience is possible in the words, " In Christ Jesus."

In a glance back to the fifth chapter we may read:

" Being now justified by His blood, shall we be saved from the wrath of God through Him. For even while we were enemies, we were reconciled to God through the death of His Son, much more, being reconciled, shall we be saved by His life."

The thought of the apostle here would be much more accurately understood if we accept the marginal reading of the last words in that quotation, namely, " shall we be saved in His life." There the movement is clearly marked. Justified, so saved from the wrath of God, and reconciled. Being reconciled, we are saved in His life. Therefore, " there is no condemnation to them that are in Christ Jesus."

It is an amazing statement, which at times we find hard to believe, and yet it is the supreme truth; and when we are tempted to doubt it, it is well to remember that one pregnant line in F. W. H. Myers' poem:

> " God shall forgive thee all but thy despair."

The redemption provided is plenteous redemption. The reconciliation is a perfect reconciliation. Through His death all the resources of His life are at our disposal; and so far as the Divine provision goes, there is no condemnation.

Then following that first inclusive statement, the writer gives further interpretation of it. Everything is of grace, as he had already shown (chapter five).

> " Through our Lord Jesus Christ . . . we have had our access by faith into this grace wherein we stand."

Standing there, there is no condemnation. Those, however, who live in that sphere have entered into a realm where they have found a new law as well as a new life; or shall I rather say, a new law, which is the necessary result of a new life. Indeed that law is described as " the Spirit of life." The law is kept as those who, having received this Spirit of life, walk after the spirit, that is, such as are obedient to a mind no longer flesh mastered, but mastered by the spirit. The fall or failure of humanity resulted in a descent into life under the dominion of the flesh. Salvation brings man back into the true adjustment where life is mastered by the spirit.

Jeremiah saw the age of the new covenant when men should depend no longer on law exhibited externally, but should find the law written on their hearts. The writer of the letter to the Hebrews shows how that foretelling was fulfilled in Christ. Standing in grace always means that this becomes definite, an experience. There are senses in which it is perfectly correct to say that those who live in this sphere of grace do not need the ten commandments hung up before their eyes. That is not for a moment to suggest that the words of those commandments are abrogated. If, however, we walk by the spirit, and not by the flesh, when that spirit is under the dominion of the Spirit of life, the law is known. Our responsibility consists in response to it. That is the realm and experience of sanctification.

Moreover the phrase, "the Spirit of life," as describing the new law refers also to the Energy whereby we are enabled to walk according to that law. The Spirit of life interprets the law to the spirit of man, and then energises him in order that he may obey its revelations. The difference between humanity, whether Jew or Gentile failing in righteousness, and the believer in Christ in process of sanctification, is that the former lives in a realm where the mind is completely dominated by the flesh or the physical, and the latter lives in a realm where the mind is dominated by the spirit, under the mastery of the Spirit of God.

Wherever human nature is examined, irrespective of clime or race, it is never found without some glimmer of light shining amid the darkness. Let it at once be said that that light, the light which lighteth every man, is of no value save as it is obeyed; and the whole catastrophe of human life is that it is not obeyed.

Accepting the Biblical history of man, we find him made in the image and likeness of God, that is, a spiritual being, inhabiting a body and having a mind. The fall of man in his rebellion against the Divine government meant his descent from the level of the spiritual to that of the fleshly. Justification puts man back in right relationship with God within his own personality, that is, puts the spiritual side of his nature again in its proper place of ascendancy, and makes the flesh or physical side, subservient. When that is so, the mind,—the consciousness, the outlook, the thinking,—is mastered from the spirit realm, and not from the flesh realm. Sanctification means the complete subjugation of the spiritual in man to the Spirit of God.

All this possibility is created for man in regeneration. It is true that in human experience, perhaps in the majority of instances, this experience of sanctification is not entered upon immediately; but its possibilities are all created in the new birth.

The obligation resting upon us is then clearly marked as the apostle wrote:

"So then, brethren, we are debtors, not to the flesh, to live after the flesh; for if ye live after the flesh, ye must die; but if by the spirit ye mortify the deeds of the body, ye shall live."

"We are debtors," is a simple and yet illuminative declaration. We all understand, theoretically at least, what it is to be in debt. It simply means that we owe something to someone. The apostle here says then we owe nothing to the flesh, but we do owe everything to the Spirit. By yielding to the indwelling Spirit Who interprets the law, energises the life, transforms all thinking, we abide in the realm of sanctification. Living there is to live where there is no condemnation.

Passing to the section dealing with progress to glorification, we find the apostle beginning with the affirmation " I reckon." It is as though he had been casting up his accounts, and finding a balance. Or we may say he had been taking stock, and now declared the result. He had been putting certain things on one side, and other things on the other side. The things on the one side were summarised by the phrase, " the sufferings of this present time "; the things on the other side summarised by the phrase, " the glory that shall be revealed." As he surveyed these two sides he declared that the things of glory completely outweighed the sufferings. The sufferings, he declared, were not worthy to be compared to the glory.

Nevertheless he was careful to show that the suffering was necessary in order to the finding of the glory. In this connection we are at once reminded of the words our Lord spoke to His disciples in His last conversations with them:

" In the world ye have tribulation; but be of good cheer; I have overcome the world."

Paul in the earlier part of the letter had said, " Let us also rejoice in our tribulations." Here the reason for such rejoicing is revealed as the apostle contemplates suffering, and sets it in relation to the ultimate glory.

To summarise the movement here, we see him looking out upon a suffering world, with which is associated a suffering Church, with which is associated a suffering God. That is revealed in his use of the word " groaning " three times over.

" The whole creation groaneth and travaileth in pain together until now."

" And . . . ourselves also . . . groan within ourselves, which have the firstfruits of the Spirit."

" The Spirit Himself maketh intercession for us with groanings which cannot be uttered."

It is a suffering world. " The whole creation groaneth "; the Church is not exempt from that suffering, but identified with it. We " ourselves . . . groan within ourselves "; and then, reverently but daringly, " the Spirit . . . with groanings which cannot be uttered."

When Mrs. Browning described the tragedy of the suffering and death of the sea-mew, and said:

> " Our human touch did on him pass,
> And with our touch our agony " ;

she was realising the relationship between the suffering of creation and the wrong-doing of humanity. Because of that relationship the Church must remain identified with the suffering of creation. Far more wonderful than the words of Mrs. Browning were those of our Lord, in which He showed the identification of God with the fallen sparrow, as He said that:

> " Not one of them shall fall on the ground without your Father,"

thus clearly showing that in all the suffering of creation God has His part.

But the teaching of the apostle here is that this very suffering is leading to the glory. He says the creation is waiting for the revealing of the sons of God. Whereas that statement may and certainly does include the ultimate deliverance in connection with the second Advent, it has a processional value. Wherever the sons of God are manifested, who are living within this sphere of grace, they bring healing to the suffering creation. That has its constant revelation in all true missionary work. It is not merely a Gospel proclaimed by its messengers, but the lives of these messengers that bring relief to the suffering creation.

Thus these men and women, justified and sanctified, and moving towards the ultimate glory, share in the groaning as they, too, are waiting for the final realisation.

Through all such processes towards the ultimate glory, the weight of which outweighs all the suffering, they live in the fellowship of the Spirit, Who makes intercession for them with groanings which cannot be uttered.

It is in this connection that the apostle wrote the words so often quoted, and perhaps too often inadequately understood,

> " To them that love God, all things work together for good."

That is the process, in sanctification, towards glorification.

Finally, on the basis of what he has already said, the apostle looked out and challenged all the facts of the universe. He cried:

> " What then shall we say to these things? "

His reference is to the great things included in the Gospel, the experience of justification, the process of sanctification through suffering, the hope of the glory which excels.

" What then shall we say to these things? "

He answers his own enquiry by asking four more questions:

" Who is against us? "
" Who shall lay anything to the charge of God's elect? "
" Who is he that condemneth? "
" Who shall separate us? "

In asking these questions, he was looking out, and looking up, looking down, looking on, and looking back. He was investigating the whole universe, and challenging it. He began the teaching at this point by the declaration:

" There is therefore now no condemnation to them that are in Christ Jesus."

Now he says:

" If God is for us, who is against us? "

and he interprets what it is to have God for us in the words:

" He that spared not His own Son, but delivered Him up for us all, how shall He not also with Him freely give us all things? "

Seeing this God upon our side, his enquiry, " Who is against us? " is a declaration of the futility of all opposition.

But there are foes. There are those who will still traduce us, accuse us; and at the head of the iniquitous host is the accuser, whose methods are revealed in the book of Job. This being so, the apostle asks:

" Who shall lay anything to the charge of God's elect? "

and answers:

" It is God that justifieth."

Whatever accusation may be made, God is seen as the Vindicator; and as all the previous argument of the letter shows, He justifies in perfect justice.

That being so:

" Who is he that shall condemn? "

The justification of God is the answer to all possible condemnation.

" It is Christ Jesus that died, yea, rather, that was raised from the dead, Who is at the right hand of God, Who also maketh intercession for us."

Christ died, Christ was raised, Christ was exalted, Christ is interceding: Who will condemn?

All this ends with the final challenge:

" Who shall separate us? "

and here he rises to the ultimate height, and surveys every possibility; and doing so declares:

" Nay in all these things we are more than conquerors through Him that loved us."

What an amazing declaration, " more than conquerors." How is it possible to be more than a conqueror? We are more than conquerors when we take hold of the very things that threaten us, and transmute them into ministers of grace. We are conquerors when we defeat opposition; but if we are able to take hold of the opposing force, and turn it into that which helps instead of harms, we are more than conquerors. And this we are able to do through grace, with tribulation, anguish, persecution, famine, nakedness, peril, the sword. The history of Christianity experimentally is the history of men and women who have taken hold of all these things that threaten, and have not only mastered them, but have changed them into allies of the soul.

The ultimate climax of the apostle is reached in his declaration of certainty as he wrote, " For I am persuaded," by which he means he is assured, and certain, that there can be no separation. In surveying the things that might separate he refers to " death," to " life," which is more dangerous than death as a separating force; to the unseen powers, " angels, principalities," to all the facts of life to-day, " things present," to all the possibilities of the future, " things to come "; to " powers " of any sort; to " height," to " depth "; and, at last, in a phrase full of significance, " nor any other creature," he declares that there can be no separation " from the love of God which is in Christ Jesus our Lord."

In that phrase, " nor any other creature," which would be more fittingly rendered, " any other creation," the apostle recognised all the things referred to in the last analysis are within the authority of God; and thus declared that nothing now existing, and nothing that may come into being, can by any means separate us from the love of God.

I CORINTHIANS XIII

PAUL's first letter to the Corinthians was evidently written to correct failure in the Church, and was called forth by a letter which he had received from the Church. At the seventh chapter he refers to that letter. Evidently his having received it, gave him the opportunity to write on matters that were on his heart. Taken as a whole, the letter falls distinctly into two parts, the first being corrective, and the second constructive. The Church was failing, and its failure was due to the fact that it had been invaded with the carnality of the city, and lost much of its spiritual power. It is with these things that the apostle was dealing in the first eleven chapters.

Having dealt with them, he turned to the constructive section of his letter. The first phrase in our translation reads,

" Now concerning spiritual gifts."

I think it is a great pity that the translators introduced the word " gifts " there. It is not found in the text. While it is quite true that the subject of gifts is dealt with, that is not the only subject. The Greek word, pneumatika, may, very literally, be translated " spirituals," or for our understanding of the thought, " spiritualities." The phrase then indicates the fact that the apostle was here turning from dealing with the carnalities which had hindered, to the spiritualities which are the secret of power in the life of the Church.

The first of these was that of the unity of the Church, his dealing with which is found in chapter twelve. The first evidence of the carnality of the Church had been that of its divisions, and over against these he set the great fact of the unity of the Church under the figure of the body, with its diversities of gifts and operations and energies, but its oneness of life. He ends this subject by the words:

" Desire earnestly the greater gifts. And a still more excellent way show I unto you."

Whereas this sentence is in many ways a simple one, it has had some difficulties for the translator. Lias renders it:

"I show you an eminently excellent way."

Beet translates it:

"A surpassingly good way I show you."

It will be seen that the thought is identical. I suggest yet another rendering, namely:

"The most excellent way show I unto you."

That is to say, while urging them to covet gifts, he says that he would show them the most excellent way of desiring and exercising gifts; and that is what he does in chapter thirteen. We may summarise by saying that he is here showing that the one law of life within the Body of Christ, which is the Church, is the law of love. The whole chapter consists of what we may venture to describe as a spectrum analysis of love. Love has within it all colours, in combination, as light has. The rainbow is the spectrum analysis of light. The colours that are ever present therein are only seen as they are revealed in the myriad raindrops.

I propose here to turn aside for a matter which is technical, and yet which is of supreme importance, that namely of the change made in the Revised Version, in the adoption of the word "love" instead of the word "charity" as found in the King James' Version. The Greek word here is one unknown in classic Greek literature, the word agape. It is found in the Greek Version of the Old Testament. When Wiclif translated from the Vulgate, he transliterated the Latin word caritas, and so we have the word charity. The Roman Catholic translation found in the Rheims Version did the same thing. The King James' translation followed suite. Tyndale, the first to translate from the original languages into English, rendered it love. Cranmer followed this also, using the word love, and so did the Geneva Version.

We may now go back and enquire why Jerome used the Latin word caritas instead of amor. I think there can be no doubt as to the reply to that question. The word amor had earthly and sensual connotations, and so to avoid the suggestiveness of that word, he employed the word caritas, which had no such suggestiveness. In his case, therefore, caritas was of great value as drawing this distinction. Since the King James' translators did their work, the word charity has very largely changed in meaning, and has come to suggest the activity of pity. This is far short of the meaning of the Greek word, and it was certainly better to go back to the word love.

It may be pointed out in passing that this word for love is ever used when the love of God is referred to. The thought has been defined as :

"An affection, embracing judgment, and the deliberate assent of the will as a matter of principle, duty, and propriety."

Whereas that definition is somewhat laboured, it is nevertheless very full and accurate. There is a love which is purely emotional. The love represented by this word is emotional, but suggests the activity of the emotion, resulting from intellectual apprehension, and reinforced by volitional action. It is that conception of love which runs through this chapter.

An examination of the chapter shows that it naturally falls into three movements. In verses one to three the apostle shows the values of love. In verses four to seven he describes the virtues of love. In verses eight to thirteen he shows the victories of love. In the first movement the apostle is emphasizing the necessity for love, and in doing so shows us its values. In the second movement he describes the fruitfulness of love, and so reveals its virtues. In the third he declares its duration, and so shows its victories.

The values of love are that it is the strength of service, that it is the energy of equipment for service, that it is the dynamic of devotion.

"If I speak with the tongues of men and of angels, but have not love, I am become sounding brass or a clanging cymbal."

That is a brief and yet tremendous statement. The apostle declares that we may speak with eloquence, and yet become merely an instrument, devoid of power, of personality, apart from love. An old Puritan writer on this verse made a quaint and yet forcible remark:

"What is the good of a fiddle without a player?"

That is the thought of the apostle. To speak, whether with the tongues of men or angels, except under the inspiration of love, is only to make a noise. The deduction is inevitable. When speech is love-inspired, it will be speech reinforced by the complete surrender of personality.

"And if I have the gift of prophecy, and know all mysteries and all knowledge; and if I have all faith, so as to remove mountains, but have not love, I am nothing."

The arresting matter here is that the apostle is not referring to low things but high things, things which are in themselves distinct gifts of God to men; prophecy, the knowledge of mysteries, and all knowledge; and even victorious faith. The apostle, moreover, was superlative. He says, " If," and we are inclined to say that the suppositions are tremendous suppositions, that if one were possessed of such gifts, surely nothing more could be desired. The apostle, however, declares that the possession of these gifts without love, cancels the value of them, as he says, If I have these without love, I have nothing. Again the self-evident deduction is that through love the supreme energy in equipment, prophecy uttered under its mastery, knowledge of mysteries governed by its inspiration, a faith acting under its direction, the true place of power and of influence is reached.

" And if I bestow all my goods to feed the poor, and if I give my body to be burned, but have not love, it profiteth me nothing."

In these words the apostle refers to two proofs of devotion, the first being the impoverishment of self for the enrichment of the poor; and the second being conviction so mighty as to create consent to martyrdom. Again we mark the superlative nature of the suggestion, and then listen as the apostle says that even if these things be so, if love be lacking, "it profiteth me nothing." Motive is everything in the matter of the bestowment of goods, and in that of consent to martyrdom.

Again to look at this from the opposite side, it means if love be the impulse of my giving, and the master power of my devotion to truth, the devotion is of value.

Turning to the second movement, dealing with the virtues of love, we find an exquisitely beautiful passage. A careful examination of this section will reveal the fact that there are seven statements dealing with love as to the individual, and seven concerning love in its relationships. Let it at once be recognised that in dealing with love from the standpoint of the individual, it is always seen in relation to others, and in dealing with love in its application to others, it is always seen as victorious in the individual.

Let us first simply read the first seven sentences:

" Love suffereth long, and is kind."
" Envieth not."
" Vaunteth not itself."
" Is not puffed up."
" Doth not behave itself unseemly."
" Seeketh not its own."
" Is not provoked."

" Suffereth long, and is kind." That is the overplusage of patience, not merely suffering long, that is patience; but being kind afterwards at the point when your patience might naturally be exhausted. It is a curiously constant habit to refer to the " third time " as marking the limits. In connection with this we may remind ourselves of how upon one occasion Peter wonderfully exceeded that idea as he suggested he should forgive his brother seven times; to which our Lord replied:

" I say not unto you, Until seven times; but, Until seventy times seven."

Only love is capable of this.

There is a poetic illustration of this, full of beauty in the Old Testament, when Jacob was dealing with his sons, referring to Joseph, he said:

" Joseph is a fruitful bough,
A fruitful bough by a fountain;
His branches run over the wall."

A fruitful bough is a beautiful thing, but when it is so fruitful that it does not confine itself within walls, but runs over, then we have love in its overplusage.

" Love envieth not."

If we return for a moment to the preceding chapter, where Paul was dealing with the diversities of gifts and operations and energies within the one body, we find him saying:

" If the foot shall say, Because I am not the hand, I am not of the body; it is not therefore not of the body. And if the ear shall say, Because I am not the eye, I am not of the body; it is not therefore not of the body."

Imaginatively here, the foot is envying the hand, and the ear the eye. This envy is impossible to love. Where love is, the foot rejoices in the dexterity of the hand, and the ear in the brilliance of the eye. There is no envy.

" Love vaunteth not itself."

The whole emphasis, of course, of that statement is on the little word " itself." Love does not boast in the fact of its own existence. The old Roman who said to one who was protesting his love for him overmuch, " Friend, I doubt thee," gave expression to a feeling which was justified. Love never vaunts itself.

" Love . . . is not puffed up."

This word goes a little deeper than the former, and shows the reason why love does not vaunt itself. The statement reveals the sweet unconsciousness of true love. It does not think of itself as something of which to be proud.

" Love . . . seeketh not its own."

That necessarily is the profoundest word concerning the self-emptying capacity of pure love. When that test is applied, it is found to be the most searching, for very much that goes by the name of love in the last analysis is self-seeking. True love, however, " seeketh not its own."

Finally:

" Love . . . is not provoked."

The King James' Version read at this point:

" Is not easily provoked."

This is a very illuminative fact. The word " easily " is not in the text; it is not found in any MS. There can be very little doubt that those godly men who were remarkable scholars, felt Paul was going a little too far, and so slipped in the word " easily." As a matter of fact multitudes of people have gone through life since 1611 excusing their evil tempers by saying they are not easily provoked. Love is not provoked at all. The declaration describes patience in the presence of irritants. So far then we have an analysis of love in its effect upon personality.

Then follow the seven phrases in the second movement.

" Taketh not account of evil."
" Rejoiceth not in unrighteousness."
" Rejoiceth with the truth."
" Beareth all things."
" Believeth all things."
" Hopeth all things."
" Endureth all things."

As we have said, the individual, of course, is here, but all the while is seen in relation to others.

" Taketh not account of evil."

This may very bluntly be expressed by saying that love does not keep a ledger in which wrongs are entered, to be dealt with on some future day.

" Rejoiceth not in unrighteousness."

That, of course, is the other side of the thing already said. Love does not take account of evil, because it cannot find satisfaction of any kind in the wrong thing done. This is expressed in the sentence, it " rejoiceth not in unrighteousness."

" Rejoiceth with the truth."

Once more this is the reason of the inability to be glad in the presence of unrighteousness. It rejoices in the truth.

An interesting commentary on these first three things may be found in Paul's letter to the Philippians, when he said:

" Whatsoever things are true, whatsoever things are honourable, whatsoever things are just, whatsoever things are pure, whatsoever things are lovely, whatsoever things are of good report, if there be any virtue, and if there be any praise, think on these things."

The last phrase of that passage, " think on these things," might accurately be rendered, " Take an inventory in these things." That is in perfect harmony with:

" Love taketh no account of evil; rejoiceth not in unrighteousness, but rejoiceth with the truth."

" Beareth all things."

Here we have a pictorial word, the point of which may be lost. The thought of the word is that of putting a shield over, so as to keep those underneath that shield in safety. Love " beareth all things " in that sense, canopies another so that he is safe from the perils that are threatening him. Love is for evermore busy thus covering those in danger, and protecting them from the harm that might come to them.

" Believeth all things."

That is not the credulity of the easily deceived, but the absence of suspicion from the nature. This is a sure activity of love.

" Hopeth all things."

This description quickly following upon the other, suggests that perhaps there may be some reason for suspicion, some warrant for it. In that case love " hopeth "; that is, love is ever the inspiration of optimism, hoping for the best against all appearances.

Love:

" Endureth all things."

Or to render that in another form, it means that love remains strong through all processes. It stays under in sustaining power, whatever may happen. It is good to link this word " endureth "

with an earlier one, " beareth." " Beareth " means to put over;
" endureth " means to stay under.

Then comes one brief sentence. Our translators follow it
with a semi-colon. It would be good to follow it with a full-stop,
thus leaving it in its completeness.

" Love never faileth."

That summarises all that has already been said. Literally
it means that love never falls out of its course. It never becomes
inefficient. It cannot lose its life principle and motive power.
This little Pauline sentence gave Shakespeare warrant when he
wrote those simple and yet sublime words:

> " Love is not love,
> Which alters when it alteration finds."

Having summarised everything in the one sentence, the
apostle comes to the final movement in the chapter, in which the
victories of love are revealed. He shows what these are by comparison with other high things, as he says:

> " Prophecies . . . shall be done away; tongues . . . shall
> cease; knowledge . . . shall be done away."

He illustrates his meaning by describing the passing of childhood into manhood. Prophecies are done away in the sense that
they are worked out to fulfilment. Tongues as signs and methods
of praise cease when the necessity for such ends. Knowledge as
enquiry is done away as it merges into the knowledge of fuller
revelation. All the things referred to are great things, and things
that tend to edification, but which cease when the edifice is
completed.

But there are things which will abide. Faith will abide.
In one of our hymns we sing of a day when faith shall be lost in
sight. Whereas there is a sense in which that is true, there is
a sense in which it is not so. The eternal principle of life for
finite beings will ever be that of faith in the infinite God. Faith
will abide, and be triumphant.

Hope will abide, because there will always be new realms
into which men can enter. It was Paul who said:

" Who hopeth for that which he seeth? "

Hope will have to do with the constant consciousness of new
unveilings to be granted. We shall never exhaust God; therefore
hope will abide.

Love necessarily will abide. The arresting thing here is that Paul declares that the greatest of these abiding things is love. When the statement is considered, we find that love is the reason and strength of faith and hope. If love should fail, faith would falter. If love broke down, hope would fade away. Therefore to the boundless ages, love will remain, the strength of faith, and the inspiration of hope.

The first sentence in the following chapter really completes the thirteenth. It is the injunction:

" Follow after love."

A study of this thirteenth chapter of First Corinthians must inevitably produce in all of us a sense of failure. If this indeed be love, how far we come short. And yet we thank God for the measure in which we do know its values, its virtues, and its victories. Realising, however, human failure, the apostle says:

" Follow after love."

His word rendered " follow " indicates necessity for something that is strenuous. He used the verb in his Philippian letter as he described himself as persecuting the Church, and later on, as following after, pressing on, pressing toward the mark. In every case there is the idea of effort, and the necessity for diligence. The word connotes a passionate devotion and a determined effort. We have not yet attained to the perfection of the love-mastered life, but we may, and must " follow after."

> " . . . we covet most
> Of Thy gifts at Pentecost,
> Holy, heavenly love."

I CORINTHIANS XV

OUR chapter falls within the second section of the letter, in which Paul was dealing with the spiritualities.   Having described the unity of the Church, and shown that its unfailing law was that of love, he turned to the subject of its ultimate victory, that of resurrection.   In this chapter we find the central, classical passage dealing with the subject in the New Testament.   Its outlook is historic, dealing with the resurrection of Christ.   It is also prophetic, looking on to the resurrection of the saints.   I think it will be conceded that in all literature, there is no greater passage in diction, in dialectic, or in dynamic.   It is characterised by logical acumen, and yet it is the chapter with which we are most familiar in the darkest hours of life, when our loved ones pass out of our sight.

In the present meditation, realizing that the one subject is that of resurrection, we shall take one method of consideration. It will be found that its teaching gathers round four words, words occurring quite incidentally, but nevertheless creating the foci of the light that shines in the chapter.   The words I refer to are " Gospel " in verse one; " Kingdom " in verse twenty-four; " How? " in verse thirty-five;   and " Immortality " in verse fifty-three.

The method thus suggested may seem at first to be capricious, but I nevertheless believe that it does help us to gather the full scope of the teaching.   The argument of the writer gathers around these words, that is, of course, around the statements in which they occur.   The whole teaching may thus be summarised in its fourfold movement.

First, the resurrection ratifies the Gospel (1–19).

Secondly, the resurrection assures the Kingdom (20–34).

Thirdly, the resurrection harmonises with natural law (35–49).

Finally, the resurrection pledges immortality (50–57).

The main teaching of the chapter is dealt with in the first, second, and fourth of the divisions suggested.   The third division is devoted to answering the question, " How? " and consists of an argument as to the inherent possibility of resurrection in itself, both in the case of Christ and of those who are believers in Him. Thus verses thirty-five to forty-nine in a sense constitute a great parenthesis of argument.

" Some will say, How? "

and Paul pauses to answer them.

The first section dealing with the resurrection and the Gospel is very arresting, because in it the apostle in a remarkable way, summarises the Gospel message.

" I make known unto you, brethren, the Gospel which I preached unto you, which also ye received, wherein also ye stand, by which also ye are saved. I make known, I say, in what words I preached it unto you, if ye hold it fast, except ye believed in vain.

" For I delivered unto you first of all that which also I received, how that Christ died for our sins according to the Scriptures; and that He was buried; and that He hath been raised on the third day according to the Scriptures."

That is the Gospel. It may be stated in many other ways quite accurately, and perhaps more fully and more in detail; but everything is summarised in the declaration that Christ died for our sins, and Christ was raised again. These are the two elemental facts constituting the Gospel. They interlock and are inter-related. The fact that Christ died does not in itself constitute the Gospel, save as it is linked with the resurrection. The resurrection demonstrates the value and the meaning of the death. Thus it is seen how that resurrection ratifies the Gospel. This the apostle makes very clear as he says:

" If Christ hath not been raised . . . ye are yet in your sins."

Necessarily we are saved by His death, but what proof have we that that is so? The proof is found in the resurrection. Others have died, and in certain senses others have died for other men's sins. Others have died in loyalty to holiness through the sinning of men against them. There is no Gospel, however, in the fact. Christ, however, died and was buried. As we stand imaginatively before the tomb containing that dead Body we are without hope, for we have no demonstration that His death was more than the death which others have died. The resurrection means that we are, as Peter has it, begotten again unto hope. It ratifies the Gospel. If there be no resurrection, the apostle twice affirms that our faith is vain, that is that it is mere superstitious credulity.

Moreover, if there were no resurrection it means that the dead have perished, that is, been completely destroyed. The resurrection is the demonstration of the fact that in the mystery of His dying He dealt with sin. Thus the resurrection provides for the world the ratification of the Gospel. How is the questioning heart of man, dissatisfied with the mere trivialities of intellectual debate, but concerned with the moral necessity of cleansing from sin, to know that the death of Christ on the Cross was of any value? The answer is He was raised from the dead. Apart from that resurrection we have no answer to this quest for moral cleansing. Any belief in Jesus as a Saviour from sin is superstitious credulity if those are right who declare that He was laid in a Syrian tomb, and never rose therefrom.

Following this teaching we have a passage of stupendous import. Paul starts with an affirmation. He had been supposing what would happen if the resurrection of Christ as a fact in history could be disproved. There was no doubt about the fact in his own mind. Therefore he now affirmed positively:

" But now hath Christ been raised."

Having made the affirmation, he proceeded to show the ultimate issue of the fact:

" By man came death, by man came also the resurrection of the dead. For as in Adam all die, so also in Christ shall all be made alive. But each in his own order; Christ the Firstfruits."

Then we have the revelation of an outlook which, for prophetic insight and foresight is in some senses the greatest in the Bible. No Hebrew prophet ever saw so far ahead as Paul did when he wrote this passage. It is equally true that no prophetic teaching in the New Testament reveals a vision so far-reaching. John, in Patmos, had granted to him an unveiling of the Lord in His glory and in His government up to the point of final victory on the earth level, when the city of God is built and the Kingdom of God is established. It was indeed a marvellous vision, and was inspired. Paul, however, writing to this Corinthian Church, was lifted to a height in which he saw further ahead than any Hebrew prophet or New Testament seer. When he wrote, " Then cometh the end," he was looking on to the consummation seen by Hebrew prophets and New Testament seers, but he saw beyond. What follows shows that what is in certain senses the end, is by no means the end, but only the beginning. The consummation or end is the initiation and beginning of a new eternal order. When the end comes:

> " He shall deliver up the Kingdom to God, even the Father."

The question arises, when will that be? The apostle distinctly answers that question in the words:

> " When He shall have abolished all rule and all authority and power. For He must reign, till He hath put all His enemies under his feet. The last enemy that shall be abolished is death."

When that consummation or end is achieved:

> " He shall deliver up the Kingdom to God."

There is a sense in which He will reign through all the ages, but not in mediatorial fashion. His reign to-day is that of the Messiah, that is, the One in Whom the offices of King and Priest merge. When the priestly function is perfectly fulfilled, then His mediatorial reign will end, and He will deliver up the Kingdom to His Father, with Whom He was and is and will be eternally associated. The vital connection between that and the resurrection is revealed in the statement that:

> " The last enemy that shall be abolished is death."

He was the Firstfruits of resurrection; and the ultimate harvest will be the destruction of death completely, when He has put down all rule and authority and power, when all the forces exalting themselves against the Kingship of God, are subdued, abolished. The assurance therefore of the ultimately perfected Kingdom being delivered to God is found not in the fact that He died, though that was the way of its restitution, but that He rose from the dead. The resurrection of our Lord therefore assures us of the ultimate answer to the prayer which He taught us to pray:

> " Our Father Who are in the heavens,
> Thy name be hallowed,
> Thy Kingdom come,
> Thy will be done
> On earth as . . . in heaven."

When that hour of ultimate triumph comes, He will deliver up the Kingdom to God, that God may be all and in all.

There are times when it seems difficult to believe that such a consummation will ever be reached. If we simply examine situations, and consider human consultations and the breakdown of human conferences, there would seem to be little hope. How then do we know that there must be such victory? We know it because He rose from the dead. That resurrection, the most stupendous supernatural wonder in all human history, is the ratification of the faith that His reign will at last bring in a perfect Kingdom, and restore completely in human history and experience the reign of God.

And now we come to what we have described as the parenthetical division, which is purely dialectic. Paul voices the questioning of those who will say, " How are the dead raised? " Moreover, he at once shows the reason for the question in that those who ask it also say:

" With what manner of body do they come? "

Let it at once be said that these are perfectly natural questions, and I will go further, and say perfectly legitimate questions. Whether we are thinking of the resurrection of Christ, or of the resurrection of others, we are thinking of the fact of resurrection in itself. Now it is of the utmost importance to consider what answer can be given to such questions.

The apostle commences with what is practically an exclamation. The Authorized Version rendered it " Thou fool." The Revisers have moderated it into, " Thou foolish one." The word literally means one without understanding. Wiclif rendered it, " Unwise man." The apostle was not suggesting that the question was an improper one in itself, but he was suggesting that it was not a question of high intellectuality.

There is a sense in which Paul does not answer the question, but there is a sense in which he very fully answers it. He took the questioner into the realm of Nature, using the illustration of the " bare grain," which put into the ground, dies, and yet comes up again. That " bare grain " coming to life again, comes not in the body in which it was put into the ground, but in a new body. Paul who sees the operation of God in Nature as well as in grace, says of that grain:

" God giveth it a body, even as it pleased Him."

Let us imaginatively look at this carefully. He reduces our looking to one grain. At his suggestion we drop it into the earth. Now, says the apostle, the thing that happens when it comes again is that it has received a new body from God. The continuity of identity is marked by the word " it." What? The " bare grain." From that which is essential in its being, presently it comes again, but in new formation and new fashion, because God hath given it a body.

All this reminds us that in the presence of the questions which are perfectly fair in themselves, the fundamental answer is God. When that is realized, whereas much of mystery remains as to the way, the possibility is at once recognised.

That, of course, is the story of every harvest time. Men:

" Plough the fields, and scatter
The good seed on the land."

All such scattering means death in the case of the seed, but over against that statement we make another quotation:

" He makes the grass the hills adorn,
And clothes the smiling fields with corn."

In every case it is He Who gives the new body for the same life principle, which has never been lost. The application of this to the fact of resurrection is self-evident. Whether our thought is concerned with the body of our Lord, or with the bodies of those who have passed from this life, the possibility of resurrection is demonstrated by the fact and activity of God.

At this point the apostle turned aside to declare the diversities of bodies. Bodies are always secondary things, however necessary they may be, and they are diversified. There is flesh of man, of beast, of bird, of fish, all different, as God pleases; and created in every case for the life principle. Again he says there are bodies celestial and terrestrial. There are different interpretations of the apostle's meaning at that point. Personally, I believe by bodies celestial he was referring to those which we have on the other side of resurrection, the body for instance, which our Lord had after His resurrection; and by bodies terrestrial he was referring to those in which we are limited by the terrestrial or earth life, such as the body of our Lord in the days prior to His Cross and resurrection.

Moreover, he says there are different glories, the glory of the sun, of the moon, of the stars. In saying that, he was not emphasizing degrees, but differentiation of quality. Here he passed to the celestial spaces to illustrate a great truth. Even in the life beyond, the bodies of the saints will differ in glory. Thus to summarise, he teaches that in the resurrection there will be continuity of personality, but a change of body; and this is wonderfully illustrated in the stories we have in the Gospels, of our Lord in the forty days following His resurrection. We read them, and we say we cannot understand them, and it is perfectly true; but when we base upon our lack of understanding, a refusal to believe in the facts, surely Paul would address us as he did the imagined asker of the questions, as Ye foolish ones. In this case also, what we know not now, we shall know hereafter. In the meantime, however, we are called upon to recognise that the whole conception of resurrection harmonises with the laws of the universe from the bare grain which we cast into earthly soil to the varied splendours of the stellar spaces.

Returning to the more positive teaching concerning the resurrection, the apostle began by declaring that the bodies of earth are unfitted for the Kingdom of God in its fullness, as he said:

" Flesh and blood cannot inherit the Kingdom of God."

Again it may be difficult to explain exactly the meaning of that statement; but without desiring to be dogmatic, it is very interesting to remember that after our Lord's resurrection, when He appeared to His disciples in His resurrection body, proving its identity by the signs He gave them, and referring to that body, He said:

" A spirit hath not flesh and bones as ye behold Me having."

Again we may not understand that, but the contrast is arresting between the statement of Paul that flesh and blood cannot inherit the Kingdom of God, and our Lord's description of His own body as " flesh and bones."

Continuing, he declares that resurrection will create a complete change as to our bodies. Whether we may have fallen on sleep ere the hour of the ultimate resurrection of the saints, or whether we remain, and are alive at the coming of the Lord, we shall all be changed. It is in that hour that death will be swallowed up in victory. It will be then that we shall reach immortality or deathlessness. In writing to Timothy, that is the word, *athanasia*, which Paul used with reference to God. None of us has attained to that yet, nor shall we, until the resurrection; and apart from resurrection, we have no proof of ever attaining to immortality in that sense of deathlessness in every regard.

It was as the apostle contemplated that ultimate issue of the resurrection of the saints, following and resulting from the resurrection of the Lord, that he uttered his double challenge:

" O death, where is thy victory? O death, where is thy sting? "

And having declared that the sting of death is sin, and the power of sin is the law; he finally affirmed:

" Thanks be to God, which giveth us the victory through our Lord Jesus Christ."

Very full of beauty are Bishop Taylor's lines on that passage.

" Death, the old serpent's son,
  Thou hadst a sting once, like thy sire,
  That carried hell and ever burning fire;
  But those black days are done;
  Thy foolish spite buried thy sting
  In the profound and wide
  Wound of our Saviour's side;
  And now thou art a tame and harmless thing;
  A thing we dare not fear,
  Since we hear
  That our triumphant God, to punish thee
  For the affront thou didst Him on the tree,
  Hast snatched the keys of hell out of thy hand,
  And made thee stand
  A porter at the gate of life, thy mortal enemy."

It is significant that this great chapter ends with the injunction:

" Wherefore, my beloved brethren, be ye stedfast, unmoveable, always abounding in the work of the Lord, forasmuch as ye know that your labour is not vain in the Lord."

Thus, the final appeal of the resurrection is to stedfastness in that work of the Lord wherein and whereby the purpose of the Gospel shall be accomplished, the victory of the Kingdom brought in, and the experience of immortality secured.

If Christ be raised, our Gospel is ratified, the coming of the Kingdom is assured, immortality is a certainty.

EPHESIANS I

THE full context of the first chapter in the letter to the Ephesians is contained in that whole letter, together with the letter to the Colossians. These two letters constitute the crown and completion in the matter of teaching of the Pauline system. The foundation letter is that to the Romans, wherein Salvation is the theme. These two letters, Ephesians and Colossians, are, or may be, described as twin epistles. They are closely related. In Ephesians the subject is the Church, as to its nature and vocation. In Colossians the subject is the Christ, as to His glory and His grace. It goes without saying that Ephesians also deals with the Christ, and Colossians with the Church. The supreme emphasis, however, is as we have stated it.

With regard to Ephesians, it may be said that it is the full and final commentary upon the words of our Lord uttered at Cæsarea Philippi:

"I will build My Church; and the gates of Hades shall not prevail against it. I will give unto thee the keys of the Kingdom of heaven; and whatsoever thou shalt bind on earth shall be bound in heaven; and whatsoever thou shalt loose on earth shall be loosed in heaven."

The letter to the Ephesians tells of the building of the Church, of the conflict of the Church, and of the moral responsibility and power of the Church. In the first three chapters the apostle dealt with the nature of the Church, and the last three with its vocation during its earthly pilgrimage.

The second part of the letter commences with the words:

. "I, therefore, the prisoner in the Lord, beseech you to walk worthily of the calling."

What that calling is, had been shown in the first three chapters. These three chapters may be described as dealing first with the predestined purpose of the Church; secondly, the processional building of the Church; and thirdly, the perfected vocation of the Church. Or more briefly, chapter one, predestination; chapter two, edification; chapter three, vocation.

Our present study is concerned with the first chapter, in which is contained the first movement, that namely of the pre-destined purpose of the Church. The chapter may be set out thus:

> Introduction and Salutation, verses 1 and 2.
> Inclusive Preliminary Benediction, verse 3.
> The Predestined Purpose, verses 4 to 6.
> The Predestined Process, verses 7 to 14; and
> The Parenthetical Prayer, verses 15 to 23.

The epistle opens with Paul's introduction of himself to his readers, and his description of those readers. He began as he so constantly did, by emphasising his authority as " an apostle of Christ Jesus through the will of God." It is impossible to read Paul's writings without realising that in a certain sense he had constantly to insist upon that right. I think it may be safely conceded that he was never *persona grata* with the Church in Jerusalem.

He described those to whom he addressed his letter as:

> " The saints which are at Ephesus, and the faithful in Christ Jesus."

It is possible that this letter was sent to a group of Churches. Many MSS. omit the words " at Ephesus." The matter is of no vital importance. We may certainly be sure that if it was sent to a group, Ephesus was one of that group. In any case, whether at Ephesus or elsewhere, those to whom he wrote were:

> " Saints . . ., and the faithful in Christ Jesus."

It may be well to pause at this point to say that this description may produce in the mind of some of us a feeling that the letter is not for us; by which I mean that we are prone to be afraid of the word " saint," and to declare that we are not saints. It is good, therefore, that we should at once remind ourselves that if we are not saints we are not Christians. Saintship means separation to God, and that separation is created when we believe, and in response are born again. It is the word which describes the position into which we are brought. It may be that we do not always walk worthily of the fact. In the course of this letter to these same people, he uses the phrase, " As becometh saints " (verse 3), when he is urging them to a life that harmonises with the fact of their saintship. To that word " saints " he added the phrase:

> " the faithful in Christ Jesus,"

and it is important that we should understand that the word " faithful " here does not necessarily mean that their life was one of complete fidelity, but rather that the principle of their life was that of faith in Christ Jesus.

He greeted these people with the salutation which he often used, " Grace to you, and peace," the grace being the source from which everything proceeds, and peace the ultimate result in experience of all that flows from grace. Practically the last thing our Lord said to His first group of disciples was:

" My peace I give unto you."

Thus Paul greeted the saints and those who live upon the principle of faith with these two words, marking as we have said, the source from which everything proceeds, and the issue in experience. Finally, he declared the source and channel both of grace and peace in the words:

" From God our Father, and the Lord Jesus Christ."

When we come to the third verse we have what we have described as an inclusive preliminary benediction. It is in the nature of a doxology, and is full of significance; as in itself it gathers up and gives expression to the full activity of the Church. It is as though at this point Paul, as member of that Church, broke out into the true eucharistic function of its priesthood. Perhaps one should turn aside to say that the word eucharist refers to the function of worship and praise.

" Blessed be the God and Father of our Lord Jesus Christ, Who hath blessed us with every spiritual blessing in the heavenly places in Christ."

In this doxology we are arrested by the recurrence of the word " blessed." It is first applied to God:

" Blessed be the God and Father of our Lord Jesus Christ."

It then has reference to us:

" Who hath blessed us with every spiritual blessing in the heavenly places in Christ."

The apostle is uttering the words that expressed his reverence, his worship, his gladness.

" Blessed be the God and Father of our Lord Jesus Christ ";

and he gives his reason for this ascription of praise in his own experience, in common with that of all believers, as he says that this God:

" Hath blessed us with every spiritual blessing in the heavenly places in Christ."

In considering the first ascription of praise to God, personally I would like to leave out the word " be." It does not occur in the Greek New Testament. There are senses of course in which it is permissible, but to me something is gained in leaving it as a great exclamation, " Blessed the God and Father." It is not that in any sense he is conferring anything upon God, but recognising the fact of His blessedness. Personally, if it is necessary to supply a verb, I should suggest that instead of " Blessed be," we should read, " Blessed is." The exclamation is the confession of the recognition of the essential fact concerning God.

It is a matter of more than passing interest that in thus uttering the word of worship, he described God as:

" The God and Father of our Lord Jesus Christ."

Necessarily the words indicate relationship, but it is at least a very interesting fact that if one takes the story of Jesus, as found in the Gospel narratives, it will be found that these were His two names for God; God and Father. It is quite true that in certain places He is recorded as having referred to God as Lord; but in all such cases He was quoting from the Old Testament. It would seem as though Paul were familiar with this fact when he spoke of God in these terms. The God addressed is the One Who in the consciousness of Christ, was ever God and Father, and Who was revealed by Christ in His Godhead and in His Fatherhood.

On the ground of personal experience of that God, resulting from what had been accomplished in His revealing by the Lord Jesus Christ, he uttered the doxology, and spoke of the things accomplished as he said: He

" hath blessed us with every spiritual blessing in the heavenly places."

In that great doxology, or Benediction, there is incidentally revealed, as we have remarked, the fact that the supreme function of the Church is that of declaring the blessedness of God as it is realised and revealed in the blessedness which has come to the Church from Him, through the Lord Jesus Christ.

We now pause to glance at the three movements following, and the first has to do with the predestined purpose of God. We notice that the writer goes straight on from the doxology, with the words:

" Even as He chose us in Him."

That is to say, the spiritual blessings in the heavenly places are now to be further interpreted. We approach this subject with care, and our care is concern with what it really says. The declaration is that God:

> "Chose us in Him before the foundation of the world, that we should be holy and without blemish before Him in love."

A very clear distinction must be made between this statement and that interpretation which declares that He chose us in order to be saved. The declaration is that He chose us that we should be holy and without blemish before Him in love. The choice of God was concerned with the character of those to whom the apostle was writing, in common with all saints:

Continuing, he said:

> "Having foreordained us unto adoption as sons through Jesus Christ unto Himself, according to the good pleasure of His will, to the praise of the glory of His grace, which He freely bestowed on us in the Beloved; in Whom we have our redemption through His blood, the forgiveness of our trespasses."

In these words we are shown who it was that He chose to this character. They are such as He foreordained to adoption as sons, and these are such as have redemption through His blood. Those chosen then are those who have become sons, and those who become sons are those who have believed; and by that act of faith have become saints. These He chose to be holy. Here then was the predestined purpose, that saints should be holy, and that in order to the praise of the glory of His grace.

Immediately following this revelation of predestined purpose, we have teaching concerning the predestined process. That process is revealed in the words already quoted:

> "In Whom we have our redemption through His blood, the forgiveness of our trespasses, according to the riches of His grace."

The people predestined to the realisation of this character are first of all redeemed, and that through blood. The redemption through blood means the forgiveness of trespasses, of course in the full sense of that phrase as it is revealed throughout the apostolic writings.

To summarise on this teaching, we find the order of experience is first:

> "Redemption through His blood, the forgiveness of our trespasses."

This is followed by a revelation, or making known of these things, the interpretation of the ultimate reach of the experience of the saints, as they become:

" A heritage, having been foreordained according to the purpose of Him Who worketh all things after the counsel of His Will."

Writing thus to these Gentile believers, the apostle says:

" Having heard the word of the truth, the Gospel of your salvation,——in Whom, having also believed, ye were sealed with the Holy Spirit of promise, which is an earnest of our inheritance, unto the redemption of God's own possession, unto the praise of His glory."

Once again to summarise on the teaching. It first declares the predestined purpose of God to be the creation of an instrument composed of men and women, " saints," " faithful in Christ Jesus," chosen to holiness and the love-mastered life, in order that they might show forth the praise and glory of the grace of God. That predestined purpose is carried out as to process in a redemption which sets free from sin, and a revelation which interprets the will and the purpose of God. These people first heard, then believed, then were sealed. All such as may be thus described, constitute that instrument of God for the revelation of Himself, and the accomplishment of His purposes.

Following, the teaching gives what we described at the beginning as a parenthetical prayer, in which the apostle turned aside to tell them of his concern for them. Here he began by recognising the things they possessed, and he did it in the words:

" Having heard of the faith in the Lord Jesus which is among you, and which ye show toward all the saints."

That is, in itself, an arresting description. The proof of the faith of the saints in the Lord Jesus Christ is found in their manifestation of faith in the saints. This, of course, does not suggest that belief in the saints is equivalent to belief in the Lord Jesus, for belief in the saints has no saving value; but belief in the saints is demonstration of belief in the Lord Jesus. It is again to be observed that the same thought was brought out by the apostle when writing to Philemon, he said:

" Hearing of thy love, and of the faith which thou hast toward the Lord Jesus, and toward all the saints."

Thus he recognised that faith in the Lord Jesus finds its manifestation in belief in each other. Of course, ultimately, that means that our faith in Christ is faith in what He can do for all the saints, which creates confidence in them. It may often be in spite of much which seems to come short of the realisation of the highest.

Now while recognising that they have this faith, Paul declared that he was still praying for them, and we enquire, What was it that he was desiring on their behalf? Glancing down the paragraph, we see the recurrence of the word " that," in verse seventeen and in verse eighteen. Thus there are two movements in his prayer.

The first is expressed in the words:

" That the God of our Lord Jesus Christ, the Father of glory, may give unto you a spirit of wisdom and revelation in the knowledge of Him; having the eyes of your heart enlightened."

Then next a declaration that shows the reason of that movement in the prayer:

" That ye may know what is the hope of His calling, what the riches of the glory of His inheritance in the saints, and what the exceeding greatness of His power to us-ward who believe."

In the teaching we have a declaration of God's purpose and process. In the prayer he recognised the faith that existed in the saints, and declared his thankfulness for it; but expressed his desires for them in this double movement.

The first desire is that they might have granted to them the spirit of wisdom and revelation. He desired that they might not be satisfied with the mere fact of relationship, but that they might have the vision, enabling them to grasp the significance of the things they believed, and the purposes of God therein.

We may turn aside for a moment to say that perhaps it is there where we are in danger of constantly coming short in the life and work of the Christian Church. We do not give time enough to examine our own experience in Christ, and to understand all that is the purpose of God therein. We are satisfied merely with the fact of forgiveness of sin. I am not suggesting that that is not subject for profound satisfaction and constant joy; but it is of importance that we should consider and understand the meaning and issue of that blessing in the purpose and economy of God.

Continuing, he shows why this enlightened intelligence is important. In this connection there occurs that which is, in itself, an arresting and an amazing suggestion. The apostle prayed that they might know what is:

" The riches of the glory of His inheritance in the saints."

Some thirty years ago, in what was intended to be a popular rendering of the New Testament, that sentence was rendered:

" That ye may know what are the riches of the glory of our inheritance in Him."

That was a most unfortunate rendering, and I may say was subsequently corrected. Paul was not here declaring his desire that they should know the greatness of their inheritance in God; but that they should know the riches and glory of God's inheritance in them.

As I have already said, this is a most arresting and amazing sentence, its meaning being that there is a sense in which God gains something in His Church of value to Him. Perhaps the truth may be bluntly stated thus, that there are things in the very Being and nature of God which found no expression or interpretation in the universe, amid all the wonders of His creation; and that these things were found possible of being revealed in that universe through His redeemed and ransomed Church. In that sense God Himself gains an inheritance in His people. The idea ever seems to me to have a remarkable expression in the poem by Elizabeth Barrett Browning, entitled " The Seraphim." In this she describes two of them watching the Christ, and the process of His work in the world, including the Cross, angels desiring to look into these things. As they watched they saw whereunto that work was proceeding, and one of them said to the other, looking down upon the ransomed and redeemed sons and daughters of the earth:

" Hereafter shall the blood-bought captives raise
The passion song of blood."

To which the other seraph replied:

" And *we* extend
Our holy vacant hands towards the Throne,
Crying, ' We have no music.' "

And that does tell the story. Neither angel, or archangel, cherubim or seraphim, or any of the heavenly host, can ever reveal the deepest truths concerning God as can ransomed humanity.

The parenthetical prayer closes with a recognition of how these eternal purposes of God concerning His people, are to be realised in the words:

"The exceeding greatness of His power to us-ward who believe, according to that working of the strength of His might."

Everything will be accomplished by what the apostle describes as "the exceeding greatness of His power"; and he gives the supreme illustration of that power as it was manifested in the resurrection of our Lord, declaring that in that resurrection He wrought, "according to the working of the strength of His might." The three words in their combination here are arresting, "working . . . strength . . . might." The last named, " might " refers to the essential fact. The previous one, " strength " refers to that might at its mightiest. And the first one, " working," refers to that same might in its activity.

This power was so great, that raising Christ from the dead, it placed Him in authority over all things, and gave Him to be Head over all things to the Church, of which the apostle now speaks as:

"His body, the fulness of Him that filleth all in all."

It is well to remind ourselves at the close, of that supreme word:

"God so loved the world that He gave His only begotten Son ";

and to remember that in order to the accomplishment of His purpose through the Son He creates His body, the Church, which is:

"The fulness of Him that filleth all in all."

EPHESIANS II

THE second chapter of the letter to the Ephesians carries forward the teaching found in the first chapter. Having revealed the purpose of God concerning the Church, the apostle now proceeded to show how God builds the Church, and fashions the instrument for the carrying out of His purpose.

The purpose of God concerning His Church being that it should be the instrument through which the work of His only begotten Son Whom He gave, because He loved the world, should be carried forward. That Church consisting of all such as believing on the Son, receiving the gift of life, He predestined to holiness and love.

Having thus dealt with the predestination of God concerning His Church, the apostle proceeded to show how God builds His Church. The chapter for purposes of examination may be divided into two parts. In the first ten verses we have a description of the materials out of which the Church is built, and a declaration concerning the Divine activity which builds. From verses eleven to twenty-two the process of the building to its completion is dealt with.

We turn first, therefore, to consider the apostolic description of the materials out of which the Church is built. We have to bear in mind that the apostle was writing to Gentiles, and that fact was in his mind throughout. He himself was a Jew, and as a member of the ancient people of God recognised the privileges that were those of his own people. He was conscious, however, that what God had done for his people, He had done for the Gentiles also.

Having declared that God had put all things in subjection under the feet of Christ, and given Him to be Head over all things to the Church, which is His body, the fullness of Him that filleth all in all;—going straight forward, he said:

" And you did He quicken, when ye were dead through your trespasses and sins, wherein aforetime ye walked according to the course of this age, according to the prince of the power of the air, of the spirit that now worketh in the sons of disobedience; among whom we also,"

Jews, as well as Gentiles

"All once lived in the lusts of our flesh, doing the desires of the flesh and of the mind, and were by nature children of wrath, even as the rest."

In that paragraph we have a description of the material out of which God builds His Church. A consideration of it will show that it is a description of people living absolutely contrary to the purpose and thought and will and character of God. It may be said that such people would appear to be the most hopeless material out of which to create an instrument for the accomplishment of the Divine purpose. Their condition before God is briefly stated in the declaration that they were dead in trespasses and sins; that is to say that they had no knowledge of God, or relationship with Him. Nevertheless, of such people He builds His Church, and creates His instrument for the fulfilling of His purpose. Moreover He has predestined those very people to holiness and love.

As the paragraph is examined more particularly, we are brought face to face with the dominant forces in the lives of these people. The first is that of the world:

"Wherein aforetime ye walked according to the course of this age,"

that is, they were conformed to the spirit of the times, to its material outlook, in which the dominant force was that of the world.

This being so, the deeper truth is declared, that they were under the dominion of Satan, for they

"Walked according to the prince of the power of the air, of the spirit that now worketh in the sons of disobedience."

The result of such a view of life, and such a mastery of Satan was that life was lived in the realm of the flesh, as the apostle says:

"In the lusts of our flesh, doing the desires of the flesh, and of the mind."

The result of all this was that these people were the "children of wrath." The Divine attitude towards such life could be none other than that of displeasure.

These are the people whom God takes hold of in order to the building of His Church; people dead towards God, that is towards all spiritual things; dominated by the outlook of the age, limited by earthly considerations; under the control of the spirit of evil. Looking at men thus, there would seem to be nothing whatever in them capable of fulfilling the vocation of revealing God, or of manifesting His holiness, or showing forth His grace. The description is humbling, and revealing, and amazing, in the light of the declared purpose of God. Nevertheless it harmonises perfectly with that saying of our Lord Himself:

> " I came not to call the righteous, but sinners to repentance."

Out of such material the Church is being built.

When we turn to consider the teaching concerning the Divine activity, we are at once arrested by the disjunctive " But," drawing as it does a sharp line between the conditions of the materials described, and that which is to follow. Men are first seen as helpless and useless in the economy of God. Then we meet with the " But," and the next word is " God." That in itself is a revelation. The only hope for man is found in God. If God does not act, humanity is hopeless and helpless.

When, however, we have the word " God," we recognise a possibility. The apostle then proceeds to show the source of the Divine activity. This he does in the words, " God, being rich in mercy." That is the essential truth concerning Him. He is " rich in mercy." Were this not so there would be no hope of redemption. Were God only the God of holiness, or the God of strict justice, there would be no deliverance for a people dead, under the mastery of the world, Satan, and the flesh, children of wrath.

The next phrase refers to the activity of that mercy in the Being of God, " For His great love wherewith He loved us." Carefully observe the connection. " Being rich in mercy . . . He loved us." Here we have brought together, if we may reverently say so, cause and effect. In one of the old Methodist hymns the lines occur:

> " He hath loved, He hath loved us,
> We cannot tell why."

That is perfectly true so long as we are looking at ourselves; but when we think of God, we may say at once, because of what He is, " being rich in mercy," He could none other. He loved us. This love of God towards man is emphasised by the writer as he declares that it operated not as the result of restoration, but as the reason of it.

> " He loved us . . . even when we were dead through our trespasses."

This is the love of God, and it is this quality in it which is different from, and transcends all other love. Sometimes a sublime truth may be illustrated in a simple story. A boy in a Sunday School class, perhaps troubled over some wrong-doing of his own, asked his teacher, " Teacher, does God love naughty boys? " and the teacher answered, " No, He certainly does not." The answer was hasty, and entirely false. It is those who are dead in trespasses and sins that He loves.

Recognising these truths concerning the Being and activity of love in God, the apostle proceeded to show how He acts with regard to those upon whom His love is thus set. The first declaration is that He quickened us, the second is that He raised us up, and the third is that He seated us in the heavenlies. Everything begins in what is here described as quickening, and that together with Christ, which, of course, self-evidently is another way of describing the new birth. By that quickening He raised us, placing us over the forces which had mastered us; and finally He seated us in the heavenlies with Christ, in the place of fellowship and authority.

The teaching is perfectly clear that all these things come to us in and through Christ Jesus. The repetition of the preposition " with " is arresting. He quickened us with Christ, He raised us with Christ, He made us sit with Christ. In doing this He deals with all the matters of our disability. We who were dead are now alive with Christ. We who were under the mastery of the destructive forces of the world, the flesh, and the devil, are now raised with Christ, and seated in the heavenly places of full and final authority. Thus the material, so impossible of anything high and holy, is taken hold of, and being brought into living relationship with Christ, passes into the realm of life, and into that of freedom from all destructive forces.

All this brings us to a statement which is at once simple and yet arresting and amazing.

" That in the ages to come He might show the exceeding riches of His grace in kindness toward us in Christ Jesus."

Thus it is stated that God quickens us, and raises us, and seats us in Christ, in order that He may show " the exceeding riches of His grace in the ages to come."

In this declaration the apostle was looking on to the ultimate purpose of God in the creation of the Church. Whereas the Church has its clearly defined responsibility in the world to-day, the ultimate meaning of its creation is found in the ages to come.

Out of material so unlikely, so useless for the display of the Divine glory, God creates an instrument through which in all the coming ages He may show the riches of His grace. These words of the apostle are words of inspiration, and like all such, they demand the breath of the Spirit upon them to interpret them in all their fullness. That reference to the ages to come is suggestive and amazing. What are the ages to come? Who shall tell? The phrase gathers all within itself which we speak of as the future. It is an outstanding truth that the Bible is always poetically suggestive concerning the future, rather than mechanically dogmatic. We use the phrase " for ever," and are justified in doing so; but what does " for ever " mean? When the question is asked, we have to admit the impossibility of anything like a mathematical reply. A little later, in this same letter, we read:

" Unto Him be glory in the Church and in Christ Jesus unto all generations for ever and ever. Amen."

The final words more literally rendered would be:

" Unto all the generations of the age of the ages."
This is indicated in the margin of the Revised. In the presence of that phrase we may allow our imagination to work. The generation refers to the births of the ages, and yet the writer includes all in the phrase, " the age of the ages."

God is creating a Church, the purpose of which is that in those ages, whatever they may be, however long their duration, or whatever their characteristics, it shall be the supreme medium for revealing to them His grace. That is the ultimate meaning of the Church, as to God's purpose concerning her.

In passing we may say that it has sometimes been declared that this kind of teaching is not practical, because it is too other-worldly. Let it at once be said that when the Church of God loses her sense of her heavenly nature and calling, and ceases in that sense to be other-worldly, she loses her power to touch the earth with saving grace. It is, therefore, of the utmost importance that we should never forget that the ultimate meaning of our salvation, and of the Church of God is relationship to the mystery of the coming ages, which ages will learn the riches of His grace through the kindness shown towards us in Christ Jesus.

The final movement in this section reveals the fact of the Divine activity, producing these results.

" For we are His workmanship, created in Christ Jesus for good works, which God afore prepared that we should walk in them."

The word workmanship is an arresting one, in that while it does refer to activity, it introduces a touch of artistic beauty. The word itself is the word *poema*, which does refer to works, but has in it the suggestiveness that the works are in themselves things of beauty and of excellence.

Whatever may be the things which we see to-day in the Church, which are things of blemish and of failure, it remains true that all the things of true beauty that are found in the life of men to-day, are things that have come to them through the grace of God, and through His Church. It is well to remember, moreover, that as yet the perfect beauty of the Church has never been revealed. It is still in process of building, and consequently is surrounded, if we may follow the figure for a moment, by much of scaffolding. Sometimes one feels that our differences and divisions are the result of the scaffolding. If we can only look through, or behind all these things, we shall see already the beauty of the edifice, which God is creating, and which is to find its final functioning in the ages to come.

The closing section of the chapter (verses eleven to twenty-two) passes from the examination of the material and the Divine activity as to individuals, and deals with the union of such individuals into the complete Church. All those who were dead, mastered by the world, the flesh, and Satan, and children of wrath, having been renewed by God Who is rich in mercy, and therefore quickened, raised, seated, are built into one great institution.

Again writing from his standpoint of relationship with the Jew, and addressing himself to these Gentiles, he says:

" Wherefore remember, that aforetime ye, the Gentiles in the flesh, who are called Uncircumcision by that which is called Circumcision, in the flesh, made by hands, that ye were at that time separate from Christ, alienated from the commonwealth of Israel, and strangers from the covenants of promise, having no hope and without God in the world."

That was the condition of the Gentile world. Here, then, occurs another disjunctive " But."

" But now in Christ Jesus ye that once were far off are made nigh in the blood of Christ,"

and so on, to the words including Jew and Gentile:

" For through Him we both have access in one Spirit unto the Father."

Thus the great apostle to the Gentiles, himself a Jew, who had been living and serving among these Gentile people, he who had recognised the dividing line between them and the Jew, saw how all the things that separated were broken down through Christ. The opposing factions and forces were ended, and peace was created. This peace was the peace of the reconciliation of all to God; and the consequent reconciliation of each to the other, of Jew to Gentile; and indeed, the reconciliation is applicable to all the differences which have divided humanity, as humanity has been separated from God. In Christ men are brought to God, and being brought to God are brought to each other. That was the constant burden of Paul's interpretation. In Christ there is neither Jew nor Gentile. In Christ there is neither bond nor free. In Christ there is neither male nor female.

That threefold declaration is in itself, a very revealing one when we remember that Paul was a Pharisee, and we know how the Pharisees day by day uttered the words:

" O God I thank Thee I am not a Gentile, that I am not a slave, and that I am not a woman."

In Christ there are no dividing lines which create separation and bitterness. In the Church all are brought together; and continuing, the apostle says:

" So then ye are no more strangers and sojourners, but ye are fellow-citizens with the saints, and of the household of God."

Finally, he shows that that building is erected upon the foundation of the apostles and prophets. It is important that we should understand what is meant by that phrase. It does not suggest that apostles and prophets constitute the foundation, but rather refers to the foundation upon which the apostles and prophets built. In his first letter to the Corinthians, Paul said:

" According to the grace of God which was given unto me I laid a foundation; and another buildeth thereon. But let each man take heed how he buildeth thereon. For other foundation can no man lay than that which is laid, which is Christ Jesus."

That is what Paul meant when in this Ephesian letter he speaks of building on the foundation of the apostles and prophets.

Here he completes the reference by the arresting figure of speech:

" Christ Jesus Himself being the chief corner-stone."

The value of that expression is only found when it is recognised that the figure employed is that of a pyramid. In a pyramid the corner-stone is the key to the whole building. From it the complete height and dimension of the erection can be gained. The lines of the corner-stone run up to the apex, and in that sense Christ is the chief Corner-stone.

Continuing, he speaks of each several building, thus recognising diversity; but speaks of them also as being " fitly framed together," thus recognising their unity. Of the building he says it ˇ

" Groweth into a holy Temple in the Lord; in Whom also ye are builded together for a habitation of God in the Spirit."

The ultimate then is this holy sanctuary, this indwelt sanctuary, which is to be the medium through all the ages to come for the manifestation of the grace of God. Through those ages, as we have said before, whatever may be their duration or characteristic, it is through the Church that God will interpret His grace. That Church He is building out of material which, when He took hold upon it, was utterly unlike Him, utterly antagonistic to Him. But He, being rich in mercy, loved us, quickened us, raised us, seated us in the heavenlies.

That Church then becomes in its very nature, and of necessity, an unveiling of God in His redeeming grace. The Church is created for this eternal vocation by the transmutation of hostile and helpless material into an instrument of beauty and of glory in its revelation of the grace of God.

EPHESIANS VI

THIS closing chapter in the letter to the Ephesians constitutes the climax to the section in which Paul was dealing with the earthly conduct of the Church, in view of its heavenly calling.

In the earlier part of the letter (chapters I. to III.), having dealt with the predestination, edification, and vocation of the Church, the apostle turned to the matter of the Church's conduct, commencing with the words:

" I therefore, the prisoner in the Lord, beseech you to walk worthily of the calling."

While the ultimate calling of the Church is a heavenly one, she has an earthly responsibility consequent thereupon. The Church's first responsibility is concerned with the recognition of her unity and of her growth. Then, turning to matters concerning the individual, the family, and the household, he showed in every case what conduct is worthy of the heavenly calling.

In this particular chapter we have the subject of parents and children, and masters and servants dealt with. This brings us to the ninth verse. Our chapter then may thus be divided: teaching concerning conduct (verses one to nine); the subject of conflict (verses ten to eighteen); the conclusion (verses nineteen to twenty-four).

The teaching concerning conduct is concerned with the relation between children and fathers, and servants and masters. Necessarily, any consideration of it must depend upon a recognition of what has preceded in chapter five, where in practical application, he begins with wives and husbands.

As to children, two injunctions are given which are closely related, and yet must be considered in separation. The first is the simple command to obey parents; but it must be remembered that in the Christian household this is qualified by the expression " in the Lord." The simple command to children to obey their parents is a re-emphasis upon the demand made by Hebrew law. Carefully considered from the standpoint of the child, it is at once seen how gracious and beneficent a command it is. It provides that in the earliest years, children should not be called upon to think, or arrange, or plan, but walk in ways appointed for them. The very mystery of the constitution of human nature in experience inclines to objection to that way of life. Its beneficence however is undoubted. As the years of life pass on, when responsibility must inevitably be assumed, and when each for himself or herself must come to personal decisions, hours will often arrive when one longs for some authority that sets one free from responsibility. A weakness of childhood is revealed in its objection to authority. The weakness of age is often revealed in desire for it. Happy indeed is the life of the child, who, when set free from responsibility except that of obedience, can express itself with all freedom.

In this connection, however, it is most important that we bear in mind the qualifying phrase already referred to, " in the Lord." Here is perhaps a startling, but nevertheless a clear recognition of the fact that if a child recognises that some command laid upon it, violates its personal relationship to the Lord, it is not called upon to obey.

The second word concerning the responsibility of children is found in the words:

" Honour thy father and mother (which is the first commandment with promise), that it may be well with thee, and thou mayest live long on the earth."

In the development of the life of a child the moment does and must arrive when obedience to external authority, even that of parents, must cease when the child comes to years of personal, volitional activity. But the duty to honour parents never ceases. It is of the utmost importance that we should remember that an hour does arrive when simple and unquestioning obedience must cease. When the boy or girl comes to what we now speak of as the period of adolescence, the hour when will becomes the central factor of personality and affirms itself, that is the time when we should no longer ask for unquestioning obedience. I have often, in the course of my work, suggested a formula for parents at such a period. It is, " Quit commanding, and begin communing." All that being granted, the hour never arrives when children should cease to honour father and mother.

Turning to parents, the apostle writes:

" Ye fathers, provoke not your children to wrath."

It is noticeable that while fathers and mothers are referred to in the command, " Obey your parents," when the apostle was speaking of the responsibility of parents, he names fathers only. This is in itself a matter of importance, especially in view of the facts as they exist to-day. It often seems to me that the fathers within the Church of God are failing, perhaps all unconsciously, but nevertheless definitely in the matter of their highest responsibility for their children. They feed them, sometimes wisely, always well; they clothe them, sometimes properly, always adequately. They give them a good education, but they neglect entirely their responsibility in spiritual matters.

The particular command laid upon fathers is certainly arresting and almost startling. It does seem to suggest that fathers are in danger of doing that very thing. The simple meaning is that they are charged not to act towards their children in such a way as to create in the heart of the children resentment against either the command issued, or, much more likely, against the means taken to enforce obedience. Bear with a very homely illustration, which perhaps comes out of one's own past experience. I confine myself to the thinking of a boy, with which I am most familiar. Your boy stands in front of you, and you are annoyed to see that his pockets are bulging in an ugly way. Manifesting your annoyance, you command that he take out of his pockets all the things stored therein, the half-penny, the broken knife, the bit of string, the pebbles. If you watch your boy as he unloads, you will see that he is annoyed. You are offending his dignity, and you have no right to do so. It is quite possible to have the pockets dealt with by drawing his attention to the fact that they are a disfigurement, and requesting that he himself shall go and investigate their contents, and deal with them. Fathers are terribly in danger of walking among their children on stilts. Let them get down by the side of their boys and girls, and entering into their feelings, refrain from provoking them to wrath. There is no surer way of provoking them to wrath than by being satirical in the presence of their ambitions. We wrong the child when it tells us of its dreams, and we remark with supercilious superiority that it is merely building a castle in the air.

All that is negative, and the apostle immediately passes to the positive injunction, which in itself is inclusive and final on the matter of the training of children.

" But nurture them in the chastening and admonition of the Lord."

Three words are employed here, " nurture," " chastening," " admonition "; and every one has its distinct value. The word nurture is excellent, if we really understand its meaning. The Greek word, *ektrepho* simply means to straighten out. The idea is that there is something involved, which must be evolved. The word postulates a starting point, and indicates a process which leads to culmination. That reveals our responsibility concerning the child. It is not that of putting something into a child that is not there, but finding what is there and leading it out to full realisation. At this point we inevitably think of the word in the

Old Testament, which is so often quoted, and so often misunderstood.

" Train up a child in the way he should go,"
a very misleading rendering of the thought in the Hebrew. It should be rendered:

" Train up a child according to its way."

The command recognises that in every child there is a way, a potentiality, a possibility. The business of those responsible for the child is that of discovering it, and leading it out to full realisation.

How this is to be done is revealed in the other words:
" in the chastening and admonition of the Lord."

The word chastening might be properly rendered disciplining. Discipline is not necessarily painful. It simply marks a necessary method. It recognises that the child is malleable and needs discipline in order to the realisation of its own powers. The word admonition, which means informing the mind with intention, cannot be improved upon. Thus the whole philosophy of training is revealed. First, education, the bringing out of what is there, and continuously instruction, the putting in of what is lacking.

The relationship between servants and masters is simply stated:

" Servants, be obedient unto them that according to the flesh are your masters, with fear and trembling, in singleness of your heart, as unto Christ; not in the way of eyeservice, as men-pleasers; but as servants of Christ, doing the will of God from the heart; with good will doing service, as unto the Lord, and not unto men."

Three simple phrases are revealing, " as unto Christ," " as servants of Christ," " as unto the Lord." If these phrases are understood by those who serve, they shed a glory upon all such service. George Herbert declared that it was possible to sweep a room and make it, that is the room, and the action, that is the sweeping of it, fine.

Turning to masters, he said:

" Ye masters, do the same things unto them, and forbear threatening; knowing that both their Master and yours is in heaven, and there is no respect of persons with Him."

Thus the attitude of masters towards servants is to be that of the recognition of the mastery of Christ, over all. A recognition of the mastery of Christ is to be the inspiration of the service of the servant; and it must also be the inspiration of the mastership of the master. Where these ideals are realised we have the Christian home.

Having thus dealt with these applications of the Christian calling to what we may perhaps call the commonplaces of life, the apostle turned to the subject of conflict. It goes without saying that for such a people in such a world as this, still under the dominion of Satan, conflict will be inevitable. It is impossible to live the heavenly life on earth as it is to-day, without knowing conflict. Our Lord Himself had distinctly told His first disciples:

" In the world ye shall have tribulation."

With that fact the apostle now deals. In doing so he commences with a general injunction:

" Finally, be strong in the Lord."

I think the marginal reading is better here. " Finally, be made powerful in the Lord." Or perhaps once more, slightly to change it, " Finally, be strengthened in the Lord, and in the strength of His might." This injunction, of course, flashes its light back upon the things already enjoined, and forward upon the subject of the conflict which must inevitably result from obedience. In order to walk worthily of the calling, and in order to the strife consequent upon the worthy walk, we need to be strong or made powerful in His strength.

That general injunction is then interpreted. He describes in some detail the equipment provided for us, and gives the reason why we should be thus equipped. The equipment is inclusively named first in the command to put on the whole armour of God; and the reason is given in the words:

" That ye may be able to stand against the wiles of the devil."

It is interesting in passing to notice that this is the only place in all the writings of Paul where he definitely names Satan. He constantly recognised the fact of his existence, and over and over again refers to the nature of the world over which Satan reigns. Here he definitely names him, and we are brought to the recognition of the age-long conflict in which we too are involved. It is a conflict between God and Satan, between those on the side of God and those under the mastery of Satan.

The apostle interpreted this conflict in remarkable language as he said:

" For our wrestling is not against flesh and blood."

It has been suggested that by the use of the word wrestling, Paul has broken down in his figure of speech, passing from the military to the athletic. I think, however, that shows an inadequate interpretation of the real thought of the word wrestling. As a matter of fact it suggests hand-to-hand fighting. Paul says that our hand-to-hand fighting is not against flesh and blood; that is not the realm of our conflict. When he himself was beaten with stripes, he did not resist. When they put him in the stocks, with his body lacerated, leaving stigmata upon him, he did not resist.

> " Our wrestling is . . . against the principalities, the powers, against the world-rulers of this darkness, against the spiritual hosts of wickedness in the heavenly places."

Thus he recognised the whole realm of the underworld of evil spirits under the mastery of Satan, and creating the earthly antagonisms.

In view of that conflict we are to " put on the whole armour of God "; but more, we are to " take up the whole armour of God." It is self-evident that there is a difference between putting on and taking up. Putting on is dressing for parade. Taking up is for actual conflict. His description of the armour is graphic, and we shall not attempt to deal with it in detail. Truth for the loins, righteousness for the breastplate, readiness in the Gospel of peace for the feet, faith for the shield, salvation for the helmet, the Word of God for the sword, prayer and supplication which make the armour effective.

The expression " the whole armour of God " is in itself a remarkable one. The word which we have rendered " whole armour " is the word *panoplia*, which in our language we have Anglicised into panoply. If we read the statement, " the panoply of God," I think we recognise at once that whereas it refers to something provided for us, it has a deeper meaning. In passing, we may notice that there is only one other place in the New Testament where the word occurs. It is found in the Gospel according to Luke (xi. 22) when Jesus, Who had been charged with casting out demons by Beelzebub, in His answer said:

> " When the strong man fully armed guardeth his own court, his goods are in peace; but when a stronger than he shall come upon him, He taketh from him his panoply wherein he trusted, and divideth his spoils."

Our Lord was there claiming that what He was doing was that of robbing the strong man of his panoply. Thus the only occurrences of the word in the New Testament are that in which it is applied to Satan and this in which it is applied to God.

The significance of the phrase is that it describes the things which make God invincible against all attacks. This very armour of God, this panoply which makes Him thus invincible, is all placed at our disposal in the conflict with the hosts of wickedness. We are certainly able with confidence to sing:

> " Jesus is stronger than Satan and sin,
>   Satan to Jesus must bow.
> Therefore I triumph without and within,
> And Jesus is saving me now."

While this panoply of God is placed at our disposal, and put on and taken up renders us invincible, the attitude in which we are able to employ it must ever be that of supplication and prayer. When this attitude is maintained, and we are able to use the armour, there can be no question as to the issue of the conflict. The reading of the whole paragraph shows the confidence of the apostle. We are to put on the armour that we may stand. We are to take it up that we may withstand. Then comes the final exultant note, " having done all, to stand."

Thus, the heavenly people, with a heavenly calling, and a heavenly testimony, living in a world still largely under the dominion of the evil one, must know conflict against these fiery forces of evil. But in the conflict, with such a panoply, they become invincible against all the attacks of the foe.

The conclusion of the letter is first personal. The apostle speaks of their being in prayer and supplication for all the saints, and adds the revealing words, " and on my behalf."

All ends with the benediction:

> " Peace be to the brethren, and love with faith from God
> the Father and the Lord Jesus Christ. Grace be with all
> them that love our Lord Jesus Christ in uncorruptness."

The outstanding words in the benediction referring to the experience desired for the saints are the words " peace " and " grace." Peace describes the possible experience of all who, conscious of their heavenly calling, are walking worthily thereof, and waging a conflict against the forces of evil. In the midst of all, peace is to be theirs, combined with love. The ultimate secret of that peace is the grace which is bestowed upon them.

Thus the concluding benediction harmonises with the opening salutation:

> " Grace to you, and peace, from God our Father and the
> Lord Jesus Christ."

PHILIPPIANS II

THE letter to the Philippians is unique among the writings of Paul in the personal note which runs through it. It was written from prison, as also were the letters to the Ephesians, Colossians, and Philemon; and evidently all were written about the same time. This particular letter was addressed to the saints in Christ Jesus, which were in Philippi. It was there that the apostle's work in Europe had begun, and that, while he was a prisoner there. He was now writing to these people, gathered to Christ in connection with his imprisonment in Philippi, from a prison in Rome. The letter is one of love and song from beginning to end, full of references to his personal experiences, and of exhortation to these children of his love concerning their experiences. The word " sin " is not found in the letter. The flesh is only mentioned once in order to be dismissed. There seems to be no ruffle upon the calm and sunlit waters, except that there would appear to have been at the time some little misunderstanding of some kind between two good women, Euodia and Syntyche, to whom the apostle said:

"I exhort Euodia, and I exhort Syntyche to be of the same mind in the Lord."

The chapter now under consideration follows closely upon an exhortation found at the twenty-seventh verse of the previous chapter:

" Only let your manner of life be worthy of the Gospel of Christ: that, whether I come and see you or be absent, I may hear of your state, that ye stand fast in one spirit, with one soul striving for the faith of the Gospel; and in nothing affrighted by the adversaries; which is for them an evident token of perdition, but of your salvation, and that from God; because to you it hath been granted in the behalf of Christ, not only to believe on Him, but also to suffer in His behalf; having the same conflict which ye saw in me, and now hear to be in me."

The first word of our chapter is " If," which of course links all that follows with what he had thus already written. In that paragraph he called these people to a manner of life or citizenship worthy of the Gospel, and described that manner of life as being first standing fast in one, secondly being in nothing affrighted; and finally, as suffering with Christ. In this chapter, then, we find what are the secrets of the manner of life enjoined.

The chapter falls into two parts; first an interpretation of the secrets of the manner of life in verses one to eighteen; and secondly certain matters concerning Timothy and Epaphroditus in verses nineteen to thirty. This second section is purely personal, very beautiful; and all the way through moving in the realm of the truth the apostle had been dealing with in the first section. In our examination we shall content ourselves by brief reference to it in conclusion. Necessarily we are principally concerned with the movement found in the first eighteen verses, dealing with the manner of life worthy of the Gospel. This section has three distinct movements, first a general exhortation (verses 1–4); secondly, the central interpretation (verses 5–11); and thirdly, the final application (verses 12–18).

Necessarily the central section is that which arrests and holds us as supreme in its values. In verses five to eleven we have a passage concerning which I do not hesitate to say there is nothing more surpassingly wonderful in the whole of the Scriptures of truth. As we are following a series of selected chapters, it is interesting and valuable to remember that our next study will be concerned with the first chapter of the letter to the Colossians. It is important because that chapter is distinctly the correlative to this. This will be understood more clearly when we come to deal with the Colossian chapter.

As to the general exhortation, it is well that we have it before us in fullness:

" If there is, therefore, any comfort in Christ, if any consolation of love, if any fellowship of the Spirit, if any tender mercies and compassions, fulfil ye my joy, that ye be of the same mind, having the same love, being of one accord, of one mind; doing nothing through faction or through vainglory, but in lowliness of mind each counting other better than himself; not looking each of you to his own things, but each of you also to the things of others."

The apostolic appeal opens with a series of suppositions, each commencing with the word " If." The very reading of these sentences makes it evident that the suppositions are intended to be affirmations. " If there be any comfort in Christ." As we

read this, let us bear in mind the strength of that word " comfort."
It literally means holding together in strength. It is self-evident
that the apostle knew the comfort of Christ in that sense. " If
any consolation of love." This goes beyond the idea of holding
together in strength, and conveys the idea of comfort in the other
sense. Paul knew well what consolation in this sense was found
in Christ. " If any fellowship of the Spirit," and that phrase
describes the reason and power of all discipleship. " If any
tender mercies and compassions," and these words reveal the
inevitable consciousness of such as have the love of God shed
abroad in their hearts. These great suppositions then, as we
have said, are references to facts in Christian experience.

Upon the basis of these great facts the apostle makes his
appeal:

" Fulfil ye my joy, that ye be of the same mind, having
the same love."

A reference to the things we have dealt with will show that
the mind is the mind of Christ, of the Spirit, and of the Father,
and that it is the mind of love.

Continuing, he shows how that mind expresses itself in self-
abnegation:

" Doing nothing through faction or through vainglory,
but in lowliness of mind, each counting other better than
himself; not looking each of you to his own things, but each
of you also to the things of others."

The general exhortation is that in view of the fact of comfort
and consolation in Christ, of the fellowship of the Spirit, of the
tender mercies and compassions of God, our life is to manifest
the power of all these things. The supreme manifestation of
them in life must ever be that of self-abnegation. That then, is
the great injunction, interpreting the manner of life worthy of the
Gospel.

Then, in that connection, the apostle summarises everything
as to the secrets of obedience in the simple, but stupendous
sentence:

" Have this mind in you, which was also in Christ Jesus."

This great word is immediately followed by a paragraph
which we read almost with bated breath, for in it Paul, by the
Spirit of God, unveils or interprets the mind of Christ.

Closely following the injunction, " Have this mind in you, which was also in Christ Jesus," is the word " Who," leading to this unveiling or interpretation of the mind of Christ. As we approach it, it is well to draw attention to a fact of vital importance, that, namely, of the recognition throughout, of the continuity and identity of the Person. Glancing back, we notice the juxtaposition of title and name and relative pronoun, " Christ Jesus; Who." Quite evidently then, the " Who " refers to the One named " Christ Jesus," and everything subsequently to be said, refers to the same Person. There is no point in the process of the unveiling in which the identity of the Person is lost. In order to clear apprehension we may divide the passage into two parts, the first revealing the mind of Christ in its outworking (verses 5–8); the second declaring the issue of the mind of Christ (verses 9–11).

When dealing with this mind which was in Christ Jesus, the apostle passes back into the mystery of the past, and refers to what we may call, for the lack of a better phrase, the pre-existence of this same Person, that is, His existence prior to His coming into human life and human history. " Who, being in the form of God." The conception is identical with that which is found in the Prologue of John, when he said:

" In the beginning was the Word, and the Word was with God, and the Word was God."

The word which Paul employed here, and we have rendered " form " is the Greek word *morphe*, which has a fuller signification than our word " form " might suggest. Whereas it does mean a manifestation, and so refers to the form of the manifestation, it also includes the idea of reality, and thus refers to that which was manifested. " Being in the form of God," then does describe the fact of the past. In that past, however, we may conceive of it, and we really can only do so by speaking of eternity, this Person was essentially God; and at the same time was the one method of the Divine manifestation. We shall reach the same idea when dealing with the Colossian chapter we find Paul saying, "Who is the Image of the invisible God," where the tense is that of the eternal present.

Thus the reference being to that eternal relationship, the apostle declares that then He:

" Counted it not a prize to be on an equality with God." That statement might with accuracy be rendered as to its meaning and value, that He did not count His equality with God a thing to be grasped and held for Himself. Using the only language possible to us, that of our earth-bound thinking, we may say that there was an utter absence of personal ambition in the mind of Christ in those eternal relationships.

The outcome of this was that He " emptied Himself." This passage is the one which is described by theologians as the passage of the Kenosis, which means the passage of the Self-emptying. When we consider it, it is of the utmost importance that we should remember that when He thus emptied Himself, He did not empty Himself of Himself. There are those who have suggested that in the Incarnation, our Lord divested Himself of His essential Deity. This was by no means so. He emptied Himself of one form of manifestation in order to the taking of another form. That is at once seen if we read the declaration concerning the self-emptying as it is written, in close connection with what follows.

" He emptied Himself, taking the form of a Servant."

That declaration, of course, is one of something that is:

> " . . . too bright,
>   For the feebleness of a sinner's sight ";

so tremendous that human intellect cannot completely grasp it. Nevertheless, it is a simple and sublime declaration that He emptied Himself of one form of manifestation to take another form of manifestation. The eternal form had ever been that of Sovereignty. Emptying Himself of that, He took the form of a Servant.

Then the revelation runs on, and deals with the form of the Servant which He became. God has many servants, such as cherubim, seraphim, arch-angels, angels. None of these did He take. His Self-emptying was in the interest of humanity, and therefore again continuing, the words are found, " being made in the likeness of men." So far we are in the presence of heights and depths transcending the possibility of final apprehension; and yet all are made evident by the declaration; and the movement brings us to the point of the human level, " Being made in the likeness of men." There again the harmony is seen between Paul and John, as we remember John's words, " The Word became flesh, and tabernacled among us."

And now we have reached the point of historic visibility:

> " And being found in fashion as a Man."

That is more than a reference to the fact of the birth of our Lord. It includes the period of innocence, and of victory over temptation, until at last He stood metamorphosed, transfigured upon the mount, having arrived at Manhood's full and final estate and glory.

Now the question comes, What will be the next stage in the Divine procedure? And the answer is found in the words:

" Being found in fashion as a Man, He humbled Himself."

Thus the perfect human realisation in the perfect Manhood is revealed as synchronising exactly with the facts stated in the essentials of Deity:

" Being in the form of God, emptied Himself."

" Being found in fashion as a Man, He humbled Himself."

That Self-emptying in His Deity, expressing itself in the humbling of His humanity, reached its ultimate as He was " obedient even unto death."

Death was not inherently necessary to human nature within the Divine ideal, but became necessary as the result of sin. Therefore being found in fashion as a Man, He humbled Himself, and went all the way with humanity in its sin, bowing even to death. That death is described with reverent reticence in the words, " yea, the death of the Cross."

Let us remind ourselves at once that all this unveiling followed upon the injunction:

" Have this mind in you which was also in Christ Jesus ";

the mind that stoops from sovereignty to slavery, from the realisation of perfect Manhood to the shame and agony of the Cross.

So far the apostle has been dealing with the mind of Christ in its outworking. Now he shows the issue of that outworking.

"Wherefore also God highly exalted Him, and gave unto Him the name which is above every name."

Here it is patent that the " Wherefore " links all now to be said with what had been said concerning the Cross. The issue of the Self-emptying, of the humbling, of the death, was this exaltation by God, and the giving to the exalted One of a name. There are differing opinions as to the name referred to. Personally I cannot see any reason for doubt that the name is the name Jesus, for the apostle runs on:

" That in the name of Jesus every knee should bow."

The name Jesus was given to Him in the historic hour of the Incarnation, and its value was declared in the angel announcement:

" Thou shalt call His name JESUS; for it is He that shall save His people from their sins."

This was heaven's choice of a name for the Incarnate Son of God. When He received it as a Babe, it was a prophetic name, a declaration of the ultimate meaning of His coming into human history. The mighty work being accomplished, and the accomplishment being ratified by the resurrection, He having ascended on high, God gave Him the name in all fullness of executive authority. That right to authority is expressed in the words which declare the purpose of God:

> " That in the name of Jesus every knee should bow, and every tongue should confess that Jesus Christ is Lord, to the glory of God the Father."

The bending of the knee is the attitude of submission, and the confession of the tongue declares the consent of the submission. The consent is to His Lordship, and the consent to His Lordship is in order to the glory of God the Father.

Once more we remind ourselves that the whole unveiling of the mind of Christ is in order to emphasise the injunction:

> " Have this mind in you."

Thus the simple things of individual life are linked to the sublimities of eternity. The attitudes and thinking and action of the human are linked with the attitudes and thinking and action of God.

This brings us to the familiar passage (verses 12–18), in which the apostle shows what is the human responsibility, and how it is linked with Divine power. Human responsibility is revealed in the words:

> " Work out your own salvation with fear and trembling."

That, in itself, reminds us that Christianity is not an easy thing. It must be wrought out, and that with fear and trembling. If, however, it is not an easy thing, it is nevertheless true that all necessary power is ours, for:

> " It is God which worketh in you both to will and to work, for His good pleasure."

Our responsibility is that we work out what God is working in.

The practical application of that is that when we are obedient, we:

> " Do all things without murmurings and disputings ";

that we

> " May be blameless and harmless."

" Blameless " refers to personal character, and " harmless " to relationship with others. As we pause at that point we may be inclined to say that we shall reach that experience in the life that lies beyond. If we are tempted so to think, we are sharply pulled up by the next words:

"Children of God without blemish, in the midst of a crooked and perverse generation, among whom ye are seen as lights in the world, holding forth the words of life."

The term, "a crooked and perverse generation" does not apply to heaven, but to the earthly places where we now live. We are to be as lights in the world.

The remainder of the chapter deals, as we said at the beginning, with personal matters, having special reference to Timothy and Epaphroditus. A reading of it will show two men living in the power of the things revealed in the earlier part of the chapter. Timothy and Epaphroditus were certainly men having the mind of Christ, hazarding their lives for the sake of others. Thus, while Paul sent these two men to the Philippians that they might know about him, and that presently he might know about them; there is no doubt that the principal reason was that they might have contact with these living witnesses of what it means to have the mind of Christ.

COLOSSIANS I

WHEN considering the first chapter in the letter to the Ephesians, we referred to the relation between that letter and the letter to the Colossians, claiming that the Ephesian letter was concerned with the Church, its nature and glory; and the Colossian letter with Christ, His glory and His grace.

There can be no doubt whatever that in this chapter we have the apex of the Pauline interpretation of the Person of our Lord. Nevertheless all the glories of Christ are set forth as at the disposal of the Church. It may be said that two sentences taken from the Colossian letter reveal its purpose, and give a summary of its content. The first of these is found in this chapter:

" For it was the good pleasure of the Father that in Him should all the fullness dwell."

The second is found in the next chapter:

" In Him ye are made full."

In our last study we were occupied with the second chapter in the letter to the Philippians, in which the glories of Christ in one particular are so marvellously revealed, that, namely of the Self-emptying of the eternal Son. That chapter is often called the chapter of the Kenosis. In this chapter from the Colossian letter we find what should ever be considered in connection with the chapter of the Kenosis, for this is the chapter of the Pleroma. In the Incarnation there was a Kenosis, " He emptied Himself." But it is equally true that in that Incarnation there was a Pleroma. In the tenth verse of the second chapter we read:

" In Him dwelleth all the fullness of the Godhead corporeally."

The word " corporeally " there does not mean in all fullness, but in bodily form. It was in the Word made flesh that all the fullness of the Godhead dwelt.

The theme of this chapter is that of the fullness or Pleroma which thus dwelt corporeally in Christ. For purposes of study it may be broken up into three movements. The introduction is found in the first thirteen verses. From the fourteenth verse through the twentieth, we have the particular passage setting forth the glories of the One Who is referred to as " The Son of His love." From verse twenty-one to the end, the Church is in view.

The introduction falls into three parts; a salutation, an apostolic thanksgiving, and an apostolic prayer. In the salutation Paul names himself as:

" An apostle of Jesus Christ through the will of God "; and associates with himself in the letter, Timothy, whom he describes as " the brother."

Having thus saluted the Colossian Christians, he told them that he was giving thanks for them, and praying for them, in the words:

" We give thanks to God the Father of our Lord Jesus Christ, praying always for you."

It is well to notice that here are two distinct movements, first that of his thanksgiving, and secondly, that of his prayer. The thanksgiving itself is found in verses three to eight, and in the reading of them three words stand out as revealing the things causing his thankfulness. He was thanking God for their faith, their love, their hope. These are the cardinal elements of true Christian experience, and they were all manifest in the lives of these Colossian Christians.

The arresting matter is that while he was giving thanks for these things, he was nevertheless still praying for them. We might be inclined to say that if these people had faith and love and hope in such a measure, that as the apostle thought of them he was filled with gladness, and gave thanks to God for them, what more could he desire on their behalf? The answer to that enquiry is found in verses nine to thirteen. We may summarise by saying that he was praying that they might have first the knowledge of the will of God, and unquestionably through that the knowledge of God Himself. That same desire found expression in each of the letters that Paul wrote during this period of imprisonment, and its true significance is gained as we recognise the force of the word that the apostle used, which we have rendered " knowledge." It is not the ordinary word for intelligent apprehension, but that word strengthened; not *gnosis*, but *epignosis*, that is, full and complete knowledge. They had faith, they had love, they had hope, and the apostle thanked God that it was so; but he knew that they had not arrived at the fullness of their Christian life, or at understanding concerning that life. This was only to be reached progressively by fuller understanding of the will of God, and of the truth concerning God Himself. For this the apostle prayed on their behalf.

Our common Christian experience responds to the suggestions of that prayer. We have faith, we have love, we have hope; but we realise there are depths unplumbed, and heights unreached, and breadths unembraced in the glory of our God, and in the perfection of His will; and there is nothing more important than that we should follow on to know the Lord.

The introductory section runs straight on into that dealing with the glories of Christ. Declaring that those to whom he wrote had been delivered out of the power of darkness, he also said that they were translated into the Kingdom of the Son of His love, and with that phrase, " the Son of His love " commences the setting forth of the glories of His Person.

This phrase, " the Son of His love " is in itself an arresting one. In its wording it is unique. We do not find it occurring anywhere else, although of course its equivalent is found, and the suggestion it makes is in harmony with the whole New Testament revelation. In writing to the Ephesians the apostle spoke of our Lord as " The Beloved." Here, however, stands a phrase full of simplicity, and yet charged with sublimity. It declares the relationship of Christ to God in two ways. In His nature He is His Son, and He is the Object of the unqualified love of God. The word employed here for love is *agape*, referring to a love which is not merely affection, but affection based upon complete approbation. It will at once be recognised that the phrase is in itself a confirmation of what God had said when He broke the silence at the baptism of Jesus, declaring of Him:

" This is My beloved Son in Whom I am well pleased."

Having used the phrase, the apostle immediately proceeded to statements concerning the One thus referred to.

The first declaration made concerning Him reads:

" In Whom we have our redemption, the forgiveness of our sins."

That statement interprets something which the apostle had said, and which led up to the description " the Son of His love." He had declared that we are:

" Delivered . . . out of the power of darkness, and translated . . . into the Kingdom of the Son of His love."

That transference from the power of darkness to the Kingdom of the Son came by the way of a redemption, which consisted in the forgiveness of sins. That is where all true Christian experience begins, and this is an experience which comes to us by the action of God. By that moral cleansing we enter into a Kingdom over which the Son of His love reigns.

What that means in all its fullness is revealed, as continuing, the apostle shows us Who this Son of His love is, into Whose Kingdom we pass. The interpretation is contained in verses fifteen to nineteen, as He is set before us in a threefold relationship; His relation to God, His relation to the whole creation, His relation to the Church.

His relation to God.

" Who is the Image of the invisible God."

His relation to the creation.

" In Him were all things created, in the heavens and upon the earth, things visible and things invisible, whether thrones or dominions or principalities or powers; all things have been created through Him, and unto Him; and He is before all things, and in Him all things consist."

His relation to the Church:

" And He is the Head of the body, the Church; Who is the beginning, the Firstborn from the dead; that in all things He might have the pre-eminence. For it was the good pleasure of the Father that in Him should all the fullness dwell."

The declaration concerning His relationship to God is one that should be very carefully observed:

" Who is the Image of the invisible God."

The word rendered " image " is the Greek word *eikon*, and always means representation as the result of derivation. As the Image of the invisible God He is the One Who represents God, because directly deriving from God. God is here spoken of as invisible, and so again the apostolic recognition harmonises with the declaration of John:

" No man hath seen God at any time; but the Son, Which is in the bosom of the Father, He hath declared Him."

In this phrase of Paul and this declaration of John the verb is employed in the present tense. " Who is the image of the invisible God," " Who is in the bosom of the Father." This is by no means an undue emphasis upon the use of the present tense. We may accurately speak of it as the eternal present tense. Paul here was not looking back merely to the Incarnation, and declaring that in the days of His flesh He was the Image. It is an eternal relationship that is indicated. God is for ever invisible to all created things, except through the manifestation of Himself in His Image, that is, in the Son of His love. Whether in what we may speak of as the past eternity, or in the processes of time, or in the coming eternity, God is only seen in His Son. In Him He can always be seen, but only in Him.

So far as we are able to measure eternal things in the terminology of time, or to think of the passing of events in the heavenly sphere by the methods of time, we may say that during the period in which the Son was incarnate in this world, heaven had no manifestation of God, save in the measure in which it was able to see Him on the earth level. He had been eternally manifested in the Son. Now the Son, the Medium of manifestation, emptied Himself of the form in which He had been manifested, to take another form of manifestation. Reverting thus to the Philippian passage, we are reminded again that *morphe* rendered " form," indicates a manifestation as well as a condition of being. Having emptied Himself of the eternal form of manifestation, and thinking of heavenly conditions by earthly measures, we may say that for three and thirty years heaven had no manifestation of God, except as we have said, upon the earth level. We are told that angels desire to look into these things. The angels then, in so far as they watched the process of the earthly life of the Son of God incarnate, saw God there. This statement of relationship then is that of the eternal fact concerning the Son of His love. He is the One and the only One through Whom God has been, is, or ever will be manifested:

> " God manifestly seen and heard,
>   And heaven's beloved One."

Continuing, the apostle dealt with the relation of the Son of His love to creation. Inclusively that relationship is described in the words, " The Firstborn of all creation." When we read the word " Firstborn " however, we must remember that it has no time value at this point. It does not suggest that He was the first created Being. That view constituted one of the early heresies of the Christian Church. The word suggests the highest, the fullest, the most glorious, because He is the Archetype of all created things. Paul's prepositions in this connection are arresting, " In Him, " through Him," " unto Him." That is, He is the Sphere, the Agent, the Goal of all creation. The inclusiveness of the statement is discovered in the repetition of the phrase, " All things."

"In Him were *all things* created."

" He is before *all things*, and in Him *all things* consist."

" That in *all things* He might have the pre-eminence."

" Through Him to reconcile *all things* unto Himself."

His relation to the origin of creation is revealed in the statement:

" In Him were all things created."

Again the eternal present tense is used in the statement that He " is before all things "; and this is immediately followed by a declaration that shows His perpetual relation to creation:

" In Him all things consist ";

which may be rendered with perfect accuracy, " In Him all things hold together."

The inclusiveness of all this is very arresting. There is no flower that decks the sod that is not conformed in its being in some measure, to the glory that is found in the Son of His love. There is no far-flung splendour of the stellar spaces but that is expressing something of the originating wisdom and might and continuing power and authority and ultimate glory of the Christ.

Passing to the subject of His relation to the Church, we find a touch of threnody vibrating in the music. He is the Head of the Church, and in this connection the word " Firstborn " is again used, but in a remarkable way. He is " Firstborn from the dead." When we consider that phrase we discover that it is far more amazing than the earlier phrase, " Firstborn of creation." That suggests superabundance and infinitude and beauty of life in its freshness and virility. This brings us face to face with reconstruction, redemption, regeneration. That is what He is to the Church.

Then the ultimate as to purpose is reached in the words:

" That in all things He might have the pre-eminence." To render that literally may be for the moment to rob it of its poetic beauty, but such rendering has its value. What Paul wrote was that " in all things He might become, being first." Being first, He is Firstborn from the dead, in order that He might realise that which is His original place and position, in spite of all failure.

The great interpretation ends with the declaration that:

" It was the good pleasure of the Father that in Him should all the fullness dwell."

That is the fullness of original creation, of redemption, and of ultimate realisation; and so:

" Through Him to reconcile all things unto Himself, having made peace through the blood of His Cross; through Him, I say, whether things upon the earth, or things in the heavens."

Final exposition of that great statement is perhaps impossible. It speaks of a reconciliation which means a change reaching ultimate completeness. The declaration is a recognition of disorder or chaos, and the declaration is that of the restoration of order, or the bringing in of the cosmos. This applies, " upon the earth," " in the heavens." We can follow the thinking suggested by the phrase " on the earth." That means human history. When we read " in the heavens " we stand in awe. At least we may remember that the reconciliation may be more than a moral one; it may be an intellectual one. It is conceivable that among the heavenly orders questions would arise in view of the failure of the human race. Through Him all things will be reconciled, interpreted, explained. Whatever question may have been raised, they will be answered, and that " through the blood of His Cross."

And so we come to the last section of the chapter, dealing with the Church. Writing to these Colossian believers who were Gentiles, he said, referring to their past:

" And you, being in time past alienated and enemies in your mind in your evil works,"

and continuing, declared their present position:

" Yet now hath He reconciled in the body of His flesh through death, to present you holy and without blemish and unreproveable before Him; if so be that ye continue in the faith, grounded and stedfast, and not moved away from the hope of the Gospel which ye heard, which was preached in all creation under heaven; whereof I Paul was made a minister."

Thus, through the Son of His love, those who were alienated, are reconciled, and constitute the Church. In referring to the Church, he said:

" Even the *mystery* which hath been hid from all ages and generations; but now hath it been manifested to His saints, to whom God was pleased to make known what is the riches of the glory of this *mystery* among the Gentiles, which is Christ in you, the hope of glory."

This reference to the Church, however, must be completed by a glance on to the next chapter, in which Paul says:

> " For I would have you know how greatly I strive for you, and for them at Laodicea, and for as many as have not seen my face in the flesh; that their hearts may be comforted, they being knit together in love . . . that they may know the *mystery* of God, even Christ."

If for a moment we take the concluding passage of the first chapter in conjunction with the opening passage of the second, our attention is at once arrested by the threefold occurrence of the word " mystery "; the mystery of the Church manifested, the mystery of that which composed the Church, individuals of whom it is said:

> " Christ formed in you, the hope of glory."

and the ultimate mystery, the mystery of God, which is Christ.

Paul was here arguing from that which is outward and self-evident, through processes, towards the deepest secret of all. If we transpose the order of his statement, we have first the mystery of God, even Christ; secondly, the mystery of the individual Christian, Christ formed in you, the hope of glory; thirdly and consequently, the mystery of the Church.

Thus the mystery of God is Christ, Who is the Image of the invisible God, the Firstborn of all creation, the Firstborn from the dead, and Head of the Church. That One, formed within men and women, constitutes the mystery of the new birth. The sum total of all those in whom He is thus formed, is the Church.

Thus the glories of the Son of His love are revealed, and all are at the disposal of the Church. To quote again in conclusion, the two sentences from the letter, quoted at the beginning:

> " It was the good pleasure of the Father that in Him should all the fullness dwell."

> " Ye are made full in Him."

HEBREWS I

IN the course of our meditations on these great chapters of the Bible we have several times had to overleap boundaries, beginning our chapter in an earlier one, or else carrying on into the next. When we come to this first chapter in the letter to the Hebrews it is more than usually difficult to consider it as a whole. We want less, or more. The more would include the whole of the second chapter, which carries out to completion a line of argument which commences at the fourth verse of chapter one, concerning the superiority of the Son of God to the angels. Or we need less, and the less would patently be the first three verses only, which constitute a complete statement. However, we will take the chapter, without going on with the second, but we will give our special attention to the first three verses, glancing briefly at the relation of the last eleven to these first three.

The whole chapter, then, may thus be divided. In verse one, and the first part of verse two, we find the introductory declarations of the writer. Beginning in the middle of verse two and running through verse three we have his setting forth of the glories of the Son. The rest of the chapter is occupied with a contrast between the Son and the angels. These last eleven verses are illustrative, argumentative, and in some senses secondary. In the first three we have fullness and completeness of statement. Indeed, they constitute an introduction to the whole letter, everything that follows being dependent upon the statements made at the beginning.

In these verses we have sentences full of significance, and indeed, almost blinding in their glory. It is impossible not to refer to the connection, in our sequence of studies, of this chapter with the two preceding ones. In the first of these we were considering the chapter of Paul's Philippian letter dealing with the Kenosis or Self-emptying of our blessed Lord. Then we passed to the Colossian letter, and considering its first chapter, found not the Kenosis, but the Pleroma, or complete fullness of the Son in all His glory. In the present chapter we have a briefer statement of the glories of the Son, but its significance harmonises perfectly with the things found in Philippians and Colossians; viewing them, if we may state it so, from a slightly different angle. Unquestionably in these three passages we have the supreme statements of the New Testament concerning the Person of our Lord.

We begin then with the sentences contained in verse one and part of verse two, constituting the introductory declarations.

" God, having of old time spoken unto the fathers in the prophets by divers portions and in divers manners, hath at the end of these days spoken unto us in His Son."

The simplest statement of the declarations made is that " God . . . hath . . . spoken unto us in His Son." All the rest is full of importance, but that does find its central declaration.

In that declaration the word " His " does not occur in the Greek. The revisers in the margin say, " Greek: a Son." As a matter of fact the word " Son " has no article at all prefacing it. Quite literally the declaration is, God has spoken to us in Son. In the idiom of our own language, that is somewhat obscure. It is perfectly proper therefore to insert the word " a "; and, moreover, it is not inaccurate to employ the word " His " instead of " a." That certainly is the truth declared. The Greek form of expression, however, means that the emphasis of the statement made is for the moment on the fact of relationship, rather than on a Person. Almost immediately we shall find the Person is referred to, and unquestionably that Person was in mind; but I repeat, it is the relationship between the Son and the Father that is emphasised. The speech of God comes to us now, not through prophet or angel or leader, but through One Who is Son. That emphasis on relationship immediately suggests a difference in quality between anything that had been said by God to what was now said.

The method of making the statement demands our attention. The writer began by looking back to all that had preceded the particular method of God with which he was now dealing. In doing this we discover what I will resolutely describe as the philosophic assumptions of the writer, and also the nature of the contrast between the past and the present.

In referring to the philosophic assumptions of the writer, we find that they are distinctly Hebrew. We are not concerned with the matter of who the writer may have been. Such matters are interesting, but not vital. Whomsoever it may have been, it is evident that philosophically two things were assumed. They are not stated formally. They are not argued for. The first is the fact of God. Here is no argument for His existence; no attempt to prove it. Unless that fact be accepted as a fact, there is no meaning or value at all in anything that follows.

The second phase in the philosophic assumption is that God not only exists, but that He makes Himself known to men. He spake in times past; He speaks still. Much later in the epistle, in another way, the writer declares the necessity for these very assumptions in the words:

" He that cometh to God must believe that He is; and that He is a Rewarder of them that seek after Him."

The next movement is that of the contrast instituted. God had in time past spoken unto the fathers by divers portions and in divers manners. The first fact that arrests us here is the verification of the past. The writer declares that the messages of the past were messages which had come from God; and he describes those messages as consisting of " divers portions," coming in " divers manners." The reference to the prophets here means far more than those whom we have described very often in the past as major and minor prophets; including all those through whom the messages of God had come to man through men; leaders, priests, and those more ordinarily referred to as prophets. In the history written, the prophecies uttered, the psalms sung, God was ever speaking to men. The portions were diversified, and the methods different; but through all, the speech of God had come to man.

It was a conviction that this was so on the part of those to whom the letter was addressed, that created their difficulty. It seemed to them that with the passing of the splendour of the old economy, things were being lost that were of value. Therefore the writer began by asserting the authority of the things already said.

Still looking back, the writer covered everything in the expression, " of old time," the word thus translated indicating something that was now over; and suggesting that God's method of speech was changed. It was a method of God in which He made Himself known, but that method was for ever past.

This is further emphasised by the phrase introducing his statement concerning the new method, when he says " at the end of these days," that is, after the days in which the method of His speech had been that of divers portions and divers manners in prophets to the fathers.

The new method is declared as we have seen, in the words, He " hath spoken unto us in His Son." The method of the past had been processional and diversified. The new method would be final and unified. In the past the method had been line upon line, precept upon precept, here a little and there a little. The principle of that progressive speech of God was revealed in the words of our Lord concerning His own teachings of His disciples when He said:

> " I have yet many things to say unto you, but ye cannot bear them now."

The opening declaration, therefore, of the letter means, quite bluntly, this, that God has nothing more to say to humanity than He said when the Word became flesh, and He spoke to us in His Son. Someone will say, But surely God has not given up speaking to men. The fact is that He has done so, in that He has no more to say than is said in His Son. Necessarily there is a great difference between the finality of the speech of the Son and our understanding of all that was said through the Son. I am not for one moment suggesting that we understand completely the speech of God that came to men through His Son. Those most familiar with that speech will be the first to acknowledge how much more there is waiting their apprehension. The fact, however, remains that nothing can be added to what has been said by God to men in His Son. There can be no other teacher who will carry the thinking of humanity, or instruct the spirit of man on higher levels than those which came to men through the Son. Still we go forward progressively in our understanding of what was thus said. If supposed progress of thought leads away from Christ, or into a place where we begin to question whether His message is final, we are not really making progress, but losing ground, and falling back. I cannot forbear using here an illustration I have used before in the course of my teaching, and certainly shall use it again. In the book of Revelation, when John tells of his vision of the Son of God in glory, as he saw it in Patmos, among other things he says:

> " His voice as the voice of many waters."

That is poetry, but it is interpretation on the highest level. It is impossible for me ever to forget the moment when that illustration came to me with singular power for the first time, quite unexpectedly. It was when I stood by the Falls of Niagara, and listened to the music of the waters. As I listened, my mind worked backwards from the point of the falling of the waters to the sources whence they had sprung. Immediately behind was the great lake, pouring itself over; but further back, the rivers were found pouring themselves into the lake; and yet still following, to travel by the route of the rivers, was to find them being created by brooks and rivulets, all merging in the rivers' waters, and so proceeding by the way of the lake to Niagara's voice of " many waters."

God had spoken in times past in divers portions and divers manners. The streams had moved on and ever on, until at last He spoke in His Son, Whose voice was as " the voice of many waters." We listen to the music of the streams, but nothing is finished, nothing is complete. The voices of the past through prophets all uttered the speech of God; but finality came in the Son, in Whom all the streams met and merged.

Thus the letter opens with its recognition of God, of the fact that He speaks; and in the declaration that in the past He had spoken positively but progressively and partially, and that now at last He has spoken in His Son, and finality and fullness is reached, never to be superseded.

Then in order to emphasise the tremendous significance of that fact, the writer immediately proceeded to show the glory of that Son through Whom God now speaks.

" Whom He appointed Heir of all things, through Whom also He fashioned the ages; Who being the Effulgence of His glory, and the very Image of His substance, and upholding all things by the word of His power, when He had made purification of sins, sat down on the right hand of the Majesty on high."

What the speech of God through the Son really means is revealed in a remarkable way in that paragraph dealing with the Person of the Son. The introduction of pronouns shows that the writer is now passing from the fact of relationship to the fact of Personality. The pronouns I refer to, of course, are " Whom," " Whom," " Who," " He." We read these pronouns, and do not find the name Jesus, nor the title Christ until later on; the name Jesus first occurring in ii. 9 and the title Christ in iii. 1. It is perfectly evident, however, that everything is moving towards that name and title, and it is significant that the nature of the One Who bore them is dealt with so fully in this paragraph. There is a sense in which our very familiarity with the name Jesus, and the title Christ, may rob us of all the mystic lights and shadows, the gleaming glories revealed concerning the Person in this paragraph.

We may say that we have a sevenfold description, as He is referred to as:

"Heir of all things."

"He fashioned the ages."

"The Effulgence of His glory."

"The very Image of His substance."

"Upholding all things by the word of His power."

"Made purification of sins."

"Sat down on the right hand of the Majesty on high."

To take out of that description simple statements made concerning Him we find first that He is appointed by God; secondly, that He is the Agent of God. He is further described in His activity; and finally, in His administrative position.

He is appointed by God, "Heir of all things." That statement almost baffles any attempt at apprehension. Perhaps the most helpful exposition is to be found in the Colossian chapter where the same phrase "all things" occurs four times over. The Divine appointment is to an inheritance of all things. Heirship means ultimate possession. To this He is appointed by God, and it follows inevitably that because He is so appointed, He must come into full possession.

Again, He is the Agent of God. That particular word is not used, but it is certainly permissible, for the declaration is that through Him also "He fashions the ages." The old version and the Revised read "He made the worlds," an unhappy failure to catch the real significance of the writer's declaration. The revisers have drawn attention in the margin to the fact that the Greek word signifies "ages." This then is a stupendous thing. We speak of ages in the scientific realm, the Stone Age, the Iron Age, and so forth. The Biblical revelation deals with a succession of ages, the Age of Innocence, of Obedience, the Abrahamic Age, the Noahic Age, the Mosaic Age. Of all these the Son is the Fashioner, that is, He presides over all the movements which we call movements of time, towards the consummation.

Passing beyond the activities of the Son the writer now deals more definitely with His Personality, in the words:

"Who being the Effulgence of His glory, and the very Image of His substance."

In the presence of this declaration our mind goes back inevitably once more to the Philippian and Colossian writings. As to the

actual phrases here employed; first, " the Effulgence of His Glory."
The word " effulgence," and that of which it is a translation means
something far more than a brightness or a brilliance. It means
that brilliance as it shines forth. The Son, then, is the outshining
of the glory of God. As we read the words we are once more
inevitably taken back to John's prologue.

> " We beheld His glory (glory as of the only begotten
> Son of the Father) full of grace and truth."

Moreover the word rendered effulgence in the Greek is prefaced
by the definite article, so that the statement is not that in the
Son there is an outshining as though it were one of many, but it
is *the* effulgence, standing alone, and complete.

The second phrase concerning the Person is that He " is the
very Image of His substance." The Revised marginal reading
suggests that this should be rendered " the impress of His
substance." In the presence of the word " image," and the
suggested word " impress " we tarry a moment, perhaps half
wondering whether something might not have been gained if
instead of translating, we had transliterated and read, " the
Character of His substance." We at once recognise that that
would not really be adequate, because our word character now
means something in some measure different from what it meant
in the Greek language. Perhaps after all then the margin is most
helpful, if we remember that impress does not mean a mark left
by pressure, but the pressure that produces the mark.

He is, then, the very Impress, that is the One Who produces
the imprint, and can produce none other. The whole idea is
that the substance of Deity is there, and through Him, impresses
the truth concerning itself upon the mind. Therefore, for the
moment realising the limitation, I dare to use the word again,
and say, He is the very Character of God, manifested and
impressed.

The last movement concerning the glories of the Son is
concerned with His activities. The first of these is expressed in
the words:

> " Upholding all things by the word of His power."

Concerning this there are differing interpretations, and while I
respect others, my personal conviction is that the " all things "
here does not refer to the cosmic order, but to the moral order.
By the word of His power, He maintains the moral order, and
prevents its disruption.

Secondly, in one simple but inclusive word, he describes the second phase in His activity.

" He made purification of sins."

In that, of course, is included not merely the life and teaching of our Lord, but supremely His Cross and Passion.

The final activity is described in the words:

" He sat down on the right hand of the Majesty on high."

Thus the Son is seen, Heir of all things, fashioning the ages, being in Himself the Effulgence of the glory of God, and the very Impress of His substance, upholding all things by the word of His power, making purification for sins, and passing to the place of ultimate and supreme authority as He sits on the right hand of the Majesty on high. This is the One through Whom God has uttered his final speech to man.

The rest of the chapter, as we said at the beginning, constitutes the commencement of the writer's argument showing the superiority of the Son to the angels. He shows this superiority by quotations of the most remarkable kind, dealing with the nature of the Son, and that of the angels; with the mission of the Son, and that of the angels; and how by reason of His nature and mission His speech must for ever be superior to that of the angels.

HEBREWS XI

THE eleventh chapter of the letter to the Hebrews may be described accurately as a record of witnesses to the truth of a principle already declared by the writer.   This principle is found in the tenth chapter where it occurs as a quotation from the prophecy of Habakkuk:

" My righteous one shall live by faith,"

or in the form found in the King James' Version:

" The just shall live by faith."

These words are also found quoted in Paul's letter to the Romans, and in his letter to the Galatians.

It is necessary that we tarry with this statement ere proceeding to survey this chapter.   Perhaps in the whole Bible we have no more concise declaration of the profound meaning and value of faith.

In Habakkuk it occurred as the word of God to the troubled soul of His servant when it seemed to him that prevailing conditions were so terrible that God was doing nothing.   Under stress of perplexity concerning these conditions, the prophet had declared that it seemed to him that God was inactive.   To this God had replied by declaring He was acting, but if He told the prophet how, he would probably not believe.   Nevertheless He did tell him that He was raising up the Chaldeans, and girding Cyrus to do His work, because His people were breaking down.   This declaration filled the prophet with a new wonder.   How could God use one outside His people, and especially such an one as Cyrus?   Then it was that God gave the prophet a double declaration, the first part referring to the unrighteous, described as " puffed up," and therefore destined to destruction; the second part being this declaration:

" The just shall live by his faith,"

the immediate application being that the Chaldeans were used, but that their ultimate destruction was inevitable, because of their pride, whereas those who act upon the principle of faith, live.

This statement implicates the spiritual nature of personality. Life has dimensions other than those that can be encompassed by the senses, and into those dimensions nothing can enter except the principle of faith. Therefore life in all its fullness is a result of faith as it acts in the realm that lies beyond the activity of the senses. The sum total of consciousness which neglects these realms and this method, constitutes something less than life. If we live by the things we see and touch and hear and smell, life is not fulfilled.

That principle having thus been declared, the writer proceeds to deal with the subject of faith, and as we have said, this eleventh chapter consists of a definition of faith, and illustrations of the working thereof. Our previous study was concerned with the first chapter in this letter, with its declaration that God has spoken to man finally in His Son. From that point the argument of the letter has been concerned with the superiority of the Son to all others: angels, leaders, priests, prophets; and the consequent fullness and finality of the speech of God to man through Him. The argument throughout is that if men had believed as the result of the messages of angels and others, we have now something far surer as a foundation for faith, and our faith ought to be active and powerful in a greater degree.

The definition of faith is found in the words:

"Faith is the assurance of things hoped for, the proving of things not seen."

To this definition we must give some careful attention. As a matter of fact it is the only definition of faith found in the Bible. Whereas the whole history is that of men living by faith, or failing to live by reason of its absence, and whereas in the course of the writings we are constantly taught what faith is able to do, here is the one place in which it is defined.

In this definition two spheres of action are named, those namely of "things hoped for," and "things not seen." "Things hoped for" are things not yet possessed, but desired and expected. "Things not seen" are things beyond the sphere of the possible demonstration by the senses.

In the definition two qualities of faith are referred to. The Revised Version reads:

"Faith is the assurance of things hoped for, the proving of things not seen."

The King James' Version reads:

"Faith is the substance of things hoped for, the evidence of things not seen."

The words employed by the writer in thus describing the two qualities of faith are rendered "assurance" or "substance," and "proving" or "evidence."

Now the first of these Greek words from the standpoint of etymology does mean exactly *substance* in the sense of something standing under. To render it *assurance* is certainly to come a little nearer to its value in use. I suggest at least that the thought would be more accurately conveyed in the language of to-day if we rendered it *certainty*, or that which certainty creates, namely *confidence*. This, by the way, is the marginal reading of the Authorised Version.

" Faith is confidence concerning things hoped for."

The second of these words rendered " proving " or " evidence " does not refer merely to a method by which proof of faith is obtained, but rather to the fact that faith is in itself the proof which brings conviction.

Therefore the simple sense of this definition of faith may thus be expressed. Faith is confidence in things hoped for, the conviction of things not seen.

In the definition then the writer moves from effect to cause. Confidence in things hoped for, results from conviction concerning things not seen. If we state this in the order of experience we shall say that the cause is conviction of things not seen, and the effect, confidence in things hoped for.

Now we may enquire what are the things not seen? That enquiry might be answered speculatively. It is better, however, to seek the answer within the chapter itself; and we shall find it suggested in two statements. The first of these is in verse six:

" He that cometh to God must believe that He is, and that He is a Rewarder of them that seek after Him."

Later in verse twenty-seven, we read of Moses:

" He endured as seeing Him Who is invisible."

Thus the things unseen are the fact of God and the activities of God. With the senses, " No man hath seen God at any time," but faith is conviction, that He is, and that He acts on behalf of man.

That conviction of unseen things creates hope. The nature of that hope is referred to in the phrase, " things hoped for." Again we say, What are the things hoped for? Once more our reply is not speculative, but found in an appeal to the writing itself as it deals with the activity of faith producing hope on the level of human history. Of Abraham it is said:

" He looked for the city which hath the foundations, Whose Architect and Framer is God."

When this was written of Abraham the reference was not to the life that lies beyond the present one. At the end of the chapter we are distinctly told that those who have acted by faith have not received the promises, that is, the fulfilment of them. Again we are told that these people desired "a better country, that is, a heavenly." Thus all those referred to in the illustrations of the chapter are seen as having a conviction of faith which inspires hope of the ultimate realisation of the Divine purpose in human history, the coming of the hour when the prayer our Lord taught His disciples shall find full and final answer in the hallowing of the Name, the coming of the Kingdom, and the doing of the Will of God, on earth as it is done in heaven.

It may be well here to turn aside to say that this interpretation does not for a single moment undervalue the ultimate fact and glory of heaven. It does, however, emphasise the truth that our concern is not that we should win heaven, but that God should be glorified on earth. Faith, then, is the certainty of God, and the consequent conviction that this high hope will yet be realised.

The rest of the chapter is occupied with illustrations of the working of this principle of faith in human life and human history. It is necessarily impossible to consider these illustrations in detail. We may, however, see the general movement of verses two to forty. We have first illustrations in the cosmic realm, verses two and three; then illustrations in the realm of history, verses four to thirty-eight; and finally, a declaration of the postponement of the ultimate realisation, verses thirty-nine and forty.

Bearing in mind, then, the definition of faith which perhaps may be restated a little more bluntly as being a conviction of God, and a consequent certainty of His victory, the writer begins with what I have described as a cosmic illustration. The first word, " Therein," of course has reference to faith, and the statement is:

" *Therein* the elders had witness borne to them."

That declaration shows that it was in answer to faith that those who have written the story of origins, received a revelation. Immediately following, the writer says:

" By faith we understand that the ages have been framed by the Word of God, so that what is seen hath not been made out of things which do appear."

Thus, we are taken back to the origin of the things of which our senses are conscious. We are told first that the account of the origin of these things was given in answer to faith, and that our understanding of the account is possible to faith. The elders received a good report, which does not at all mean that they were well reported of, but that the report or information granted to them was trustworthy. Here again we are face to face with the

fact that there are realms that do not yield themselves to the
investigation of the human mind. The work of the scientist is
marvellous work, never to be spoken of slightingly, but it has its
limitations. There are facts which are not discoverable by its
activities. This applies equally to the work of the philosopher,
who is ever attempting, and quite properly, to solve the riddle
of the universe. He never, however, is able to do that until faith
comes to conviction concerning the unseen God. Certainty of
God prepares man for receiving a report from God.

Through that report we understand that the ages have been
framed by the Word of God. We may take that word " ages "
in any sense that appeals to us. We may employ it as the scientists
have employed it when they speak of the Stone Age, or the Iron
Age. We may employ it in its more Biblical sense of appealing
to the history of humanity through the age of innocence, the age
of conscience, and so forth and so on. Whatever the method of
our thinking concerning the ages, faith declares that they are
fashioned, that is, that they have arisen and passed, under the
dominion of God. In the opening of the letter, referring to them,
the writer said of the Son, " through Whom He fashioned the
ages." Here the same truth is declared in the words:

" The ages have been framed by the Word of God."

The deduction from this is made in one profoundly
philosophical statement:

" What is seen hath not been made out of things which
do appear."

It is very arresting to realise that science itself is recognising the
truth of that fact. Whatever it may have to say concerning
evolution, it is being driven to the recognition that evolution
postulates involution. That is to say, it is inevitably being forced
to the recognition of the spiritual as behind and beyond the
material. By faith, then, man transcends the proof possible to
his senses, and grasps the infinite and the spiritual. The elders
obtained the revelation because they believed in God, and we by
that same faith understand that beyond all the things revealed to
the senses, God Himself is found.

Then follow the illustrations from history. It is by no means
an exhaustive list, but it illustrates the operation of the principle.
By faith Abel worshipped, Enoch walked, Noah wrought.
Every statement is worthy of close consideration, but that is not
possible in a rapid survey.

By faith Abraham obeyed, going out, not knowing whither
he went, but knowing perfectly well why he went; he obtained

the promises, not their fulfilment, but the word from God which assured him concerning the future. By faith he offered his son.

By faith Sarah conceived, that is, by her conviction of God, and her certainty that He would fulfil any hope inspired in the soul by faith.

By faith Isaac blessed, and Jacob blessed, and worshipped, leaning upon his staff. In each case these men were convinced of God, and therefore confident as to the future, in spite of all apparent difficulties.

So Joseph also by faith foretold the future, and demonstrated his perfect confidence therein when he commanded that the children of Israel, leaving Egypt, should carry up his bones with them.

The parents of Moses acted upon the same principle of faith, conviction of God and certainty as to the issue.

" By faith Moses, when he was born, was hid three months by his parents, because they saw he was a goodly child; and they were not afraid of the king's commandment."

Moses, the great leader and law-giver, acted throughout on the same principle. Brought up as he was in the court of Pharaoh, as the son of Pharaoh's daughter, and possibly heir-apparent to the throne of Egypt, he presently refused that position, choosing rather to be " evil entreated with the people of God, than to enjoy the pleasures of sin for a season." By faith also " he kept the Passover," that one brief sentence which tells the whole story of the bringing of the people out of Egypt, and the constituting of the new nation.

By faith presently the walls of Jericho fell, and at that point the writer introduces the figure of a woman outside the covenant, a harlot withal, whose faith fastened upon the fact of God and His activity, and so she was delivered, and lived by the same principle.

The writer then seeing that time fails him to deal in detail, gives a group, naming them only. It is interesting to take that group of names, and go back to the stories concerning each. In doing so we may be surprised at the inclusion of some, and yet the very surprise makes us reconsider and discover in each case, the operation of faith.

" Gideon, Barak, Samson, Jephthah, David, and Samuel."

We may read the story of these, and find in them evidences of frailty and of failure; but we shall have to recognise the contribution they made to the purpose of God, and find it was always the result of the activity of faith.

In that list the writer also puts "the prophets," and the phrase brings back the memory of the heroisms of these men as they proclaimed the Word of God in dark times, and were faithful to the messages committed to them. The secret of their heroism and fidelity is declared to be that of faith.

Having thus grouped together these names, the writer passed from persons to deeds. We read the phrases as they follow one by one, and feel their tremendous suggestiveness:

"Subdued kingdoms, wrought righteousness, obtained promises, stopped the mouths of lions, quenched the power of fire, escaped the edge of the sword, from weakness were made strong, waxed mighty in war, turned to flight armies of aliens."

All these were active.

Continuing, he referred to the victories of faith in which those referred to were passive:

"Women received their dead by a resurrection; and others were tortured, not accepting their deliverance, that they might obtain a better resurrection; and others had trial of mockings and scourgings, yea, moreover of bonds and imprisonments; they were stoned, they were sawn asunder, they were tempted, they were slain with the sword, they went about in sheepskins, in goatskins; being destitute, afflicted, evil entreated."

At this point the writer evidently conscious of the might and the majesty of these victories, whether active or passive, said of these people:

"Of whom the world was not worthy."

In conclusion he refers to the fact that faith moves ever forward towards a postponed accomplishment:

"These all, having had witness borne to them through their faith, received not the promise, God having provided some better thing concerning us, that apart from us they should not be made perfect."

This concluding statement reminds us that the activity of faith is not over, that it is still proceeding, and will continue to do so until the purposes of God are fully realised in human history, and that by faith, and by faith alone, can we be workers together with Him towards that consummation.

HEBREWS XII

THIS chapter contains the great appeal of the letter to the Hebrews. Its opening word, " Therefore " links its message to everything that has already been written. The appeal is finally contained in the words:

" See that ye refuse not Him that speaketh."

The great declaration in the opening of the letter was made in the words:

" God . . . hath . . . spoken unto us in His Son."

The connection between this opening declaration and the closing appeal will at once be seen. The whole argument of the letter has been that God has spoken in His Son fully and finally, and that therefore He has no more to say than He had said in Him. The argument has proceeded to deal with the superiority of the Son over angels, leaders, priests, and prophets, and upon the basis of that proved superiority the charge is given:

" See that ye refuse not Him that speaketh."

At the beginning of the letter it will be remembered that the writer asked:

" How shall we escape if we neglect so great salvation? " In this chapter he declares that:

" If they escaped not, when they refused Him that warned on earth, much more shall not we escape, who turn away from Him that warneth from heaven."

Thus from affirmation to appeal, the letter has proceeded, that appeal reaching its final message in the words:

" See that ye refuse not Him that speaketh."

The chapter falls into two parts. The first is brief (verses one to three) and yet is of supreme value. The second (verses four to twenty-nine) consists of an interpretation and application of all stated in the first part.

With the first three verses of this chapter we are most familiar, and I think it may be said that in the reading of them, there is always a consciousness of their close connection with the previous chapter. The opening word, " Therefore," while as we have said, linking this chapter to the whole epistle, connects it especially with chapter eleven. The reference to the cloud of witnesses is to such as have been referred to, either by name, or by achievement in the eleventh chapter. The call in itself simply stated, is a call to run the race. The writer begins with matters preliminary, the laying aside of " every weight, and the sin which doth so easily beset us "; and so reaches the final, the running of the race. The word " also " shows a connection, and the reference is to the fact that all those named in chapter eleven were running in this race, the appeal to us being that we should run in the same race. To this company of those referred to as having run this race by faith he refers as " a cloud of witnesses." A company had been named, and deeds had been recorded both active and passive, and the whole movement of the eleventh chapter shows that the list was not intended to be exhaustive, but to illustrate a principle.

It is important here that we clearly understand that the meaning of the writer is not that these are witnessing us in the sense of watching us, but rather that they are witnessing to us concerning the power of faith in life and service, in suffering and toil, and in victory.

The eleventh chapter ended with the remarkable statement that:

" These all, having had witness borne to them through their faith, received not the promise, God having provided some better thing concerning us, that apart from us they should not be made perfect."

It is of the utmost importance that we recognise that the appeal is to that of continuity in a movement towards an ultimate goal. What that goal is, is revealed in the eleventh chapter as being the establishment of a city, Whose Builder and Maker is God; the coming to " a better country, that is a heavenly." This reference to a heavenly country is not a reference to heaven, but to earth, when the prayer is fully answered:

" Thy name be hallowed, Thy kingdom come, Thy will be done, On earth as it is in heaven."

That goal has not been reached. All those of the past died, having moved towards the great ultimate, but without having reached it. It is not reached yet. Hence at once the importance and urgency of the appeal to us to be true to the principle and purpose of the past, to run the race that leads toward the full and final realisation.

The conditions for the running of the race are expressed in the words:

"Let us . . . lay aside every weight, and the sin that doth so easily beset us."

The question quite properly arises as to what the writer means when he refers to weights. A sufficient answer to the enquiry is that the reference is to anything and everything which would hinder our running in the race. There was an occasion when Paul, writing to the Galatians in another connection and application said:

"Ye were running well, who did hinder you?"

That is the principle involved in this reference to weights. The things which may hinder are not necessarily low or vulgar. They may be in themselves noble things, intellectual things, beautiful things, but if our participation in any of these dims our vision of the ultimate goal in the purpose of God, halts us in our running, makes our going less determined or steady, they become weights which hinder. It is always a dangerous thing to try and name weights which are hindering others. Indeed, I think it may safely be said that one weight that often hinders, is that of attempting to find out what another man's weights are. Let it be repeated then that anything that hinders the running is a weight.

It is not only weights that are to be laid aside, but:
"The sin which doth so easily beset us."

This is the old and familiar rendering. The words, "doth so easily beset us" constitute the translation of one word in the Greek, *euperistaton*. In the Revised Version two marginal alternatives are suggested, "doth closely cling to us," or "is admired of many." The second of these can by no means be considered accurate translation, but it certainly is accurate interpretation. We may accurately render the Greek word, "in good standing around." The revisers suggest that that means something which "is admired of many." Whereas that may go a little far, it certainly expresses the idea. I say a little far in that the thought of admiration is not necessarily included, but certainly that of approbation is. In either of the words it suggests a sin which is not looked upon as being reprehensible. Quite naturally the question is forced upon us as to what the particular sin is to which the writer refers. The answer is found by remembering that the one sin against which this letter is uttering its persistent warning is that of unbelief as opposed to faith. Unbelief unnerves, and devitalises running. It may be said that such unbelief is the girdle on which all weights are hung. When it is laid aside, the weights drop off. Or to put that positively, when faith is full, all secondary things become unimportant, and the supreme matter of the ultimate goal becomes the secret of the patient running of the race.

All this leads to a declaration of the supreme inspiration for running such a race. This is declared in the words, " Looking off unto Jesus." The Greek word commonly rendered " looking " is an arresting one, seeing that this is the only occasion when it occurs in the New Testament. It is a word suggesting a vision that surprises, captures, masters.

The interpretation of that vision is given in the following sentences. Jesus is first presented as the " Author and Perfecter of faith." The word " our " in that connection has been introduced, and is really misleading. While it is true that He is the Author of our faith, and that He will perfect it, that is not the thought in the mind of the writer. It is rather, to translate literally, that He is the File Leader and Perfecter in the sense of Vindicator of faith. He is the One Who takes precedence in the revelation of the meaning of faith. Seeing the witnesses, we are told to look off to One Who outreaches them all, in the revelation and the meaning of the value of faith.

The next words give us a further vision of Him:

" Who for the joy that was set before Him."

That joy was ever that of His ultimate purpose of bringing about the complete accomplishment of the purpose of God in a redeemed humanity.

In order to the accomplishment of that purpose:
" He endured the Cross, despising shame."

He is finally presented as One Who completes the triumph as the writer says He:

" Sat down at the right hand of the throne of God."

Having thus described the vision, the writer calls for special attention to the central matter of the Cross, in the words:

" Consider Him that hath endured such gainsaying of sinners against themselves."

The Old Version here read, " Against Himself." The alteration was made on the basis of MS. examination. Perhaps we have no right to be dogmatic in the matter, seeing some of the old MSS. give one reading and some another. Yet the words, " against themselves " more clearly state the principle of the Cross. What our Lord endured was not something against Himself, but that contradiction of Himself by sinners in its reaction upon themselves.

One may now glance at the rest of the chapter. The interpretation of appeal falls into three parts. First in verses four to seventeen the perils that threaten the life of faith, are stated. Then in verses eighteen to twenty-four the encouragements to the life of faith are recorded. Finally, in verses twenty-five to twenty-nine, the great appeal reaches its climax, commencing with the words:

> " See that ye refuse not Him that speaketh."

The perils threatening the life of faith are two. The first is that of failure to respond to chastening. The second is that of falling short of the grace of God. In introducing the first of these perils, the writer utters words of rebuke.

> " Ye have not yet resisted unto blood, striving against sin; and ye have forgotten the exhortation, which reasoneth with you as with sons."

The introduction of this rebuke seems to prove conclusively that this letter was sent to some particular group of people of whom such a statement would be true. Its principle is of persistent application. Of chastening the writer declares that it is of God, that it is a proof of sonship. If we have no chastening, no discipline, then he declares with great boldness we are not sons, but bastards. Chastening is a process of pain:

> " All chastening seemeth for the present to be not joyous, but grievous.";

but it is a process which leads to purification:

> " Afterward it yieldeth peaceable fruit unto them that have been exercised thereby, even the fruit of righteousness."

There is always a danger that we resent chastening. If we fail to respond to it, because we fail to understand it, we fail to gather the values which it is intended to create. That is one peril which ever threatens the life of faith. Let us ever be careful, in the midst of trial of sorrow, of heart-break, of disappointment, lest we resist the chastening of the Lord, and so fail to learn the lessons He has to teach. In such failure faith is challenged and weakened, and the running of the race ceases to be what it ought to be.

The further peril is described in a paragraph in which the recurrence of the word "lest" three times, is arresting.

"Looking carefully *lest* there be any man that falleth short of the grace of God; *lest* any root of bitterness springing up trouble you, and thereby the many be defiled; *lest* there be any fornicator or profane person, as Esau, who for one mess of meat sold his own birthright."

Here is a threefold warning.

The first is expressed in the words, "falleth short of the grace of God," that is, falling short of fellowship with the heart of God that ever desires to bestow blessing upon others; falling short of the activity of God, which by the way of the Cross made possible this conferring of blessing upon others. Falling short of the grace of God is not a question of falling from grace, but it is a question of falling so far below the profound meaning and ultimate value of grace as to fail in our running of the race; because it is only through grace that the ultimate goal can be reached.

When we thus fall short of the grace of God, the result is that instead of that grace, a root of bitterness springs up, whereby the many are defiled. Thus failure in fellowship with the grace of God reacts upon the communion of such as are running in the same race. There is no need to emphasise the fact so constantly seen in the history of the people of God, that roots of bitterness have halted and hindered the work of the Kingdom of God.

Finally:

"Lest there be any fornicator or profane person, as Esau."

The illustration is a very solemn one of the fact that falling short of the grace of God, issuing in bitterness, may bring us to the hour when we are willing to sell our birthright for a mess of pottage.

It is by the chastening of the Lord that we are to be delivered from these very perils. By such chastening, a process of pain, never

joyous, but grievous, we are saved from falling short of the grace
of God, and from the bitterness which produces defilement, and
the tragedy of selling our birthright.

If these are the perils, in the passage which follows, the
writer shows the great encouragements to faith. A glance at the
passage will show a contrast. One picture begins, " Ye are not
come "; the second, " Ye are come."

Writing to Hebrews, with a knowledge of all their past
history, and how it began, he refers to the mount that might not
be touched, the surroundings and atmosphere of which were
terror and majesty, of which the material symbols are named.
It was a Divine economy, but transient. Of the glory and the
majesty of it there was no question, but it was one that filled the
heart with fear. To that, says the writer, those under the rule of
the Son are not come.

Instead of terror and majesty we have tenderness and mercy.
Instead of the material symbols we have the spiritual facts.
Instead of the shadow we have the substance. Instead of the
Divine which was transient we have the Divine which is
permanent. These are the great sources of encouragement. We
are come to Mount Zion, the city of the living God, the heavenly
Jerusalem, innumerable hosts of angels, the general assembly
and Church of the firstborn who are enrolled in heaven, to God
the Judge of all, and to the spirits of just men made perfect, and
to Jesus the Mediator and the blood of sprinkling.

All this, then, leads to that simple and yet inclusive final
injunction:

" See that ye refuse not Him that speaketh."

Once more he contrasts the speech on earth and the speech
from heaven. The speech on earth was the speech of God through
human instruments, for God in times past, spoke unto the fathers
through the prophets. That was the speech on earth. Now
He speaks in His Son. It is speech from heaven in a new way.

Therefore:

" If they escaped not,"

who were disobedient to the speech on the earth level:

" how much more shall not we escape,"

who are disobedient to the speech that has thus come in this
new way, directly from heaven.

Therefore he ends:

" Let us have grace whereby we may offer service well-pleasing to God with reverence and awe."

The great appeal ends with the tremendous word:

" For our God is a consuming fire."

That has indeed an arresting and almost terrible sound, and yet it is wholly beneficent. A very illuminating commentary on the fact declared may be found in the end of the Old Testament literature. If we read the last chapter in Malachi, we discover two remarkable and contrasting descriptions of the same fact, both referring to the ultimate things in the Divine economy. First:

" The day cometh, it burneth as a furnace."
Second:

" The sun of righteousness shall arise with healing in his wings."

" Our God is a consuming fire." The effect of the fire depends upon our relationship to Him. It destroys all stubble and all dross; but it purifies and heals all those who are in right relationship with Him.

REVELATION I

THIS chapter is complete in itself, constituting as it does one division of the book of Revelation. The theme of that book is stated in its opening phrase, "The Revelation of Jesus Christ." We often speak of the book as the Apocalypse, which word is a transliteration of the Greek word, *apokalupsis.* This word literally rendered means unveiling, so that the theme of the book is announced as being that of the Unveiling of Jesus Christ.

That unveiling moves quite naturally along three lines. In the first we have an unveiling of the Person of Jesus Christ (chapter i.); in the second, an unveiling of Jesus Christ in relation to His Church (chapters ii., iii.); and finally, an unveiling of Jesus Christ and the processes of the Kingdom of God to consummation (chapters iv.–xxii.). That movement may be expressed in other words by saying we have an unveiling of Jesus Christ in His glory, in His grace, and in His government.

In that sense, therefore, this chapter is complete in that before portraying Jesus Christ in grace or in government, He is presented in His personal glory, in language of symbolic suggestiveness.

The actual description of the glory of the Person is contained in verses twelve to sixteen. This section is preceded by an introduction, occupying the first eleven verses, and is followed by an account of the commission given to John in verses seventeen to twenty.

The introduction falls into four distinct parts. First the prologue in verses one to three; then the salutation in verses four to six; next an enunciation of central truths in verses seven and eight; and finally a declaration by the writer concerning the occasion of his writing.

In the prologue we have a clear statement as to the nature, the origin, and the method of the book. The nature of the book is, as we have already seen, revealed in the opening phrase, "The Unveiling of Jesus Christ." It is impossible to lay too much emphasis upon this fact. Whereas the book in its entirety contains revelations of conditions on the earth level, and in the heavenly places, of conflict, and oftentimes of terror, moving ever on until the consummation is reached, the one purpose of its writing is the presentation of the vision of Jesus Christ Himself.

The origin of the book is then stated, and in terms that demand careful consideration. The statement is made that this unveiling of Jesus Christ, " God gave Him to show unto His servants." The force of the word " gave " there is that it suggests authorisation. We might with perfect accuracy as to intention, read the statement that " God authorised Him to show unto His servants." Whatever is found in the book afterwards, we are to understand that it is an unveiling, especially intended for the servants of God, and one given upon the authority of God Himself.

This authorisation was given to Jesus Christ, of Whom the book constitutes the unveiling. He having received this authority:

"Sent and signified it by His angel unto His servant John."

There has been much controversy as to the authorship of the book. The simple reading of this introduction shows who the writer really was, for running on, it says:

"His servant John, who bare witness of the Word of God."

This is surely a reference to the Gospel narrative, which commences with the declaration:

"In the beginning was the Word, and the Word was with God, and the Word was God,"

and presently affirms:

"The Word became flesh."

Later on (verse 9), the writer refers to himself again in the words:

"I John, your brother and partaker with you in the tribulation and Kingdom and patience which are in Jesus, was in the isle that is called Patmos, for the Word of God, and the testimony of Jesus,"

thus accounting for his imprisonment by the fact that he had been a witness to " the Word of God."

The method, then, was that having received this authority from God, Jesus Christ gave the revelation to John through an angel. John receiving, wrote. Such is the nature, origin, and method of the book.

The prologue ends with an arresting beatitude:

" Blessed is he that readeth, and they that hear the words of the prophecy, and keep the things which are written therein; for the time is at hand."

It has often been pointed out that this is the only book in the Divine Library which opens with a definite blessing pronounced upon those who read, and hear, and obey. In considering it, it is a significant thing that the Greek word employed for reading is not the ordinary one. To translate quite literally, we should read:

" Blessed is he that readeth aloud, and they that hear the words of the prophecy, and keep the things written therein."

The picture presented then is that of a reader reading aloud to a group of listening people; and the beatitude is for that reader and for those who are listening. It must be observed, however, that the blessing is not only upon the reading and the hearing, but upon the keeping of the words. That is to say any reading which is merely one of curiosity as to programme and dating, is of little avail. Where the reading has as its purpose the discovery of the principles of life revealed, and a determination to conform to those principles, the blessing is granted.

This brings us to the salutation (verses 4–6). This salutation is two-fold. The writer first salutes the Churches to whom the writing is to be sent, and then salutes the One Who is the Subject of the writing. In saluting the Churches he uses words which are full of meaning, and yet so constantly in use, " grace and peace "; declaring in remarkable language, the source of this twofold blessing:

" From Him Which is and Which was and Which is to come (the Father); and from the seven Spirits which are before His throne (the Holy Spirit); and from Jesus Christ, Who is the faithful Witness, the Firstborn of the dead, and the Ruler of the kings of the earth."

In saluting the One concerning Whom he is writing, he uses the words " glory and dominion," with the qualifying phrase, " for ever and ever." Thus to the Churches grace and peace, and to the Lord Himself glory and dominion.

The enunciation of central truths follows immediately This opens with the declaration:

" Behold, He cometh with the clouds; and every eye shall see Him, and they which pierced Him; and all the tribes of the earth shall mourn over Him. Even so, Amen."

That is a glance to the ultimate, to that to which everything is moving. It is not without significance at this point to remind ourselves that in the days of His flesh our Lord declared:

> "Blessed are they that mourn, for they shall be comforted."

The reference in each case is to a mourning that leads to the establishment of right relationships with God through Christ.

In connection with that statement concerning the ultimate, the announcement of that which is continuous is made:

> "I am the Alpha and the Omega, saith the Lord God, which is and which was and which is to come, the Almighty."

This is the abiding fact which gives assurance of the ultimate victory. It may be observed at this point that that phrase, " I am the Alpha and the Omega " occurs three times in the course of the book, here, and in xxi. 6 and xxii. 13.

The occasion upon which John received the revelation is then declared:

> "I John, your brother . . . was in the isle that is called Patmos . . . was in the Spirit on the Lord's day."

He thus refers to two environments. First, he was in Patmos, an exile, separated by the waters of the Sea from kith and country. But he was in the Spirit. His local situation was that of a prisoner. His spiritual consciousness was that of the freedom of the Spirit. Under these circumstances, and in these conditions, he heard behind him the voice, and turning to see, beheld the vision of the Person of the Lord.

As we turn to observe the vision, we remember that it is the last description historically of Jesus found in the New Testament. In the Gospel narratives we have the presentation of Him as seen by those who wrote. Of these Matthew was certainly an eye-witness, as also was John. Mark in all probability also had seen Him in bodily form, though he was not an apostle. Luke's description is one which he had derived, as he tells us, from those who had been eye-witnesses. All these portray Him as a Man of sorrows, and acquainted with grief. They saw Him in the midst of earthly limitation, living in comparative poverty, divested of everything that earth considers glorious. Now John who had seen Him during that period, and companied with Him in a close relationship, describes how he saw Him in Patmos. The description is characterised by Eastern imagery from beginning to end; and the whole picture is marvellous in its glory and in its beauty. It was so great a vision that John says when he saw Him, he fell at His feet as one dead. If only we could see the vision as John saw it, if our imaginations could be captured and cleansed by the Holy Spirit, we also should fall at His feet in the light of the glory.

As we have said, the description is that of the imagery of the East, and it is well to remember that figures of speech are always employed to describe that which is finer than the figures can be. As John looked upon the vision of the Lord, he saw His robing, beheld His hair, His eyes, His feet; listened to His voice; looked also at His hand, and at His mouth; and all he saw could only be conveyed to us through these wonderful Eastern figures.

When he turned, that which first arrested his attention was a vision of seven golden lampstands, that is seven luminaries, from which light was proceeding. The general scene, therefore, was a night scene, and in the midst of the darkness these lamps were burning. Yet in a very remarkable sense it is a day scene, for presently John records the fact that:

" His countenance was as the sun shineth in his strength."

All this in itself is full of symbolic suggestiveness. Lampstands are for the night, and these by the interpretation of the Lord Himself represent the Churches. They are instruments intended to give light in the midst of the night. The light they give is derived directly from the glory of the countenance that shineth as the sun. That shining is for the Churches themselves, and its glory can only be revealed to the world through the lampstands.

That, however, which supremely arrested John was not the vision of the lampstands, but that of the One he saw in the midst of them. This One he speaks of as being " Like unto the Son of man." The text reads " Like unto a son of man." As a matter of fact there is no article in the Greek, so that either reading may be appropriate. It is almost impossible to escape from the conviction that when John employed that phrase to describe the One he saw, he was remembering that during the earthly ministry of our Lord, His constant title for Himself was the Son of man. The phrase occurs in the records no less than eighty-five times, eighty-three of them being occasions when our Lord used it Himself. Thus when John employed the phrase as expressing the first impression made upon him when he turned to observe the Person uttering the voice, it was one which was our

Lord's own description of Himself. That description, moreover, is found in the book of Daniel:

> "I saw in the night visions, and, behold, there came with the clouds of heaven One like unto a Son of man."

That was the phrase which our Lord had taken and appropriated to Himself. Thus in effect John says that when he turned, the One Whom he beheld was the One Whom he had known, and about Whom he had previously written.

He then proceeded to describe Him, and he did it in a fourfold movement of symbolism; first, the symbolism of function; secondly, that of character; thirdly, that of activity; and, finally, that of glory.

The symbolism of function is found in the words:

> "Clothed with a garment down to the foot, and girt about at the breasts with a golden girdle."

Here the symbolism is most distinctly Eastern, and definitely describes function. The garment to the foot was always interpretive of judicial authority; and the golden girdle, that of Kingship. Thus as John saw Him, he beheld Him in full and complete authority. The garment might also suggest priesthood. This garment was held in place by the golden girdle of kingly supremacy.

The next phrases give the symbolism of character.

> "His head and His hair were white as white wool, white as snow; and His eyes were as a flame of fire."

Here again we have the distinct Eastern symbolism, suggesting both purity and eternity. The words already quoted from Daniel, "The Ancient of days," have the same suggestiveness, not of age as of One Who had become aged, but that of abiding age. The words, "His eyes were as a flame of fire," suggest such piercing, penetrative looking that sees accurately and truthfully, and consequently finds verdicts that cannot be gainsaid. The symbolism of character, therefore, sets Him forth as One of absolute purity, strength, and complete knowledge.

Then follows the symbolism of His activity:

> "His feet like unto burnished brass, as if it had been refined in a furnace; and His voice as the voice of many waters. And He had in His right hand, seven stars; and out of His mouth proceeded a sharp two-edged sword."

In Eastern symbolism the feet were always symbolic of procedure, and the description of them " like unto burnished brass," refers to the strength and purity of all His government.

His voice as " the voice of many waters " is suggestive of a concord of sounds, differentiated and yet harmonious. It is a graphic poetic declaration that all the voices that had sounded were gathered up and harmonised in His speech.

The vision of the seven stars held in His right hand had its explicit interpretation in the words of Jesus to John uttered presently. " The . . . stars are the angels of the . . . Churches." The holding of them in His hand spoke of His power and protection.

Finally, under this symbolism of activity, John declared:

" Out of His mouth proceeded a sharp two-edged sword,"

a poetic revelation of the fact that He utters the truth, and finds verdicts and passes sentences, which are in strict accord therewith.

Finally, everything of the glory of the vision is summarised in a sentence which speaks of that glory alone.

" His countenance was as the sun shineth in his strength."

This, then, in its entirety, as we have said, is the last picture of the Son of man in Holy Scripture. It is full of the light and colour and glory and beauty of Eastern symbolism. Familiar as we are with the vision of the Son of man in the days of His flesh, as a Man of sorrows, concerning Whom we may use the words of the ancient prophecy and say that His face was more marred than that of any other man; it is well for us to remember that the only description which is perfect concerning Him to-day is that His countenance is as the sun shineth in its strength.

In the last movement of the chapter we have the record of the effect produced upon John by the vision.

" When I saw Him, I fell at His feet as one dead."

What a tremendous sentence that is. In the presence of that supernal glory, the consciousness of self was ended, and it was as though the watcher had died. Then the exquisite beauty of that which followed. As we read it let us keep in mind the radiant wonder of the Personality, and the fact that in His right hand, the seven stars were resting. Then we watch as He placed that hand upon the prostrate form of His servant, and said to him:

"Fear not, I am the first and the last, and the Living One; and I was dead, and behold, I am alive for evermore; and I have the keys of death and of Hades."

In these words He declared Himself to be the Origin and Consummation of all things; declared moreover that He had passed into the dereliction of human experience due to sin, but that He was now alive for evermore, holding the keys of complete authority.

In view of these facts John was commanded to write. Thus came to him the commission for the writing of the book.

This was followed by a general word of interpretation of the surroundings. He was in the midst of the lampstands, which were symbols of His Churches. The next movement in the book contains the messages which He sent to the Churches. As we read them, with this radiant vision of the Person in mind, we see how different aspects suggested by the vision, are used in application to the diversified needs of these very Churches. Thus the unveiling of the glory of the Lord prepares for the unveiling of His grace in His presence with, and presidency over, His Church; and reveals the secrets of His power and authority in the unveiling of His glory in government, until the purposes of God are fulfilled in human history, and the city of God is built.

REVELATION XXI—XXII, 5

IT is necessary in dealing with this chapter to read in connection with it the first five verses of chapter twenty-two, which complete the presentation of the city of God. This section closes the book as to its unveiling. The rest of chapter twenty-two constitutes an epilogue full of meaning and of value, referring to the writing thus completed. I am not proposing to enter into any discussion as to the question of dating, save to say that I think there are evidences that this book was the final writing of John, and thus completes the Literature of the Divine Library.

That Library in the order in which we have it, began with the words:

"In the beginning God created the heavens and the earth,"

and then tells the story of a garden in which man was placed. This final movement in the last book commences:

"And I saw a new heaven and a new earth,"

and proceeds to describe the city which is the centre of the new earth. Thus we may say that the whole of the Library began with a picture of potential beauty, and closes with an account of the realised potentiality.

In the economy and purpose of God, all the potentiality of the ultimate was found in that garden, when man was placed there. In that same economy the ultimate outworking of the forces placed within the garden is seen in this chapter.

Browning was certainly familiar with the whole movement of the Biblical Literature, and he expressed his conviction in the words so often quoted:

"My own hope is, a sun will pierce
    The thickest cloud earth ever stretched;
That, after Last, returns the First,
    Though a wide compass round be fetched;
That what began best, can't end worst,
    Nor what God blessed once, prove accurst."

In this Biblical Literature then, we repeat, we have the account of processes stretching over centuries and millenniums; and in this chapter we have the portrayal of the ultimate of the new heaven and the new earth, with a special vision of the city of God, which reveals the conditions established on the earth.

The purpose of God was ever the city, and the powers for the city were resident in the garden. The whole Literature opens in a garden, and closes in a city. When we say that the city lay potentially in the garden, we are simply referring to something that is true of all cities. London is the outcome of a garden, for there is nothing in it that did not come out of the garden. Everything that is unhealthy and ugly in the cities results from the prostitution of the forces which, rightly used, would have made for health and beauty. The ultimate purpose of God is the realisation of the meaning of human life in all social inter-relationships, and in such conditions as are full of strength and of beauty. It is well to remind ourselves that it was in order that man might reach such conditions, and arrive at such a city, that God confused the project of man at Babel, and scattered the people, in order to the larger ingathering. It was to reach this city that Abraham turned his back upon Ur of Chaldea. The purpose of God was clearly seen by the prophet who, when the material walls of Jerusalem were broken down, and the gates burned with fire, declared that God was saying:

" Thy walls are continually before Me."

He never lost sight of the ultimate purpose and victory. There is surely great significance in the words spoken about our Lord, when it is said of Him that " He stedfastly set His face to go to Jerusalem." Jerusalem was then doomed, and He had uttered its doom; but He saw through the gloom to the glory, and moved onward towards the city of God.

The city then portrays the metropolis which is to be the centre of the realised ideals of God for men. It is a portrayal in figurative language of the centre of the new social order.

" Lift your eyes, ye sons of light,
　　Zion's city is in sight."

It is vital that we should remember that the picture is not the picture of heaven, but of a city which comes out of heaven; a city which is the centre of the Kingdom of God established on earth. The presentation portrays a city wherein the full and final answer to the prayer which Jesus taught His disciples, and which the Church has been praying, is seen as reached:

" Our Father, Who art in the heavens,
　　Hallowed be Thy name,
　　Thy Kingdom come,
　　Thy will be done.
　　　　On earth as in heaven."

The answer to that prayer has never yet come in all fullness, but it is coming; and here in figurative language, we have the description of the answer.

In our consideration of the revelation, we shall adopt a general rather than a detailed method. The first thing which is clearly revealed is that the city of God as described, is the city of which God is the Architect and Builder. It comes out of heaven. That city will not be the result of evolution in any sense. It will result from revelation, producing revolution on the earth level. Looking over the whole portrayal, then, there are four things that become self-evident. The first is that it will be the city inter-national; secondly, that it will be the city redeemed; third, that it will be the city holy; and finally, that it will be the city beautiful.

This city of God will be international. This is most distinctly revealed in the statements that the nations are to walk in the light of it, and are to bring their glory and their honour into it. Its gates swing open to every point of the compass, and everything is suggestive of this unifying of the nations. The unifying of the nations does not mean the ending of national life, but rather the co-ordination of all nations in a great harmony. Diversity will remain, for it is part of the wonder and majesty of human nature, as God has created and governed it, in spite of all its own blundering and failure. The wide open gates speak of this possibility and realisation of perfect inter-relationship.

The outlook suggests a complete change in international affairs from conditions obtaining to-day. That change may be briefly expressed by declaring that when the city of God is built, national relationships will not be competitive but co-operative. It is a revelation at once of humanity's greatness and weakness, in that everywhere men are seeking for some such inter-relationship, and are entirely unable to bring it about. Competition is still mastering the policies of statesmen, and selfishness dominating the counsels of the nations. When the Kingdom of God is come, with this city as its metropolis, the nations will still exist, but their inter-relationship will be that of fellowship, and not of strife. Every nation in the Kingdom of God will still have its own peculiar deposit; but no nation will hold that deposit as for itself alone. It will hold it on trust for the rest of the world.

As we look over world conditions to-day we realise how revolutionary all this is; and yet it is to that consummation that the Kingdom of God is moving, and of its realisation the picture is given in this presentation of the city.

Thus will be realised the true communism. Naturally, we are afraid of that word to-day because as it is interpreted, it is not communism at all, but a protest against possession by some, with an attempt to secure the same possession by others. The inspiration of such false communism is ever selfishness, whereas the true communism as here revealed, is inspired by love and service.

The question naturally arises as to how such conditions can ever be brought about, and this unveiling answers the question. The declaration is made that the light of that city in which the nations walk, is the glory of God, and that the lamp, or centre from which that light will shine, will be the Lamb. That reference sends us back to the beginning of the book, particularly to the fourth and fifth chapters. In the fourth chapter we have a vision of the eternal Throne. In the fifth chapter we find that the One occupying the Throne eternally, is seeking someone to administer the affairs of the earth, so as to bring in the realisation of the Divine purpose. The question asked is:

" Who is worthy to take the book, and to open the seals? " As John records this, in a personal aside, he declares:

" I wept much, because no one was found worthy to open the book, or to look thereon."

It was then that it was said to him:

" Weep not; behold, the Lion that is of the tribe of Judah, the Root of David, hath overcome, to open the book and the seals thereof ?"

Then we have something than which there is nothing more startlingly dramatic in literature. He turned to see the conquering Lion, and he saw " A Lamb standing, as though it had been slain." The Executive of the Throne is the Lamb.

We now come to this picture of the city of God, and are told that its light is the glory of God, and that of that light the Lamp is the lampstand. Thus the city international, is a redeemed city. No conclaves of statesmen, attempting to bring about a true order, without a recognition of the Throne of God, and of the redemptive work of the Son of God, will ever succeed in establishing true internationalism.

In describing the gates and the foundations of the city we have a suggestive revelation of this fact of redemption. On the gates are the names of the twelve tribes of the children of Israel. Perhaps nowhere is the truth concerning these twelve tribes more clearly revealed than in the dying words of Jacob, found in the book of Genesis. The sons of Jacob were indeed men characterised by weakness and failure and sin. Nevertheless their names are inscribed upon these gates, and the fact symbolises the truth that the burgesses of the city of God are redeemed men.

If we look at the foundations we find the names of the twelve apostles of the Lamb. These men were also men of like passions with ourselves, men who blundered and failed oftentimes. Nevertheless their names are here, once more showing that all the conditions of life in the city are founded upon ransomed and redeemed humanity.

Because the city is a city redeemed, it follows that it is a city holy. That fact is made clear in the description of the things which are excluded from the city of God. All the things which have broken up and scattered humanity, creating false nationalism, mastered by selfishness, are excluded. The conditions excluded are tears, death, mourning, crying, pain. These are excluded because of the character excluded, that of the fearful, the unbelieving, the abominable. Continuing, the description shows the conduct which is excluded, no murderer, no fornicator, no sorcerer, no idolater, no liar will be found therein. As we read, we find further references to the things excluded, as we are told there will be no night there, the opportunity of evil; nothing unclean, the occasion of evil; nothing that makes a lie, the occupation of evil; and no curse, the outcome of evil.

In the description we have no list of things included in the city of the same kind, but these, of course, are at once to be deduced from the things excluded. If no tears, no death, no mourning, no crying, no pain; then merriment, life, abounding joy, will be there. We may summarise by declaring that all the positives that evil has negative, will be found in the city of God. In our attempt to understand this we may revert to the earlier writings of John, and remind ourselves of the three great words of which he constantly made use, the words life, and light, and love. In the course of those writings we find the clear-cut definitions of God, " God is love," "God is light." Whereas the statement that God is life is not made in the same form, that is a self-evident truth. The order of heaven may be summarised by saying that its law is for ever love, that its intelligence is perfect light, and that its power is age-abiding life. In the city of God then, love will be the one impulse, light the perfect guidance, and life the adequate power.

Once more the city of God will be the city beautiful. In the statement that the city will have no need of the sun and moon, we have teaching which is mystical, and yet full of suggestiveness.

The glory of God is the light pervasive, and casting no shadows. The statement is one of poetry defying, it may be, anything like material interpretation, but remaining in all beauty of suggestiveness.

As we look at the foundations, they are described as garnished with all manner of precious stones. As we attempt to understand that, we are conscious of the flaming beauty of the merging of colours. All rainbow tints are found therein. Unquestionably the language here is figurative, and yet as always the figurative is intended to convey the idea of a beauty that defies any other method of expression.

Once again looking, we see presented to us a river and trees. The trees are described as:

"Bearing twelve manner of fruits,"

a different one for each month. Of these trees it is said:

"The leaves of the tree were for the healing of the nations."

It is important that at this point we understand the real meaning of the word rendered "healing." The idea would be more correctly conveyed by the use of a word which is now obsolete, but which we find in Old English literature, the word "healthing." Healthing means preventing sickness, whereas healing may mean restoration to health from sickness. The idea, therefore, is that in the city of God there will be provision made for the maintenance of perfect health. We thank God for all the ministry of healing that is being carried on in the world to-day, but far greater than healing will be a prevention of the need for it. Some years ago I heard Dr. Saleeby say in this regard, when arguing the importance of preventing disease:

"A fence at the top of the cliff is more valuable than an ambulance at its foot."

In reading this account we are arrested by the statement as to the dimensions of the city. It is described as being:

"Twelve thousand furlongs; the length and the breadth and the height thereof are equal."

In other words, we have the portrayal of a city consisting of a cube of twelve thousand furlongs. Now let it be at once recognised that the mathematics of that statement carry us beyond the possibility of complete apprehension. The one idea thus superlatively and overwhelmingly suggested is that of its infinite space, of the vastness, the joyous vastness of the city and the Kingdom of God.

Any contemplation of the conditions revealed in this apocalypse of the city of God while we are still living in the midst of world conditions with which we are familiar, must lead to the enquiry, How can these things be brought about?

The answer to that enquiry is found in the great statement:

> " He that sitteth on the Throne saith: Behold, I make all things new."

That is the guarantee of the ultimate realisation. Abraham left Ur to seek a city, Whose Architect and Maker is God; and now at last the great word is heard, spoken by God Himself:

> " I make all things new."

From none other would such a statement have any convincing significance. He Who is God from everlasting to everlasting, cannot be outreached. He antedates evil, and is beyond it. Whatever the processes may be, He is before, and He is beyond. Moreover, He cannot be overcome, and this not merely because of His eternity and absolute might, but because He has overcome, and by the mystery of redemption is Victor.

Thus, as amid all the clouds and the darkness, the mysteries and the disappointments of to-day, we pause and lift our eyes toward the ultimate, the vision makes a threefold appeal to us. The first is that we should accept the ideals revealed in the portrayal. The second is that we take part in the process that leads to the realisation, and that is always the way of the Cross. The third is that we should allow no questionings to arise in our minds as to the certainty of the issue. In this case in very deed:

> " To doubt would be disloyalty,
> To falter would be sin."

However perplexing the outlook may be to-day, it is ours to sing the song of the coming victory with all confidence:

> " Your harps, ye trembling saints,
>   Down from the willows take;
> Loud to the praise of love Divine
>   Bid every string awake.
> Blest is the man, O God,
>   That stays himself on Thee;
> Who waits for Thy salvation, Lord,
>   Shall Thy salvation see."

REVELATION XXII, 6—21

IN our survey of Revelation xxi., we included the first five
verses of this chapter, as we were bound to do. That which
remains of the chapter constitutes an epilogue, and is concerned
with the whole book, and its value. The apocalyptic unveiling
was completed with the revelation of the ultimate in the government
of our Lord, as the city of God is presented, descending out of
heaven, established on the earth, with the whole Kingdom of God
fully established around it.

The movement of the book, as we have seen, is the unveiling
of Jesus Christ, first in His personal glory in chapter one; then
in His infinite grace in chapters two and three, as He deals with
the Churches; and finally in the august majesty of His government,
from the point in chapter five where He is seen taking the book
for the loosing of the seals, to the consummation in the city of
God.

We come then to a consideration of this epilogue concerning
the book in its entirety. This may be divided into two parts, the
first having to do with the ratification of the book (verses 6–16);
and the second forming a definite conclusion (verses 17–21).

In the first part, then (verses 6–16), there are three distinct
movements. In verses six and seven we have the record of
words of Jesus. That they are so, is evident from the declaration
made therein, "Behold, I come quickly." In verses eight to
eleven we have what may be described as an historical interlude,
as John tells what took place between him and the angel, after
he had completed his work. In verses twelve to sixteen we find
again the words of Jesus; and the whole constitutes a ratification
of the book.

The section begins with the words, "And He said unto me,"
and the question arises as to whom John was referring. An
angel had been speaking to him, and these words are generally
treated as though spoken by this angel. That, however, is not
really tenable when we notice what was said:

"These words are faithful and true; and the Lord, the
God of the spirits of the prophets, sent His angel to show
unto His servants the things which must surely come to
pass. And behold, I come quickly."

Quite evidently that final word is not the word of an angel, but
of the Lord Himself. Consequently we have in these words the
ratification by the Lord of all that had so far been written.

The statement made is first that "these words are faithful and true." The phrase "faithful and true" is found earlier in the book, and is given as the name of the Lord Himself, first in the letter to Laodicea, and again in the nineteenth chapter, where He is described as the victorious One. The phrase moreover occurs once again in application to the writing itself in the previous chapter (xxi. 5).

"He that sitteth on the throne saith, Behold, I make all things new. And He saith, Write, for these words are faithful and true."

Thus the phrase is used as the name of the Lord twice, and as descriptive of the value of the writings twice.

This is an arresting fact, and calls for an examination of the words. The phrase does not constitute a repetition of the same idea in differing words. The words rendered "faithful" and "true," have differing signification. The word rendered "faithful" has the sense of trustworthy, that is, quite evidently, some one or some message which is worthy of complete confidence. The other word rendered "true" is a very significant one. The literal meaning of it is something which is not hidden. The real idea is conveyed by a phrase of which we sometimes make use, namely, "the naked truth"; the idea being that of truth unadorned, truth with no embellishments. Perhaps the formula of an oath in our courts of law may be helpful. "The truth, the whole truth, and nothing but the truth." Our Lord, then, in those words referred to this writing that He had been authorised by God to show unto His servants, and which He had sent and signified by an angel unto John, and declared that the things written are to be depended upon, that they are words of unadorned and naked truth.

Continuing, the source of the words is then declared in the remarkable statement:

"The Lord, the God of the spirits of the prophets, sent His angel."

The King James' Version reads here:

"The Lord God of the holy prophets sent His angel,"

which was a rendering based upon the Greek Text of Stephens. It is now, however, generally agreed that the text should be as here translated, "The God of the spirits of the prophets."

The statement, then, is that that which has been written has come from the One Who is here described as "the Lord," that is the One Who is "the God of the spirits of the prophets." That description has value as a recognition of all that God had

said to men through the prophets. The commencement of the
Hebrew letter at once occurs to mind, with its declaration that
God had spoken in times past unto the fathers through the
prophets. The declaration now is that that same God is the
One from Whom the things written in this book have come, and
that the medium had been the Son, Who sent His angel, as was
stated in the opening of the book (i. 1, 2).

Having thus ratified the authority of the writing, our Lord
made the great affirmation:

"Behold, I come quickly."

Seven times over in the course of the book is that affirmation
repeated. It gathers up in itself the whole truth revealed in the
unveiling. It is important that here we recognise the real value
of the word " quickly." It does not mean soon. To so interpret
it would be to introduce a time element, which must for ever be
cancelled when the Divine activities are under consideration. The
word rather suggests promptness. There are those who would
render it suddenly, but it does not seem to me that that really
catches the significance. Personally, I would unhesitatingly
render the statement, " Behold, I come on time," that is quickly,
in the sense of coming at the right moment. That is the perpetual
revelation of Scripture concerning our Lord. When He was born
of a Virgin, as Paul says, He was sent " in the fulness of time."
God never comes too soon, and never comes too late. The whole
teaching of this book in its unveiling of the glory and the grace
and the government of Jesus Christ emphasises that fact.

Necessarily the principal thought is contained in the thought
" I come," where our Lord used, as He so constantly did, what
we cannot describe better than the eternal present tense. He
came when He was " made flesh." He came when the Holy
Spirit came. He is coming again to bring in the consummation.
In every case His coming is quickly, that is with promptitude,
always on time.

The words of our Lord close here with the Beatitude:

" Blessed is he that keepeth the words of the prophecy
of this book."

The book opened with blessing pronounced upon the man who
reads aloud, and the people who hear and keep the things written
therein. This Beatitude, then, restates the same thing. The word
rendered " keepeth " has a very definite meaning, and might be
rendered with perfect accuracy " he that observeth." This, of
course, means far more than reading them, and does not at all
mean defending them. To keep in the sense of to observe is
necessarily to read and be familiar with them, but it is to be
obedient to them, to square life by them.

This ratification, ending with this Beatitude, emphasises the fact that a study of this book is only of value in so far as the vision of the Lord in His glory, His grace, and His government reacts upon life in such way as to produce the attitudes and activities which, recognising the glory, appropriate the grace, and yield to the government.

It is interesting here to remember that in the days of His flesh when our Lord enunciated His ethical code, we find the cluster of beatitudes at the beginning, and these all refer to the attitudes of life which fulfil these very conditions. To recognise His glory is to submit the life to Him, and that in the power of His grace, and under the constant authority of His government. In these words of our Lord, then, we have His ratification of the whole book.

In verses eight to eleven we have what we may in some senses describe as an interpolation, containing the ratification of the book by John himself, as he tells of his experiences with the angel. He first of all in a sense signs his document, as he writes:

" I, John, am he that heard and saw these things."

This final statement by the writer inevitably takes us back to that to which reference had already been made, the statement at the beginning:

" The Unveiling of Jesus Christ, which God gave Him to show unto His servants, . . . and He sent and signified it by an angel unto His servant John."

At the beginning we read that our Lord said to John "Write." He now declared that at the close of this period in which the angel had communicated to him the things he had been commanded to write, that in his own words:

" I fell down to worship before the feet of the angel which showed me these things."

This statement is a clear revelation of what it had meant to John, that period in Patmos, during which the angel had accompanied him, and given him vision after vision, first of glory, then of grace, and then of government, on to the consummation, and the building of the city of God. It is not to be wondered at that he took up this attitude; and yet it was a mistaken one; and he records how the angel at once refused to accept the worship. He did so in the remarkable words:

" I am a fellow-servant with thee and with thy brethren the prophets and with them that keep the words of this book."

Thus the angel linked himself with John and all the prophets. Having thus refused the worship, he uttered the sentence, " Worship

God," showing that the temptation to render homage to an instrument, whether angel or man, is wrong. God alone is to receive worship.

Continuing, the angel declared that the words of the book are not to be kept privately. They are not to be sealed up, " for the time is at hand." In that declaration " the time is at hand," we have again insistence upon immediateness, which has no reference to a date, but breathes the same thought as we have seen found in the word " quickly."

Then followed the arresting declaration:

" He that is unrighteous, let him do unrighteousness still; and he that is filthy, let him be made filthy still; and he that is righteous, let him do righteousness still, and he that is holy, let him be made holy still."

These particular words of the angel, as all scholars will agree, are not easy to translate, and yet the one matter of supreme value revealed in them is that of a movement towards permanence in courses of unrighteousness, or of righteousness.

It must remain an arresting fact that these words are found recorded here as uttered by this announcing angel, in close connection with what has gone before concerning the unveiling of Christ. If the glory be unrecognised, the grace not responded to, and the government disobeyed, the result of such failure to keep the words must result in an ever deepening degradation.

In verses twelve to sixteen once more we have the words of the Lord Himself:

" Behold, I come quickly, and My reward is with Me," constituting a reaffirmation of the great fact, and a declaration of its issue and purpose. The effect of the coming of the Lord is ever thus. For the moment I would change the word " reward," and substitute the word " award." The word reward may confine our thought to blessing, whereas it is equally true that His award deals with righteousness or unrighteousness. His coming always means discrimination, the finding of verdicts, and the declaration of the inevitable issues.

In connection with this the great affirmation is once again made:

" I am the Alpha and the Omega, the first and the last, the beginning and the end,"

which is a threefold statement of the same fact. The first phrase " Alpha and Omega " consists, as we all know, of the first and last letters of the alphabet, and between these all literature is contained. " The first and the last, the beginning and the end," that is, the

Garden of Genesis, and the City of Revelation; origin and consummation of life; and in these words the Lord claims relationship with everything.

In view of this statement concerning Himself the words were then uttered:

"Blessed are they that wash their robes, that they may have the right to come to the tree of life, and may enter in by the gates into the city. Without are the dogs, and the sorcerers, and the fornicators, and the murderers, and the idolaters, and every one that loveth and maketh a lie."

Then the old and familiar name is used, " I Jesus," but we must not fail to interpret it by the description before employed. Jesus is the Alpha and the Omega, the first and the last, the beginning and the end. The declaration now made is that He is responsible for the book:

"I sent Mine angel to testify unto you these things for the Churches."

Once more descriptive words are employed:

"I am the Root and the Offspring of David."

"The Root," out of which David came; "the Offspring," the fruitage of all that David meant; and lastly:

"The bright, the morning Star,"

or, more literally:

"The bright morning Star."

Thus we come to the conclusion of the whole book, and I think it is important that we should examine it somewhat technically. The first statement is:

"The Spirit and the bride say, Come."

Now it is important to remember that that is not the voice of the Spirit and the bride to the world. It is rather the call of the Spirit and the bride to Christ. It expresses the consent of the bride, through the interpretation of the Spirit to the great declaration made by the Lord: "Behold, I come "; and the expression of desire for the realisation in fullness of that great word.

This is followed by the sentence:

"And he that heareth, let him say, Come."

This is generally taken to mean that those who have heard the call of Christ are to repeat it to others. I do not so understand it. Rather it is still the voice of the Church appealing to Christ to continue His call to humanity. The Spirit and the bride desiring the coming of Christ, and working towards that great consummation, are appealing to Him that He will continue calling men to Himself. He that heareth, that is heareth the call of the Church, let Him still continue to say as He did in the long ago, " Come unto Me, all ye that labour."

Then suddenly in this poetic final movement the voice of the Lord is heard:

"He that is athirst, let him come: he that will, let him take the water of life freely."

It is almost impossible to escape the conviction that as John recorded those words, he was remembering the great call of Jesus, which he had recorded in his Gospel, when in the last day of the great feast He said, " If any man thirst, let him come unto Me, and drink." He heard that voice still uttering that same call.

It is in this connection that he wrote the solemn words:

" I testify unto every man that heareth the words of the prophecy of this book, If any man shall add unto them, God shall add unto him the plagues which are written in this book; and if any man shall take away from the words of the book of this prophecy, God shall take away his part from the tree of life, and out of the holy city, which are written in this book."

John then once more records the fact that:

" He which testifieth these things saith, Yea, I come quickly."

These are the last recorded words of the Lord, and it is the seventh occurrence of the great declaration in the course of the unveiling.

To this declaration of the Lord the answer of John is recorded, and it is the answer of the Church:

" Amen, come, Lord Jesus."

Thus the epilogue is completed. There remains only the benediction, and here it is found in its simplest form.

" The grace of the Lord Jesus be with the saints."

The proportion in which that benediction becomes the experience of those who hear and keep the words of the prophecy is the proportion in which the glory of the Lord is known and His government obeyed. By the way of His grace we share His glory, and enter into the victories of His government.

DEUTERONOMY XXXII

THE last nine verses of this chapter constitute history, first recording the words of Moses to the people concerning the song, and secondly the words of Jehovah to Moses concerning his death.

The great poem recorded herein has been described as the Swan Song of Moses. This is not strictly accurate, if by Swan Song is meant the last song before death, because in the next chapter we have the blessing of Moses which is also in the form of a song. The two taken together may be accurately described as constituting his Swan Song. It is in itself an arresting fact that Moses completed his work by composing two songs.

His life had fallen into three clearly marked periods: the first forty years at the court of Pharaoh, during which he was trained in all the learning of the Egyptians; the second forty years spent in the magnificent silences and solitudes of the desert as a shepherd; the last forty years amid the turbulence of the people, whom he was guiding and governing under the Divine authority.

During this last period he had received the great ritual of their religion, and the system of laws, finally delivering a series of farewell discourses, recorded in this book of Deuteronomy. Then when all was done, he wrote two songs and left them to his people, and so to us for all time. It is almost certain that these were not the only songs that he wrote, for the ninetieth psalm must be attributed to him, and personally I think he also wrote the ninety-first.

There are senses in which these two chapters should be considered together. To do so is to discover a remarkable and arresting contrast between the Song of chapter thirty-two and the Blessing of chapter thirty-three. The Blessing sets forth the glories of Israel ideally considered. In it there are no shadows, no clouds upon the horizon. Its closing stanza opens with the revealing exclamation:

" Happy art thou, O Israel."

In the Song now under consideration we have something entirely different. It is full of shadows and of storm-clouds; but shadows and storm-clouds are alike set in the light of a glorious background. The storm and shadows are created by the poignant confessions of the faithlessness of Israel, while the foreground of glory is found in the celebration of the faithfulness of God. All the way through we are conscious of these two matters, set one over against the other. The Song celebrates the faithfulness of God, and confesses the faithlessness of His people. That, of course, is a general summary.

The Song may thus be broken up into its constituent parts. In verses one to three we have an exordium; in verses four to six the theme is stated; in verses seven to twenty-eight a historic survey is given in illustration of the theme; in verses twenty-nine to forty-three we have a terrible prophetic outlook, ending with one sentence which illuminates the gloom.

I propose dealing with the Song in general outline, pausing with certain focal points of light and beauty. The exordium is full and important:

> " Give ear, ye heavens, and I will speak;
> And let the earth hear the words of my mouth;
> My doctrine shall drop as the rain,
> My speech shall distil as the dew;
> As the small rain upon the tender grass,
> And as the showers upon the herb,
> For I will proclaim the name of the Lord;
> Ascribe ye greatness unto our God."

When we recognise that this is the introduction of all that the song is to celebrate, we are conscious of what we may speak of as the audacity of the singer. That audacity, however, is vindicated before he has done. I suggest that no other poem can be found where the poet begins by challenging the heavens and the earth to listen, and by declaring that the effect of what he has to say will be fertilising as the rain and as the dew. His warrant for such a declaration is found in the last movement:

> " For I will proclaim the name of the Lord;
> Ascribe ye greatness un.:o our God."

The force of the word " For " there is Because. That is to say, he dares to make the statement he does about his song, on account of the theme thereof, that of the name of Jehovah, and of the greatness of God.

The theme of the song is then elaborated, and its force may be gathered by observing the first words of verse four, " The Rock," as they stand in contrast to the first word of verse five, " They." Concerning the Rock, he declares that His work is perfect, and His ways are judgment; that He is in Himself, a God of· faithfulness and without iniquity, just and right. Concerning the people represented by the word " They " he declares that they have dealt corruptly with Him, and are a perverse and crooked generation. Thus it is seen that the theme is, as we suggested at the outset, that of the faithfulness of God contrasted with the faithlessness of the people.

Necessarily all the previous ˙history enables us to understand this contrast as Moses realised it. For forty years he had been with these people, and was familiar with their tendencies and their attitudes, and saw how they had been characterised by unfaithfulness and disobedience; whereas, in his own communion with God, whom as the historian declares subsequently, Jehovah knew face to face, he had discovered nothing but faithfulness, justice, and righteousness.

We pause for a moment with the arresting phrase " The Rock." Our translators have properly capitalised the first letter in the word " Rock." If we glance on down the chapter to verse eighteen, we have the words:

" Of the Rock that begat thee thou art unmindful,"

where again the word is spelt with a capital letter. This is repeated in the thirtieth verse, in the words:

" Except their Rock had sold them."

In the next verse we have the statement:

" Their rock is not as our Rock,"

where the first word rock is not spelt with a capital letter, while the second is. Here emerges then in the Scriptures a figurative expression referring to God.

This is a matter of arresting value, because of its bearing on the Song, and, indeed, on all the subsequent Scriptures. This is the first occasion, then, where the word Rock is used as a figure of speech. If we follow through the Old Testament, and make a list of the places where the word Rock is used figuratively, we shall find about forty such occasions, and invariably it is used as a figure representing Deity. Someone investigating this matter may refer to the passage in Isaiah:

> " A man shall be . . . as the shadow of a great rock in a weary land."

The question immediately arises as to who the man is referred to. We need not tarry with that. The word thus reserved to represent Deity is employed in this chapter when the reference is to false gods. It is at that point that the translators have spelt it with a small r. Everywhere else it is a figure applicable to God Himself. It is well to bear this in mind when, in the course of our reading, we come to the point in the history where our Lord said:

> " On this Rock I will build My Church."

The theme of the Song, then, may be said to be the stedfastness of that Rock, and the instability of the people who, nevertheless, claim that God is their Rock.

The theme having been thus stated, the Song passes to historic survey. This opens with an appeal.

> " Remember the days of old,
> Consider the years of many generations;
> Ask thy father, and he will shew thee;
> Thine elders, and they will tell thee."

The appeal, therefore, is to remember and to consider.

This historic survey, then, falls into three parts. The first is found in verses eight to fourteen, in which Jehovah and His doings are recorded. In verses fifteen to eighteen, the response of the people is put on record. In verses nineteen to twenty-seven, the attitudes of Jehovah are described.

In a passage characterised by great tenderness and beauty of poetic suggestiveness, the primal relation of Jehovah to His people and His constant care of them, are set forth.

> " He found him in a desert land,
> And in the waste howling wilderness;
> He compassed him about, He cared for him,
> He kept him as the apple of His eye."

This is followed by that wonderful illustration of the eagles. On the human level Moses had gained this illustration from his sojourn in the Siniatic peninsular as a shepherd for forty years. In the loneliness of that work undoubtedly, he had often watched the eagles and now employs the figure. It is well, however, to remember that forty years before, when God was calling him to be His instrument in the deliverance of this people from their bondage, He had used the same figure.

> "Ye have seen what·I did unto the Egyptians, and how I bare you on eagles' wings, and brought you unto Myself" (Exodus xix. 4).

Then, at the beginning, Moses would understand the figure, because of his familiarity with the methods of the eagles. Now in his Song he makes use of it.

In examining this, we need to be careful to observe the pronouns employed, as to their gender.

> "As an eagle that stirreth up her nest,
> That fluttereth over her young,
> He spread abroad his wings, he took them,
> He bare them on his pinions."

Let it first be recognised that the whole of that is descriptive of the eagles. The first couplet reveals the action of the mother bird:

> "As an eagle that stirreth up her nest,
> That fluttereth over her young."

The second couplet describes the action of the father bird:

> "He spread abroad his wings, he took them,
> He bare them on his pinions."

The picture is that of an eagle eyrie, with the young eaglets in the nest. The mother and the father are both there. The activity of the mother is that of disturbing these birds, stirring up the nest, and then hovering or brooding over the eaglets. The intention of the mother bird is that of disturbing them, and flinging them off the height into the air. Then, as thus disturbed and flung out, they begin to fall, the father bird spreads his wings, swoops beneath them, and catches them on his pinions, and bears them back to safety.

This process Moses unquestionably had often watched, and now he says that it represents the way in which God deals with His people, flinging them out into new and unexpected places, disturbing them, but evermore catching them, and bearing them on His pinions. We realise that this process goes forward in the case of the eaglets until they have found the use of their wings, and are able to exercise them in flight.

The biting satire of the sentence opening the next section is almost terrific:

> "But Jeshurun waxed fat, and kicked."

Then, as though the poet were looking at Jeshurun, continuing, he said:

> " Thou art waxen fat, thou art grown thick, thou art become sleek."

The prosperity of the people is thus described, a prosperity resulting from the fact that Jehovah had made them ride on the high places of the earth, had enabled them to suck honey out of the rock, and oil from the flinty rock; had provided them butter of kine, and milk of sheep, the fat of lambs, rams of the breed of Bashan, and goats, the fat of kidneys of wheat, and the blood of grapes.

> " But Jeshurun waxed fat, and kicked."

In spite of all the manifold blessings bestowed, producing prosperity, there had been rebellion against God. The application of this inclusive and satirical statement runs on through verse twenty-seven, and the whole thing is finally summarised in the words:

> " They are a nation void of counsel,
> And there is no understanding in them."

The goodness of God had produced the pride of possession, and His disciplines were not understood. The Rock is revealed as stedfast; the people as failing in fidelity.

All this brings us to the final movement beginning with verse twenty-nine, that, namely, of the prophetic outlook. Moses was going. He was looking on down the years into the subsequent history of these people. He began with a great sigh:

> " O that they were wise, that they understood this,
> That they would consider their latter end ! "

If they would do so, they would be an invincible people.

> " How should one chase a thousand,
> And two put ten thousand to flight,
> Except their Rock had sold them,
> And Jehovah had delivered them up? "

All failure in the future would be due to the fact that God would hand them over for the time being, because they were trusting in false gods. It is here that he refers to those false gods under the figure of rock, putting them into contrast with the true God, under the same figure, in the words:

> " Their rock is not as our Rock,
> Even our enemies themselves being judges."

A description of the life of such as trust in the false rock follows:

" For their vine is of the vine of Sodom,
And of the fields of Gomorrah;
Their grapes are grapes of gall,
Their clusters are bitter;
Their wine is the poison of dragons,
And the cruel venom of asps."

Then follow the tremendous declarations of God's determination to deal in judgment with His own, and with all the surrounding nations. The declarations reveal a necessity created by the faithlessness of those for whom God has done such wondrous things.

That terrible story of coming judgment and punishment ends with the strange and arresting words:

" Rejoice, O ye nations, with His people;
For He will avenge the blood of His servants,
And will render vengeance to His adversaries,
And will make expiation for His land, for His people."

These words reveal judgment proceeding to mercy. The purpose of all the discipline is the ultimate realisation of the highest well-being of His people. He will avenge, and will make expiation. It is possible that a later singer in Israel, one of the psalmists, had been contemplating this song with spiritual intelligence, when he broke out into the great words:

" I will sing of mercy and of judgment."

We are all ever ready to sing of mercy. The heart is reluctant to sing of judgment. Nevertheless, if we know God, and understand His discipline, we shall realise that through all the circumstances of sorrow and of trial, the purpose of every judgment is the ultimate realisation of the highest.

We close our meditation on this great Song by one or two general observations. It celebrates the goodness of God to His people. Originally He found them in the waste howling wilderness. Processionally He trains them, and brings them through discipline, for the development of His own purpose concerning them. In discipline the goodness of God is as clearly marked as anywhere else. He will not allow His people to settle down to their own failure and their own disaster. He will not permit them to settle into the lethargy of comfort, but will disturb them, in order to the discovery of their powers, and the realisation of them.

This Song cannot be studied without a discovery being made of the grief of the heart of God in the presence of the infidelities of His people.

Let us close by glancing back for a moment to the previous chapter, where at verse nineteen, we read these words:

" Now, therefore, write ye this song for you, and teach thou it to the children of Israel; put it in their mouths, that this song may be a witness for Me against the children of Israel."

Then glance at the last verse of that chapter:

" And Moses spake in the ears of all the assembly of Israel the words of this song, until they were finished."

This backward glance will show us the reason of the Song. Moses was commanded by God to write it, and to commit to the people. To me the suggestive fact in all this is that when Moses had given them the ritual, had given them the law, God commanded him to give them a Song.

Over and over again, a song will live longer in the memory, and produce more results than ritualistic observance, or ethical codes. The songs of the ages are the supreme instruments for keeping in the memory of man the faithfulness of God, and compelling him to face his own faithlessness.

PROVERBS VIII

A NY consideration of this chapter demands a recognition of its place in the whole of the inspired Literature. The book of Proverbs constitutes a part of what we often accurately describe as the Wisdom Literature of the Old Testament. We have only three books which can strictly be placed in that category, the book of Job, the book of Proverbs, and the book of Ecclesiastes. Scattered through the Psalms we may find songs of the same nature. In the Apocrypha there are two books, one called the Wisdom of Solomon, and the other Ecclesiasticus, which are also strictly Wisdom books.

The word Wisdom, as thus used, is the equivalent of our word Philosophy. These books, then, constitute the philosophic writings of our Bible. It is important, however, that we make a distinction when we speak of philosophy generally, and of the philosophy of the Bible. Philosophy, as we understand the word to-day, in the last analysis, consists of the asking of questions, and a sincere attempt to discover true answers to the questions. If we take a broad outlook on the history of philosophy, going back, shall we say to Anaxagoras, following through the first living three centuries, and then travelling through the comparatively barren centuries until philosophy had its re-birth with Descartes and Bacon, we shall find that in every case the starting point is a perfectly proper and legitimate question. Arrestingly enough, it is the very question which Pilate asked Jesus: " What is truth? "

Now Hebrew philosophy did not begin with a question. It began rather with an affirmation. It affirmed God, and as a result of that affirmation, it further assumed that all wisdom is to be found in Him. From these positions it drew a deduction, namely, that for man, " The fear of the Lord is the beginning of wisdom." If we think of this matter from the standpoint of the thought processes of these Hebrew philosophers, we may thus describe it. They said that everything in the realm of being must have been first a conception, or a thought, and that thought pre-supposes a thinker. They therefore assumed God as the Thinker, and His thoughts as preceding all phenomena. These Hebrew philosophers therefore said, in effect, There is no unsolved riddle of the universe, that if the mind of man has not yet full knowledge, that knowledge does exist in the mind of God. Therefore, for man "the fear of the Lord is the beginning of wisdom."

It may be remarked in passing that in these Wisdom books, the conception of God is universal rather than Hebrew. By that I do not intend to suggest that there was any clash between the Hebrew theology and the Hebrew philosophy. The ultimate conception of God found in the Hebrew theology was of Him as revealed in the great name Yahweh, or Jehovah. That name is found repeatedly in the book of Job, and more often in the book of Proverbs. Interestingly enough, in Ecclesiastes, where the author had lost the conception of God suggested in the name Jehovah, that name is not found. In these Wisdom books there is utter absence of reference to the Mosaic law, or the Mosaic ritual. The moral is emphasised rather than the ceremonial. Therefore the moral standards are human rather than Jewish, and so the whole range of human experience comes into view.

The book of Proverbs consists first of a series of discourses on Wisdom (i.–ix.). These are followed by a collection of Proverbs x.–xxiv.). The next section contains a second collection of Proverbs made in the days of Hezekiah (xxv.–xxix.); and the book ends with an appendix containing the words of Agur, and the oracles of Lemuel (xxx.–xxxi.).

The eighth chapter in the first section is a complete discourse in itself, and is really climacteric to these discourses on Wisdom. In it Wisdom is personified and is made to speak for herself. She is introduced in the first three verses, and then her message is recorded in the rest of the chapter. That message has four distinct movements. In the first, Wisdom introduces herself (verses 4–9); in the second she describes her treasures (verses 10–21); and in the third she utters her claims (verses 22–31); and in the last makes her final appeal (verses 32–36).

The introduction reads:

> " Doth not wisdom cry,
> And understanding put forth her voice?
> In the top of high places by the way,
> Where the paths meet, she standeth;
> Beside the gates, at the entry of the city,
> At the coming in of the doors, she crieth aloud."

In these words the writer is introducing Wisdom. Immediately following them her voice is heard commencing:

> " Unto you, O men, I call:
> And my voice is to the sons of men."

In this introduction two words are made use of, "wisdom" and "understanding." Wisdom refers to complete knowledge, absolute truth. Understanding describes perfect intelligence, that is apprehension of wisdom in completeness.

Wisdom is described as standing at the centre of the highways, at the place to which all roads are beating up. She is standing, moreover, at the gates, at the entries, at the doors, at all the starting places. Her voice, then, is to be heard at all the converging centres, and at every point where the roads start towards these centres. In other words, the declaration is that the speech of Wisdom is everywhere. If imaginatively we take the idea and apply it to London, it would be possible to say that Wisdom is here speaking at the Mansion House, the Exchange, the Bank of England, and talking at every gate or entry whether North, South, West or East, along which traffic moves to the centre. The conception is that Wisdom is for evermore speaking in the open. In her method there is no hiding, no whispering, no lurking-places. Wisdom has a universal language.

In this connection we glance back for a moment to the previous chapter, and find something standing in striking contrast. In that chapter evil is personified as a woman, and all the terrible figurative language of the ways of evil are found therein. The real value in the portrayal of evil is that it is seen hiding in lurking-places, breaking through surreptitiously, and dealing treacherously. The contrast is arresting and complete.

So we pass to a consideration of what Wisdom has to say, and we observe her declaration is to those to whom she speaks:

"Unto you, O men, I call:
And my voice is to the sons of men."

The voice of Wisdom, therefore, is speaking to humanity, and that fact distinguishes man from all below him in creation. Nothing beneath man can hear the voice of wisdom. That in itself assumes the marvel and majesty of human nature.

Continuing, Wisdom cries:
"O ye simple, understand subtilty;
And ye fools, be ye of an understanding heart."

Thus while Wisdom talks to men, its appeal is made to the simple. We are arrested by that word "simple," because in our common use of it, it has lost its old value. When the King James' translators did their work, and rendered the Hebrew word "simple" it did not mean one devoid of intelligence. The literal meaning of the word refers to having an open mind. Wisdom is also speaking to the fools, and the word there translated does suggest a person stupid in action. Wisdom therefore has a message to humanity, and she appeals to the open-minded. However stupid they may be in some senses, it is the recognition of a capacity for hearing.

Wisdom then utters "excellent things." They are the things of right. They are the things of truth. In her speech there is no wickedness, nothing crooked, nothing perverse. In what she has to say, the moral principle is supreme. When Wisdom speaks to man she ever tells him the truth about himself, tells him, for instance, that he is a fool if he is a fool, does not allow him to hide himself, and think of himself as clever when he is but a fool. The voice of Wisdom invades the realm of human nature, and interprets the actual facts. Someone has said that " God is the God of things as they are," a very profound statement. Wisdom is the voice of God to the soul of man, declaring the facts. In its message there is no deceit, no contortion, nothing out of harmony with truth. So Wisdom introduces herself.

The next movement in the address of Wisdom is that in which she puts herself into comparison with things which men hold valuable, and declares that there is nothing that has any value at all by comparison with Wisdom. The things named are silver, gold, rubies, all things held to be valuable by men. Concerning these, she says:

"Receive my instruction, and not silver;
And knowledge rather than choice gold.
For wisdom is better than rubies."

Thus naming three, the sum totality of all things conceived of as being valuable, is referred to, and the declaration is made tha all the things that are to be desired are not to be compared to Wisdom.

The things which Wisdom offers are knowledge, prudence, purity. These are the secrets of all true authority. Kings, princes, nobles, judges, rule by such wisdom. It may be said that kings have not always done so, and nobles and judges have failed. The reply is that in so far as they have thus failed, they have failed in authority. It is only when those who occupy places of authority, exercise authority according to wisdom, that their authority is valid.

Continuing, Wisdom claims that durable wealth is her gift, and honour is her gift, and urges obedience to her voice, because of its advantage.

Following on, Wisdom utters her claims, and if one were inclined to make distinctions between the different parts of this chapter, we might say that this section contains its supreme movement.

> " The Lord possessed me in the beginning of His way,
> Before His works of old."

A distinction between " way " and " works " is to be noted. We call to mind a passage from an ancient Psalm:

> " He made known His *ways* unto Moses,
> His *acts* unto the children of Israel."

In each case the way precedes the work; the thought comes before the deed. Now Wisdom says that in the beginning of the way of God, Wisdom was possessed before His works. We read as we open our Bible, " In the beginning God created." Wisdom now claims that she was with God in the beginning, before the creative acts.

The great truth is then repeated in another form in the words:

> " I was set up from everlasting, from the beginning,
> Or ever the earth was."

As we think of these things, our minds travel from Genesis i. 1 to John i. 1. In each of these passages we have that phrase, " In the beginning." In John the declaration is made that " The Word was with God." The Hebrew philosopher says that Wisdom was with God, and the idea is identical, and thus its claim that behind all creation was this activity of Wisdom.

At this point the description is so full of beauty that it is well to quote it again.

> " When there were no depths, I was brought forth;
> When there were no fountains abounding with water.
> Before the mountains were settled,
> Before the hills was I brought forth;
> While as yet He had not made the earth, nor the fields,
> Nor the beginning of the dust of the world.
> When He established the heavens, I was there;
> When He set a circle upon the face of the deep;
> When He made firm the skies above;
> When the fountains of the deep became strong;
> When He gave to the sea its bound,
> That the waters should not transgress His commandment;
> When He marked out the foundations of the earth;
> Then I was by Him, as a master workman;
> And I was daily His delight,
> Rejoicing always before Him."

Thus Wisdom personified, takes us back behind all created things, and to the activity of creation, claiming that in the processes thereof, it was with God; that is to say, that all the ways of God and the works of God were conditioned in this Wisdom. In all such activity, Wisdom was daily His delight.

Closely connected, indeed running straight on, Wisdom speaks of its own joy as it says:

" Rejoicing in His habitable earth,
And my delight was with the sons of men."

The movement here is arresting. Wisdom is the delight of Jehovah, and Wisdom is seen rejoicing before Jehovah in the finished creation, but ultimately delighting in the sons of men.

Thus Wisdom takes us away beyond all creation, and declares that it was the delight of God, and that as the processes of creation moved forward, and culminated in man, the delight of Wisdom was realised. The whole movement emphasises the fact that there can be no deviation between Wisdom and God, and makes the tremendous declaration that in all the processes of creation the central purpose and ultimate meaning was man.

Thus we reach the final appeal. Again the words are addressed to man.

" Now, therefore, my sons, hearken unto Me;
For blessed are they that keep my ways.
Hear instruction, and be wise,
And refuse it not.
Blessed is the man that heareth me,
Watching daily at my gates,
Waiting at the posts of my doors.
For whoso findeth me findeth life,
And shall obtain favour of the Lord."

All this means that if we hearken to Wisdom, and obey, we are putting our lives into touch with the eternal things, with the wisdom that existed before creation, that presided over the processes of creation, which culminated in man himself.

What we have done is self-evident, that of taking a very general survey of this great chapter. In conclusion let us attempt to recognise the things which are clearly revealed therein.

First of all, then, the creation is seen to be cosmic, not fortuitous. Whatever we are conscious of in creation is here revealed to be the result of the operation of Wisdom. God is the God of creation, and He is the God of law and of order.

Again, it is impossible to read this chapter without being brought face to face with that to which I have already referred, namely, the centrality of man to the cosmic order. That is a matter which has been much debated; and indeed, by many rejected. It was at this point that Darwin and Wallace parted company. Wallace insisted that man is central to the universe. It has been objected that man is too insignificant to be considered in that way. Have we, however, any right to speak of man as insignificant? We turn over for a moment to one of the Hebrew poems, in which the singer said:

> " When I consider Thy heavens, the work of Thy fingers,
> The moon and the stars, which Thou hast ordained;
> What is man that Thou art mindful of him?
> And the son of man, that Thou visitest him? "

That singer was unquestionably conscious of the apparent insignificance of man in comparison with the cosmic order which he referred to in the lines:

> " When I consider Thy heavens, the work of Thy fingers,
> The moon and the stars."

But the singer celebrates the greatness of man rather than his insignificance, for the singer saw that God was mindful of him, and visited him in ways different from and transcending completely anything else to be found in the splendours of the cosmic order.

Again, another supreme truth revealed in this message of Wisdom is that of the supremacy of the moral in the cosmic order. The laws of Nature are the thoughts of God, and they are all in accord with righteousness and holiness. The ethical principle everywhere obtains.

Once more we turn to that to which we have already referred, the prologue to the Gospel according to John, in which we find complement and completion of the truth revealed in the eighth chapter of Proverbs. The great ideas of the Wisdom message are now seen revealed in an actual Person.

In this connection I want to quote from the Apocrypha a passage of the Wisdom literature. It is found in the Wisdom of Solomon.

> "She is a breath of the power of God,
> And a clear effluence of the glory of the Almighty;
> Therefore can nothing defiled find entrance into her,
> For she is an effulgence from everlasting light,
> And an unspotted mirror of the working of God,
> And an image of God's goodness.
> And she, being one, hath power to do all things;
> And remaining in herself, reneweth all things;
> And from generation to generation passing into holy souls.
> She maketh men friends of God and of prophets,
> For nothing doth God love save him that dwelleth with
>   wisdom.
> For she is fairer than the sun,
> And above all the constellations of the stars."

Thus the Wisdom literature celebrates Wisdom. Presently there came Philo, that Palestinian Jew, saturated with Greek philosophy, and he spoke of the Logos. Finally there came John, not influenced by Philo, but correcting Philo, and he declared that the Logos was in the beginning with God, and was of the very nature of God ; and that the Logos became flesh. Here we see then the true meaning of Christianity. Christ was made unto us Wisdom from God.

JOHN XXI

THE fascination of this chapter is universally felt. It is interesting from the fact that it certainly is an appendix to the Gospel, and is complete in itself. The first scheme of this book was completed at the twenty-ninth verse of chapter twenty, and immediately followed by the writer's foot-note of explanation of his book, in verses thirty and thirty-one. Then later, how much later it is impossible to say, John added this chapter. That is merely to deal with the literary form. The chapter in itself for us is an integral part of the Gospel according to John, completing the account of the risen Christ, which commenced in chapter twenty.

A study of the chapter makes it perfectly plain that in writing it the design of John was not to prove the fact of the resurrection. That had already been done in chapter twenty. The purpose is rather to reveal the risen One. The key to the consideration is found in the opening verse:

"After these things Jesus manifested Himself again to the disciples at the sea of Tiberias; and He manifested on this wise."

The arresting word is the word "manifested," "Jesus manifested Himself . . . He manifested on this wise." The verb in the Greek is in the active voice, which at once suggests that whatever is found in the chapter is the account of a manifestation of Jesus made by Himself. The thought of the word "manifested" is that of a shining forth, or a causing to shine forth. Here, then, John is recording an event in which the Lord came to a certain group in order to reveal Himself to them in certain ways. Quite evidently, then, whatever we may find in the chapter, its supreme value is some revelation of the Lord Himself, which He, of set purpose, gave to these men.

The manifestation was given in the early hours of the morning on the shore of the lake which here is called Tiberias. This, of course, was the Sea of Galilee, and so the place was familiar to these men, for they had often trodden its shores with their Lord. Our purpose, then, is that of attempting to see Him clearly as He was manifested, remembering that the manifestation was intentional on His part. He manifested Himself.

The chapter falls naturally into three parts, the last two verses constituting the third division, contain the conclusion of the book. The two main divisions are found first in verses one to fourteen, where the Lord is manifesting Himself to that representative company, and so to the Church to the end of the age. Then in verses fifteen to twenty-three we still see Him manifested, in dealing with two individuals, Peter and John.

At the risk of being monotonous, I want once more to insist upon the fact that whatever we see here, the supreme value is His intended manifestation of Himself. He caused Himself to shine forth upon those gathered around Him. Whether in the first movement of manifestation to the group, or the second manifestation of His dealing with two individuals, the whole thing is microcosmic, having distinct value for all time. He is manifested dealing with a group, representing His Church, and with two individuals, constituting units in the unity of the Church. The group is in many ways representative, as we shall see; and the individuals, utterly dissimilar in temperament, are also representative.

As to the first movement, the group in itself is a very interesting one. John Ruskin has pointed out in his criticism of Raphael's cartoon of this scene, how mediæval art failed in accurate representation of the facts. In the first place he gave an Italian background to Tiberias. In the second place he portrayed twelve apostles as standing round the Lord, and these by the way, robed in full ecclesiastical garments. Of course, Raphael painted under the mastery of ecclesiastical and theological interpretations current at the time. Dismissing much of this criticism, the one thing to be observed is that the twelve apostles were not there. There were seven in the group. Five of them are named, and we have been made familiar with them if we have been reading through John's story: Simon Peter, Thomas, Nathanael, and the sons of Zebedee, that is James and John. Beyond these there were two others, and many expositors have indulged in speculation as to who these were, some suggesting Andrew and Philip. I think not. Seeing that they were both apostles, had they been there they would in all probability have been named. They were, and remain, anonymous; and so are representatives of the anonymous multitude which creates the real strength of the Christian Church.

We look, then, at the scene with this small company gathered together, with the Lord in the midst, and so representative of the Church.

Their condition arrests our attention. Quite evidently they were restless, and what wonder. They had been passing through the strangest experiences; first that which must have appeared to them as the tragedy of the Cross, followed by the mysterious fact of the resurrection, and the strange appearances and disappearances of Jesus. Simon, who was ever a leader in many ways, unquestionably voiced this restlessness when he said: " I go a fishing." It was an expression of his own desire for some activity to ease the strain. This great soul who had blundered so terrifically, but who had been restored in a private interview with Jesus, sought some method which should give him relief. It was as though he had said, This suspense is becoming intolerable. I am going back to the old job. That his feeling was shared by the others is proven by the fact of their ready response as they said, " We also come with thee."

The writer then says, " That night they took nothing." I think the emphasis should be on the word " that." It was not normal for these fishermen to spend a night on the lake without taking fish. They knew the waters. They knew where to cast the nets. They knew how to do it, but " that night" they caught nothing. It was to them, then, under such circumstances, that He manifested Himself, and we immediately become interested in the nature of the manifestation. The first thing we observe is that He offered no word of rebuke. Opinions differ as to whether they were right or wrong in going fishing, and I am not prepared to dogmatise on the subject. Personally, I do not think that they ought to have done so. They had been distinctly told by their Lord to tarry until they were clothed with power from on high; but they had yielded to restlessness. In the very fact that He did not rebuke them He is manifesting Himself in His infinite understanding and patience. Even though their restlessness may have led them somewhat astray, He understood that restlessness, and said no word of rebuke.

On the other hand, He entered into the immediate experience resulting from their action. It was an experience of entire failure. " That night they took nothing." Standing on the shore Jesus' addressed them quite literally as " Little children," and asked them, " Have ye aught to eat? " The enquiry, of course, was as to whether they had taken fish. We can imagine how the Figure standing on the shore in the dim light of the breaking day was indistinct. Quite evidently they did not recognise the voice, and answered the enquiry with the simple negative, " No." He then commanded them " to cast the net on the right side of the boat," and told them, " ye shall find." As one reads the story it is at least an arresting fact that they obeyed. There must have been some sense borne in upon them that the Stranger had some reason for His command. In obedience they cast the net, and lo ! the failure of the night was turned into the success of the morning. Thus He manifested Himself. They saw Him as interested in them, in their fishing; and, moreover, as able to give them success, even in that work.

It was this manifestation which brought to John the conviction which he expressed in the words, " It is the Lord "; and directly he had so said, Peter evidently also recognising the Person:

" Girt his coat about him . . . and cast himself into the sea,"

and reached the land.

It is almost impossible to read this story without remembering a previous occasion on which our Lord had granted to these men success in fishing. The story is told in Luke five, and it is quite certain that on that occasion they had no right to have been fishing. He had called them to follow Him, and in some interval of waiting, they had gone back to their fishing nets. When He found them there, as now, He did not rebuke them, and yet produced in the mind of Peter a consciousness of failure, so that he said to Him:

" Depart from me, for I am a sinful man, O Lord."

To that cry, which was a confession of his failure, the Lord had replied:

" Henceforth thou shalt catch men alive."

There, then, coming into their commonplace lives, He had revealed His ability, and lifted it on to the highest level as He forecasted their ultimate business. Exactly the same thing took place here. Thus He manifested Himself.

It was this revelation which caused Peter to feel that he must get to the Lord, and so he cast himself into the sea, and swam to the shore. It is interesting to notice in passing that on the earlier occasion he had said to Jesus, " Depart from me," and now his anxiety was to get near to his Lord.

The manifestation continued as they came to land. There they found a charcoal fire burning. Quite evidently it had been built and lit by the Lord Himself. On that fire they found fish already laid, and bread was there. Thus He manifested Himself, building a fire, preparing a breakfast, and then calling them to break their fast, He Himself handed to them the bread and the fish. Thus He manifested Himself.

When all this is considered in the light of the world enterprise which was on the heart of Jesus, it becomes the more radiantly beautiful. The vastness of His purpose did not divorce Him from the immediate necessities of His own. He showed Himself as interested in, and able to help in the ordinary business affairs of life. He manifested Himself as interested, and having

fellowship with all the commonplace things necessary to the
sustenance of physical life. Thus He manifested Himself.

And so we pass to the second movement in the manifestation
in which we see Him dealing with two individuals; more directly
and particularly with the one, but indirectly and quite definitely
with the other.

The two, Simon and John, are entirely different in many ways.
Simon was the man of action, John the man of contemplation;
Simon the practical man, John the poet. As we consider the story
we observe that all the way through, while dealing with the
individual, He was recognising the relation of the individual to
others. The value of personality never lies wholly within
personality. It is rather to be discovered in its worth to others.
No individual has value simply on account of physical strength
or mental ability, or spiritual experience. The value of the
individual is always that of its worth to others. As we watch the
scene and listen to the converse between the Lord and Simon, we
first of all discover in the mind of the Lord, His concern in the
words:

" Feed My lambs . . . shepherd My sheep . . . feed
My sheep."

How are we to understand these words, " My lambs," " My
sheep? " One expositor dealing with this chapter, has described
this as the moment when our Lord handed to Peter the crozier,
that is the staff of the pastoral office; and continuing, declared that
he was now appointed a shepherd within the Church. That,
however, is altogether too narrow an outlook. He was not thinking
merely of those gathered within the fold; but of those who were
out on the mountains cold and bare. We may with perfect warrant
interpret this story by one paragraph in Matthew, which it is well
to quote:

" When He saw the multitudes, He was moved with
compassion for them, because they were distressed and
scattered, as sheep, not having a shepherd."

That declaration concerning Him reveals Him as looking upon the
unshepherded and distressed, as still being His sheep. It was
an outlook upon humanity generally, and such were in His mind
when He now used the phrases, " My sheep," " My lambs."

In the expression, moreover, there is an evidence of royalty
and Kingship. All those upon whom He thus looked, and whom
He saw distressed and scattered, He spoke of as " *My* sheep,
My lambs." They were His by the right of creation, but supremely
by the right of redemption. He stood there among this little
group of men, talking to one of them as " the good Shepherd,"

and had declared " the good Shepherd layeth down His life for the sheep." Because of that great vision and purpose of His heart, He now manifested Himself to Simon, and revealed to him what his work should be, what the qualifications necessary for doing it; and, moreover, what the programme set before him was.

The work of shepherding the sheep may mean a journey over the mountains, coming into grips with the wolf, being wounded in order to save. It was to this work that Simon was called.

The story of the revelation of qualification is very full of beauty, and perhaps does not need that we should tarry long with it. Suffice it to say that the question which Jesus asked of this man twice over can only be accurately interpreted for us by the change of the word from " Lovest thou Me? " into the question. " Art thou devoted to Me? " It was a very searching question, and evidently Peter felt it to be so. He had passed through experiences which had put an end to his boasting. Therefore he replied:

" Lord, Thou knowest that I love Thee,"

using a word full of emotional value, but not daring to use the word which Christ had used which expressed complete devotion. The third time our Lord asked him the question He adopted Peter's word, " Lovest thou Me? " Simon was grieved, not because he was asked three times, but because on the third occasion even though he dared not rise to the height suggested by our Lord's enquiry, his Master had now taken the simpler and more emotional word. The manifestation of the Lord is full of beauty, in that while He sought for the highest devotion, He was willing to accept this confession of love; and upon the basis of it, to give to Simon his work.

Having done so, He told Peter what his programme should be. Looking on in effect He declared to him he would prove more than his love, his devotion, for he would finally complete his service in a surrender that would bring him to death.

In doing so, He reminded him of what he had been, as He said:

" When thou wast young, thou girdest thyself, and walkedst whither thou wouldest."

It was a recognition of his natural characteristics, a strong will, strong determination. Now he was a different man, and the issue was declared in the words:

" Thou shalt stretch forth thy hands, and another shall gird thee, and carry thee whither thou wouldest not."

In close connection with that foretelling, He uttered to him once more the words, " Follow Me."

Here it is well that we remember that Simon had protested against our Lord's going to His Cross; but He had gone, and He had risen from the dead. Now said the Lord to him, " Follow Me." You also are going to the cross, but by that way you shall come to triumph, as I have done.

The story, so full of matchless beauty, ends with a revelation of the continued weakness of this man, Simon, and incidentally shows our Lord's dealing with another, John. The conversation between Peter and his Lord being over, Peter caught sight of John, and said:

" Lord, and what shall this man do? "

He was quickly, sharply, definitely rebuked, as our Lord said to him:

" If I will that he tarry till I come, what is that to thee? Follow thou Me."

In this word spoken to Peter He was manifesting Himself also in His understanding of John. The very language He employed was poetic, mystical. Evidently it was such, because it was not understood generally, and the writer is careful to declare the fact of that misunderstanding, and to correct it. In correcting it, however, he leaves the statement mystical and unexplained. I think there can be no doubt that John caught the spiritual significance of what the Lord had said about him. Be that as it may, the manifestation is that of Christ as understanding John, and uttering a word which revealed that understanding.

Thus He manifested Himself. Interested in, and associating Himself with the commonplaces of every-day life for His own, incorporating all these commonplaces into the sublime and the supreme; interested in fishermen fishing, and leading them into the place of success when they had failed; providing for their hunger and satisfying it; and then in a conversation, revealing to that group of men the desire of His heart, and the purpose of His enterprise; and calling them into fellowship with Him both in that desire, and in the service of accomplishment. Thus He manifested Himself.

ROMANS XII

IN this series of studies we have surveyed chapters five and eight in the Roman letter. As we have said before, this letter is the supreme document of the Bible concerning salvation. It faces human corruption, and interprets God's way of redemption. It explains how God can be just and the Justifier of the sinner. In common with all the inspired writings, it is ethical in purpose, showing the relation between doctrine and duty, truth and triumph, redemption and righteousness.

While the first movement in the letter (i.–xi.) is occupied with the interpretation of salvation, the second movement beginning with this chapter, and running to the end, is occupied with the ethical values of salvation. This portion of the letter begins with the appeal found in the earlier sentences of this chapter, and then shows how obedience to the appeal will affect personal and relative life. Here we have the appeal, and a personal application. Therefore, there is a sense in which the whole value of the chapter is contained in the first movement. In our consideration, therefore, we deal principally with the appeal, glancing at the personal application more briefly.

In the appeal contained in the first two verses, three things demand our attention. It reveals a purpose; announces a plan, and utters a plea. That statement is a result of reading the whole, and beginning with the final words which reveal the purpose.

"That ye may prove what is the good and acceptable and perfect will of God."

The plan is revealed in the words:

"To present your bodies a living sacrifice, holy, acceptable to God, which is your reasonable service. And be not fashioned according to this age; but be ye transformed by the renewing of your mind."

The purpose is fulfilled by the carrying out of that plan. This takes us to the opening words, which contain the plea:

"I beseech you . . . by the mercies of God."

We may restate that in the order of writing. First the plea:

"I beseech you . . . by the mercies of God";

secondly, the plan:

"To present your bodies a living sacrifice, holy, acceptable to God, which is your spiritual service. And be not fashioned according to this age; but be ye transformed by the renewing of your mind";

finally, the purpose:

"That ye may prove what is the good and acceptable and perfect will of God."

Commencing our consideration with the purpose then, we pause with the word "prove." We might render the word so translated quite accurately and helpfully, put to the test. In the last analysis the word prove is better, because it indicates not merely the process of putting to the test, but the result thereof.

As we read these words, we find that Paul is perhaps for the moment unconsciously revealing the deepest conviction of his heart, which is that the will of God is good and acceptable and perfect. He desired that those to whom he was writing, should discover this great fact. His letter was addressed to those whom he had described as "beloved of God, called saints." Those so described were dwelling in Rome. Paul was himself a Roman citizen, and he knew that at the time Rome was the centre of the world. He had greatly desired to visit Rome, and had been hindered; and because of this, he sent this letter to those in Rome described in the words we have already quoted, "beloved of God, called saints." The whole letter was intended to interpret to them their life, their experience, to show them all its meaning, and the value of it. As he came to the end of his writing to those, he expressed his supreme desire for them, and it was that they might realise to the full the goodness and acceptability and perfection of the will of God. It is evident that to him the knowing of the will of God, and the doing of it, are the supreme things. Thus in his appeal he was revealing his own personal conviction; but that conviction was of no value to them, save as it became their own conviction.

Nevertheless, the words he uses here to describe the will of God are wonderfully revealing. He says that will is good, and that needs no interpretation, for it means exactly good, intrinsically good. He says that will is acceptable, that is fitting, suitable. The will of God is not only good, but is completely suited to the need of human nature. Therefore His will is

perfect. Being in itself intrinsically good, and being of such a
nature as to meet completely the needs of man, it is perfect.

Faber expressed the truth in that great hymn which, in part,
finds place in nearly all our hymn books to-day, and in which
these stanzas are found:

" I worship Thee, sweet Will of God!
And all Thy ways adore,
And every day I live I seem
To love Thee more and more.
I love to kiss each print where Thou
Hast set Thine unseen feet;
I cannot fear Thee, blessed Will!
Thine empire is so sweet.
He always wins who sides with God,
To him no chance is lost;
God's Will is sweetest to him when
It triumphs at his cost.
Ill that He blesses is our good,
And unblest good is ill;
And all is right that seems most wrong,
If it be His sweet Will."

That conviction of the apostle, thus expressed by Faber, is
of supreme truth and importance; and yet it is one which even
Christian people find it hard at times to believe. My memory
goes back to one of the old days at Westminster. One evening
after a Service there came a young man into my vestry. He had
just graduated at Oxford. His people were Christian people.
He himself had never made a personal surrender to the claims of
Christ. As he came into the vestry, he approached me, and with
a stern, set face, he said, " I have come to tell you I am going to
be a Christian." He said it as though he were surrendering himself
to the stake, and perhaps in some senses he was, for following
Christ ever means taking up the Cross. Taking his hand I told
him of course I was glad to know of his decision. Then he said,
" Yes, I must do it, notwithstanding the fact that it goes against
the grain." I realised that he had at once delivered himself into
my hands, and I said to him, " No, you have been going against
the grain all your life. You are now going with it." The man
who lives outside the will of God is cutting across the grain of
capacity and possibility. The man who launches out into the
will of God, at whatever cost, is able to sing with Faber:
" I worship Thee, sweet Will of God!
And all Thy ways adore ",
for he finds with Paul that the will of God is good and acceptable
and perfect.

The assumption, then, of Paul is that the will of God for man means the conditioning of his life in order to the realisation of its highest and its best. The purpose of the appeal is that they should so act as to prove this great fact for themselves. If men will hear the appeal, and follow the plan, they will prove the will of God to be good, to be acceptable, to be perfect.

This being the purpose, we now turn to consider the plan as revealed.

" To present your bodies a living sacrifice, holy, acceptable to God, which is your spiritual service. And be not fashioned according to this world; but be ye transformed by the renewing of your mind."

As we approach this consideration we pause to notice that it is based on an arresting conception and analysis of human nature. He was writing to dwellers in Rome, men and women " beloved of God, called saints." An examination of some of the names appearing in this letter will show that some remarkable people were found in the group. There is no question that among the rest, British princes were present. I may remark, in passing, that the idea that the Church of God was planted in Britain by the coming of Augustine is entirely false. Ere he arrived, there were already Christians found in the land. In the group there were others, as for instance we know of a runaway slave named Onesimus, who arrived there later; and there can be no doubt that in the company there were rich and poor, learned and illiterate. They were all human beings, and his appeal approaches them from this conception of human personality.

We observe the pronouns as he uses them in addressing them:
" I beseech *you* . . . to present *your* . . . *your* reasonable service . . . *your* mind, that *ye* may prove."

Now that is a curious and almost grotesque grouping of phrases. It is done to show that his recognition of personality was that of something beyond the physical, or the mental. They were called upon to present the body. Evidently therefore the body is not, in itself, the essence of personality. He refers also to the mind. They had minds, but once more, the essence of personality did not lie within the mental. The mind was to be brought under control, guarded from wrong ideas and relationships. They were not to be conformed to the age, but transformed by the renewing of their mind. Thus Paul, writing to these people, and indeed to us, calls us to the attitude where the body and mind are brought under control. The essential fact, therefore, of human personality is the spiritual fact. A man is a spirit, and he has a mind and a body.

An incidental word occurring in the letter to the Hebrews is a very revealing one. The writer said:

" We had the fathers of our flesh to chasten us, and we gave them reverence; shall we not much rather be in subjection unto the Father of spirits."

A distinction is made there between " fathers of our flesh," and " the Father of spirits." The fathers of our flesh are not our fathers in the deepest sense of personality. God is the Father of all spirits, and the spirit is the essential thing. That is true whether for good or ill, whether for righteousness or wickedness; and whether the one or the other depends upon the relationship of that spiritual essence to the will of God. Body and mind are essential, but secondary, and need to be brought under the control of the spirit. Of course the supreme teaching is that the spirit must be under the control of God. To this essential fact of personality he makes his appeal in his use of the pronouns already quoted. The spirit is called upon to present the body, and to see to it that the mind is renewed.

In writing to the Thessalonians the apostle incidentally gave a final analysis of personality as he said:

" May your spirit and soul and body be preserved entire."

The word there rendered " soul " might be accurately rendered mind. Taking that analysis then, and applying it personally, I may say I am not a body, but I have one; I am not a mind, but I have one; I am a spirit, and in this appeal in the Roman letter I am called upon to present that body to God, holy and acceptable to Him. That is the responsibility of the spirit life; but it is necessary to remember that Paul was writing to those who in the spirit life were renewed, born again, and therefore had the power to do that which he was appealing to them to do.

All this is equally applicable to the mind. The mind may be dominated by fleshly desires or spiritual aspirations. The Biblical interpretation of man gives the account of how he descended from the realm where the spirit governs, under the authority of heaven, into a realm where the flesh governs and the mind is thus degraded. In regeneration the spirit is placed back in right relationship with God, and so is enabled to bring under control both body and mind. It is important to realise that Paul does not call for the mutilation of the body in any sense, but rather its mastery. The whole conception that a man might develop his spiritual life by the mutilation of his body is anti-Christian. No man ever became more spiritual by the wearing of a hair shirt, or the flaggelation of his flesh. The body is to be presented not a dead or mutilated thing, but alive, and holy, and so acceptable to God. The mind is not to be conformed to the age in which we live. "Demas forsook me, having loved the present age." That is to say, he loved the things near, and allowed himself to be blinded to the splendour of the spiritual and the eternal. His mind was conformed to the present age, and not submitted to the Spirit of God.

If, therefore, we desire to test the will of God, and to discover whether it is good and acceptable and perfect, this is how we must do it. The first necessity is the recognition of our spiritual entity, which issues in the presentation of the body, "living, holy, acceptable to God"; and the guarding of our intellectual activities, seeing to it that they are not conformed to the spirit of an age which is evanescent; but rather conformed to the spiritual facts and forces.

The plea is urged in the words:

"I beseech you . . . by the mercies of God."

Here I do not suggest that I can improve upon the word "mercies," but we may change it for the sake of interpretation, and render with perfect accuracy:

"I beseech you . . . by the compassions of God."

If we retain the word "mercies" we may properly enquire what was in the mind of the apostle? We often declare that the mercies of God are fresh every morning, and new every evening; and when we do so, we are thinking of the blessings that come to us constantly from His hand. I do not think Paul at the moment was thinking in that way. He had rather in mind those great mercies, or compassions which had been dealt with in the earlier part of his letter; the mercies of God as manifested to a world sunk in darkness and death, the mercies which provided a way of release and redemption. We may properly summarise them by the use of three great words, standing for the subjects already dealt with; justification, sanctification, glorification.

Justification restores the spirit life to right relationship with God. Sanctification transforms the thinking of the mind concerning all things. Glorification refers to the ultimate issue of justification and sanctification. In another of his letters, Paul writes:

"He shall fashion anew the body of our humiliation, that it may be conformed to the body of His glory."

That is glorification.

Thus the whole of personality is included. In justification, the righteousness of God in Christ is imputed on the basis of His redeeming work. In sanctification, that same righteousness is implanted progressively in the personality of the believer. In glorification that righteousness will be completely imparted, so that spirit, mind, and body are brought into eternal conformity with Christ, and so with God. These are the mercies of God.

It is interesting to observe here that nothing is said concerning ethical standards, or rules, or regulations. Nevertheless it is impossible to ponder this matter without discovering that the purpose is ethical from beginning to end. The spirit life rightly related to God, controlling the body, and making it the instrument of fellowship with God, refusing to listen to the syren voices of a passing age which would seduce it, is a life ethical and holy. Thus our consideration has been so far confined to the first movement of the chapter.

We may now glance at the personal application found in what remains. That commences with the words:

" For I say, through the grace that was given me, to every man that is among you, not to think of himself more highly than he ought to think; but so to think as to think soberly, according as God hath dealt to each man a measure of faith."

The first result, then, of obedience to the appeal in the power of the compassions of God is that of a life characterised by humility, and humility means the lack of self-consciousness. We are to think of ourselves in a certain sense, but not above that which we ought to think. We are to think of ourselves as God thinks of us, which is only another way of saying that we constantly face all the truth concerning ourselves. To do that is to be kept in the position of a true humility; while nevertheless we are privileged constantly to remember that the thought of God for us was expressed in the Cross, and our true value is revealed therein.

Continuing, he shows that such humility results in a recognition of our relationship to all the rest. To show this the apostle employed the figure of the body having many members, having different offices, but yet constituting one body. It is impossible to live a lonely life in this fellowship of faith and consecration. Each is bound up with others. Each has gifts, and we are told how they are to be used. The gifts named are first spiritual: prophecy, ministry, teaching, exhortation. Then gifts that operate within the realm of the material; serving tables, giving, ruling, showing mercy. These are to be exercised in the interest of others, and in our sense of oneness with them in the mystery of life which is in Jesus Christ.

From the ninth verse to the twenty-first we have the apostle's description of the condition that will result. The great principle flashes forth again in the words:

" Let love be without hypocrisy; abhor that which is evil; cleave to that which is good."

Furthermore, he shows what the practice of those thus obedient to his appeal will be towards the outside world. That section is characterised by great clarity, and we need not tarry to deal with it in detail.

The chapter as a whole is a revelation of Christian ethics. All that is enjoined is infinitely more than merely cold rectitude. Everything is rooted in love, and that is the love of God. Its appeal is based upon the compassions of God, and the answer to the appeal is a life mastered by these compassions. That does not make anything less exacting, but rather more so. It calls for serious diligence.

Granted the life, the responsibility is supreme. Yielding to it completely, presenting the body, and guarding the mind, we prove what is the good and acceptable and perfect will of God.